COMING TO TERMS WITH THE Qur'ān

A volume in honor of

Professor Issa Boullata

McGill University

COMING TO TERMS WITH THE Qur'ān

A volume in honor of

Professor Issa Boullata

McGill University

Edited by

Khaleel Mohammed & Andrew Rippin

Islamic Publications International | North Haledon, New Jersey

Islamic Publications International
5 Sicomac Road, Suite 302, North Haledon, NJ 07508
Telephone: 800-568-9814
Fax: 800-466-8111
Email: ipi@onebox.com
US Website: www.islampub.com
UK & Europe website: www.ipimizan.co.uk

Director of Publications: Moin Shaikh
Book Design: Windesheim Design, San Francisco, CA
Book Layout : David Van Ness
Index: Melody Englund

Printed in the United States of America

Library of Congress Cataloging-in-Publication Data

Coming to terms with the Qur'an : a volume in honor of professor Issa Boullata, McGill University / edited by Khaleel Mohammed & Andrew Rippin.
p. cm.
ISBN 978-1-889999-47-0 (pbk.) -- ISBN 978-1-889999-48-7 (hardback)
1. Koran--Criticism, interpretation, etc.--History. 2. Koran--Hermeneutics.
I. Boullata, Issa J., 1929- II. Moḥammed, Khaleel. III. Rippin, Andrew, 1950-
BP130.45.C66 2008
297.1'226--dc22

2007028152

Professor Issa J. Boullata

TABLE OF CONTENTS

III. The Qur'ān in the Modern World

ABOUT THE CONTRIBUTORS

Asma Afsaruddin is Associate Professor of Arabic and Islamic Studies at the University of Notre Dame. Her fields of research are Islamic political and religious thought, Qur'ān and *ḥadīth*, Islamic intellectual history, and gender issues. She is the author or editor of four books, including *Excellence and Precedence: Medieval Islamic Discourse on Legitimate Leadership* (Leiden 2002) and *The First Muslims: History and Memory* (Oneworld 2007). She has also written numerous articles and essays on various aspects of Islamic thought and has lectured extensively in this country and abroad. She previously taught at the Johns Hopkins and Harvard Universities and is a member of the editorial boards of the *Oxford Encyclopedia of the Islamic World* and the *Bulletin of the Middle East Studies Association*. Afsaruddin's research has been funded by the Harry Frank Guggenheim Foundation, among others, and she was recently named a Carnegie Scholar for 2005 by the Carnegie Corporation. She came to know Issa Boullata during her stint as co-editor (with Mathias Zahniser) of a festschrift for Georg Krotkoff at the Johns Hopkins University and they have developed a collegial relationship over the years.

Carl Sharif El-Tobgui holds a BS in Arabic Language from Georgetown University and an MA in Islamic Studies from McGill University with a joint concentration in Islamic thought and Islamic law and legal theory. He is currently ABD in Islamic Studies at McGill and is writing a doctoral dissertation on reason and revelation in the thought of Ibn Taymiyya. Since September 2004, El-Tobgui has taught Arabic full-time at Harvard University. El-Tobgui had the honor of taking courses on Qur'ānic *tafsīr* and the *iʿjāz* of the Qur'ān with Issa Boullata during his time in residency at McGill University.

Rizwi Faizer received her basic degree in the University of Peradeniya, Sri Lanka, in 1970. After working for a couple of years under Neelan Tiruchelvam at the Asian Council for Law and Development she obtained a grant to enter the University of New Brunswick in 1982. Having completed her MA on "Muslim Ethno-Politics in Sri Lanka," she then entered McGill for an MA in Islamic Studies. It was Issa Boullata who first welcomed her to the department in 1984 and taught her in two courses, one on Modern Approaches to the Qur'ān, and the other on *tafsīr*. She obtained her PhD in 1995, after completing her dissertation "Ibn Isḥāq and al-Wāqidī Revisited," under the supervision of Donald Little. Since then she has taught Islam as a Sessional Lecturer at Carleton University, Ottawa, and written articles for scholarly journals, as well as for the *Encyclopaedia of the Qur'ān*, *Encyclopaedia of Islam and the Muslim World* and the *Encyclopaedia of Medieval Islamic Civilization*.

Alan M. Guenther is Assistant Professor of History at Briercrest College and Seminary in Saskatchewan. He received his PhD from the Institute of Islamic Studies, McGill University, writing his dissertation on the subject of "Syed Mahmood and the Transformation of Muslim Law in British India." In the course of his academic program, he had the opportunity to participate in two seminar courses on the exegesis of the Qur'ān led by Issa Boullata, and prepare research papers on the subject in connection with his own field of study, the historical development of the Muslim communities in South Asia. His paper on the Tablīghī Jamāᶜat and the Qur'ān included in this volume is one of those papers. He has published "Hanafi *Fiqh* in Mughal India: The *Fatawa-i 'Alamgfrt'*" in Richard Eaton's *India's Islamic Traditions, 711-1750* (2003) and other papers in *Oriente Moderno* (2002), *Muslim World* (2000), and *Islam and Christian-Muslim Relations* (1999).

Eltigani Hamid is an Associate Professor of Islamic Political Thought. He received his doctorate from the University of London (SOAS). He has taught and carried out research at several universities including the University of Khartoum, the International Islamic University(Malaysia),and the Graduate School of Islamic and Social Sciences (USA). He is the author of *The Qur'ān and Politics: A Study of the Origins of Political Thought in the Meccan Qur'ān* (London, 2004). His research interests covers Qur'ānic hermeneutics, Islamic reform movements and political philosophy. He currently teaches at Zayed University, United Arab Emirates (UAE). He is a great admirer of the works of Issa Boullata.

Soraya Mahdi Hajjaji-Jarrah is a PhD candidate in the Institute of Islamic Studies, McGill University, working on controversial Qur'ānic verses on women. Previously she taught in the Faculty of Education, University of Libya. She has studied with Issa Boullata and has published "Women's Modesty in Qur'anic Commentaries: The Founding Discourse" in *The Muslim Veil in North America: Issues and Debates*, edited by Sajida Alvi, Homa Hoodfar and Sheila McDonough and "The Enchantment of Reading: Sound, Meaning, and Expression in *Surat al-ᶜĀdiyāt*," in *Literary Structures of Religious Meaning in the Qur'ān*, edited by Issa Boullata.

Qamar-ul Huda is the Senior Program Officer in the Religion and Peacemaking Program at the United States Institute of Peace. His work focuses on Islamic thought and Islamic philosophy on violence, non-violence and conflict resolution. He holds a PhD in Islamic intellectual history from the History department at the University of California-Los Angeles and has taught Islamic Studies and Comparative Theology in Boston College's Theology department and at the College of Holy Cross and Brandeis University. Given his interest in theological studies, Issa Boullata suggested to Huda to systematically examine the medieval texts of Suhrawardī mysticism and their Qur'anic hermeneutics. He published his work as *Striving for Divine Union: The Spiritual Exercises of Suhrawardi Sufis* (2003). Recently he organized a USIP conference on "Islamic Reform relating to Conflict and Peace" at which scholars of Islamic studies explored interdisciplinary approaches to peace-building.

Roxanne D. Marcotte holds a BA in Philosophy from l'Université du Québec à Montréal and an MA and PhD in Islamic Studies from the Institute of Islamic Studies, McGill University; Issa Boullata was on the committee for her PhD oral defense. She publishes mainly in the field of medieval Arabic and Persian Islamic philosophy, but also on contemporary Muslim thinkers (in Syria, Morocco, Iran and Egypt) and on women's issues. She lived for five years in Tunisia and Jordan, as well as in Syria and Iran where she pursued doctoral research (1993–4) and held a Postdoctoral fellowship (2000–2002) at the Institut français d'études arabes à Damas and at the Institut français de recherche en Iran and Tehran University.

She is currently Lecturer in Studies in Religion at the University of Queensland in Australia.

Sheila McDonough is Professor Emerita at Concordia University. She completed her PhD in 1963 as the first female graduate of McGill University's Institute of Islamic Studies. She has published over 30 chapters and articles and four books, most recently *Gandhi's Responses to Islam* (1994) and *The Flame of Sinai: Vision and Hope in Iqbal* (2002). She has worked with the United Church of Canada to foster interfaith dialogue and promote Christian-Muslim relations. She is a neighbor and sometimes colleague of Issa Boullata.

Khaleel Mohammed is Associate Professor in the Department of Religious Studies at San Diego State University. He is also a core-faculty member of that institution's Center for Islamic and Arabic Studies. He studied Islamic law at the Imam Muhammad bin Saud University in Saudi Arabia and did his graduate education in Canada, obtaining his PhD from McGill University in 2001. He also completed a post-doctoral fellowship in Islamic studies at Brandeis University. His research areas are Islamic law, exegesis and Judaic-Islamic interaction throughout the centuries. He was a student of Issa Boullata at McGill University in classical and modern exegetical approaches to the Qur'ān, and both of his research papers from those courses have been published.

Yusuf Rahman was one of Issa Boullata's students at the Institute of Islamic Studies, McGill University. Rahman, an Indonesian, studied at the Institute from 1993 to 2001 in order to complete his MA and PhD degrees with the scholarship from CIDA and McGill-Indonesia Project of which Issa Boullata was one of the directors. He wrote his MA thesis and PhD dissertation under Boullata's supervision. The article in this book is a part of his dissertation entitled "The Hermeneutical Theory of Naṣr Ḥāmid Abū Zayd: An Analytical Study of His Method of Interpreting the Qur'ān." He currently teaches at the State Islamic University (UIN) Syarif Hidayatullah in Jakarta, Indonesia.

Andrew Rippin was a student at the Institute of Islamic Studies, McGill University, from 1974 to 1981 for his MA and PhD, during which time Issa Boullata joined the staff. He remembers formative classes with Boullata on Arabic stylistics and the Qur'ān. He was also fortunate to be a colleague of Boullata as a visiting professor at the Institute in 1990, and enjoyed his hospitality and graciousness during that year. Rippin is the author of *Muslims: their Religious Beliefs and Practices* (third edition 2005) and has gathered together some of his articles in a volume *The Qur'ān and its Interpretative Tradition* (2001). He is also the editor of many works on Islam and the Qur'ān. He is currently Dean of the Faculty of Humanities and Professor of Islamic History at the University of Victoria in British Columbia.

Sahiron Syamsuddin is a lecturer at the Sunan Kalijaga Institute of Islamic Studies, University of Yogyakarta, Indonesia. From 1996 to 1998 he studied at McGill University for his MA degree. During that program, he took several seminars offered by Issa Boullata on the Qur'ān and Arabic Stylistics, Modern Arabic Literature: Bint al-Shāṭi', and Qur'ānic Exegesis (Classical). He wrote his MA thesis entitled "An Examination of Bint al-Shāṭi''s Method of Interpreting the Qur'ān" under Boullata's supervision. He has published several articles resulting from his study at McGill including a chapter in *The Dynamics of Islamic Civilization* (1998), as well as in *Islamic Quarterly* (1998) and *Journal of Qur'anic Studies* (1999). From 2001 to 2006 he studied for his PhD at the Otto-Friedrich University of Bamberg, Germany. He wrote a dissertation on the inner-Islamic discussion on Muḥammad Shaḥrūr's hermeneutics under the supervision of Rotraud Wielandt.

Seth Ward teaches Islamic history and religious studies at the University of Wyoming at Laramie. He was Director of the Institute for Islamic-Judaic Studies at the University of Denver. He received his academic degrees from Yale University, with additional studies at Hebrew University and at the Jewish Theological Seminary. His PhD was on "Construction and Repair of Churches and Synagogues in Islamic Law." His academic interests include the Jews of Muslim Lands, Jewish-Muslim relations, and other aspects of Islamic-Judaic Studies. He has published widely in a number of scholarly journals.

ABBREVIATIONS

BSOAS	Bulletin of the School of Oriental and African Studies
EI1	*Encyclopaedia of Islam*, First Edition (Leiden 1913–38)
EI2	*Encyclopaedia of Islam*, New Edition (Leiden 1954–2005)
IBLA	Revue de l'Institut des belles lettres arabes
IJMES	International Journal of Middle East Studies
JAOS	Journal of the American Oriental Society
JRAS	Journal of the Royal Asiatic Society
JSAI	Jerusalem Studies in Arabic and Islam
MIDEO	Mélanges de l'Institut Dominicain d'études orientales du Caire
ZDMG	Zeitschrift der Deutschen Morganländischen Gesellschaft

INTRODUCTION

Current popular attention to the Qur'ān often includes observations concerning the absolute authority of that document and the lack of freedom in interpreting it. The image has been received that Muslims simply accept their scripture with little thought and little question. The reality is far different. Not only is there an active scholarly community involved with detailed study of the Qur'ān in every conceivable way, but Muslims around the world have been and are constantly questioning, reinterpreting, and interacting with the Qur'ān. Coming to terms with the Qur'ān is not a matter of reconciling oneself to the obvious sense of the text but is a process of examination and understanding.

This collection of essays, organized as a part of the celebration of the seventy-fifth birthday [February 25, 2004] of Professor Issa J. Boullata of the Institute of Islamic Studies, McGill University, is devoted to elucidating the many dimensions of understanding the Qur'ān. Issa Boullata has spent his scholarly career teaching and writing prolifically on Arabic literature in general and especially the Qur'ān, inspiring a generation of scholars in their reflections and analyses of the qualities of the Muslim sacred text. Many of those students, along with a groups of friends, have contributed essays all of which are devoted to explicating the Qur'ān in its historical and contemporary contexts. They constitute, as a group, a fitting tribute to the way in which Issa Boullata has affected the academic study of the Qur'ān in Canada, the United States, Indonesia, and around the world. Boullata's students know well his insistence on concise presentations, his embodiment of the Arab saying *Khayr al-kalām mā qalla wa dalla*—"The best of speech is that which is concise and instructive." With this in mind, the editors of this volume consider the following essays fitting to honor Issa Boullata as a reflection of the field of study that his irenic approach has cultivated. When the Middle East Studies Association awarded its 2004 Mentoring Award to Boullata, he was commended for being "an outstanding mentor who has introduced so many to the joys of scholarship and who has, through his generous sharing of knowledge, encouraged the careers of generations of students and colleagues." The fourteen essays of this volume are testimony to that, each of them devoted to explicating the Qur'ān in its historical and contemporary contexts.

The material in this volume has been separated into three main categories: (1) Problems in reading the Qur'ān; (2) The Qur'ān in history; and (3) The Qur'ān in the modern world. The four articles in the first section underline the issue of dealing with problematic usages. Eltijani Hamid examines the several terms in the Qur'ān, with particular focus on the root *iṣlāḥ*, to propose a theoretical construct for reformation within Islam. Most scholars interested in Islamic reform look to the teachings of such writers as Muḥammad ᶜAbduh and Rashīd Riḍa. Instead, Hamid argues one should look at how the Qur'ān refers to "reform" (*iṣlāḥ*) and where the attributes of *ṣāliḥ* and its opposite state, *fasād*, are discussed. These terms refer to more than what the Arabic lexicon defines as "righteousness" or "mischievousness." God created humans in the best possible form, *aḥsan taqwīm*, and gave them the ability to balance right and wrong. This dynamism between *iṣlāḥ* and *fasād* within the individual is present in the external world as well. *Iṣlāḥ* promotes a personal behavior and social responsibility to maintain the balance necessary for a just social order.

Next, Khaleel Mohammed argues that Muḥammad's contemporaries would have understood certain Qur'ānic terms differently from later Muslims. He reveals the changes in interpretation that have occurred regarding the term *ahl al-dhikr* (Q. 16:43, 21:7). While early scholars perceived the term as referring to Jews only, later exegetes widened it to include Christians as well. The widespread contemporary understanding is that *ahl al-dhikr* refers to learned Muslims, and this is further restricted in Shīᶜī circles to their *imāms* only.

Andrew Rippin examines the use of the words for "blind" in the Qur'ān and notes that while the words do, in some instances, clearly refer to those who are physically blind, it also becomes associated with a metaphorical usage with a sense of doubt, error, dark, lacking understanding, and sickness. These connotations, then, convey an attitude towards the blind that associates those who are characterized physically this way with these metaphorical connotations. So, despite the positive view of those who are physically blind that is contained in the Qur'ān, the passages which may or must be read metaphorically will always convey their connotations back upon the physiological nature of blindness. Rippin argues that the power of metaphor and of language as a product of its own time and space to convey social attitudes and perspectives is clear, but also highly problematic for contemporary interpretation.

In the final entry in the first section, Seth Ward examines certain verses of the Qur'ān showing that, within the Islamic scripture, there is room for interpretation that could set the foundation for a peaceful coexistence between Muslims and Jews in Israel. Acknowledging the Qur'ān's affirmation of the chosenness of Jews and their claim to the Promised Land is a necessary step to be taken by those who seek an Islamic-Judaic discourse, Ward suggests. Passages in the Qur'ān support the idea that God considered Jewish people as chosen, and He ordered them to dwell in the land. The question of which land has various different interpretations; it is generally considered to be the land of Abraham and Jacob. An analysis of *asbāb al-nuzūl* shows that it was the later Medinan *sūra*s that reflect negative changes to the position that Jews hold in the Qur'ān.

"The Qur'ān in History"—the second section—consists of four articles that seek to cast light upon hitherto problematic areas. Rizvi Faizer examines the inscriptions on the Dome of the Rock (dated 72/692) which include sections from the Qur'ān, raising issues related to the date of the canonization of the Qur'ān. Despite the caliph ᶜUthmān's best efforts to canonize a single version of the Qur'ān, the inscriptions in the Dome, ascribed to the Umayyad Caliph ᶜAbd al-Malik, appear to be taken from one of several versions of the text that continued to be used. The inscriptions—which include references to the nature of Christ/Jesus—reflect one such version that assigns a more important role to Christian beliefs, Faizer argues.

Asma Afsaruddin shows the different ways in which Qur'ānic verses were used by Shīᶜī and Sunnī polemicists in their support of their respective claimants to the caliphate. The Sunnī and Shīᶜī dispute regarding whether Abū Bakr or ᶜAlī was more qualified to lead the Muslim community (as caliph or *imām*) is a debate that is based on two Qur'ānic passages, Q. 9:40, *āyat al-ghār* ("the verse of the cave") and Q. 2:207, *āyat al-mabīt* ("the verse of the night stopover"). The *ghār* verse refers to the Prophet's and Abu Bakr's refuge in a cave while escaping from the Meccans; Abū Bakr's role is seen by the Sunnīs as a testament to his preeminent stature. The *mabīt* verse refers to ᶜAlī's substitution of himself in the place of the Prophet—a testament of his rights to leadership according to the Shīᶜa.

Carl El-Tobgui explains the idea of *muḥkam* and *mutashābih* verses in the Qur'ān according to the exegesis of the twelfth-century Fakhr al-Dīn al-Rāzī. Al-Rāzi is shown to view as sheer presumption any attempt to specify the exact meaning of *mutashābih* ("unclear" or "metaphorical") verses that deal with fundamental creedal matters whose details, in some instances, remain known exclusively to God—a remarkably conservative position, at the end of the day, for a thinker as philosophically inclined as al-Rāzī. El-Tobgui argues that this more than anything, perhaps, confirms that al-Rāzī—notwithstanding his reputation as a thinker who ventures into the outer bounds of philosophical speculation—remains, when all is said and done, firmly within the worldview of classical Ashᶜarism.

In the final essay of this section, Qamar-ul Huda shows how the scholars of the Suhrawardī school of mystical Islam use an esoteric approach in explicating the Qur'ān and *ḥadīth*. This approach to authoritative sources seeks an understanding of the inner spiritual messages found in these sources. Huda shows that al-Suhrawardī (d. 631/1234) taught strict observance of the *sharīᶜa*, a model to emulate the Prophet's conduct, and the use of *ᶜaql* ("intellect") as a tool of *taṣawwuf*. Al-Suhrawardī's disciple, Zakariyyā (d. 660/1262) followed in his master's footsteps and emphasized prayer, as well as the receptivity of the heart, for spiritual guidance. Zakariyyā differs from al-Suhrawardī in that he was not as concerned with linking *taṣawwuf* to the *sharīᶜa* as was his teacher.

The six papers in the final section, "The Qur'ān in the Modern World," all testify to the changes that different exegetical approaches affect on the Qur'ān. Roxanne Marcotte deals with the pioneering work of Bint al-Shāṭi' ᶜĀ'isha ᶜAbd al-Raḥmān (1913–98), the Egyptian professor whose departure from the traditional exegetical approaches can be said to have provided the grounding for the foundations of a feminist hermeneutic. Bint al-Shāṭi' was an early advocate of women's rights, despite her opposition to leftist ideologies. Marcotte shows that Bint al-Shāṭi' explains that women's inferior status is the result of the prior generation's "harem society," where men assumed responsibility for women's moral virtue. The modern woman has the obligation to assume that responsibility for herself; her salvation is, after all, a consequence of her personal actions. A woman's right to education is integral to Muslim concepts of humanity. By virtue of her education, a woman can play an active role in religious interpretation, a role that is especially attested to in *ḥadīth*.

Yusuf Rahman's focus is on the theories of the contemporary Egyptian scholar Naṣr Abū Zayd, whose radical stance of viewing the Qur'ān as a literary text like any other text led to his exile from his homeland to Europe. Rahman shows that Abū Zayd has benefited in particular from modern and postmodern theories of interpretation, but his theory falls within the category of modernism rather than postmodernism; Abū Zayd insists that, with his theory, one can reach an objective understanding of the text because of the humanity and historicity of the revelation itself. Although the content of the Qur'ān is from God, Abū Zayd argues, it is expressed in human language, and therefore it is correlated with cultural and historical contexts.

Soraya Hajjaji-Jarrah illustrates the evolution in the exegesis of Sayyid Quṭb (d. 1966), focusing on the diametrical changes in his views on the inimitability of the Qur'ān. In his writings in the 1940s, Qutb advocates a literary approach to Qur'ānic studies and to the inimitability *(iᶜjāz)* of the Qur'ān. He discusses the power that *taṣwīr* ("portrayal") and *takhyīl* ("imagery") have in their appeal to the emotions and senses of those reading the Qur'ān. In his later writings, however, he condemns literary approaches in a change of point of view that Quṭb himself acknowledges. When his political position has more bearing on his interpretations, he emphasizes a more doctrinal interpretation. The *iᶜjāz* of the Qur'ān becomes seen as a testimony to the Qur'ān's exceptional message.

Sahiron Syamsuddin examines the exegetical approach of Muḥammad Shaḥrūr, a contemporary Syrian engineer whose new theories have led to the banning of his books in many Arab countries. Shaḥrūr uses a semantic method focused on inner-Qur'ānic exegesis, and

Syamsuddin examines his approach by looking first at his theory of revelation and then at the way in which he understands the nature of God through the ideas of *rubūbiyya* ("world mastery", "lordship") and *uluhiyya* ("worshipped-ness", "divineness"). He then examines Shaḥrūr's attitude of pluralism as displayed through his understanding of the word *islām* and *īmān*.

Sheila McDonough examines the different perceptions of the Qur'ān by two of the Asian sub-continent's most famous contemporaries Muḥammad Iqbāl and Gandhi, and how those perceptions impacted on their religious outlook. Gandhi and Iqbāl are shown to share a common readiness to appreciate religious experience as a human possibility not restricted to any one tradition. They differed, however, in their attitudes to the possibilities of genuinely new developments taking place within historical time. Gandhi showed little interest in the question as to whether anything new could happen. For Iqbāl, however, this notion was central. It meant, for him, that individuals and societies could learn from past mistakes, and go on to create better human institutions. The essential characteristic of human consciousness, in Iqbāl's view, was that the present could be transcended, and the new could be created; this was the lesson of the Qur'ān.

Finally, Alan Guenther focuses on the Deobandi-Ṣūfī approach to interpreting the Qur'ān by two of the Tablīghī Jamāᶜat's most revered proponents, Muḥammad Ilyās (1885–1944) and his nephew, Muḥammad Zakariyyā (1898–1982). The Tablīghī Jamāᶜat movement supported *taqlīd* ("following traditional interpretations") rather than *ijtihād* ("independent reasoning"). Both men were heavily influenced by Ṣūfism. Ilyās initially established elementary religious schools, but later turned his attention to the parents of those children and appealed to them to join Jamāᶜat in order to learn the fundamentals. He rejected the traditional role of the *ᶜulamā'* whom he considered to be too far removed from the masses. Zakariyyā was more scholarly than his uncle and gained a reputation for his work on the *ḥadīth*.

This collection of works, then, with its vast array of themes, is a fitting tribute and testimony to the way in which Issa Boullata has affected the study of the Qur'ān the world over. The book has taken several years to bring it into published form and the editors would like to thank the contributors for their patience; their dedication to the idea of being a part of this book honoring Issa Boullata kept them all committed, despite the various delays. The editors also wish to thank Mona Sedky Goode, currently a PhD student in Victoria but also a holder of an MA from McGill University's Institute of Islamic Studies, for her editorial help in making the completion of this volume possible. Finally, Moin Shaikh of Islamic Publications International has been everything one could hope for from a publisher: prompt, efficient, helpful, and generally a pleasure to work with. His support of this project is greatly appreciated by everyone involved in it.

— *Khaleel Mohammed & Andrew Rippin*

Problems in reading the

Qur'ān

Chapter 1

The Concept of Reform in the Qur'ān

Eltigani Abdulqadir Hamid

In recent years there has been growing interest among students of Islam in discerning the intellectual roots of the current Islamic resurgence. Most studies, however, have not gone beyond the nineteenth and early twentieth century ideologies of reform and renewal—especially the ideology of reform advocated by Muḥammad ᶜAbduh and Rashīd Riḍā. Reform has, consequently, been defined as "the orthodox reformism of the type that emerges in the doctrinal teachings of Muḥammad ᶜAbduh, in the writings of Rashīd Riḍā and numerous Muslim authors who are influenced by these two masters."[1]

Works of ᶜAbduh, Riḍā and their disciples are important, but they cannot become the Islamic frame of reference, or the single formulation of the Islamic social theory. To discern that frame one has to go farther back to the Qur'ānic foundations of Islamic thought and try to unfold the intricate conceptual system embedded therein prior to any ideological presuppositions. Without knowing that conceptual system, neither the scholars nor the linguists and lexicographers on whom they rely can give a satisfactory definition of *iṣlāḥ,* "reform." Al-Fīrūzābādī (d. 817/1415) and Ibn Manẓūr (d. 711/1311), the two renowned Arab lexicographers, define *iṣlāḥ* as the opposite of *fasād*. But *fasād* itself is defined by them as the opposite of *iṣlāḥ*[2] thus leading us in a circle. Such negative definitions are sometimes useful, as we shall see later, but they are certainly insufficient.

The verbal roots *ṣaluḥa* and *fasada* are, indeed, opposites, but we cannot know what exactly they mean by simply turning to a dictionary. One way of analyzing the Qur'ānic terms *iṣlāḥ* and *fasād* is to trace them back to their roots. The basic meaning subsiding in the verbal root remains a unifying common element to which all derivatives can be traced in the same way that members of a family are traced back to their common ancestor. All members of a family share some minimum common attribute which stems from the family root. To apply the basic meaning to a member of a family is to make a generalization, that is, to form a concept in the etymological discourse.

The problem with such an etymological definition is that it is not always fruitful, as in this case of *ṣaluḥa*. Sometimes it turns out that the source of derivation for some words is beyond analysis, such that one can hardly take any generalization from it. This is the reason that has prompted some creative linguists, such as Ibn Jinnī (d. 392/1002), to invent what he calls the great derivation (*al-ishtiqāq al-akbar*)[3] which was a new technique whereby the letters of the verbal root are rearranged repeatedly to yield new ways of looking at ideas or objects.

If this fails, however, one is bound to go beyond the province of etymology to that of syntax where one can look at the text as a whole and into the linguistic structure within which the word occurs. Such a focus on relations within language is not, of course, a new thing. All linguists know that a sense of a term can be conveyed by other elements of language within a certain structure. This is a common feature in classical Arabic literature and most commentaries have applied it to the Qur'ānic text. But again this is not always sufficient; the Qur'ān is not a simple text. A Qur'ānic verse sometimes includes numerous allusions to other verses or other sources that stand as explanatory texts within the text. A reader of the Qur'ān who fails to see such intertextuality may fail to grasp the deeper Qur'ānic meanings. This compels anyone who attempts to fully understand the Qur'ān to shift the focus from the structures of words and language (that is, etymology and syntax), and delve into the Qur'ānic structure. The underlying assumptions here are that the Qur'ān is a phenomenon and, like all natural phenomena, it has an internal structure; that Qur'ānic words and verses occupy specific positions within that internal structure; and that the Qur'ān is self-reflective such that it explains itself by referring to other patterns of usage within its own system where additional information can be obtained. But if the Qur'ānic internal structure itself does not yield sufficient information, one has to look into the wider context from which the Qur'ānic metaphors are drawn, and towards that to which they refer. This wider context can be either the social and cultural environment within which the discourse has taken place or the natural phenomena that surround them.

By adopting this approach to the text of the Qur'ān, language is not overlooked, but neither is the focus exclusively on words. Our focus will be on relations between the language and the world, that is, on the situations and occasions in which the term is employed, rather than on relations within the language. We will attempt to perceive the word as a stimulus that might lead us beyond the linguistic structure, and refer us either to other sources of information within the Qur'ān, or to the wider social and/or natural environments; we will seek the context from which the accompanying images, linkages and associations that contribute to the formation of the unifying concept are drawn. In fact, this is exactly the function of metaphor in all languages. If we could pinpoint the images and associations of Qur'ānic metaphors, we may be in a position to discern the Qur'ānic conceptual system and sub-systems. Our purpose is twofold: to explore the possibility of employing the concept of *iṣlāḥ* as a key-concept that might lead to a network of interrelated Qur'ānic concepts, and to see whether we can construct, on the basis of such concepts, a sound framework that would serve as an explanatory tool for examining social and political phenomenon.

Qur'ānic descriptive definitions of *ṣāliḥ*

The word *ṣaluḥa* and its derivatives occurs 180 times in the Qur'ān. It would be impracticable, even undesirable, to pursue all of these occurrences. Fortunately, some of these terms have been used repeatedly, either to emphasize or to expand some basic meanings. Deleting these repeated meanings (162 verses), we are left with eighteen verses.[4] This group will, then, constitute the field of our study, and we will begin our research by examining the descriptive definitions that the Qur'ān provides.

The term *ṣāliḥ* is usually translated as righteous, or virtuous, which is correct as far as the Arabic lexicon is concerned. However, in addition to what the dictionary says, one needs to know much more about the properties of a *ṣāliḥ* person, about the types of actions he performs, and the kind of relations in which he is engaged. It is our objective in this study to re-examine the eighteen verses where the term *ṣaluḥa* and its derivatives occur, so as to find out whether the Qur'ānic text can, independently, provide significant information that would help in specifying the referent.

There are at least two occasions (Q. 3:113–4 and 4:34) where the Qur'ān's inbuilt system of definitions provides more specific information about the characteristics of those described as *ṣāliḥ*. The Qur'ān observes that not all of the People of the Book are alike; some of them are an *umma* that stands for the right; they rehearse the signs of God all night long, and they prostrate themselves in adoration. They believe in God and the last day; they enjoin what is right, and forbid what is wrong; and they hasten (in emulation) in all good works: they are in the ranks of the *ṣāliḥūn* (Q. 3:113–114).

In this passage, the term *ṣāliḥūn* has been explicated by way of using it as a label for a pattern of behavior that has been clearly reported in the text. Instead of describing the *ṣāliḥūn* only as righteous or virtuous, we have an extended description of their personal performances, convictions, purposes, types of public actions, and interactions, as could be summarized in the following list:

1. they believe in God, the Last Day, and they establish prayers; that is, they have a vision about the human destiny, the good life, and they have a vision about the means of achieving it;
2. they are an organized group within the broader society;
3. they stand for truth and justice;
4. They enjoin what is right, and oppose what is wrong;
5. They hasten in all good deeds.

This is in fact a verbal definition of the term *ṣāliḥ*, which is so illuminating that one would hardly need any additional information from an Arabic lexicon.

The second passage Q. 4:34 where *ṣāliḥūn* characters are identified reads, "Therefore the *ṣāliḥāt* (righteous women) are devoutly obedient, and guard (in the husband's) absence what God would have them guard." Here again we have a verbal definition where more information is given about the characteristics and behavior of the righteous women:

1. they stand firm in their beliefs and worship;
2. they adhere strictly to moral codes in their private life;
3. they guard their husbands property and reputation.

A wife who violates any of these requirements would degenerate from the position of the *ṣāliḥāt* to that of betrayal, as is explicitly mentioned in Q. 66:10, "God sets an example for those who disbelieve: the wife of Noah and the wife of Lot: they were (respectively) under two of our *ṣāliḥ* servants but they betrayed their husbands." Betrayal here is tantamount to eroding the foundations of the family.

We have been able, so far, to gather some basic information that helps in identifying the *ṣāliḥūn* in the Qur'ānic perspective. But that is not all. In addition to these Qur'ānic inbuilt definitions, there are other clues which are equally important, although they are not as explicit as the former descriptive definitions. One such clue resides in the Qur'ānic style of informing, emphasizing and evaluating by way of comparison and contrast. The Qur'ān urges its reader to understand the meaning of *iṣlāḥ* by looking into its opposite form, *fasād*.[5] Like *iṣlāḥ*, the word *fasād* is used with great frequency in the Qur'ān. To know what types of conduct are generally regarded *ṣāliḥāt* and what types of personalities referred to as *ṣāliḥūn*, the Qur'ān refers its reader to the characteristics and actions of the mischief-makers, *mufsidūn,* who are highlighted occasionally in various passages in the Qur'ān. The *mufsidūn* are everything that the *muṣliḥūn* are not. The two groups are in complete contrast, representing two diametrically opposed characteristics and conduct in private and public life.

Verses 8 to 18 and 204 to 206 of the second chapter of the Qur'ān give the longest and most elaborated description of the conduct of the *fasād*-makers. A brief analysis of these verses is in order:

> (1) And of the people there are some who say: we believe in God and the Last Day, but they do not (really) believe. They think to deceive God and those who believe, but they deceive none but themselves; and they perceive not. In their

> hearts is a disease, and God has increased their disease. A painful doom is theirs because they lie (to themselves). And when it is said to them: make no *fasād* in the earth, they say: we are only *muṣliḥūn*. Are not they indeed the *mufsidūn* (mischief-makers) but they perceive not. (Q. 2:8–18)
>
> (2) There is the type of man whose speech about this world's life may dazzle thee, and he calls God to witness about what is in his heart; yet is he the most contentious of enemies. When he turns his back, his aim everywhere is to spread *fasād* through the earth and destroy crops and progeny but God loveth not the *fasād*. When it is said to him, "Fear God," he is led by arrogance to more crime. (Q. 2:204–6)

These are strong statements about the hypocrites who oscillate between the believers and non-believers, trying to get the best of both worlds. It is an example of the shameful divergence between an acclaimed vision and reality, and it is exemplified in this group of hypocrites who pride themselves on being virtuous and reasonable, though they fail to internalize these values. The standard definition of a hypocrite is the one whose words and outward appearances contradict his true internal reality. Failing to internalize the core Islamic values, a person can neither attain internal peace nor can he be qualified to play the role of peacemaker in the external world (the *muṣliḥ)*. That is why the Qur'ān emphasizes that the hypocrites cannot be agents of peace.

Briefly outlined, the characteristics of the *mufsidūn* are:

1. they do not believe sincerely in God and the last Day (i.e., they have no definite conception about the ultimate human destiny);
2. they have disease in their hearts, and their perception of right and wrong is somewhat clouded, their perception—both of themselves and of the others—is distorted;
3. they make mischief on earth by destroying crops and progeny;
4. they pretend to be peacemakers, but they stir up quarrels;

5. they are arrogant and insincere, though they have smooth tongues.

By identifying these characteristics of the *mufsidūn*, it has become now much easier to immediately identify the characteristics of their opponents, the *muṣliḥūn*, who are the exact opposite of this list. Briefly stated, the *muṣliḥūn* are sincere believers who have no disease in their hearts; they perceive the realities around them accurately; they work towards protecting the crops and progeny; they refrain from stirring quarrels and wars; and they are humble and straightforward in their words and deeds. But if the *muṣliḥūn* and *mufsidūn* are so different, as indeed they are, what is then the basis of comparison? The answer, one may venture, is that both of them make claims to leadership, seek to occupy the public place, and call for moral integrity and sound behavior.

When we add these characteristics to the earlier ones that have been provided through descriptive definitions, we are in a position to make the claim that we have pinpointed the core meaning of the concept of *iṣlāḥ* that dominates all other peripheral meanings in the Qur'ān's internal structure. What is implied here is that the core meaning of *iṣlāḥ* will refer us, mainly through the usage of metaphor, to the peripheral meanings. The task ahead, then, is to try to discern those peripheral meanings of *iṣlāḥ* by way of seeking clues in the Qur'ān's style of description.

What is striking is that some of the descriptive definitions we have isolated are cast in metaphoric style. The hypocrites, for instance, are described as having disease in their hearts, they do not perceive, and the result of their excessive behavior is the destruction of the crop and progeny. In contrast to the *mufsidūn* who have disease in their hearts, we have the *ṣāliḥūn* who possess pure hearts, as is explicitly stated in the Q. 2:89 and 37:84. These metaphors are obviously drawn from the field of living organisms, human physiology, production and reproduction, but what does that imply? Are there any associations and linkages between these people's behavior and their physiological systems and environmental surroundings? Are these sources from whence the *ṣāliḥūn* and *mufsidūn* derive their strength, weaknesses and special skills? Does this imply that the qualities of *ṣalāḥ* and *fasād* are attributable, for instance, to the environmental circumstances and genetic endowment?

Obviously there is no quick answer to be found in the list of characteristics we have so far compiled, but it certainly does contains some useful metaphorical clues on the bases of which we can fairly conclude that the quality for which this type of people has earned praise is a quality that is related to the field of consciousness and inner virtues; for the heart in the Qur'ānic usage is the place of feelings, conscious, understanding and wisdom (see Q. 7:179; 22:46; 50:37). Staying unaffected by the diseases that afflict the *fāsidūn*, the perception of the *ṣāliḥūn* has not been distorted; hence, they are capable of knowing themselves, others and the world accurately.

These ideas are certainly the province of psychological and behavioral sciences, which would direct our attention to study the possible bio-psychical basis of *iṣlāḥ*, as well as to the environmental contingencies under which a person is induced to stand for truth, justice and the common good, or oppose them. But according to the methodology we are following, we should be aware that whatever findings we may arrive at will be peripheral meanings that are governed by the core meaning of *iṣlāḥ*.

The bio-psychical basis of *iṣlāḥ*

There is a reference in the Qur'ān to man's physiological composition and how God has fashioned him in due proportion (*sawwā*) (Q. 32:8–9). But there are also many hints in the Qur'ān to biological qualities, or genetic endowment, as a basis for a person being a *ṣāliḥ*. A number of verses lie within a context of biological reproduction. These verses are Q. 7:189–90, 11:46, 21:90 and 46:15. All of them occur within a context of childbearing, fertility and sterile couples who either lack the physical ability to reproduce or who are worried about bearing children who would be born with physical deformities.

Q. 7:189 reads "It is He who created you from a single *nafs*, and made his mate of like nature, in order that he might dwell with her (in love). When they are united, she bears a light burden and carries it about (unnoticed). When she grows heavy, they both pray to God their Lord, saying: 'If You give us a *ṣāliḥ* child we vow we shall ever be grateful'." In this verse (and the next one) a couple is invoking God to grant them a child who is *ṣāliḥ*. No precise information about the identity of the couple, their social or historical background is given in the text because, according to some accounts, the reference here is to Adam and Eve,[6] the founders of human race prior to whose existence there was no society or history to talk about. The couple was not sure, due to the lack of experience, whether their first-born would be a human being or another species. They prayed that if God would grant them a newborn of like nature, they would be grateful. Within this context, *ṣāliḥ* is probably an equivalent of *aḥsan taqwīm,* and both of them are used, according to the opinion of the classical authority Ibn ᶜAbbās (d. 68/686),[7] as a reference to man's bodily structure. Following Ibn ᶜAbbās, many of the earlier commentators conceived this *aḥsan taqwīm* in physical terms; that is, man has been created in the best physical structure, being bipedal in contradistinction to other animals which are either quadrupeds or reptiles crawling on the ground.[8]

There is, admittedly, an emphasis in the Qur'ān on the makeup and functioning of the human body; what conclusions can be drawn from this emphasis is a matter for debate. In another occasion, the Qur'ān draws our attention, for instance, to the clot which clings in a mother's womb and how God fashioned it (*sawwā*) in *aḥsan taqwīm* ("due proportion"); and how He made two sexes out of it, male and female (Q. 75:38–9). This could also be construed as a direct reference to the basic biological unit of life, where growth and multiplication take place. Almost everyone today holds that a human being springs from a single cell and that this original cell contains a great number of distinct and separable parts, each of which performs an important function in the overall living process.[9]

Can we, then, define *ṣalāḥ* in terms of corporeal structure and physique-biological fitness? And what does physical fitness mean? It is not possible to give a definite answer to this question at this preliminary stage of inquiry but it may be sufficient to state for now that physical composition is the prime part of the meaning of (*ṣāliḥ*) in this context. However, some later commentators and theologians have shown dissatisfaction with this interpretation, and suggested some modifications. Ibn ᶜAṭiyya (d. 546/1151) summarizes the issue in this way:

> People have differed on the meaning of *aḥsan taqwīm*. According to al-Nakhāᶜī, Mujāhid and Qatāda, it means the beauty of his shape and senses; to others it means the erection of his stature. It was Abū Bakr ibn Ṭāhir who said, as quoted in al-Thaᶜlabi's book, that it is man's mind and cognitive power that makes him beautiful and able to distinguish between things. The truth is that all these together convey what is meant by the beauty of his form.[10]

In this vein, al-Ālūsī (d. 1854) also interprets *aḥsan taqwīm* as meaning that man has been created in the best possible form, which includes a beautiful stature, functioning senses and mind. [11]

Ibn ᶜAṭiyya, al-Ālūsī and the authorities on whom they relied wanted to give support to what they believed to be the rational dimension of man. By relating the physical form of man to his mental soundness, these commentators have added a rational element to the meaning of the concept *aḥsan taqwīm*. Whether this idea is a result of a profound reflection on the Qur'ān or disguised Aristotelian orientation[12] we cannot immediately ascertain. In other places in the Qur'ān, the concepts of *taswiya* and *taqdīr* are obviously used to convey the meaning of bodily structure. No mention of the mind as distinct from body is made. Hence, it would be fair to conclude that the Qur'ānic term *sawwā* is a reference to the balanced combining of different organs or systems (nervous, digestive, respiratory, etc.) of which the human body is composed. We need to have a closer look into one of the passages where the fullest exposition of the process of Divine creation is given, Q. 32:7–9: "He who created all things in *aḥsan taqwīm*, and He began the creation of man from clay, and made his progeny from quintessence of despised fluid, and He *sawwā* him, and breathed into him from His spirit, and He gave you (the faculties of) hearing and sight and understanding (*af'ida*)—little thanks do you give." Here the concept of *taswiya* is added to the earlier concept of *aḥsan taqwīm*. The past tense *sawwā* means "made a thing equal, uniform, even, level, straight or rightly directed."[13] *Taswiya*, however, does not mean merely that some one (God) brought different things together, but it means that he combined them, skillfully, in a highly balanced and carefully weighed ratio. In the view of the classical exegete al-Ṭabarī (d. 310/923) *taswiya* means straightening up (*taᶜdīl*).[14] Thus, one cannot do justice to the concept of *aḥsan taqwīm*, in which a human being is created, without taking into account the concept of the balanced bodily design (*qadar/taqdīr*).

These verses bear clear references to the creation of the human body, but in addition to that they also refer to the infusion between the Divine breathe and the human body. The outcome of this infusion is to be the human *nafs,* which can safely be translated as the human psyche—not mind or soul, as they are usually but mistakenly used. So the *nafs* is partially composed of the same stuff, out of which the natural world is made, but it also contains a portion of the divine breath—whatever that might be.[15] The central meaning that these verses convey is the balanced physical-psychical wholeness of a person. For one can hardly be described as *ṣāliḥ* or in his *aḥsan taqwīm* if his physical composition is totally out of proportion to his psychical system.

We have now reached a point where the relations between the body, *nafs* and divine breath have to be specified. What is clear in the Qur'ānic narrative is that the human body and human *nafs* are closely related, if not made up of the same substance. To be sure, *nafs* is not the body, but it could be a reference to the system of stimuli (or drives) which is connected with the various senses and organs of the body and which persistently seeks gratification. This system of stimuli is often referred to in the Qur'ān as the *hawā* (pleasure or lower desires). Following it blindly is seen as a cardinal mistake or sin that leads to failure, corruption and destruction: "But as for him who feared to stand before his Lord and restrained his *nafs* from *al-hawā*, his abode will be the Garden" (Q. 79:40–1).

Hence, unlike the hedonist, a *ṣāliḥ* is a person who submits himself to the *hudā* (or God's guidance), and refuses to succumb to his *hawā* (or lower desires). He refuses the unconditional gratification of his physiological drives, which means he is able to restrain his *nafs* (physiological demands) and put it under the command of his *qalb* (moral vision) and rational imperatives. This process of restraining the *nafs*, is equated with the process of maintaining the *mīzān* (balance) within one own self, as well as with the outer environment. So important as it is, this concept of *mīzān* is elaborated in the following passage: "We sent aforetime Our messengers with clear signs and sent down with them the Book and the *mīzān* (or the balance of right and wrong), that men may stand forth in justice; and We sent down iron, in which is great might, as well as many benefits for mankind" (Q. 57:25). In the opinion of Ibn ᶜAbbās and some of his disciples (Mujāhid and Qatāda), *mīzān* means justice. Most of the later commentators (e.g., al-Ṭabarī, al-Zamakhsharī, and al-Rāzī) have accepted this opinion and reproduced it in their works.[16] To them, the *mīzān* is a reference to the principles of justice which have to be understood in the most general sense that covers moral as well as legal instructions.

There are three things explicitly emphasized in this Qur'ānic verse: the book, the balance, and iron. They stand as symbols of three elements that would hold the society together: faith, justice, and material power respectively. But justice, of course, has to be maintained and upheld within an actor's own *nafs* before attempting to do that in the outer environment. Those who claim to uphold justice in the wider society without upholding it in themselves are the hypocrites who spread the *fasād* on earth.

In this context, the self is not to be seen as monolithic entity, but as an arena of various contending drives, each of which is pushing towards its own satisfaction. The *ṣāliḥ* person is a one who has acquired an ability of self-restraining. But self-restraint is only the first step in a long route of *tazkiya* (self-purification and self-governance); this is another important concept that comes immediately as a concluding remark in Q. 91:1–10: "By the sun... By the moon... By the night. ...and the heaven and by the *nafs* and the proportion and order given to it.... Truly he succeeds who has *zakkāhā* (purified it), and he fails who corrupts it." This is probably one of the rare occasions upon which Qur'ānic cosmology, psychology and sociology are brought together. The purpose is twofold: one, to draw the attention to the fact that the contending forces of *iṣlāḥ* and *fasād* within the human psyche are not unique—similar opposing forces do also exist in the cosmos and in societies; and two, to emphasize that the internal *fasād*, resulting from the triumph of the *hawā* (lower desires) within the *nafs* is connected with the greater *fasād* in the external world. This link between the internal psychical *fasād* and the external global one is so important that it has been re-emphasized explicitly in Q. 23:71 and 30:41. So, there is no room for a crude environmentalism in which man's behavior is thought to be totally shaped by his environment; nor is there a room for the autonomous man who is believed to be totally unaffected by the environment and unchangeable. There are internal, psychical dynamics that affect the external human behavior but there are also external contingencies that affect the inner human psyche.

But if everybody is created *ṣāliḥ*, and in *aḥsan taqwīm*, why then should these parents feel worried at all? Does this imply that there were infants who had been born with natural defects and deformities, as the worries of these two parents attested to and as the medical conditions in prehistoric times could be imagined. We may suspend judgment on this issue till we examine more occasions.

The case of Zakariyyā'

"And remember Zakariyyā' when he cried to his lord: O my Lord, leave me not without offspring, though Thou art the best of inheritors. So We listened to him and we granted him Yaḥyā: We *aṣlaḥnā* his wife for him" (Q. 21:89–90). This is a case of a person who is somewhat frustrated about his own condition because he was getting old, his wife was barren, and he was aspiring for a son to carry on his line. He cried out, "O my Lord, leave me not without offspring." As a reply to his prayer, God cured his wife's barrenness. For that process of curing barrenness the Qur'ān uses the word *aṣlaḥnā*, which implies that there was a prior state of physiological defect.

Muslim scholars and interpreters have differed on the meaning of *aṣlaḥnā*. Some of them have concluded that it is a reference to the divine act of curing Zakariyyā''s wife who had been *ᶜaqīm* (barren). Others thought that the woman was ill-mannered and God enhanced her manners. In al-Ṭabarī's opinion, both meanings are possible because the verb *aṣlaḥnā* has been used in the general sense. No one has a right, al-Ṭabarī says, to restrict it to one particular meaning to the exclusion of the others.[17] This view, however, can hardly be accepted since Zakariyyā''s wife is praised elsewhere in the Qur'ān (Q. 21:90), and her piety and devotion are emphasized. In fact, it is her barrenness and not her ill-manners which has been explicitly mentioned in the Qur'ān (Q. 3:40). But what were the possible causes of that woman's barrenness? Was it, for instance, a result of purely physiological (or genetic) malfunctioning, or would it be possible to assume a kind of connection between her infertility and her psychical conditions? For if we assume that there was a psychical basis for that woman's disease, then we will not need to restrict the general meaning of *aṣlaḥnā*, as both al-Ṭabarī and al-Zamakhsharī would insist. It could be argued that prior to her religious commitment, which earned her the Qur'ānic praise, Zakariyyā''s wife had undergone some psychical disturbances that affected her fertility as well as her manner. But through communal prayers, family support, and sincere devotion, she regained her self-confidence and, accordingly, she was healed of both psychical and bodily diseases.[18]

It is interesting to note, however, that as all things—and not only humans—have been created in *aḥsan taqwīm*, so all things also are vulnerable to some kinds of infertility. This concept of *ᶜuqm*, or barrenness, is often mentioned in the Qur'ān; but not only as a feminine or a human condition. A wind that does not cause clouds to produce rain is *rīḥ ᶜaqīm*,[19] and a land that is incapable of production is also *ᶜaqīm*. In Q. 2:223 wives are likened to lands that are ploughed up for sowing. In the likeness of one sowing seeds on the ground, he also drops his sperm in his wife's womb, thus sowing his offspring (note the same metaphor of *ḥarth* and *nasl*).

Focusing on the structures and functions of the human body and psyche (as we did in the two aforementioned cases) has, thus, drawn attention to the structure of the natural world. The creation of human beings and their *iṣlāḥ,* is not totally different from the creation of the natural world and its *iṣlāḥ*; nor is the *fasād* in the human psyche totally isolated from the *fasād* in the natural world. To clarify this observation, we need to map the wider cosmological horizons of *iṣlāḥ* and *fasād*.

The Cosmological Dimension of *iṣlāḥ*

In many occasions the Qur'ān speaks about the *iṣlāḥ* of the earth and the skies and urges people not to do mischief on them. Q. 7:56 says, "Do not do mischief on earth after it has been set in order (*iṣlāḥihā*)." The word *iṣlāḥihā* is highly important. It suggests two things: one, that the natural world has been structured according to the right order; and two, that its human inhabitants have been provided with principles and values, referred to in the Qur'ān as *mīzān* (or balance), which would keep the world in a state of *ṣalāḥ* (harmony, or balance), provided that these principles and values are sincerely followed.

So, in addition to the earlier concept of *disease in the heart*, we are now witnessing the emergence of a new concept, the *fasād fī'l-arḍ* ("corruption in earth"). *Arḍ* here could be a reference to the physical system of the cosmos and, in that sense, *fasād* on earth could be explicated ecologically to mean the waste, excessive use, and abuse of natural resources and other actions of deforming nature. There is a reference in the Qur'ān to this: "and the earth We have spread out (like a carpet); set thereon mountains firm and immovable; and produced therein all kinds of things in due *balance* (*mawzūn*)" (Q. 15:19). This is, according to the translator Abdullah Yusuf Ali, a direct reference to how the mineral kingdom supports the vegetable and they, in their turn, support the animal. There is a link of interdependence between these systems where excess is eliminated; the waste of one is made the food of another, and vice versa.[20] On the other hand, *iṣlāḥ* on earth would normally stand for the opposite meaning, that is, maintaining, preserving, and developing natural resources. However, *arḍ* could also imply a reference to the social system found in the human relations and, in that sense, *fasād* and *iṣlāḥ* on earth could mean social disruption and social reform respectively. But if people are created in the right set up, why do they really make mischief on earth? A clue for answering this question is given in the concept of *qalb* (or heart) which we have come across earlier. The people who make mischief on earth are described in these verses as people who have " disease in their hearts," So, *fasād* on earth and in society are closely related with the human psyche. The *fasād* on earth is not a disease of nature alone; it has its counterparts in the psychosocial domains.

The issue that now raises itself forcibly is what is man and what is the universe in the Qur'ānic conception? Are they related, and, if that is the case, in what way does the conception of the cosmic universe determine or shape men's conception of themselves, as well as their concrete actions and social relationships? And in what way does the conception of the human's self and the cosmic universe contribute to the formulation of an Islamic social theory?

It is noteworthy that this same issue of conceiving the cosmic universe, particularly the existence of disorder and evil in this world, as well as in the human psyche, has been a central question among non-Muslim religious scholars as well. The ancient Israelites, for instance, "did not conceive that God could create a disordered world. Therefore the evident disorder in the existing world cannot be due to the inability of God to create a world worthy of Himself, it must be attributed to the rebellion of man, (in the story of Adam and Eve) to man's refusal to recognize the true character of the deity. This rebellion of man is primeval and universal. Because of it man suffers in his family life, in his struggle with nature, in his strife with his fellow man (cf. Gen. LV) and finally in death."[21]

This appears to be a point of significant difference between Judaeo-Christian theology and Muslim theologians on the one hand, and Greek philosophy (particularly Plato and Aristotle) on the other. Muslim theologians agree that there is evident natural contradiction and affliction in the world, manifested in several forms of sufferings, injustices, evil occurrences and ugly creatures, but this is not due in any way to the rebellion of the first couple (Adam and Eve). As early as the tenth century, al-Māturīdī (d. 333/944) developed a concept of evil parallel to Plato's concept of beauty and Aristotle's concept of order such that God is the cause of beauty in objects and that God is the cause of order in objects. In al-Māturīdī's opinion, the existence of disharmony and disorder in the world demonstrates that it did not create itself but must have a maker. If the world had come out into being of its own will, it would have not settled down with less than the best of conditions and the best of qualities for itself.[22] There is no substance, he says,

> Which can be reduced to a single quality, be it negative or positive; good or bad; bless or distress. Anything that we describe as bad can also be described as good, though in an aspect other than that for which it has been designated as bad. This is true for all qualities and conditions of all things. They do not remain useful permanently, nor do they remain useless forever. This shows that the All-administering force is one, and that He has combined in each (substance) all aspects of good and bad.[23]

Within this view, the co-existence of the opposites as, for instance, in *ṣalāḥ* and *fasād,* and fertility and infertility, is not a problematic issue.

This idea of co-existence of good and evil has also re-emerged centuries later in the work of Ibn Taymiyya (d. 728/1328). He notices that there is disorder and misfortune in the world but he contends that there is always a *ḥikma* ("divine wisdom") behind creating ugly, harmful and evil things in the world.

> Behind all calamities that occur in the world there is a *ḥikma* since it is stated in the Qur'ān that He created all things in the *aḥsan taqwīm* (Q. 32:7). An evil or distress (*ḍarar*) that brings about a required *ḥikma* is not an absolute evil, though it would, of course, be a real evil according to those who are subjected to it.[24]

It is pretty clear that those two scholars were aiming to introduce and employ the notion of system and relativity. In the English language, a system can be a complex unity formed of many often diverse parts subject to a common purpose, or it can be an aggregation or assemblage of objects joined in regular interaction or interdependence; it can thus be a set of units combined by nature or art to form an integral organic or organized whole, an orderly working totality, a coherent unification.[25]

Al-Māturīdī's and Ibn Taymiyya's argument can then be formulated in this way: the world should be looked at holistically as systems of interrelated parts. Some one or something that is born ugly, harmful or defective is not totally out of place or useless; it has a function within the wider system of creation which we can discern and appreciate if only we try to go beyond appearances. This is the juncture where the Islamic tradition of theology has taken a decisive turn, and started to turn away from the classic Ashᶜarite atomistic cosmology, where the universe was seen as an occasion discontinuous of divine decrees.[26] This is also where al-Māturīdī and Ibn Taymiyya have traveled ahead of their times, started to take into account the environmental and social contingencies, and to attach, accordingly, relative values to beings, thus reformulating the Islamic theory of values and standing as forerunners of the nineteenth century structuralists/functionalists.[27]

Based on the foregoing discussion and observations, we can tentatively formulate the following hypothesis: that the world, according to Qur'ānic cosmology, is a diversified but organized phenomenon which is composed of separate but connected parts, each of which has a variety of characteristics and perform certain functions that contribute to the overall being of the world. Contradictions and disorder do exist, but they exist as parts of a system where opposites meet and adversaries coexist. This also could lead to the opinion that the initial *aḥsan taqwīm* upon which human beings are created is an open-ended universal design that contains potentialities and possibilities. A child is initially designed in *aḥsan taqwīm* in the sense that his bodily structure is quite in line with his psychical disposition, but there is no guarantee that when he interacts with the environment around him he will remain *ṣāliḥ*. A woman's womb is designed to conceive but barrenness is a possibility, since she would normally be susceptible to numerous influences; wind is supposed to cause rain but it might fail to do so due to other opposing factors. Hence a process of *iṣlāḥ*, where good is pursued and developed, and evil is suppressed and purged, is always needed. For those who are sincerely engaged in this process, God will be on their side. This will not lead to the negation of causality, but it will certainly negate all notions of absolute determinism in nature and will open the gates for change and reform.

God has sent the prophets with the book and the *mīzān*, that is, with the value-system and law. There are three types of *āyāt* referred to in the Qur'ān: the pattern of natural behavior that the cosmos follows, the pattern of biological behavior that a human body follows, and the pattern of values that human beings ought to follow. Neither the natural, nor the biological (or, for that matter, the ancestors and their inherited norms) should set the standards of wrong and right for human beings. Human beings need an "informed source" (*mīzān*) that would lay down a criterion of right and wrong. At one level this informing source manifests itself through the inspired, restraining *nafs*, which presides over the internal physiological nature; at another level this source is embodied on the revealed positive law (*sharīᶜa*), which preside over the external human behavior. Within this context, *iṣlāḥ* does not mean that we ought to just "preserve" the natural set up as we find it. It means, in addition, that we must control it and bring it into compliance with the internal as well as the external *mīzān*.

It is time now to see how these aforementioned psychical and cosmological conceptions could be related to the Qur'ānic social perspective. We need to know what are, precisely, the bases on which the human society is built, and how the human *nafs* interacts with its social environment. What are the Qur'ānic verses that address the issue of social environment where the term of *iṣlāḥ* occurs?

The Social Environment of *iṣlāḥ*: Social Interactions and Conflict Situations

These questions bring us back to our earlier list of eighteen verses where we can readily detect at least eight occasions of social conflict and conflict resolution, Q. 2:11, 2:182, 2:220, 2:228, 11:117, 27:48, 28:19 and 49:9–10, where *iṣlāḥ* is used. The central theme in all these verses revolves around conflictual situations in which town-dwellers (whether heroes or villains) are grappling with problems of power, wealth and ethnic violence. In most of these situations, actors are engulfed in an environment where a just and peaceful social order is out of reach. Various instances of injustices, corruption, and fighting are presented where ethnic groups, broken families, widows, female orphans, weak and oppressed children are pushed into the fore of the community's attention. Again and again it is impressed on individuals and groups that they must show readiness for reconciliation, concessions, and peacemaking. Rather than general references to the physical environment (land and earth) which are so common in other passages, references here are more specific and directed to the social rather than the natural world including villages and towns as dwelling places. There are also references to identifiable groups, blood relationships and extra-ethnic religious associations. An allusion to the dichotomy between ethnicity-based and religious-based associations is also made.

The Case of Noah

> "And Noah called upon his Lord and said: O my Lord, surely my son is of my family and Thy promise is true, and Thou art the most just of judges. He said: O Noah, he is not of thy family: for it is a conduct which is not *ṣāliḥ*. So ask not of Me that of which you have no knowledge. I give you counsel, so that you will not become one of the *jāhilūn*" (Q. 11:46).

In these verses Noah is presented as a kind-hearted father who is praying for the safety of his drowning son, but God's response was: "O Noah, he is not of thy family: for it is a conduct which is not *ṣāliḥ*." The Qur'ānic phrase *ghayr ṣāliḥ* is so ambiguous that commentators could not agree on its possible meaning. Some of them saw this as a moment of a shocking discovery in Noah's life. All of sudden it was brought to his attention that the child he had always considered his son was, in fact, illegitimate. According to this interpretation, *ṣāliḥ* is used here in the technical sense to denote the illegality of children born out of the wedlock.[28] Other interpreters have fervently argued against this opinion. To them, the phrase "he is not of thy family," means he is not a believer in your religion and consequently he is not a member of your religious community.[29] This, however, does not mean that he is not related to you by blood. So, in terms of blood relations, the boy was Noah's son, but in terms of spirituality he was not. Here blood (biological) and spiritual relations do not coincide; in fact, they are in direct contradiction. On another occasion, we are told that Noah's wife was also a non-believer, and that she was a dishonest wife who betrayed her husband (Q. 66:10). So, here we have a family which exemplifies disaccord and disintegration, notwithstanding the fact that the head of that family was a prophet of God. The social reality here does not match with the spiritual one.

The lesson that these verses present is that the contradiction between blood ties and religious commitment is a cause of social conflict and sufferings, even within a household headed by a prophet. This raises the broader question of the bases of a stable social order and the means of a durable social cohesion. Should individuals associate with each other to form a community along ethnic identities alone or along moral vision? The first option is turned down in the Qur'ān as *jāhiliyya*; that is, a community based exclusively on ethnicity is a community of *jāhilūn*, and that is why Noah is warned not to be one of the *jāhilūn*. The second is the option of the *ṣāliḥūn* who would ultimately be the inheritors of earth. Noah, we should recall, was the first inheritor of earth, according to the Qur'ānic narrative.

Broken Families

"Divorced women shall wait concerning themselves for three monthly periods...and their husbands have the better right to take them back in that period, if they wish for *iṣlāḥ*" (Q. 2:228). In this passage, *iṣlāḥ* is again used in the social, not the biological context. It is employed as a reference to the process of maintaining marital relations. All reconciliatory steps and concessions that might lead to an amicable settlement (or mutual adjustment) between a married couple (with divorce experiences) in order to salvage their marriage are urged and highly recommended, and labeled as an *iṣlāḥ* process, as is also emphasized in Q. 4:128. However, if a marital relation per se cannot be salvaged, as in the case of irrevocable divorce or the death of a husband or a wife, there is still a need for saving the family by way of protecting the interests of its living members (the orphans and widows). Hence, the attention and care that a guardian gives to the orphan's interests is also seen as a part and parcel of the *iṣlāḥ*. The dissolution of the family institution is a social evil that all measures should be taken to avoid, but if families did, however, dissolve, other arrangements should be sought to replace them. In the history of the Muslim societies, various substitute institutions and systems of guardianship, child adoption, and councils of trustees have gradually evolved and functioned to protect children against neglect and abuse.

Q. 2:220 is also related with the right of heirs and orphans: "They ask thee concerning orphans. Say: the best thing to do is what is for their *iṣlāḥ*; if ye mix their affairs with yours, they are your brethren, but Allah knows the man who means mischief from the man who is *muṣliḥ*". The immediate meaning of this passage centers on the formal and legal relations between orphans and their guardians. Guardians are expected and encouraged to take care of the orphan's economic affairs. Far from abuse and exploitation, guardians are urged to develop the orphan's property. *Iṣlāḥ* here stands for economic activities and social development; it means that one should consider the economic interests of his dependents, especially those who are so weak to articulate their demands or to pursue or protect their interests. But behind this formal and legal aspect, there is another important level of meaning. The Qur'ān calls on guardians, as well as on the larger Muslim community, not to dissociate themselves from orphans, or refrain from mixing with them under pretence of not abusing their properties. In a Muslim community, orphans have to be integrated into networks of relatives. The Qur'ānic word for such a process of integration is *tukhālituhum,* which literarily means to mix with them and not to set them apart, stresses the importance of the group for the psychological development of an orphaned child. Putting orphans aside in asylums or orphanages might suppress their individuality, and damage their personalities—as available evidence in modern psychology scholarship makes it amply clear.

Ethnic Violence

"Then, when he (Moses) decided to lay hold of the man who was an enemy to both of them, that man said: Oh Moses, is it thy intention to slay me as thou slewest a man yesterday? Your intention is none other than to become a powerful violent man in the land, and not to be one of the *muṣliḥūn*" (Q. 28:19). In this example the *muṣliḥ* is used in the context of individual quarrels that involve ethnic violence. The focus is on Moses, and the ancient Egyptian-Israelite struggle. Visiting the city privately, Moses intervened in a fight between an Israelite and an Egyptian, and, in the rage of the moment, Moses struck the latter and killed him. Another Israelite who saw the situation shouted at Moses, "Your intention is none other than to become a powerful violent man in the land, and not to be one of the *muṣliḥūn*." In this passage, *muṣliḥūn* could possibly be translated as those who set things right (as some translators have actually done) but that does not convey the full meaning. In this context, setting things right must be understood as a reference to resisting injustice. A resistance, which is necessarily based on principles of justice and fairness, in turn requires that the *muṣliḥ* himself act in perfect impartiality, to free himself totally from racial bias and arrogance, and not to allow himself to be swayed by his personal *hawā*, or by likes and dislikes that obstruct the process of *iṣlāḥ*. To become a *muṣliḥ* one has to transcend his own immediate interests, rid himself from his own disease of the heart and transform himself in such a way that he will be an example for others.

Organized Corruption

"There were in the city a *rahṭ* nine men of a family, who made mischief in the land, and were not *muṣliḥūn*" (Q. 27:48). The reference here is to a certain group of nine persons who make mischief on the city and fail to make *iṣlāḥ*. But to translate *rahṭ* as a group of persons does not do justice to the original word at all. *Rahṭ* does not mean just a group of persons but a blood-related group of persons; the difference between the two is too important to be overlooked. It is clear then that the reference here is to an ethnic group which is involved in organized corruption or terror. Because they were left unchecked, they brought destruction to the whole community, as the subsequent verses indicated.

Civil War

"If two parties among the believers fall into a quarrel, make ye *iṣlāḥ* between them: but if one of them transgresses beyond bounds against the other, then fight ye (all) against the one that transgresses till it complies with the commands of Allah; but if it complies, then make *iṣlāḥ* between them, with justice, and be fair" (Q. 49:9). This is an obvious case of a civil war (group quarrels) that might flare up among the believers. *Iṣlāḥ* is employed to designate a process of peacemaking between the contending factions, (based on impartiality and justice) which also implies the supremacy of the Muslim community as a whole over the quarreling factions. But how can a community perform such a function unless it possesses a kind of an executive machinery, with a peacekeeping force under its command—a government in modern political terminology? What is implied here is that the force of the community has to be entrusted to a government that would be obliged to enforce law and order on the contending factions, and to maintain the public security and welfare. Interestingly enough, Muslim jurists have developed out of this very concept of *iṣlāḥ* the important legal concept of *istiṣlāḥ* (seeking the best possible solution that serves the general interests of the community) and made it a subsidiary source of the Islamic law.

Bringing together the elements of the concept of *iṣlāḥ* conveyed in these verses and relating it to our earlier discussions, we may now draw the following three general conclusions. The first conclusion is that a society is not a monolithic block of beings, but just as there has been a cosmological multiplicity and psychological polarity, there is also a social pluralism. A society is made up of a multiple of groups which may or may not overlap, coexist, live in harmony, cooperate, or fight against each other and disintegrate. Internal conflicts and contradictions are part and parcel of human societies in the same way that they are in the human psyche and the natural world, but unless some basic values are agreed upon, some hard core of leaders stand up, and some basic institutions are maintained, the minimum level of stability will be eroded. This notion of offsetting evil with good is presented in the Qur'ān as a general rule: "And did not God check one set of people by means of another, the earth would indeed be full of mischief" (Q. 2:251).

The second conclusion is that ethnic pride and arrogance are possible sources of social conflict, and that if these sentiments are left unchecked by moral values and not tempered by religious creed they will develop into ethnic violence. The third conclusion is that broken marriages and ruined families are possible sources of resentment and bitterness (dysfunctions), and that if the weaker members in the families (orphans and divorcees) are not treated with justice and fairness, or integrated, social peace will be disrupted. In other words, there is always a great social cost for the breakdown of the family institution. Unless other substitutive social institutions are established, victims of disintegrated families might transform themselves into sub-systems that would fuel ethnic violence, or turn into organized crime, or both. And all these could lead to civil wars.

We may take yet a farther step in this direction and conclude that the *iṣlāḥ* comes to acquire in the Qur'ān a primary meaning of involvement in a process of creating a just social order, of developing it by way of trust-building and peacemaking. The *muṣliḥ* in this regard is the one who is necessarily engaged in these processes of trust and institution building and peacemaking; he is necessarily a social integrator, and a war resister. A hard core of such virtuous individuals who exemplify the core moral values and who, against all odds, are determined to resist evil and promote good, will inherit the earth, and their emergence is the necessary requirement for any process of *iṣlāḥ*.

The Inheritors of the Earth

"God has promised, to those among you who believe and do *ṣāliḥāt*, that He will, of a surety, grant them in the land, inheritance (of power), as He granted it to those before them; that He will establish in authority their religion—the one which He has chosen for them; and that He will change (their state) after the fear in which they (lived), to one of security and peace" (Q. 24:55). These verses explicitly speak of the outcome of *iṣlāḥ*, which is, among other things, the *istikhlāf* (the inheritance of the earth). *Iṣlāḥ*, as we have already seen, is multi-dimension process: it is primarily a process of preserving that God-given set up (reflected on earth, human body, human *nafs* and human relations) as healthy, pure and sound as is meant to be. This necessarily entails a counteraction against the forces of *fasād* (or mischief) and it is referred to in the Qur'ān as *amr bi'l maᶜrūf wa'l nahī ᶜan al-munkar*. It could be construed as a process of persuading and encouraging fellow-citizens to adopt the positive core values, and discourage them from following the negative ones. The other dimension of *iṣlāḥ* is a positive one. It is an attempt not only to preserve and counteract but also to develop the natural set up, albeit along the same lines of the initial *iṣlāḥ*. This is referred to in the Qur'ān as *tazkiya* (self purification) and *ᶜumrān*. There is an obvious interrelationship between these two last concepts and the earlier one, e.g. the concept of *amr bi'l maᶜrūf wa'l nahī ᶜan al-munkar*. The whole process of *iṣlāḥ* starts with the psychical *tazkiya* where the human *nafs* comes into contact with the transcendental, and starts to respond to it by internalizing its imperatives. But *tazkiya* is not an exclusive internal process; it has to be performed within the society. In fact it is through interacting with others that an individual believer strives and aspires to purify himself, that is, to cure his own "heart disease". In the same way, *amr bi'l maᶜrūf* and *nahī ᶜan al-munkar* is nothing other than a positive reaction of a believer who aspires to purify himself by way of discouraging others from doing evil and mischief on earth or on society. The expected outcome of such *tazkiya* is *ᶜumrān* (or civilization) both at the level of the individual and the society.

Conclusions

There are some scholars who believe that a meaning of a concept cannot be independently ascertained and that it can only be attained in the context of a theory.[30] This is partially true, though it is rather problematic. For a theory itself has to be formulated out of some basic, well-defined concepts. We may agree, however, that one is not justified in defining a concept without having a tentative hypothesis.

In our present endeavor to discern the meaning of *iṣlāḥ* (as it is used in the Qur'ān), we chose to look into the Qur'ānic text for possible orienting signals that might point towards a broader perspective, if not a theory, within which the concept *iṣlāḥ* is employed. What we have found, however, is more than sketchy signals; we found descriptive definitions, where the referents are clearly specified. We then took that to be what we called the core meaning of the concept *iṣlāḥ* that would, presumably, point towards possible peripheral meanings. Following the Qur'ānic metaphors embedded in those descriptions, we found that is exactly the case. It has, thus, become clear that the definition of *iṣlāḥ* that we have come across is profoundly grounded in a deeper and broader Qur'ānic world-view, where the conception of the human psyche, the cosmos, and society are carefully interwoven. We have also realized that within this Qur'ānic world-view, multiplicity is a universal phenomenon that manifests itself in all levels of existence: the physical, the psychical and the social. All these are interrelated worlds, and in each of them there are opposite forces, energies, and actors. When a just balance is maintained among these contending forces, then a condition of *iṣlāḥ* is created; if the balance is not maintained then the conditions of *fasād* are created.

It has then become easier to attempt to develop, based on this grand worldview, a set of propositions (a sub-framework or a middle-range theory)[31] within which the complex social and political relations may be comprehended. We would venture to synthesize the following four testable hypotheses to be the core of our framework.

1. Adapting the natural (whether physical or psychical) to the moral vision is the first step of *iṣlāḥ*. But such a process entails knowledge of both the natural laws and moral system.

2. Internalizing the Islamic principles and values will produce internal tensions and struggles between the forces of *hawā* and forces of truth within the human psyche; hence, a process of *tazkiya* (self-restraint, and self-development) is required. If it is attained, it will lead to the suppression of the anti-social motives;

3. Such a process of *tazkiya* does not take place in a vacuum, it has to be within a context of social interaction, hence, the *tazkiya* will likely lead to a process of amr *bi'l maᶜrūf,* and both of them will lead to growth and development, on the social and material environment. They will lead to *ᶜumrān* (civilization).

4. Those who are engaged in attaining true knowledge and disseminating it (the intellectuals and scientists), those who manage to control themselves through processes of *tazkiya*, and those who are standing for justice by way of enjoining the good and forbidding the evil in public life (law-makers,

> law enforcers, councilors, and social workers, etc.,) are the main agents and workers of *ᶜumrān* (or civilization). They would likely inherit the earth; that is, they will be able to control their environment (or public place) and change it by introducing new (*ṣāliḥ*) patterns of behavior.

In our view, these four propositions centered on these four variables (*ᶜilm*, *tazkiya*, *amr bi'l maᶜrūf* and *ᶜumrān)*, will constitute a Qur'ānic framework or theory of *iṣlāḥ*. This framework will allow us to identify areas of problems; alert us to observe keenly certain types of relations; and enable us to make some predictions for novel situations. It shows, for instance, that there is a strong relationship between the (internal) *tazkiya* and the (external) *ᶜumrān*; that the accumulated (objective) knowledge, be it knowledge about the universe, the moral system or religion, would not be transformed into a useful social action unless this knowledge is related to the internal (subject) in one way or another. The framework, however, is no more than a set of propositions waiting for empirical testing.

NOTES

1. A. Merad, "Iṣlāḥ," *EI2,* IV, 141.

2. Ibn Manẓūr, *Lisān al-ᶜArab* (Beirut 1997), VII, 384. See also al-Fīrūzābādī, *al-Qāmūs al-muḥīṭ* (Beirut 1970), I, 235. It must be mentioned, however, that Ibn Manẓūr and the other lexicographers were not unaware of the fact that words cannot be fully defined out of their contexts. In this occasion of trying to define *iṣlāḥ*, Ibn Manẓūr has made references to fifteen places in the Qur'ān, three in the *ḥadīth*, and four in Arabic poetry.

3. Ibn Jinnī, *Al-Khaṣā'iṣ*, ed. Muḥammad ᶜAlī al-Najjār (Cairo 1957), I, 12.

4. This is a list with the 18 verses, arranged according to the contexts within which they occur; (1) descriptive definitions, Q. 4:34, 3:114; (2) bio-psychical, Q. 7:189, 7:190, 21:90, 11:46, 46:15; (3) social conflict, Q. 2:11, 2:182, 2:220, 2:228, 11:117, 27:48, 28:19, 49:9–10; (4) cosmological, Q. 7:56; (5) the consequences of *iṣlāḥ*, Q. 24:55.

5. Izutsu notes that the semantic structure of an obscure word x is cleared up in terms of its negative form, not-x; knowing what types of conduct are generally referred to by the expression "this is not good" is as important for the semanticist as knowing what types of conduct are generally called "good." See his *Ethico-Religious Concepts in the Qur'ān* (Montreal: McGill-Queen's University Press, 1966), 39. This is quite in line with the Qur'ānic strategy that we are pursuing here in our current attempt of elucidating the concept of *iṣlāḥ*.

6. Reportedly, this is the opinion of Ibn ᶜAbbās and some of his disciples, but al-Ṭabarī believes that this is also the consensus of the commentators. See al-Ṭabarī, *Jāmi al-bayān* (Beirut 1987), VI, 99–101.

7. See his opinion in ibid, XII, 156.The same opinion is also reproduced in al-Suyūṭī, *al-Durr al-manthūr* (Beirut 1990), 620.

8. Ibid, 620.

9. See Robert C. Bohinski, *Modern Concepts in Biochemistry* (Boston: Allyn and Bacon, 1973), 216.

10. Ibn ᶜAṭiyya, Tafsīr Ibn ᶜAṭiyya: al-Muḥarrar al-wajīz fī tafsīr al-kitāb al-ᶜazīz (Qatar 1991), XV, 504.

11. Al-Ālūsi, *Tafsīr al-Ālūsī* (Beirut 1994), XV, 395.

12. Aristotle believes, like Plato before, that the human soul is made of two parts: the rational and irrational. Reason has, thus, become an essential part in Aristotle's moral theory. See Bertrand Russell, *A History of Western Philosophy and its Connection with Political and Social Circumstances from the Earliest Times to the Present Day* (New York: Simon and Schuster, 1945), 173.

13. E. W. Lane, *Arabic-English Lexicon* (London and Edinburgh: Williams and Norgate, 1863–1893), I, 1476.

14. Al-Ṭabarī, *Jāmiᶜ*, IX, 66; al-Zamakhsharī, *al-Kashshāf* (Tehran 1966), IV, 243.

15. It should be mentioned here that this divine/natural infusion is what distinguishes the Qur'ānic perspective from that of Positivism and Behaviorism whose exponents attempt to abolish the inner man and thereby separate the natural from the spiritual. See, for instance, B.F. Skinner, *Beyond Freedom and Dignity* (New York: Knopf, 1971), 201.

16. See al-Ṭabarī, *Jāmiᶜ*, II, 13.This opinion has been adopted by most of the commentators, like al-Ṭabarī, himself, al-Zamakhsharī, *al-Kashshāf*, II, 582, and al-Rāzī, *al-Tafsīr al-kabīr* (Beirut 1990), XV, 210.

17. Al-Ṭabarī, *Jāmiᶜ*, IX, 66.

18. It should be recalled that even in modern times, the inability to conceive could not be conclusively determined. Of all causes of infertility, only 55% may be attributable to the female, and 20% of the causes of female infertility may be attributed to ovulatory dysfunction—and this, in turn, is affected by hormone release that could be impeded by various factors among which are stress and anorexia nervosa. Hence, the suggestion that the infertility of the wife of Zakariyyā' was probably related to psychical disturbances is not farfetched. For relations between infertility and psychological disturbances, see *McGraw-Hill Encyclopedia of Science and Technology*, 8th ed. (New York: McGraw-Hill, 1997), IX, 154–6.

19. Lane, *Arabic*, II, 2117.

20. Abdullah Yusuf Ali, *The Meaning of the Holy Quran*, 17th. ed. (Beltsville-Maryland 1995), 623.

21. Encyclopedia Britannica (Chicago), I, 120.

22. Al-Māturīdī, *Kitāb al-Tawhīd*, 2nd ed., ed. Fathalla Kholeif (Beirut 1986), xxiv.

23. Ibid., 22.

24. Ibn Taymiyya, *Majmuᶜāt al-fatāwā*, ed. ᶜAbd al-Raḥmān b. Muḥammad b. Qāsim (Beirut 1398/1977), VIII, 94, 123.

25. *Webster's Third New International Dictionary*, ed. Philip B. Grove (Springfield, Mass. : Merriam-Webster, 1993), 2322.

26. See, for instance, L. Gardet, "Allāh," *EI2*, I, 413.

27. For definitions and use of these concepts, see A. R. Radcliff-Brown, *Structure and Function in Primitive Society: essays and addresses* (New York: The Free Press, 1965), chapter 9.

28. This is the opinion of Mujāhid and al-Ḥasan, see al-Ṭabarī, *Jāmiᶜ*, VII, 31

29. This is al-Ṭabarī's opinion, which is based on the opinions of Ibn ᶜAbbās, Ikrima and Saᶜīd. See al-Ṭabarī, *Jāmiᶜ*, VII, 32–3.

30. P. L. Heath, "Concepts," in *The Encyclopedia of Philosophy*, ed. Paul Edwards (New York: Macmillan, 1996), I–II, 180.

31. For a full exposition of middle-range theories see R.K. Merton, *Social Theory and Social Structure* (New York: Free Press, 1968), 39–40.

The Identity of the Qur'ān's *Ahl al-Dhikr*

Khaleel Mohammed

> *And we did not send before you except men onto whom we granted revelation—ask the* ahl al-dhikr *if you know not! (Qur'ān 16:43, 21:7)*

What does the term *ahl al-dhikr*, used only twice in the Qur'ān, mean? Using cyber-technology, if we submit the term on the "Google" search engine, we get 1430 hits, of which three are the most significant, in that they appear on sites that, for most Muslims, are authoritative. The first is the definition given by Muḥammad Nāṣir al-Dīn al-Albānī, the contemporary Ḥadīth scholar, who states: "The *ahl al-dhikr*, as we all know, are the Ahl al-Qur'aan [sic] and the Ahl al-Hadeeth [sic], those who know the authentic from the unauthentic [sic], the general from the specific, the abrogating from the abrogated, and other such principles of Fiqh and Hadeeth."[1]

The second definition is given by Muḥammad al-Tijānī, the North African Sunnī turned Shīᶜī, who writes that the term refers to the members of the Prophet's family,[2] that is Fāṭima, Muḥammad's daughter, her husband ᶜAlī b. Abī Ṭālib, and their progeny.[3] The third definition, sticking to lexical analysis, defines the term as "people of remembrance," referring to true (Muslim) scholars, whose knowledge springs from, and is steeped in, the remembrance of God."[4]

These contemporary interpretations reflect the latest stage in an evolution from the Qur'ānic usage; indeed, by the time of the earliest exegetical works known to us, reinterpretation had already commenced. In attempting to decipher the meaning of *ahl al-dhikr*, some exegetes relied on traditional reports. Others sought to explain the term by restricting themselves to the narrowest of linguistic and lexical parameters. And while few exegetes paid attention to the interaction between Jews, Christians and Muslims at the time of Muḥammad, absolutely none examined the possibility that the Qur'ānic language may instead reflect terminology well-known to Muḥammad's contemporaries.[5] With the passing of time, under the influence of new creedal developments, they embarked on a continual reinterpretation that was to distance the term far from its original meaning.

To better approach this task, this essay will focus on certain facts that have been previously researched, and are so well known that the task of detailed presentation is unnecessary here. The first of these is that the Qur'ānic language, especially in reference to matters of law and of the past, indicates a familiarity with Judaic laws and concepts.[6] This is supported by the admission of all scholars of Islam, from within and without the faith, that Medina, where the majority of such verses were revealed, had a large Jewish presence.[7] The next is that before the rise of Islam, as Muslim historians have noted, the Arabs used to ask the Jewish scholars about the past, since the latter were known to record such details.[8] The third fact is that the earliest exegetical works that have come to us are from people who wrote long after Muḥammad, in the setting of developed cities that were in no way similar to the Prophet's milieu. Their interpretations tell us primarily and reliably only what the people of their time understood, and only secondarily and sometimes unreliably about the actual views of Muḥammad and his Companions. Certainly there is the argument that the *mufassirs*[9] relied on transmissions of *ḥadīth*, the reliability of which was preserved by the highly developed science of *al-jarḥ wa'l-ta*ᶜ*dīl*.[10] These transmissions purportedly allow us to know the occasions of revelation (*asbāb al-nuzūl*) of each verse. Yet, as Andrew Rippin has shown, such literature is simply not reliable.[11]

A fourth, and very important, fact is that Arabic is from the Semitic group of languages, and in many cases, terms used in the Qur'ān are the same as, or similar to those in Hebrew and/or Aramaic, e.g. *zakāt*, *ṣadaqa*. Now, while proximity of culture and language may explain this remarkable similarity in some Islamic and Jewish terminology, it is also clear that on several occasions, the Qur'ān, in stating that Muḥammad had not come to found a new religion, but rather to re-establish Abrahamic monotheism,[12] saw fit to use the terminology known to be specific to those who identified themselves as Abraham's heirs, that is, the Jews, followers of Moses, the prophet most mentioned in the Qur'ān.[13]

Dhikr, from the root DhKR, means "remembrance."[14] In its various forms, it occurs no less than two hundred and eighty times in the Qur'ān. When affixed to *ahl* (people), the combined term could be translated as "people of remembrance." This would mean that the verse(s) quoted at the beginning of this paper, if read atomistically, indicate that Muḥammad's contemporaries were being ordered to seek out the people of remembrance from amongst themselves. But the context simply does not allow this interpretation. The first *āya* is followed by one that explains it further so that, read together, Q. 16:43–4 may be translated thus:

> And We did not send before you except men onto whom we granted revelation—ask the *ahl al-dhikr* if you know not about the Clear Signs (*bayyināt*) and the Psalms! And We sent unto you the Remembrance[15] to make clear to the people what was revealed unto them, and so that they may reflect.

The other *āya*, Q. 21:7, when read in the context of Q. 21: 3–9, may be translated thus:

> With hearts vainly occupied, they secretly confer. And the wrongdoers say, "Is this anything but a man just like you? Will you then believe in magic when you clearly perceive it? He said, "My lord knows what is said in the Heaven and in the Earth, and He is the Hearer, the Knower. But they say, "These are muddled dreams, which he has invented. Rather he is nothing but a poet. Come instead with a sign as those of old were sent with signs. Not a single township of those that We destroyed before believed. Will they now believe? And We did not send before you except men onto whom we granted revelation—ask the *ahl al-dhikr* if you know not. We did not make them beings that did not eat food, nor were they immortals. And then We fulfilled our promise unto them, and We rescued them along with those whom We wished, and We destroyed the iniquitous.

In both cases, the Muslims are being directed to address their enquiries to a specific group of people. From Q. 16:43–4, it can be understood that these people are those who are familiar with the "Clear Signs" and the Psalms. Now, the Qur'ān states that both Moses and

Jesus were blessed with "Clear Signs" (Q. 2:87, 92). Yet, for reasons that will become clear presently, I will show that the direction is to ask the followers of Moses, not those of Jesus.

From Q. 21:3–9, we understand that man being spoken about is Muḥammad and that his detractors seem to feel that a mere human cannot be a Prophet. Muḥammad is being challenged to produce miracles or portents as the Prophets of yore had done. The Qur'ān answers by pointing out that those Prophets were only human, and then exhorts the disbeliever to verify this information by asking the *ahl al-dhikr*, those who have detailed knowledge of those past Prophets. Quite significantly, the prophetology of the Qur'ān focuses on the Hebrew messengers to such an extent that only four of the persons clearly identified as prophets in the Qur'ān are not Biblical personalities.[16] It is highly improbable that Muḥammad's contemporaries were in any doubt regarding the identity of the *ahl al-dhikr* to whom Q. 16:43 and 21:7 direct them. For us then, the obvious question is: who are these people that can provide detailed information about the past prophets?

In the Hebrew Bible, *zākhar* (to remember) and its different forms occur no less than two hundred and seventy six times.[17] The imperative form (*zakhor*), as noted by Josef Yerushalmi, occurs with a hammering insistency in the Deuteronomic history and in the Prophets.[18] "Remember the days of old, consider the years of ages past" (Deut. 32:7). "Remember these things, O Jacob, for you, O Israel, are my servant; I have fashioned you, you are My servant; O Israel, never forget me" (Is. 44:21). "O My people, remember what the Balak king of Moab plotted against you" (Micah 6:5). "You may say to yourselves, 'These nations outnumber us, how can we drive them out?' But you need have no fear of them; only remember what the Lord your God did to Pharaoh and to the whole of Egypt" (Deut. 7:17). "Remember and never forget, how you angered the Lord your God in the wilderness" (Deut. 9:7).

These commands are not designed to foster nostalgia; rather the focus is to give meaning to the past and to emphasize the importance of the covenant between God and the Children of Israel. Remembering and acting in concordance with God's commandments are vital, for only then will the Divine promise be fulfilled. The Qur'ān seems to presuppose knowledge of the details of this relationship between God and Israel, and the importance of memory in this bond by using the Arabic form of the imperative (*udhkurū*) to specifically address the Jews: "O Children of Israel! Remember my favor which I conferred upon you, and be faithful to your covenant with me, and I will fulfill my covenant with you, and fear only me" (Q. 2:40). "O Children of Israel, remember my favor which I conferred upon you, and I chose you above all the nations" (Q. 2:47; 2:122).

While the Christian Testament incorporates the Hebrew Bible, the imperative to remember is not central to Christianity; rather, the focus is soteriological, in salvation through baptism and belief in Jesus, his sacrifice by the crucifixion, and his Second Coming (see Mark 16:16; John 3:17; Acts 4:12; 15:11; 16:31; 2 Thess. 1:7–10; Mark 13:27). Luke 1:72 does mention the act of remembering but puts this as a duty of "our fathers,"[19] and a few verses later, lets it be known that the covenant will be fulfilled only through belief in Jesus (Luke 1:76). The emphasis on the Second Coming makes the Christian duty lie therefore, not in remembering the past, but rather in patient waiting for a future event (Matt. 24:30–1; 25:31; 26:64; Mark 14:62; John 14:1–3, 28; Acts 1:11, Rev. 22:12 inter alia). Since, in Christian theological outlook, Jesus is the son of God, it is important to note that the *ahl al-dhikr* are supposed to provide testimony for the mortal, human nature of the prophets, and that Christian views of Jesus would not have been particularly helpful to the Qur'ānic argument. The importance and meaning of remembrance (*zakhor*, *dhikr*) is therefore specific to the Jews, *quod erat demonstrandum*. And it is with this realization that the Qur'ānic verses must be read since, as indicated earlier in this essay, the Qur'ān presupposes an awareness of Judaic laws and concepts.

Indeed, the Qur'ān seems bent on drilling into the Muslim consciousness the need for inquiry about the past, and from whom the answers are to be sought. The foregoing arguments about the identity of *ahl al-dhikr* are buttressed by verses from two other *sūra*s:

> Ask the Children of Israel how many clear signs (*ayāt bayyināt*) We have given unto them. Whosoever alters God's Grace after it has been given unto him, indeed God is severe in punishment. (Q. 2:211)

> And we certainly did allot unto the Children of Israel a fixed abode, and did provide them with the finest things; and they differed not until knowledge came unto them. Lo! Your Lord will judge between them on the Day of Resurrection concerning that wherein they used to differ. And if you (Muhammad) are in doubt concerning that which We reveal unto thee, then ask those who read the Scripture before thee. Indeed the Truth from thy Lord has come unto thee. So be not thou of the waverers. (Q. 10: 92–3)

These verses need no explanation—they offer unassailable verification of our contention that the *ahl al-dhikr* of the Qur'ān are the Jewish *mazkirim* (recorders)[20] of the past.

As pointed out earlier, Muslim historians have noted that before the rise of Islam, the Arabs would ask the Jews about history. With the rise of Islam, Q. 16:43 and 21:7 reinforced this practice; so too did the *ḥadīth*, as for example, "Relate from the children of Israel, and there is no objection in that."[21] Indeed, a special name was coined for this genre of narrations: "Isrā'īliyyāt."[22] Based on the considerable evidence of such material in the formation of early Islamic thought, Nabia Abbott concluded that the Islamic traditions came to resemble the Mishna more than any other sacred literature of the People of the Book.[23]

Quite early, however, under the rubric of Isrā'īliyyāt, several aspects of folklore that clashed with the message of the Qur'ān were imported into Muslim tradition.[24] Soon Isrā'īliyyāt evolved to indicate material that came from any non-Muslim source, and then to refer to anything that was considered seditious to Islamic belief. [25]In an effort to curb such importations, the Muslim scholars sought recourse to traditions that countered those that allowed Isrā'īliyyāt. One such example is:

> ᶜUmar said to the Prophet: We hear several tales from the Jews that we like; may we write some of them down? Whereupon the Prophet replied: Do you wish to rush to perdition as did the Jews and Christians? I have brought you white and clean *ḥadīths*![26]

It is in light of these developments that the science of *tafsīr* developed,[27] with severe repercussions for the explanations of Q. 16:43 and 21:7. The earliest exegetes, however, left us reports that may have reached them through oral tradition, or by written works that are no longer extant, and we can still find traces of the old interpretations.

In order to present the widest range of coverage possible within the limits of this paper, I have selected the works of some of the most famous exegetes, from the classical period to the present time. In dealing with Q. 16:43, Hūd b. Muḥakkam (exact date of death unknown; third/ninth century) explained that the verse was addressed to the polytheists, and they were being sent to ask the people of the two books, i.e. the Torah and the Gospel.[28] He faithfully, however, recorded a variant opinion, noting that there were those who viewed the *ahl al-dhikr* as the people of the Torah.[29] Some further refined the explanation—the reference was taken to refer to the Jews who had converted to Islam, such as ᶜAbd Allāh b. Salām (d. 43/663–4) and his companions.[30] Al-Farrā' (d. 207/822), writing in the same century as Hūd b. Muḥakkam did not record any difference of opinion, but simply stated that the reference was to the people who followed the Torah and the Gospel.[31]

By the fourth/tenth century, al-Ṭabarī (d. 310/923) could offer some light on the various opinions. He singled out Mujāhid (d. 104/722), one of the most famous *tābiᶜī* [32] exegetes, as interpreting *ahl al-dhikr* to mean followers of the Torah.[33] He however recorded that Ibn ᶜAbbās (d. 68/687) and al-ᶜĀmash (d.148/765) extended the reference to include the Christians.[34] ᶜAlī b. Ibrahīm al-Qummī (d. 328/939), the Shīᶜite commentator, provided a new explanation for *ahl al-dhikr*, and also regarding those to whom the Qur'ānic directives are addressed.[35] While it would appear that his predecessors and contemporaries had viewed the instruction as being given to those who doubted Muḥammad, i.e. the polytheists, al-Qummī now propounded that the Muslims were in fact being addressed.[36] Through a chain of tradents viewed as authoritative by the Shīᶜa, he stated that their fifth imam, Muḥammad b. ᶜAlī (d. circa 117/735) was questioned regarding the identity of the *ahl al-dhikr* as mentioned in Q. 21:7. He responded, "By God! It is us!" His interlocutor probed further, "You are the ones to be asked?" Muḥammad b.

ᶜAlī reiterated his answer, upon which his interlocutor pushed, "And is it incumbent upon us to ask you?" When he again gave an affirmative answer, Muḥammad b. ᶜAlī was asked, "And do you have to respond to us?" He responded, "No. This is up to us; if we wish, we may do so, and if we do not wish, we may leave it aside."[37]

In the next century, Muḥammad al-Māwardī (d. 450/1058) reported several views, providing the provenance for some of them.[38] Al-Ḥasan al-Baṣrī (d. 110/728), Qatāda (d. 117/735), Ibn ᶜAbbās and Mujāhid (d. 104/722) felt that *ahl al-dhikr* were the peoples of the Torah and the Gospel.[39] ᶜAlī b. Abī Ṭālib (assassinated in 40/660) viewed the term as referring to the scholars of the Muslims.[40] And one Ibn Shajara felt that it referred to the believers from the Christians and Jews.[41] Some felt that the reference was to the scholars of the Qur'ān, and Ibn Zayd felt that it was rather the followers of the Qur'ān, i.e. the Muslims.[42] It is notable that al-Māwardī cites Mujāhid as an authority for the explanation that includes Christians, whereas more than a century earlier, al-Ṭabarī had cited him as limiting the reference to the Jews. What al-Ṭabarī had done was to mention Mujāhid's (alleged) view, and then mention Mujāhid as a narrator of, not a subscriber to, Ibn ᶜAbbās's (alleged) opinion.[43] Al-Māwardī seems to have ignored this point.

Al-Ṭusī (d. 465/1073) gave the Shīᶜite interpretation mentioned by al-Qummī, now backdating the authority for the explanation from Muḥammad b. ᶜAlī all the way back to ᶜAlī b. Abī Ṭālib.[44] He also mentioned the view that the *ahl al-dhikr* are the scholars of the Qur'ān referring to an *ayah* that states, "Indeed we have sent down the *dhikr* and we will preserve it" (Q. 15:9).[45] According to him, since in this context, the term *dhikr* clearly refers to the Qur'ān, then *ahl al-dhikr* = *ahl al-Qur'ān* = scholars of the Qur'ān.[46] Strikingly, he ignored the Qur'ān's reference to other scriptures by the term *dhikr* as in, "And surely we wrote in the Psalms, after *al-dhikr*, that our righteous servants shall inherit the earth" (Q. 21:105). He also ignored the other instances in the Qur'ān (Q. 2:211; 10:92–3) where as explained earlier in this essay, the instruction was to seek information from the Jews.

It would appear that by the fifth/eleventh century, the full range of the classical exegetical views had been reached, as the subsequent *mufassirs* recounted them, changing only details of provenance for the various opinions. What is significant however, is that by the time of al-Māwardī, most exegetes seem to dismiss the view that the *ahl al-dhikr* refers solely to the followers of the Torah. In the sixth/twelfth century, al-Baghawī (d. 516/1122),[47] al-Yarūsuwī (d. 531/1137),[48] and al-Zamakhsharī (d. 538/1144)[49] omitted this interpretation; al-Ṭabarsī (d. 548/1153)[50] repeated the Shīᶜite view of al-Qummī. Like al-Māwardī, al-Ṭabarsī cited Ibn Abbās and Mujāhid as authorities for the view to include Christians. As already explained, al-Ṭabarī, two centuries earlier, had shown Mujāhid as having a different view to Ibn ᶜAbbās.

Ibn al-Jawzī (d. 597/1201) was one of the rare voices that still reported Mujāhid as provenance for the explanation of *ahl al-dhikr* as followers of the Torah.[51] Quite significantly, Ibn al-Jawzi referred to al-Māwardī, but did not explain why he omitted the latter's report of Mujāhid as sharing Ibn ᶜAbbās's view that the term included the Christians. It would appear that, diplomatic scholar that he was, Ibn Jawzī had noted the change from al-Tabarī's original report, and had chosen not to discuss al-Māwardī's apparent mistake.

By the seventh/thirteenth century, Fakhr al-Dīn al-Rāzī (d. 606/1205)[52] used Ibn ᶜAbbās as provenance for the view that the reference is to the Jews—although the earlier exegetes (al-Ṭabarī, al-Māwardī) had reported Ibn ᶜAbbās's view of *ahl al-dhikr* being the Jews and Christians. Al-Rāzī, as al-Ṭūsī had done approximately one hundred and fifty years earlier, used the Qur'ānic reference to *al-dhikr*. Unlike his predecessor who had used only the *āyas* where the term referred to the Qur'ān, al-Rāzī focused on the verse where the reference is to the Torah (Q. 21:105).[53] Al-Rāzī also reported the view that the *ahl al-dhikr* could refer to anyone who was versed in the affairs of the past.[54] Yet, after his presentations, he opined that the reference was to the Jews and Christians.[55]

Al-Qurṭubī (d. 671/1273), going against his predecessors' reports, ascribed a new view to Ibn ᶜAbbās: the *ahl al- dhikr* were the people of the Qur'ān.[56] Yet, al-Qurṭubī opted for the view that the reference was to Jews and Christians who believed in the Prophet.[57] This was, he surmised, because unlike the Arabs, these people knew the history of the prophets, and the Quraysh used to seek such information from them.[58] In apparent ignorance of the Arabia of Muhammad's time, he seemed to feel that Christians were non-Arabs, when, in fact, many Arab tribes were Christian.[59] The scholars of the later centuries did not add any truly new view to the discussion; they were content to merely report the earlier explanations. Among Shī'ite exegetes, Muḥsin al-Kāshānī (d. 1091/1680), in attempting to bolster the view that the Qur'ān was referring to the *ahl al-bayt*, used the following tradition:

> Al-Bāqir was told that some people viewed the words of God "Ask the *ahl al-dhikr*" as referring to the Jews and Christians. He said, "In that case, those people invite you to their religion." He then placed his hands on his chest and said, "We are the *ahl al-dhikr*, we are the ones to be asked!"[60]

Given the Shīᶜite focus on the probity and authority of the *ahl al-bayt*, it is surprising that not all modern Shīᶜite commentators view the *ahl al-dhikr* as referring to this honored group. Muḥammad al-Sabzawarī follows the view that the reference is to the Jews and Christians, since the disbelievers of Mecca used to ask them about details of the past.[61] Muḥammad Ṭabāṭabā'ī also holds the same view.[62] Muḥammad al-Shīrāzī also sees the instruction as referring to the Jews and Christians, although for a different reason.[63] In obvious reference to Q. 21:105, he states that the scripture of the Jews and Christians is referred to as *al-dhikr*, since that scripture reminds them of their beginnings, their end, and other areas of general knowledge.[64] He chooses to make no difference between the Hebrew Bible and the Gospel.

As demonstrated above, reinterpretation of the expression *ahl al-dhikr*, started quite early in Islamic history. From the initial Qur'ānic reference to the scholars of the Torah, exegetes extended the term to include Christians, and then further refined the expression to mean those followers of the Torah and Gospel who believed in Muḥammad—essentially referring to converts to Islam. Others viewed the term as indicating the *ahl al-bayt*, while yet others saw the reference as being the scholars of the Qur'ān. That the names of famous early personalities were selectively used was demonstrated in the cases of ᶜAlī, Ibn ᶜAbbās, and Mujāhid. This in itself was not a pioneering stratagem; the practice was well known in Jewish and

Islamic debate, with the aim being to provide clout of provenance, a *diachronie*—an authority of "pastness."[65]

It is unlikely that the findings of this research, for all their cogency, will counteract any of the modern (mis)interpretations of *ahl al-dhikr*. Yet, they raise a question that could promote research as well as the irenic philosophy of scholars like Issa Boullata: how many more terms in the Qur'ān have metamorphosed over the passage of time?

NOTES

1. www.islaam.com

2. www.geocities.com/ahlulbayt14/dhikr.html

3. Known as the *ahl al-bayt* in Arabic.

4. www.islamfortoday.com/glossary

5. As will be demonstrated in this paper, many exegetes examined Judaic influences; they give no indication, however, that they perceived the term as being already in vogue, but, rather, implied that the expression represents the first usage of the term *ahl al-dhikr*.

6. See Khaleel Mohammed, "Probing the Identity of the Sacrificial Son," *Journal of Religion and Culture*, Concordia University (13) 1999: 125–38.

7. There are several sources for this information. See Abraham Geiger, *Judaism and Islam* (New York: KTAV, 1970). Also Charles Torrey, *The Jewish Foundation of Islam* (New York: Jewish Institute of Religion Press, 1933).

8. Ibn Khaldūn, *The Muqaddimah—An Introduction to History*, trans. Franz Rosenthal (New York: Pantheon Books, 1958), II, 445. Also Akram Ḍiyyā al-ᶜUmari, *Madinan Society at the Time of the Prophet* (Herndon: International Institute of Islamic Thought, 1991), 44.

9. Anglicized plural of *mufassir,* the Arabic term for exegete. More commonly applied to the classical exegetes.

10. Literally "impugning and probity"—a science which investigated the reporters of *ḥadīth*, judging them according to their moral character, reliability of memory, inter alia.

11. "The Function of *Asbāb al-Nuzūl* in Qur'anic Exegesis," *BSOAS* 51 (1988): 1–20, reprinted in A. Rippin, *The Qur'ān and Its Interpretative Tradition* (Aldershot: Variorum, 2001), chapter 19.

12. Q. 2:135–6; 3:30, 4:47; 5:46 etc.

13. 136 times.

14. Ibn Manẓūr, *Lisān al-ᶜArab* (Cairo 1300 AH), V, 395.

15. "Remembrance" here is not related to the term under discussion.

16. Hūd, Ṣāliḥ, Luqmān, Muḥammad.

17. Brevard S. Childs, *Memory and Tradition in Israel* (Naperville IL: A.R. Allenson, 1962), 9.

18. Josef Yerushalmi, *Zakhor: Jewish History and Jewish Memory* (Seattle: University of Washington Press, 1982), 9.

19. This is a specific Jewish term. Luke seems to be implying here that remembrance is a duty not on the present generation that is to be saved by Jesus, but rather on their parents, i.e. the Jewish community to which Jesus primarily addressed his message.

20. It is significant that the office of the *mazkir* (recorder) appears in the list of officials serving under David and Solomon (2 Samuel 8:16; 20:24; 1 Kings 4:3; 1 Chron. 18:15).

21. For a particularly excellent analysis of this tradition, see M. J. Kister, "Ḥaddithū ᶜan banī Isrā'ila wa la ḥaraj" in *Israel Oriental Studies* 11 (1972): 215–39.

22. See Muḥammad el-Dhahabī, "Israilitic Narratives in Exegesis and Tradition," *Papers of the Fourth Conference of the Academy of Islamic Research* (Cairo 1970), 586. See also Khaleel Mohammed, "The Jewish and Christian Influences on the Eschatological Imagery of Ṣaḥīḥ Muslim," MA Thesis, Concordia University, 1997, 4.

23. Nabia Abbott, *Studies in Arabic Literary Papyri* (Chicago: University of Chicago Press, 1957), II, 8.

24. See S. D. Goitein, *Jews and Arabs: their contacts through the ages* (New York: Schocken Books: 1964), 195f.

25. ᶜAyyāda al-Kubaysī, "Tafsīr al-Khāzin wa'l-Isra'īliyyāt," *Journal of the Islamic University*, 1994: 37–70.

26. Reported in Ibn Mājah and Ibn Ḥanbal; see Ignaz Goldziher, *Muslim Studies* (London: George Allen and Unwin, 1971), II, 131.

27. Fazlur Rahman, *Islam* (Chicago: University of Chicago Press, 1979), 40–1.

28. Hūd b. Muḥakkam, *Tafsīr kitāb Allāh al-ᶜazīz* (Beirut n.d.), II, 371

29. Ibid., III, 63.

30. Ibid.

31. Abū Zakariyya' Yaḥyā b. Ziyād al-Farrā', *Maᶜānī al-Qur'ān* (Beirut 1988), II, 199.

32. A second generation Muslim: one who did not meet the Prophet, but met one of his Companions.

33. Al-Ṭabarī, Jāmiᶜ al-bayān fi tafsīr āy al-Qur'ān (Beirut 1986), XIV, 75

34. Ibid.

35. ᶜAlī b. Ibrahīm al-Qummī, *Tafsīr al-Qummī*, ed. Ṭayyib al-Musawī al-Jazā'irī (Najaf 1387 A.H.), II, 67.

36. Ibid.

37. Ibid.

38. Al-Māwardī, *Al-Nukat wa'l-ᶜuyūn* (Beirut 1992), III,189.

39. Ibid.

40. Ibid.

41. Ibid.

42. Ibid.

43. Al-Ṭabarī, XIV, 75.

44. Muḥammad b. al-Ḥasan al-Ṭūsī, *Tafsīr al-tibyān* (Najaf 1962), VII, 232.

45. Ibid.

46. Ibid.

47. Al-Ḥasan b. Farrā' al-Baghawī, *Maᶜālim al-tanzīl* (Beirut 1986), III, 239.

48. Ismāᶜīl Ḥaqqī al-Yarusuwī, *Tanwīr al-adhhān min tafsīr rūḥ al-bayān* (Damascus 1988), II, 458.

49. Al-Zamakhsharī, *Al-Kashshāf ᶜan ḥaqā'iq al-tanzīl wa ᶜuyūn al-aqāwīl fī wujūh al-ta'wīl* (Beirut n.d.), II, 330.

50. Faḍl b. Ḥasan al-Ṭabarsī, *Majmaᶜ al-bayān fī tafsīr al-Qur'ān* (Qom 1937), IV, 40.

51. Ibn al-Jawzī, *Zād al-masīr fī ᶜilm al-tafsīr* (Beirut n.d.), IV, 449.

52. Al-Rāzī, *Al-Tafsīr al-kabīr* (Beirut 1980), XX, 36.

53. Ibid.

54. Ibid.

55. Ibid.

56. Al-Qurṭubī, *Mukhtaṣar tafsīr al-Qurṭubī*, ed. Muḥammad Karīm Rājiḥ (Beirut n.d.), III, 253.

57. Ibid.

58. Ibid.

59. See Tor Andrae, *Les Origines de l'Islam et le Christianisme*, trans. Jules Roche (Paris: Adrien Maisonneuve, 1955); also Richard Bell, *The Origins of Islam in its Christian Environment* (London: Frank Cass, 1968); J. M. Fiey, "Naṣārā," *EI2*.

60. Muḥsin al-Kāshānī, *Tafsīr al-ṣāfī* (Beirut 1979), III, 331.

61. Muḥammad al-Sabzawarī, *Al-Jadīd fi tafsīr al-Qur'ān al-karīm* (Beirut n.d.), IV, 482.

62. Muḥammad Ḥusayn Ṭabāṭabā'ī, *Al-Mīzān fī tafsīr al-Qur'ān* (Beirut n.d.), XVII, 254.

63. Muḥammad al-Ḥusaynī al-Shirāzī, *Tafsīr taqrīb al-Qur'ān ilā 'l-adhhān* (Beirut 1980), XVI, 16.

64. Ibid.

65 William Scott Green, "What's in a Name—The Problematic of Rabbinic Biography," in *Approaches to Ancient Judaism*, ed. W. S. Green (Missoula MT: Scholars Press, 1978), 88. See also Marc Bregman, "Pseudepigraphy in Rabbinic Literature," in *Pseudepigraphic Perspectives: The Apocrypha and Pseudepigrapha in Light of the Dead Sea Scrolls*, ed. Esther Chazon and Michael Stone (Leiden: Brill, 1999), 26–41.

Chapter 3

Metaphor and the Authority of the Qur'ān

Andrew Rippin

The Qur'ān's role in the context of the academic study of world literature—both in terms of the study of history and the study of literature per se—is quite insignificant, especially in comparison with its place within the Muslim world. While the profiling of Islamic revivalism in the popular media has led to some greater acquaintance with what the book looks and sounds like among non-Muslims, it is doubtful that any significant portion of the Euro-American population has ever sat down to examine the book in any detail.

The project which this paper represents is a part of a larger research endeavor of mine dealing with the Qur'ān and its interpretation at the beginning of the 21st century. In a series of papers, I have tried to investigate the Qur'ān's use of language within the context of a contemporary literary understanding. I am especially interested in these studies in the way in which complex arrays of metaphors convey ideas about society, both in historical terms—for example, in an earlier study of the imagery associated with eschatology and its vision of the perfect society[1]—and in conceptual terms, as within this paper.[2]

This series of essays has also emphasized the element of the Qur'ān's participation within the general Near Eastern religious milieu. The emphasis in the papers falls on the extent to which the Qur'ān continues the metaphorical and idiomatic expression of its religious, social and cultural predecessors, whether that be in the stories that are recounted of past prophets, or in the way the Qur'ān speaks of the religious themes of God, eschatology, and community, or in the use of specific idioms such as "the wages of sin" or "blindness." The interpretation of the Qur'ān cannot, in my view, take place outside that context but this need not be approached in a reductive mode conceived in terms of "borrowings." Rather it should be thought of in terms of a common shared and continued heritage, a revived and re-imagined version of the monotheist heritage. This, I must admit, is not an uncontroversial position. The legacy of 19th and early 20th century Euro-American scholarship has left a deep suspicion of anything that suggests a formative relationship between the monotheistic faiths of the Near East. Many books were published in the last 100 years that attempted to catalog the "Christian Influence on the Rise of Islam" or the "Jewish Foundations of Islam," tending to treat the Qur'ān as a work which was composed of elements stolen—and often misunderstood—from earlier scripture. One reaction to that approach—which certainly is reductive and denies any sense of value to the Muslim religious imagination—was to avoid all such questions of "origins." But that then creates a situation in which the Qur'ān—which is a remarkably context-less text as we shall see—had to be interpreted within the situation which Muslims had constructed as the community's own understanding of its origins. And that is a context which was, in itself, exegetical, that is designed specifically to interpret the text. Any sense of coming to an understanding of the text as a part of the literary heritage of the Middle East, an element in the continuum of religious discourse, is undermined. My point here is that, on the contrary, we must understand the Qur'ān as part of the Middle Eastern religious imagination, a text within the midrashic genre coming from the 7th century.

Another narrative must also be told about the construction of this paper and its topic which reflects a certain personal situation within my university career. Over the years my job has involved coordination of accommodations for students with disabilities within the courses taught in my faculty. As a result, I have had a number of encounters with various disabilities, but those that have impacted upon me are those students who are blind. Their abilities and their struggles to find ways of being scholars within the sighted world, with our emphasis upon the written word and the expectation of being able to maneuver easily within physical space, have both impressed me and made me conscious of my own ingrained assumptions about the value of sight in the intellectual universe in which we live. How could I ever be who I am without my eyes? Is not the loss of vision—something which surely strikes most of us as we age and discover the need for bifocal lenses and stronger and stronger lighting in order to read—is not that loss of vision the greatest fear that a humanist academic has? The point of course is that this is not so—I have colleagues in my own field who are totally blind and succeed very well, just as we have students who prosper as well. Our fears are real but the reality around us does not confirm those fears. Trying to understand that was one of the points of this investigation; while I am well aware that, for myself, I generally research something precisely simply because I find it interesting and somehow relevant—even though that relevance may be very tangential—in this instance my motivation and the relevance of humanist scholarship became more apparent to me.

•

The observation that language embeds social perceptions and attitudes of a historical time and place hardly needs intellectual justification in most fields of study these days. Illness, it has often been remarked, has become a particular vehicle for the expression of such attitudes through its metaphorical applications. For example, we can easily see this in today's English-speaking society in our talk of "cancer" as a disease which attacks social systems, or in our attitudes towards AIDS.[3] Blindness, a physical characteristic referring to those who, for a variety of causes, do not perceive light intensity and color (or have a limited perception compared to human norms), has a long cultural history in its use as a trope. Many authors have written on this subject and the ways in which the use of "blindness" has conveyed social perceptions and attitudes. In fact, the contemporary attention being given to blindness and other bodily variations from the statistical norm is quite significant, probably reflecting specifically North American concerns with human rights and their connection to disabilities. For example, Stephen Kuusisto's *Planet of the Blind* [4] and Rod Michalko's *The Mystery of the Eye and the Shadow of Blindness* [5] are both works of contemporary authors who are themselves blind who reflect upon what that has meant and means to them. Jacques Derrida's *Memoirs of the Blind: The Self Portrait and other Ruins* [6] is another prominent example published in conjunction with a 1990 exhibition at the Louvre. Another work which builds an intellectual framework for the study of the meaning of blindness is Eleftheria A. Bernidaki-Aldous, *Blindness in a Culture of Light, Especially the Case of*

Oedipus at Colonus of Sophocles.[7] Finally, a foundational work that sets the tone for many later contemplations is Michael E. Monbeck, *The Meaning of Blindness: Attitudes towards Blindness and Blind People* [8] which is especially good in dealing with the classical and biblical texts and their use of blindness as a metaphor. Overall there has been increased academic attention to the meaning of differences in individual physical capabilities.

Monbeck provides a useful summary of the motifs of the understanding of blindness in world literature. When blindness is used as a motif in literature, it conveys one or more of the following (some of which are, in the manner of such things, mutually exclusive): deserving of pity and sympathy; miserable; in a world of darkness; helpless; fools; useless; beggars; still able to function despite their blindness [i. e., the opposite of useless yet still the object of attention and note]; compensated for their lack of sight; being punished for some past sin; to be feared, avoided, and rejected; maladjusted; immoral and evil; better than sighted people (an idealization because such people are "protected" from the horrors of the world); mysterious and connected to magic and the supernatural. Examples of metaphorical uses within these motifs are easy to cite within the patterns of everyday speech; we speak of "blind rage" and "blind chance," reflecting the attitude of irrationality that sighted people imagine to be the life of one who is blind. The blind man creates the popular beggar image of cartoons and the like, and the blind salesperson on the side of the street is a cross-cultural figure in movies for the person to be taken advantage of. Examples can be multiplied endlessly.

It is commonly held around the world that sight is the "queen of the senses." This is based on the equation that seeing equals understanding (as embedded in so many metaphorical uses), but it is important to remark that not all (if even many) blind people are mentally deficient, so the presumption of sighted people that sight equals understanding is simply wrong empirically. Regardless, sight has been deemed essential to life and essential to the definition of a full person, and it is those attitudes which pervade the metaphorical usages of blindness.

Sight is so valued by sighted people (because its function is so obvious) that we forget that all the other senses play as important a role: they are all necessary, strong, vivid and pleasurable. Yet the absence of any or all of the senses does not deny the possibility of the "examined life," of living a reflective, human existence.

What factors lead to thinking this way about sight and the blind?

Surely the clumsiness in the dark of those of us who are sighted leads us to think about the blind this way. The blind remind us of our own vulnerability even in our sightedness. Further, we discover that the blind function and are productive in society, even though we think of sight as essential to life. We end up questioning our own sense of personal productivity. Loss of vision seems the most serious deviation from the norm of "body-wholeness," thus the encounter with the functioning-blind becomes threatening, especially to our way of defining identity through physique. Some have suggested that encountering blindness makes us confront our own mortality, because of the conceptualization of vision as essential to life (and darkness as associated with death). The images which thus become associated with the blind are defense mechanisms to protect our own sense of identity and meaning.

Our image of blindness builds upon and interacts with a variety of symbols:

a) the image of light and dark: illumination, enlightenment, God is light, He is the All-Seeing[9];

b) the image of the eye: association with light, idea of the "divine/third eye"; the eye as magic/mystery/power/evil/harm; the eye as the window to the soul; the appearance of the eye as a key to the person ("dark eyes," "somber eyes");

c) the image of loss of an eye: punishment for having seen what is forbidden, transgression of the natural order—the loss of an eye is thus transformative, being associated with death and rebirth (Paul blinded on the road to Damascus); the person who is blind is guilty of "looking" (often in a sexual sense, suggesting a link between blindness and castration).

"Blindness is, therefore, a thing in itself, not an absence of sight, but the grip of darkness, the maw of the chasm, the obliteration of consciousness by the overpowering seduction of the unconscious."[10]

•

The Qur'ānic vocabulary of blindness consists of three words, with one additional idiom often connected as well. The vast majority of passages (33 total uses) employ the root *ᶜ-m-y*. In addition, there are two uses of *akmah*, understood to mean "blind from birth," and one of *ᶜashā*, suggesting blindness as related to darkness. The one additional idiom is found in Q. 12:84, in which the patriarch Jacob is described in the following way: "And his eyes turned white because of the sorrow that choked within him." [11] Jacob's grief over the loss of Joseph is described as causing his eyes to "become white with sorrow," *wa-'byaḍḍat ᶜaynāhu min al-ḥuzn*, sorrow causing blindness, which itself is characterized as showing the whites of one's eyes.[12]

The Qur'ān speaks of those who are physically blind on a number of occasions, displaying attitudes towards those members of society. Blindness is understood as an illness of major significance, one which isolates its members. But at the same time, those who are blind are subject to God's mercy and compassion. Notably, all the passages which suggest the reality of blindness can also be read symbolically, such that blindness is not only a physical trait that afflicts some people but a paradigm of human behavior.

One example of this double sense of meaning in speaking of the blind is found in the stories of the miracles of Jesus. The blind, along with the leper, are those whom Jesus can cure, a motif within the New Testament stories. In Q. 3:49 and 5:110, the word *akmah* is used, meaning "those who are blind from birth." Both passages may easily be read as symbolic but they are generally understood as reference to literal miracles and thus physical blindness. Jesus is quoted as saying, "I will also heal the *blind* and the leper, and bring to life the dead, by the leave of God." Does the reference mean Jesus brings spiritual healing to those in need or is this a reference to physically blind people? The narratives told about the people Jesus encountered in his life suggest, of course, that these were real blind people, but the additional level of meaning has always been apparent to interpreters. These passages remind us that we cannot interpret the Qur'ān simply as a document of 7th century Arabia; the Qur'ān participates in the near eastern worldview, using the stories of the past to continue to convey its messages and, in doing so, transmitting the cultural views of Judaism, Christianity and the other social forces of the earlier near eastern world as embedded in the attitudes towards the blind.

Other Qur'ānic passages appear to deal with blind people as encountered by Muḥammad or by the reader of the Qur'ān in general. Q. 80:2 suggests that the blind need sympathy perhaps: "He frowned and turned away that the *blind* man came to him. And what should teach thee? Perchance he would cleanse him, or yet remember, and the reminder profits him. But the self-sufficient, to him thou attendest though it is not thy concern, if he does not cleanse himself." More direct are a series of passages which suggest that the physical fact of blindness is not a bar or inhibitor from a relationship with God. The blind are like the lame and the sick; blindness is not to be thought of as a punishment or a spiritual handicap. Q. 48:17 (also see 24:61) states: "There is no fault in the *blind*, and there is no fault in the lame, and there is no fault in the sick. And whosoever obeys God and His Messenger, He will admit him into gardens underneath which rivers flow; but whosoever turns his back, him He will chastise with a painful chastisement." This association of the blind, lame and sick is traditional, of course, emphasizing the linkages spoken of earlier.

The following passages have a phrase which suggests that being *blind and seeing are not equal*, suggesting that it must be admitted that the blind person (physically) is not the same as a sighted person:

> Q. 11:24: The likeness of the two parties is as the man *blind* and deaf, and the man who sees and hears; are they equal in likeness? Will you not remember?

> Q. 13:16: Say: "Are the *blind* and the seeing man equal, or are the shadows and the light equal? Or have they ascribed to God associates who created as He created, so that creation is all alike to them?"

> Q. 6:50 [note the use of "Unseen" here]: Say: "I do not say to you, 'I possess the treasuries of God'; I know not the Unseen. And I say not to you, 'I am an angel'; I only follow

what is revealed to me." Say: "Are the *blind* and the seeing man equal? Will you not reflect?"

Q. 35:19 follows the same idiom but adds an extra sense of blindness as being in a shadow, shade, or even dead: "Thou warnest only those who fear their Lord in the Unseen and perform the prayer; and whosoever purifies himself, purifies himself only for his own soul's good. To God is the homecoming. Not equal are the *blind* and the seeing man, the shadows and the light, the shade and the torrid heat; not equal are the living and the dead. God makes to hear whomsoever He will; thou canst not make those in their tombs to hear—thou art naught but a warner."

Q. 40:58 treats the blind in parallel with the wrongdoer and we start to see some of the moral overtones of the metaphor of blindness: "So seek thou refuge in God; surely He is the All-hearing, the All-seeing. Certainly the creation of the heavens and earth is greater than the creation of men; but most men know it not. Not equal are the *blind* and the seeing man, those who believe and do deeds of righteousness, and the wrongdoer."

Likewise in Q. 30:53, the blind can obey God but they need guidance, like everyone else: "Thou shalt not make the dead to hear, neither shalt thou make the deaf to hear the call when they turn about, retreating. Thou shalt not guide the *blind* out of their error, neither shalt thou make any to hear except for such as believe in Our signs, and so surrender."

Q. 17:72 could perhaps be interpreted as spiritual blindness, but if taken as physical, it does suggest that the blind are further astray. "And whosoever is *blind* in this world shall be *blind* in the world to come, and he shall be even further astray from the way."

Q. 20:124 is similar to the previous passage: blinded at resurrection, implying that blindness makes one further astray, but this may also be taken in the physical sense; also see 28:66 with its use of "darkened" and 17:97, the deaf, dumb and blind whose destiny is Gehenna:

"But whosoever turns away from My remembrance, his shall be a life of narrowness, and on the Resurrection Day We shall raise him *blind*. He shall say, 'O my Lord, why hast thou raised me *blind*, and I was wont to see?' God shall say, 'Even so it is. Our signs came unto thee, and thou didst forget them; and so today thou art forgotten.'"

Blindness on other occasions can be a punishment. When God curses people he makes them blind and deaf. Q. 47:23: "If you turned away, would you then haply work corruption in the land, and break your bonds of kin? Those are they whom God has cursed, and so made them deaf, and *blinded* their eyes. What, do they not ponder the Qur'ān? Or is it that there are locks upon their hearts?"

As suggested earlier, many of these usages could be taken as symbolic in the sense that physical blindness is perhaps not the primary connotation, but there is always some lingering doubt as to the metaphoric nature of the passages. Some other passages are clearer in their metaphorical sense, however.[13]

Q. 41:17 is clear in providing the metaphorical basis; here "blindness" is the opposite of "guidance." "As for Thamud, We guided them, but they preferred *blindness* above guidance, so the thunderbolt of the chastisement of humiliation seized them for that they were earning." Clearly, such a passage is unlikely to be interpreted to suggest that the people chose to physically blind themselves (although such a historical reconstruction may not be beyond the imagination of some exegetes, I would suggest). Rather, "blindness" here means "ignorance" of spiritual reality. The question that arises in any such clear metaphorical usage must be "why blindness?" What is it about blindness which suggests that there is a relationship between ignorance and blindness which makes this metaphor work? The clear answer is that those of us who are sighted rely so heavily upon our vision for our construction of reality that we cannot conceive of a fully meaningful human existence—one which is somehow not deficient and thus ignorant—without sight.

In Q. 27:66, blindness is a metaphor for "in doubt"; note here again the use of "Unseen." "Say: None knows the Unseen in the heavens and earth except God. And they are not aware when they shall be raised; nay, but their knowledge fails as to the Hereafter; nay, they are in doubt of it; nay, they are *blind* to it."

Likewise in Q. 43:40 (also see 10:43 and 27:81), the gloss is provided between being blind and/or deaf and being in "manifest error": blindness is clearly not being used in the sense of not being able to see light but rather in that metaphorical sense of somebody who is adrift. We need to remember, when contemplating the metaphor here, that those people who are blind do not conceive of themselves (necessarily) as "adrift" in the world; the usage here does not convey a "fact" about the world, but rather conveys a sighted person's perception of what it would be like to be blind. And therein lies the essence of metaphor. "What, shalt thou make the deaf to hear, or shalt thou guide the *blind* and him who is in manifest error? Whether We take thee away, We shall take vengeance upon them, or We show thee a part of that We promised them, surely We have power over them."

Blindness in Q. 2:18 is also equated with spiritual blindness such that the removal of guidance leaves one blind or in darkness: "The likeness of them is as the likeness of a man who kindled a fire, and when it lit all about him God took away their light, and left them in darkness unseeing, deaf, dumb, *blind*—so they shall not return; or as a cloudburst out of heaven in which is darkness, and thunder, and lightning—they put their fingers in their ears against the thunderclaps, fearful of death; and God encompasses the unbelievers; the lightning well-nigh snatches away their sight; whensoever it gives them light, they walk in it, and when the darkness is over them, they halt; had God willed, He would have taken away their hearing and their sight. Truly, God is powerful over everything." Here the equation of blindness with darkness is significant. According to an insightful study by Fedwa Malti-Douglas,[14] this image is not significant in medieval Mamluk literature, even though it does seem to have a firm foundation in the Qur'ān. Second, the parallel between blindness and darkness is once again a sighted person's perception.

This goes further. Another passage, Q. 2:171, suggests that blindness is to be equated with the inability to believe, that blindness is a hindrance to reality and truth (along with being deaf or dumb): "The likeness of those who disbelieve is as the likeness of one who shouts to that which hears nothing, save a call and a cry; deaf, dumb, *blind*—they do not understand."

The inability of humans to use their capability to perceive is highlighted through the metaphor of being blind in Q. 5:71. Humans are blind to signs, but God sees:

> And We took compact with the Children of Israel, and We sent Messengers to them. Whensoever there came to them a Messenger with that their souls had not desire for, some they cried lies to, and some they slew. And they supposed there should be no trial; but *blind* they were, and deaf. Then God turned towards them; then again *blind* they were, many of them, and deaf; and God sees the things they do.

This comparison of being sighted verses being blind as the key to spiritual understanding is clear again in Q. 6:104 with its very literal use of "eyes." "The eyes attain Him not, but He attains the eyes; He is the All-subtle, the All-aware. Clear proofs have come to you from your Lord. Whoso sees clearly, it is to his own gain, and whoso is *blind*, it is to his own loss."

The blind are spiritually dead in Q. 7:64: "But they cried him lies; so We delivered him, and those with him, in the Ark, and We drowned those who cried lies to Our signs; assuredly they were a *blind* people."

The heart is linked to blindness in Q. 22:46: "What, have they not journeyed in the land so that they have hearts to understand with or ears to hear with? It is not the eyes that are *blind*, but *blind* are the hearts within the breasts."

Q. 41:44 blindness is spiritual sickness (guidance = healing) although note that this might also suggest the idea that blindness is physically an illness, that it has medical causes.

> If We had made it a barbarous Qur'ān, they would have said, "Why are its signs not distinguished? What, barbarous and Arabic?" Say: "To the believers it is a guidance, and a healing; but those who believe not, in their ears is a heaviness, and to them it is a *blindness*; those—they are called from a far place."

Q. 43:36 uses the verb *ʿashā*, the only time this term is used in the Qur'ān, with an underlying sense of "darkness." Given the parallel passages Q. 25:73 and 13:19, however, there does not seem to be any particularly distinctiveness about this usage.

> Whoso *blinds* himself to the remembrance of the All-merciful, to him We assign a Satan for comrade; and they bar them from the way, and they think they are guided, till, when he comes to Us, he says, "Would there had been between me and thee the distance of the two Easts!" An evil comrade!

•

What then, is to be made of this?

Blindness is recognized as a physical attribute that imposes restrictions upon the experience of those afflicted but does not change their status nor are they at a necessary disadvantage in front of God nor should it affect their relationship with other people. The physical trait itself is not declared impure or a legal deficiency as it is in the Bible, for example, where the blind are prohibited entrance to the temple because of their bodily difference. However, underlying this attitude are other thoughts which might even be considered to be in conflict with this explicit level. "Blind" becomes associated with doubt, error, dark, lacking understanding, sickness. These metaphorical connotations, then, convey an attitude towards the blind that associates those who are physically afflicted with these metaphorical connotations. So, despite the positive view of those who are physically blind, the passages which may or must be read as metaphorical will always convey their connotations back upon the physiological nature of blindness. It is in that observation that we see the power of metaphor and of language as a whole to convey social attitudes and perspectives. Such metaphors stand at the basis of language and illustrate the ways that historical manifestations of language are a product of their own time and space. Of course, the Arabic-speaking world is not the "source" of this conception of the blind: the metaphor is widely used, as I have suggested earlier, and the same metaphorical usage of "blind" in Biblical stories conveys the same sense in its Qur'ānic setting. This does not suggest the necessity of "borrowing": if anything, it argues against it, since for the metaphor to remain meaningful between cultures, there must be a shared understanding. The attitudes conveyed in the "blindness" metaphor may well be so universal as to be a part of common human experience, as with matters such as the perception of human skin color (but not, for example, with the shape of noses: this is important—there is nothing "obvious" or "natural" about the characteristics of human existence which isolates one element as particularly significant). It is worthy of note the extent to which the metaphor of "blindness" is linked to an entire "conceptual metaphor"[15] in language: the overwhelming use of aspects of "sight" in the sense of "knowledge" (as in the English usage of "insight," "farsighted," "I see"), something as true in Arabic as it is in English (see the words related to the root *b-ṣ-r* for an illustration "They have eyes, but perceive not with them," Q. 7:179).

Philosophically, the observation has been made that the "because the apprehension of metaphorical meaning involves, at a certain level, the *assent* of the reader, the effect of metaphor goes beyond the verbal."[16] The metaphorical use of "blindness" as equivalent to "ignorance" involves the reader in the acceptance of the equation. If we accept the metaphor, our perception of reality is skewed by it. The question must arise, then, as to whether this metaphor can be accepted at the beginning of the 21st century. What does the metaphor suggest about the status of the blind in our society today? Must our attitudes to the blind not change? And what does that do to a metaphor in a sacred text such as the Qur'ān? But that drives us to the more fundamental question: what are the implications for the value and the authority of the Qur'ān when such a metaphor is present in such a sacred text?

Much of the Muslim attention to the Qur'ān today in terms of its relevance and applicability falls on matters primarily related to law: is it in keeping with contemporary standards of morality to lash fornicators and chop off the hands of highway robbers? Should men be allowed to beat their wives if their wives do not behave appropriately? Those questions are usually dealt with through invoking well-established techniques of interpretation. The tension between the apparent meaning of the text (or the well-established meaning) and the modern sensibility is resolved through exegesis. "Beat" does not mean "beat" in a physical sense when it comes to disciplining wives; legal restrictions on marriage mean that no one should marry four wives since they cannot deal with each of them equally. Whether the desire is to change the law because of changing moral standards or to maintain the traditional interpretation of the text in upholding law as it has been in the past (something which takes just as much interpretational inventiveness), behind such strategies lies the desire to maintain the authority of the text itself. The text retains its absolute authority as applicable at all times in all situations, with the exegetical proviso that the text is "properly" interpreted.

The case of cultural standards embedded in metaphor in an absolutely authoritative text, then, is particularly interesting because of the challenge which it poses to an attitude that demands that absolute authority of the text, subject to the powers of the exegetical imagination. If one wishes to maintain the authority of the scriptural text absolutely—once again only subject to the ingenuity of the exegete but not give in to the relativity of historicizing the text—how is one to deal with the metaphorical language which challenges ethical and social standards with which the community of believers may wish to identify? The range of possible examples here is broad and certainly not limited to "blindness," and the question is not limited to the Muslim tradition either. Some fascinating struggles have gone on in the Jewish and Christian world especially with the language related to God in both its masculine bias and its vocabulary of social structures which have shifted so much in their meaning and connotations: king, master, lord in reference to God no longer sit so well with many people.

Such, it seems to me, in a very small way, is illustrative of the dilemmas that many religious people face today, especially those who wish to view their lives within the framework of the absolute authority of scripture, as most—but certainly not all—Muslims do today. Muslims have displayed unlimited creativity and uncovered the power of the linguistic sophistication of their scripture, by being able to reconcile science, evolution, human rights and most every other topic to the principles enunciated in their scripture. But the nature of language is such that the challenge posed is, in fact, far more serious. To some intellectuals within the Muslim community, these challenges seem to demand that the historicization of the text be pursued, that the text must be seen as a linguistic and cultural product of 7th century Arabia, a reflection of that situation and those perceptions; and yet so many members of the community resist, fearing that they will lose all defense against the impact of contemporary Euro-American norms if they relinquish the absolute standard of their scripture based in the theological concept of the eternal word of God.

In conclusion then, a study such as this, on a topic of very limited range and what some may consider hardly worthy of putting all the weight on it which I may be suggesting, does seem to land us up in the fundamental questions related to reading and its manifestation in language. This is not an issue that pertains to scholarship alone, nor to Muslims alone; it is a human problem, but it is one for which scholarly reflection upon the text of the Qur'ān can contribute to raising the issues to the foreground for everyone, regardless of religious and cultural orientation. In this particular instance, it may be observed that some metaphors are empowering to human thought and action (as I would claim for eschatological imagery, for example), while others may have a misleading, even prejudiced outcome. The final conclusion may well be that we need a new understanding of language which moves away from the binary metaphorical/non-metaphorical construct and directs us towards a comprehension of language as fundamentally metaphorical. What this might mean in terms of its implications for the more pragmatic aspects of our existence is a question I must leave to the philosophers of language. But that the problematic nature of human language may well be explored within the context of a subject such as Qur'ānic studies is a challenge which should not escape us as in the 21st century.

NOTES

1. A. Rippin, "The Commerce of Eschatology," in *The Qur'ān as Text*, ed. S. Wild (Leiden: E. J. Brill, 1996), 125–35.

2. Other papers include "'Desiring the Face of God': the Qur'ānic Symbolism of Personal Responsibility," in *Literary Structures of Religious Meaning in the Qur'ān*, ed. I. J. Boullata (Richmond: Curzon, 2000), 117–24; "God" in *The Blackwell Companion to the Qur'ān*, ed. A. Rippin (Oxford: Blackwell, 2006), 223–33, based on an earlier paper, "'God is King': Studying the Qur'ān and Talking of God," unpublished paper presented at a colloquium in honor of Mohammed Arkoun, Carthage 1993.

3. Susan Sontag, *Illness as Metaphor* (New York: Farrar, Straus and Giroux, 1978), is an obvious example of a work which elaborates this theme.

4. New York: Dial Press, 1998.

5. Toronto: University of Toronto Press, 1998.

6. Chicago: University of Chicago Press, 1993.

7. New York: Peter Lang, 1990.

8. Bloomington: Indiana University Press, 1973.

9. See D. Gimaret, *Les noms divins en Islam. Exégèse lexicographique et théologique* (Paris: Cerf, 1988), 262–6 for a treatment of this image within Islamic theology.

10. Monbeck, *Meaning of Blindness*, 143.

11. See my article "Colors," in *Encyclopaedia of the Qur'ān*, ed. J. D. McAuliffe (Leiden: Brill, 2001), I, 361–5, in the section dealing with "white and black."

12. See M. Mir, *Verbal Idioms of the Qur'ān* (Ann Arbor: Center for Near Eastern and North African Studies, University of Michigan, 1989), 64.

13. Al-Fīrūzābādī, *Baṣā'ir dhawī 'l-tamyīz* (Beirut n. d. reprint), IV, 102, distinguishes the "absence of sight" and the "absence of sight of the heart" and compares Q. 80:2 to 2:18 as illustrating the two meanings.

14. Fedwa Malti-Douglas, "*Mentalités* and Marginality: Blindness and Mamluk Civilization," in *The Islamic World, from Classical to Modern times. Essays in Honor of Bernard Lewis*, ed. C.E. Bosworth et al (Princeton: Darwin Press, 1989), 211–37. This insightful essay draws attention to some of the differences between the European and the medieval Mamluk attitudes towards blindness. On a legal level, the blind are treated in the same manner as women. Their sexual prowess along with their ability in memorization is highlighted more than their spiritual insight.

15. G. Lakoff, M. Johnson, "Conceptual Metaphors in Everyday Language," in *Philosophical Perspectives on Metaphor*, ed. M. Johnson (Minneapolis: University of Minnesota Press, 1981), 286–329.

16. Julie Galambush, *Jerusalem in the Book of Ezekiel: The City as Yahweh's Wife* (Atlanta: Scholars Press, 1992), 9, speaking of Lakoff and Ricoeur.

Chapter 4

The Qur'ān, Chosen People and Holy Land

Seth Ward

Much of what is written and said by Muslims today about Israel and the Jews in the name of Islam or of the Qur'ān is decidedly negative: statements about Jews and Judaism are shaped by the perceived political realities. It is easy enough to focus on a reading of the Qur'ān in which Jews are portrayed as sinners and implacable enemies of today's Muslims, and the latter are the only true spiritual descendants of the Children of Israel and followers of the Abrahamic religion. Yet many verses in the Qur'ān may be read in a broader way. God may grant land to whomever He wishes, and is ever-merciful, forgiving and rewarding those who remain steadfast. More specifically, many verses in the Qur'ān support the chosenness of Israel, and even God's specific promise of the land to the Israelites. This essay reviews the Qur'ānic verses about the chosenness of Israel and God's assignment of the Promised Land to them.

Over two decades ago, the late Ismā[c]īl Rājī al-Fārūqī noted that Jewish-Christian dialogue had had many achievements; but Muslim-Christian dialogue had little to show for itself and Muslim-Jewish nothing at all.[1] Authentic Islamic-Judaic discourse drawing on the Qur'ān could be shaped by verses describing divine promises to the Israelites, much as Christian-Jewish dialogue has been shaped by a Christian reinterpretation of the meaning they give to the old Jewish covenant with God. Muslims and Jews have much to gain by seeking a dialogue about scripture and shared values.

The Qur'ān contains several passages regarding the chosenness of Abraham's progeny and of the Israelites (*banū Isrā'īl*), most often in the context of the Exodus. In the times of Moses, son of [c]Amram (Arabic: [c]Imrān), the Israelites were saved from Pharaoh, witnessed miracles and prostrated themselves before God in true worship. We read in the Qur'ān that God was gracious to Adam and to those with

Noah. His grace extended to "the descendants of Abraham and of Israel, and of those whom We have guided and chosen (*ijtabaynā*), for when the revelations of the Merciful were recited to them they fell down to their knees in tears and adoration" (Q. 19:58)[2]. "God chose (*inna 'llāha 'ṣṭāfā*) Adam and Noah, Abraham's descendants and the descendants of ᶜImrān, above the nations" (Q. 3:33).[3] "We saved the Israelites from the degrading scourge, from Pharaoh, who was a tyrant and a transgressor, and chose them knowingly (*akhtarnāhum*) above the nations. We showed them miracles which tested them beyond all doubt" (Q. 44:30–2). "We gave the Book to the Israelites and exalted them (*faḍalnāhum*) above the nations" (Q. 45:16). "O Children of Israel: remember my favor (*niᶜmatī*) which I have bestowed upon you and that I exalted you (*faḍaltukum*) above the nations" (Q. 2:122). In each of these verses, the Qur'ān refers to Israel as chosen. The same message may be learned by noting that the Israelites were given the Book as an inheritance (*wa-awrathnā Banī Isra'īla 'l-kitāb)* (Q. 40:53); and that "the Book was bestowed as inheritance upon those whom God has chosen" (*alladhīna 'ṣṭafaynā min ᶜibādinā*) (Q. 35:32). The Qur'ān also honors the Israelites with peace, guidance and safety: "peace upon those who have followed the guidance" and "We have saved you from your enemy"—in context, both referring to the Israelites (Q. 20:47, 84).

The promise or grant of the land to the Israelites is also found in the Qur'ān 17:104: "We said then unto the Israelites: 'Dwell in the land'" (*wa-qulnā min baᶜdihī li-Banī Isrā'īla 'skunū 'l-arḍ*) This promise comes towards the end of *sūra* 17, to which we will soon turn in some detail.

The land itself is also blessed or chosen. The "blessed land" is the land in which God settled the Israelites. It was already blessed in the days of the Patriarchs: "We delivered [Abraham] and [his nephew] Lot to the land which We have blessed (*al-arḍ allātī bāraknā fīhā*)" (Q. 21:71). So, too, God enabled Solomon to bring the wind to the land "which We have blessed" (Q. 21:81). The Israelites were settled in the land after the persecutions of Pharaoh and the exodus from Egypt. Moses tells the people to have heart, as the Lord may "destroy your enemies and make you rulers in the land" (*wa-yastakhlifakum fī'l-arḍ*) (Q. 7:129). This came to pass, and "We gave the persecuted people dominion over the Eastern and Western lands, which we have blessed" (*allatī bāraknā fīhā*) (Q. 7:137).[4]

The blessed cities (*al-qurā allātī bāraknā fīhā*) of Q. 34:18 occur in the context of a narrative about the Sabaeans of pre-Islamic Yemen; the *sūra* refers to the famous breaking of the Mārib Dam. But the *qurā* are understood by Islamic commentators to refer to the cities of *al-Shām*, "Syria." In other words, this phrase, too, refers to the blessed land of the Israelites.

Israel is to find its true homeland there: The land of the Israelites is described as *mubawwa'*, "place prepared as a lodging." "We settled the Israelites in a homeland of truth (*mubawwa'a ṣidq*)[5] and provided them with good things" (Q. 10:93).

The "Holy Land," *al-arḍ al-muqaddasa*—etymologically the same as Hebrew *ha-aretz ha-qedosha*—occurs only once in the Qur'ān, and refers to the land of the Israelites. In a passage referring to the "words of Moses to his people," encouraging them when they were afraid of giants in the promised land, we read: "Remember my people, the favor which God has bestowed upon you. He has raised up prophets among you, and made you kings, and given you that which he has given to no other nation. Enter, my people, the holy land (*al-arḍ al-muqaddasa*), which God has decreed for you (*allatī kataba 'llāhu lakum*)" (Q. 5:21). Indeed, Ibn Kathīr goes so far as to consider these verses a divine command to Israel for *jihād* to enter Jerusalem, which was in their hands in the time of Jacob. Although they sinned and strayed from God, their punishment was to delay their entry for forty years—after which they were to enter the land.[6] The Israelites are also commanded to "enter the gate," which probably also refers to entering the land or entering Jericho (Q. 4:154, 5:23).

Perhaps the most striking narrative about the history of the Israelites in their land occurs in *sūra* 17. This chapter is usually entitled *al-Isrā'*, "The Night Journey;" sometimes it is called *Banū Isrā'īl*. The "Night Journey" refers to the usual Islamic understanding of the first verse (which forms a separate subject from the rest of the chapter):[7] Muḥammad was miraculously transported from Mecca to Jerusalem and thence to Heaven. This verse is the only Qur'ānic reference to this story: "Glory to Him who made his servant go from the sacred house to the farther temple (*al-masjid al-aqṣā*), whose surroundings We have blessed (*alladhī bāraraknā ḥawlahū*), that We might show him of our signs" (Q. 17:1). There is considerable discussion about the meaning of *al-masjid al-aqṣā* in this verse. It may refer to "the highest heaven;" according to some versions of Muḥammad's account of his heavenly journey, the angel Gabriel took him by the hand from where he slept directly to "the lowest heaven," leading him successively upwards, with no reference to Jerusalem at all.[8] Alfred Guillaume has argued convincingly that in its original context the verse refers to a point on the outskirts of the ancient sacred enclave around Mecca.[9] The view that has become standard in Islam, however, is that Muḥammad journeyed first to Jerusalem. This verse is therefore taken to refer either to the Jewish Holy Temple, the place from which Muḥammad is said to have ascended to heaven—in other words, the rock underneath today's Dome of the Rock—or to Jerusalem in general. The blessing of its surroundings would thus appear to be a reference to the Holy Land, as is the case with similar language used elsewhere in the Qur'ān. As for today's Aqsa Mosque (Arabic: *masjid al-aqṣā,* as in the verse), it of course did not exist in Muḥammad's time. During most of Muḥammad's prophetic career, Jerusalem was under Persian control (614–628). Byzantines returned triumphantly to Jerusalem in 629 and Muḥammad is said to have rejoiced when he learned Jerusalem was once again under the control of People of the Book.[10] After Jerusalem was conquered by Islam, several years after Muḥammad's death, Muslims in Jerusalem gathered for prayer at the southern end of the Temple Mount enclosure, the side closest to Mecca; when the mosque was built, its name recalled the verse. Interestingly, the language of blessing is different when the Qur'ān discusses the holy house in Mecca. Here the notion of "blessing" is not made to agree with "land," nor is the blessing applied to the surrounding area. "The first house placed on the earth was in Bakka (i.e. Mecca), as a blessing (*mubārak*) and guidance for the nations" (Q. 3:91).

Chapter 17 continues with a discussion of the Book given to Moses.[11] This book reminds the Israelites that they are descendants of those whom God carried on the ark with Noah, a motif we have seen from passages elsewhere in the Qur'ān. The book—

presumably a reference to the Torah—contained a promise about the land. Although the text of the promise is not mentioned at this juncture, it could hardly be other than the land. The Qur'ān notes that Moses' book contains predictions that twice the Israelites will commit evil in the land (Q. 17:4). Possibly this is a reference to the two passages of reproof (*tokaḥa*, Lev. 26:14–41, Deut. 28:15–68) read in synagogues, according to today's standard reading cycle, shortly before Shavu'ot and Rosh Hashanah. The prediction was fulfilled: the Qur'ān reviews the history of God's punishment, referring to two formidable armies who punished Israel. The first army "ravaged the land and carried out the punishment with which you had been threatened" (Q. 17:5). But God granted victory to Israel, and again Israel became rich and numerous (Q. 17:6). Then the prophecy of a second transgression was fulfilled, and God "sent another army to afflict you and to enter the temple (*al-masjid*) as the former entered it before, utterly destroying all that they laid their hands on" (Q. 17:7). The verses refer to the destruction of the first and second temples, in 586 BCE and 70 CE. The book given to Moses had predicted that God would scourge the Israelites twice; the Qur'ān envisions future forgiveness and renewal—again punishable by destruction. "God may yet be merciful unto you, but if you again transgress, you shall again be scourged. We have made hell a prison-house for unbelievers" (Q. 17:8). The end of *sūra* 17 returns to an account of Moses, and the command to "dwell in the land" noted above. The process of forgiveness and victory, transgression and destruction is to cease when the promises of the hereafter come to pass, and "We shall bring you all together'" (*ji'nā bikum lafīfan*) (Q. 17:104). The chapter ends with a call to all mankind to pray to God, calling upon him as God or as the All-Merciful or by whatever name, praying with neither too loud nor to soft a voice, and proclaiming His oneness and His greatness (Q. 17:110–11).

God has caused the Egyptians to abandon "gardens, fountains and ... a noble place (*maqām karīm*)" and "we have caused the Israelites to inherit them (*awrathnāhā*)" (Q. 26:59; see also 44:25–9 where the language is very similar and the Israelites are mentioned in the next verse). "Gardens and fountains" are also associated with the heavenly paradise. In Q. 5:12, we find the divine promise to cause them "to enter gardens under which rivers flow." This sounds like paradise to be sure, but it is also a description of Jerusalem, e.g. in al-Zamakhsharī on Q. 17:1.[12]

Even had there been no promise, God's ability to offer any land to anyone whom He chooses is underscored by the Qur'ān: "Lord... You bestow sovereignty on whom you will and take it away from whom you please" (Q. 3:26). "The earth is God's, He gives it to whosoever He chooses." And similarly, God bestows favor on whom He will and takes it away from whom He will (e.g. Q. 3:74). We have seen that the Israelites were offered the "Eastern and Western lands" (Q. 7:137), but the Qur'ān reminds us that "The East and West are God's, He guides whom He will to the right path" (Q. 2:142). God can thus offer sovereignty to anyone He wishes. Indeed, any sovereignty exists only by divine favor.

Thus, we see that there is much material in the Qur'ān which links Israelites to the "blessed" or "holy" land. Abraham came to this land when he first left his homeland; the Israelites came to this land when God brought them out of Egypt; the Temple of the Israelites stood in this land. Moreover, God may at any moment give a land to whomever He chooses, and God promised that the Israelites will be gathered together in the land just before the end-times.

Many of these passages are associated with the revelations of the Meccan period, i.e., before Muḥammad emigrated to Medina in 622 CE. Other passages in the Qur'ān, many associated with Muḥammad's Medinan period, are far less favorable to the notion of Israelite land and have a negative attitude towards the Jews; sometimes the verses cited above appear in such contexts.

Jewish discourse takes it as a given that there is an unbroken continuity from Abraham, Isaac and Jacob to the ancient Israelites to the Jewish people of Roman times, Muḥammad's times and our own days. In the Bible, Jacob is renamed Israel, and Jacob's descendants—the twelve tribes—are known as the Children of Israel, who recognize the God of Abraham, Isaac and Jacob. The Qur'ān recounts a story similar to one found in Jewish literature: The children of Jacob (also known as Israel) gather around him on his deathbed. He asked them about their loyalty to God, and together, they recited a verse, Deuteronomy 6:4, "Hear O Israel, the Lord is our God, the Lord is One."

[13] This verse, the quintessential profession of Jewish faith, mentions the negation of all other gods save God, and the profession of divine unity. In context, the verse also asserts the loyalty of the individual sons—the twelve tribes—to the people which bears the name of their father. The Qur'ān does not read the biblical narrative the same way. Ishmael joins the others as an ancestor. Jacob's children, "the tribes," swear loyalty to the God of Jacob and of Jacob's "forefathers, Abraham, Ishmael, and Isaac," and promise to surrender themselves to God, (*wanaḥnu lahū muslimūn*) i.e., to be Muslims (Q. 2:133). We read in the next verse that the people formed by the Tribes—the Israelites—is no more: "That community has passed away (*tilka 'l-umma qad khalat*)" (Q. 2:134) (compare the next section, especially Q. 2:140–141, which ends with the identical wording "Do you claim that Abraham, Ishmael, Isaac, Jacob and the Tribes were all Jews or Christians? … that community has passed away…."). Abraham himself is not seen as the progenitor of the Israelites, or even of the Israelites and the Arabs. Instead, "Abraham was neither Jew nor Christian. He was an upright man who surrendered himself (to God) (*ḥanīfan musliman*)" (Q. 3:67). Thus "those who are nearest to Abraham"—the true inheritors of Abraham's promises—are those "who follow him, this Prophet (i.e., Muḥammad) and the true believers" (Q. 3:68). God was gracious to the descendants of Abraham, and Israel; but God's grace also included others, "those whom [He] has guided and chosen" (Q. 19:58), and moreover, "the generations who succeeded them neglected their prayers and succumbed to their desires. These shall assuredly be lost" (Q. 19:59), and cannot demand divine favor: "Let the People of the Book know that they have no control over the grace of God *faḍl Allāh*" (Q. 57:29). In short, they have become enemies—and they have become unbelievers. Like the idolaters, they associate others with God, and even consider humans to be divine: the Qur'ān says that Jews believe Ezra to be the son of God (Q. 9:30).

The Qur'ān refers to the notion of covenant in several terms, including *ᶜahd* and *ayman,* as well as *mīthāq*, "covenant," which appears twenty-five times. In many instances, the term is used of those who were allied to the Muslim community. But *mīthāq* often refers to a divine covenant with a people, in chapters considered to have been revealed late in Muḥammad's career. There is the "*mīthāq* of the believers," and most particularly the "Covenant of the Israelites" in *sūras* 2, 4 and 5, and the covenant of those to whom the Book was given in Q. 3:187. In these late chapters, the Covenant is almost always presented as rejected. "The covenant of those to whom the Book was given... they sold it for a paltry price" (Q. 3:187; see also 2:40, 2:86, 2:90). Addressing the Israelites, the Qur'ān notes that the covenant was made when the mountain was held over their heads, but they have turned away from it (Q. 2:63–4).[14] The Qur'ān teaches that the promises and revelations Jews claim for themselves are forgeries, and reiterates to the Jews "you have turned away from your bonds with Allah" (Q. 2:83). This passage refers to shedding kinsmen's blood and turning them out of their homes (Q. 2:84), and God has cursed them for their unbelief (Q. 2:88). God made a covenant with the Israelites, but the Israelites said "we hear and disobey" (Q. 2:93) and have broken the covenant (*fa-bimā naqḍihim mīthāqahum*) (Q. 4:154–5, 5:12–13). They turned away from God's messengers, playing blind and deaf, even after God turned to them again in mercy (Q. 5:70–71). There is an additional reference to what must be the Covenant of the Israelites in Q. 5:7. Here, those who received the covenant say "we hear and obey" and there is no immediate reference to breaking the covenant. But it may also be noted that there is no specific reference to the Israelites or to the mountain raised over their heads.

Moreover, the covenant does not apply to evil-doers (Q. 2:123 and frequently). The Qur'ān even recounts the divine prerogative to reward the Muslims at the expense of the People of the Book: "He made you masters of their land, their houses, and their goods, and of yet another land on which you had never set foot before" (Q. 33:27). The context is no doubt that of Medina, the city of Muḥammad, and the oasis of Khaybar in what is today NW Saudi Arabia. In both places, the peoples of the book referred to were Jews, some of whom were dispossessed, expelled or slaughtered. Such verses include: Take not the Jews and Christians as friends (Q. 5:51). Regarding "those who have received a portion of the Scripture ..." i.e. the People of the Book, they purchase error, and "God knows best who your enemies are" (Q. 4:44–6). Indeed you will find that the most vehement of men in enmity to those who believe are the Jews and polytheists" (Q. 5:82). The verse about Medina and Khaybar refers to a one-time dispossession, but another well-known verse may be said to imply continuing struggle, at least until the non-Muslims have recognized the hegemony of Islam. "Fight those to whom the book has been given, who believe not in God and the last day, who forbid not what God and his Apostle have forbidden, and do not embrace the true faith, until they pay tribute (*jizya*) out of hand and are utterly subdued" (Q. 9:29).

Thus we have seen that the Qur'ān describes God's election of the Israelites, and that God granted the land of Abraham and Jacob to Israel. Some verses about the land the Israelites were to receive broadens it to "East and West"—understood as Egypt and Syria by some commentators. We also saw them inheriting "the gardens and fountains" of the Egyptians, in language similar to that used to refer to paradise. But we have also seen verses which explain why the Qur'ān is not often read this way. The Qur'ān discusses the descendants of the Israelites, and notes that Jews and Christians, or at least some of them, have fallen away from the true path, pervert scriptures, do evil and fight the believers. Yet, many of these references are in Medinan *sūra*s. Rather than understand them in broad terms, they must be seen in the context of the *asbāb al-nuzūl*, the specific history of the community of believers during that period. And the evil end which meets them is no different than that which is in store for those who claim to be Muslims yet do evil.

There is much in the Qur'ān and in Islamic tradition which allows for dialogue and common ground, or at least heated debate, even on highly controversial issues. For example, the contention that there is no connection between Judaism and the Ḥaram al-Sharīf—the Temple Mount—flies in the face of the Qur'ān, which tells the story of the destruction of both temples, as we have seen. Moreover, Jerusalem was not under Islamic control when the Prophet is said to have visited there—nor, for that matter, when he recommended his followers to visit or support Jerusalem.[15] The Qur'ān may be read to show a sense of discontinuity between Israelites of old and the Jews of today—yet the Qur'ān also records God's promise which allows for the possibility of their reinstatement.

This may be illustrated by the Qur'ān passage including the command to replace an earlier *qibla*, direction faced in prayer. The earlier *qibla* is unspecified in the Qur'ān, but always understood as facing Jerusalem. The *qibla* commanded by the Qur'ān is towards the Holy Mosque in Mecca (Q. 2:144). But this passage also recognizes that there is an arbitrariness to this, as "East and West are God's" (Q. 2:142). Addressing Muḥammad, the verse says that the new Meccan "*qibla* will be pleasing to you" (*qibla tarḍāhā*) (Q. 2:144); others are unlikely to adopt the *qibla* of the Muslims, no matter what verses or proofs are brought to bear (Q. 2:145). "Each one has the direction in which he faces … and God will bring them all together" (Q. 2:148). It is antithetical to Islam to prevent anyone from prayer to God, anywhere, facing any direction; this would include Muslim prohibition of Jewish prayer on the Temple Mount or the Western Wall, where prayer to God has been prevented several times by rocks being thrown from above.

The Qur'ān cannot be seen only as a book read by extremists to justify extremism, but also as scripture which can be used by Muslims who fight against a political interpretation of Islam that stresses armed struggle, and who reject terror and hatred as un-Islamic. The liberal tradition of modern Islam also has deep roots developed over nearly two centuries, although in contrast to "political Islam," it usually is nearly invisible to outside observers. Many Muslims stress that today, Muslims must put aside the lesser *jihād* (literally "exertion") of armed struggle to join in a "greater" and more holy struggle against the evil which lurks within ourselves. Muslims justify marriage to Christian and Jewish women not only because the Qur'ān allows them to do so but because these communities are fundamentally monotheistic: if they *really* practiced polytheism, how could religious Muslims allow their wives to continue to practice these religions? Islamic attitudes to Judaism—and to Israel—must come to stress the brotherhood of ancestry and belief, to debate the State of Israel as possibly justified by Islam, and to interpret the negative material in the Qur'ān as reflecting particular occasions in the past. As we have seen, the Qur'ān provides ample scope for such interpretations. Jewish-Christian relations have shown much success in concerted effort on both sides to find teachings consistent with religious values which overcome both Christian triumphalism and charges of deicide, and Jewish teachings about the proverbial hatred of Esau—symbolizing Christianity—for Jacob. Among the rules of reasoning which may be applied in Islam, some legal traditions recognize that rulings may be issued on the basis of such concepts as *istiḥsān* or *maṣlaḥa*: what makes life better or more suitable for the Muslims. Certainly, under the concept of *maṣlaḥa*, much benefit would accrue to Muslims by emphasizing Qur'ānic elements allowing for a peaceful coexistence with an Israeli state. This would remove a cause of much death and destruction, liberating energy to concentrate on economic advancement and intellectual development—and leaving more time and ease for prayerful devotion to the Almighty.

There can be no progress towards stopping violence without a framework for societal justification for doing so. For Arabs and Israelis, the Muslim and Jewish traditions provide important societal grounding, but the religious sources are being used most often to support highly rejectionist viewpoints; often they are re-interpreted in this way. To succeed, any peace process must re-focus use of religious sources to promote a religious justification to reject bloodshed in favor of prayer, service and harmony among men.

"Lord, make this a land of peace and bestow plenty upon its people" (Q. 2:125). The Qur'ān's blessing applies to the Ka^{c}ba in Mecca. May it be God's will that the blessings of peace and prosperity apply also to the land called holy and blessed in the Qur'ān.

NOTES

1. Foreword, *Trialogue of the Abrahamic Faiths* (Herndon: International Institute of Islamic Thought, 1991), x-xi (First edition: 1982; the lectures in the book were given in 1979).

2. Ismā^{c}īl is mentioned in Q. 19:54, without mentioning his progeny as is the case with Abraham and Israel. It is not immediately clear from the text whether the chosenness mentioned here refers to the progeny of Abraham and Israel or to Prophets from among their progeny.

3. Here, ^{c}Imrān is the father of Moses, although in the next verse of the Qur'ān, ^{c}Imrān appears as the name of the grandfather of Jesus. Most Muslims do not believe that the Qur'ān considers Mary mother of Jesus to be the same as Miriam, sister of Moses, although in the Qur'ān both are Maryam the daughter of ^{c}Imrān.

4. Al-Zamakhsharī glosses this as Egypt and Syria.

5. Al-Zamakhsharī: "a safe domicile (*manzal*), that is, Egypt and Syria."

6. Ibn Kathīr, *Tafsīr al-Qur'ān al-^{c}aẓīm* (Beirut n. d.) II, 53.

7. In the article "*Isrā',* " *EI2*, B. Schrieke noted that discussion of the original meaning of the verse and whether it was originally part of its current chapter were beyond the scope of the article. Such issues are also beyond our scope here.

8. Variant *ḥadīth* traditions have Gabriel lead Muḥammad by the hand directly from his home to the lowest heaven and thence upward, i.e. bypassing Jerusalem; others recount

how Muhammad traveled on Burāq to Jerusalem. A third possibility raised by some is that this occurred in a dream. Sources also differ about the details which might serve to assign a date to this event. Some sources imply the ascent to heaven is to be dated very early in Muḥammad's life or career; perhaps the most common dating is to c. 619, the year in which his wife Khadīja and his uncle ᶜAbbās died. The story of the development of this and other elements of the sacred biography of Muḥammad is comprehensively retold in Uri Rubin, *The Eye of the Beholder: The Life of Muhammad as viewed by the early Muslims* (Princeton: Darwin Press, 1995). On the place of Jerusalem in Islamic tradition, see S. D. Goitein, "The Sanctity of Jerusalem and Palestine" in his *Studies in Islamic History and Institutions* (Leiden: E. J. Brill, 1968), 135–148. Goitein takes issue with Goldziher about the role of the Umayyads in promoting the sanctity of Jerusalem; interestingly, the history of interpretation of the *isrā'* does not play a major role in his argument.

9. A. Guillaume, "Where was the al-Masjid al-Aqṣā?" *Al-Andalus* 18 (1953): 323–36. This is of course irrelevant to the traditional Islamic interpretation of this verse.

10. Some sources believe that Persians handed day-to-day control of Jerusalem to the Jews, which would mean it was under *Jewish* control at the time often cited for the *isrā'*. It is not clear that this should be considered historical. See M. Gil, *A History of Palestine 634–1099* (New York: Cambridge University Press, 1992), 5–10 (sections 5–11).

11. Compare *kitāb Mūsā,* "the book of Moses" Q. 11:17; here it is always simply *al-kitāb*.

12. In this context, it is interesting to note the Biblical comparison of the area of Sodom prior to its destruction as "like the Garden of the Lord, like the land of Egypt" (Genesis 13:10); the Midrash understands this as trees and agricultural lands (Genesis Rabbah 41:7). The land of Israel is not usually described as "a garden" but as a "land flowing with milk and honey." The major exception is Deut. 7:7–10 in which the land is described as having streams of water and springs, and producing agricultural products and minerals; the final line of this passage provides that the Israelites will eat and be satisfied and bless the Lord for the bounteous land.

13. Pesahim 56a; see Maimonides, *Mishneh Torah*, "Laws of reciting the Shema," 1:4.

14. This is well-known midrash is found in the Babylonian Talmud, Shabbat 88a.

15. A well known *ḥadīth* reports that Muḥammad was asked about Bayt al-Maqdis (Jerusalem) and said "Go and pray in it, for a prayer in it is the equivalent of a thousand prayers elsewhere." If one could not go there, "send a gift of oil to it in order to be lit in its lanterns, for one who does so is the same as the one who has been there." Cited by Abū Dāwūd, Ibn Māja, and Ibn Ḥanbal; see Mustafa Abu Sway, "The Holy Land, Jerusalem and Al-Aqsa Mosque in the Islamic Sources" *CCAR Journal,* Fall 2000: 63.

The Qur'ān in history

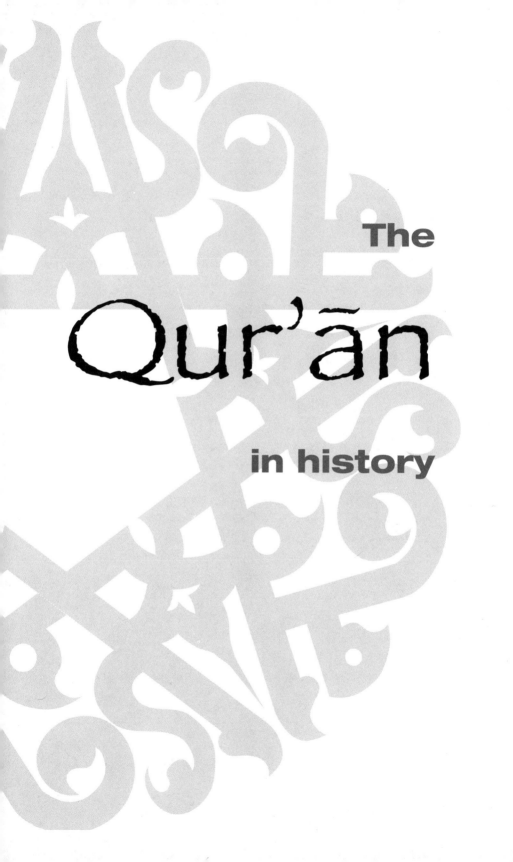

The Dome of the Rock and the Qur'ān

Rizwi Faizer

Many believe that the mosaic inscriptions of the Dome of the Rock, *Qubbat al-Sakhra* in Arabic, that edge the ambulatories surrounding its central rock are Qur'ānic.[2] The fact is that they not only encapsulate the fundamental assertions of Islam, but that much of the text of the inscriptions appears to be verses cited from that holy text. The inscriptions, which are dated 72/692 and established in a fairly developed script, are even cited by a few scholars as proof that the Qur'ān had been canonized by this date.[3] Yet, the fact that the Dome of the Rock is in Jerusalem rather than Mecca, combined with approaches to the Qur'ān that reject Muslim belief that the Qur'ān originated as the God-inspired teachings of a single Meccan, has resulted in a hesitancy on the part of most scholars to acknowledge the Qur'ānic origins of these inscriptions.[4] While recognizing that the inscriptions are not necessarily from the canon, this article will argue that they are, nevertheless, probably *qur'ānic*, perhaps even indicative of another codex, and that one may use its passages to understand Islam as it was asserted by the Umayyads of the late seventh century. Moreover, if the objection to Muslim notions of an ᶜUthmānic canon was predicated on the desire to suggest that the essential vision of Islam was not asserted until the ninth century, the date indicated by John Wansbrough[5] for the emergence of the Qur'ānic canon, this essay challenges such views to argue that by 72/692 not merely the vision of an iconoclastic monotheism, but both the centrality of Mecca and the leadership of an Arab named Muḥammad had been claimed for Islam by its followers. Furthermore, this essay uses the inscriptions' references to the nature of Christ to reawaken the notions put forward by scholars such as Richard Bell[6] who argued that Islam arose in a Christian rather than the Jewish milieu suggested by Wansbrough.

To establish the above, this essay begins by presenting the historical background to the era of ᶜAbd al-Malik, followed by a brief description of the Dome of the Rock; next, translations of the inscriptions are followed by an investigation of the nature of *qur'āns* during the time of ᶜAbd al-Malik and a discussion of the content of the inscriptions. Finally the significance of the Dome of the Rock is presented.

Historical Background

Even Muḥammad had emphasized the significance of Jerusalem for the Muslims. Muḥammad, the Prophet of Islam, had claimed that he was merely reviving the monotheistic beliefs proclaimed by Abraham, Moses, David and Jesus, so that inevitably, Jerusalem, where the temple of the Jews had once stood, was his original direction of prayer, or *qibla*. It was only after a period of constant quarrelling with the Jews of Medina that he turned towards the Kaᶜba in Mecca instead.[7]

That one should interpret the phrase *masjid al-aqṣā* or "the distant place of prayer" mentioned in Q. 17:1 as a reference to the temple grounds in Jerusalem, appears to be a logical consequence of the context in which the phrase is situated, given the esteem granted by Islam to Jerusalem, and its distance from Mecca. Thus, *al-Isrā'*, the chapter in which the phrase is included in the Qur'ān is also entitled *Banū Isrā'īl*, "the Children of Israel," and the verses immediately following the phrase *masjid al-aqṣa* (Q. 17:2–7) refer to the repeated destruction of the Temple of Jerusalem because of the "sins" of the Jews. The Qur'ān which refers to Palestine as the Holy Land—*al-arḍ al-muqaddasa*—in Q. 5:23 also refers to it as the Blessed Land—*al-arḍ allatī baraknā fīhā*—in Q. 7:137; 17:1; 21:71; and 34:18.[8] Such a regard for Jerusalem is also demonstrated by the tradition cited by al-Wāqidī (d. 207/823) according to which Maymūna, a wife of the Prophet, informs Muḥammad that she had vowed to pray at the temple in Jerusalem if God should conquer Mecca for him, and he asks her to send oil instead as he feared the Byzantines would keep her from entering Jerusalem.[9]

Muslim reverence for Jerusalem persisted after the death of the Prophet. A tradition recalled by al-Ṭabarī (d. 311/923) informs us that when ᶜUmar b. al-Khaṭṭāb (r. 13–23/634–44) arrived in Jerusalem, he proclaimed the *labbayka*,[10] a recital associated with the circumambulation of the Kaᶜba, as he stood at the gates of the temple grounds;[11] then approaching the so called *mihrāb Dāwūd* on the Temple Mount, he recited, first, the section of *sūrat Ṣād* (Q. 38: 21–25) which tells of David's repentance and God's forgiveness of his sins, followed by *sūrat al-Isrā'* (Q. 17) which tells of the "night journey" of the Prophet.[12]

Traditions tell of the Muslim embrace of the temple grounds as part of their religious heritage: When the Muslims took Jerusalem in around 17/638, the Jews who had previously taken care of the temple grounds had been exiled from Palestine for almost 500 years by the Emperor Hadrian in 135 CE; they had briefly returned in 614–17 CE with the Persian conquest,[13] only to be exiled again when the Persians were defeated by Heraclius in 628 CE and Jerusalem restored to the Christians. Since the latter felt no reverence for the temple site of Mount Moriah which Jesus had abjured,[14] the area was not only neglected, but, deliberately polluted, a site for the deposition of menstrual cloths of Byzantine women.[15]

While there is no eyewitness account of the events that saw the conversion of Jerusalem from a Christian into a Muslim centre we learn from later chroniclers that once the terms of surrender had been agreed to, the Christian Patriarch Sophronius gave ᶜUmar b. al-Khaṭṭāb a tour of Jerusalem, and indicated to him the site of the temple;[16] Kaᶜb al-Aḥbār (a Jew who had converted to Islam soon after Muḥammad's death), who was specially summoned for the occasion by the caliph, is then supposed to have carefully measured the grounds to identify the temple's exact situation.[17] The temple grounds were cleaned and perfumed by ᶜUmar and the Muslims with the help of some Jews. ᶜUmar then built a mosque on the site—the mosque of ᶜUmar (the title which was later mistakenly adopted as that of the Dome of the Rock, itself, by Western scholars),[18] in front of the protruding rock, with its *qibla* directed towards Mecca.[19]

No Muslim source records the Ḥaram's first mosque but, in the reign of Muᶜāwiya b. Abī Sufyān (41–60/660–80), the Gallic pilgrim Arculf (late 7th C) claimed he saw a rough prayer house of the Saracens built on what he understood to be the remains of the Jewish Temple.[20] It is not certain whether it was ᶜUmar or Muᶜāwiya who actually built this earlier mosque. But, as Elad points out, Arculf visited Jerusalem in 50/670 and since ᶜUmar had died in 23/644,

Muᶜāwiya may have put up the construction in the meantime.[21] On the other hand, it was ᶜUmar who appointed Muᶜāwiya governor of Syria and Palestine in 19/640, and it is plausible that Muᶜāwiya merely carried out ᶜUmar's instructions.

Be that as it may, Jerusalem came to be closely associated with Umayyad authority. When, in June 656, the caliph ᶜUthmān ibn ᶜAffān was assassinated and ᶜAlī b. Abī Ṭālib appointed his successor, it was as governor of Syria and Palestine that Muᶜāwiya protested ᶜAlī's appointment. When ᶜAlī was assassinated by a Kharijite rebel, it was the Arab tribes in Palestine who pronounced Muᶜāwiya caliph in Jerusalem in 40/661.[22] According to a Syriac source, Muᶜāwiya then visited not only the Church of the Holy Sepulcher, but the Church of the Ascension on the Mount of Olives and the Virgin's tomb in Gethsemane, as well, as a mark of respect.[23] As caliph, Muᶜāwiya visited Jerusalem frequently with his son, Yazīd, whose mother was a Christian from the Arab tribe of Kalb (largely Monophysite Christian by faith).[24] It was with Palestinian forces that Yazīd suppressed the Medinans at the battle of Ḥarra in 682 CE, plundering the town and extracting oaths of allegiance from its occupants. Later, the army marched into Mecca where at some stage in the course of the siege the Kaᶜba caught fire.[25]

With the death of Yazīd I in 64/683 followed almost immediately by the death of his son, Muᶜāwiya II, Umayyad authority was on the verge of collapse. ᶜAbd Allāh b. al-Zubayr (the son of Ibn al-Awwām and Asma bt. Abī Bakr, reportedly treated by ᶜĀ'isha, the wife of Muḥammad, as her son) who had asserted his claims as caliph soon after the death of Ḥusayn, now began to extend his authority from Mecca all the way into Iraq. Even in Syria, the Qaysī tribes recognized him as caliph, and coins issued in his name in Fars and Kirman attest to his acceptance there as well.[26]

Meanwhile, Marwān b. al-Ḥakam (son of the notorious Ḥakam b. al-ᶜĀs, himself brother of ᶜUthmān's father ᶜAffān, who was exiled by the Prophet for mocking him)[27] an Umayyad and cousin to both ᶜUthmān and Muᶜāwiya, having considered offering his allegiance to ᶜAbd Allāh b. al-Zubayr, now decided to come forward as a contender for the Umayyad-caliphal leadership, himself. Interestingly, Marwān was kept away from the court of Muᶜawiya because the latter had felt threatened by him. Yet, it was Marwān who had functioned as ᶜUthmān's scribe and keeper of his caliphal seal.[28] Recognized for his knowledge of the Qur'ān, he probably played some part in the Qur'ān compilation activities which ᶜUthmān put together. His loyalty to ᶜUthmān was evident when he was seriously wounded defending the caliph against his assassins at Yawm al-Dār (35/656).[29]

To achieve his caliphal ambitions, Marwān won over the tribes of southern and central Syria (led by the tribe of Kalb) by marrying the widow of Yazīd and having her son, Khālid, named his heir. It helped him win the battle at Marj Rāhiṭ (64/684) against the Qays, many of who supported Ibn al-Zubayr. Once appointed caliph, however, Marwān immediately reneged on his agreements, naming his own son, ᶜAbd al-Malik, mothered by his wife ᶜĀ'isha bt. Muᶜāwiya, as heir.[30] It was his new wife, the Christian mother of Khālid, who murdered Marwān a few days later.[31] Marwān's rule lasted for barely a year (64–5/683–4).

It took several more years for ᶜAbd al-Malik to consolidate his Islamic empire. Though his father, as caliph, had managed to retake Egypt, ᶜAbd al-Malik's own attempts to enter Iraq had been far from easy: his general ᶜUbayd Allāh b. Ziyād was killed (67/686) by the armies of the Shīᶜite leader, Mukhtār.[32] ᶜAbd al-Malik therefore decided to, first, consolidate his position in Syria, keeping away from both the Hijāz and Iraq while the Shīᶜites and Zubayrids battled each other. He also agreed to pay an annual tribute of 365,000 *solidi* in return for a ten year truce with Byzantium and the removal of the Christian Mardaites from Syria.[33]

In the summer of 70/690, however, ᶜAbd al-Malik's luck began to improve. He overcame Zufar b. al-Ḥarith in Mesopotamia, went on to defeat Musᶜab b. al-Zubayr (d. 72/691) in Iraq and won a significant victory against the Byzantines at Sebastopolis (692 CE). Sending his general Ḥajjāj to battle ᶜAbd Allāh b. al-Zubayr in Mecca, he then proceeded to build the *Qubbat al-Ṣakhrā* or Dome of the Rock, on Mount Moriah in 72/692.[34] According to the Mujīr al-Dīn al-ᶜUlaymī (d. 927/1521), it was Rajā' b. Haywā al-Kindī (d. 112/730), the most prominent traditionist of al-Shām, from Baysān, who was appointed in charge of the building operations; his *mawla* Yazīd b. Salām supervised the actual work.[35]

The Dome of the Rock

The Dome of the Rock, which stands on the promontory understood to be the Temple Mount or Mount Moriah, is the earliest extant monument of Islam that contains an inscription which includes today's formula of the Muslim creed: "There is but one God and Muḥammad is His Prophet."[36] One hesitates to call the Dome of the Rock a mosque, for the area covered by the Dome instead of providing space for prayer, opens up to reveal a lower chamber which houses a protruding rock emerging right from the earth's surface. It is this same *lapis pertusus* of the Temple area that the Bordeaux pilgrim, writing in 333 CE, advises us was visited annually by Jews; it is this same area that is referred to by the seventh century Armenian chronicler Sebeos who informs us that the Arabs had built a mosque at a place where the Hebrews thought they had found the Holy of Holies.[37] Inevitably, the Dome came to be associated with the Temple of Solomon or Masjid Sulaymān which the Muslims believed had once stood there.

The rock which the dome protects would generally be considered quite unremarkable except for a marking it bares, described by some as the mark of God Himself, defining it as the place from which God rose into the heavens once He had completed the creation of the world.[38] Others insist that the marking on the rock is the footprint of the Prophet Muḥammad.[39] Indeed, the spot has been represented as the navel of the earth. According to Mujīr al-Dīn al-ᶜUlaymī, "the very site of the city is holy by dint of its being the closest of the earth to the heaven, the source of all sweet water and wine on earth, the dividing line between heaven and hell. In addition it is, of course, the place of the Day of Judgment…"[40] It is believed to be the site of Jacob's ladder,[41] the place from which Jacob dreamed of meeting God, and of the Prophet Muḥammad's ascension—*miᶜrāj* means ladder—as well. The latter claim is based on Q. 17:1 combined with traditions that tell us that Muḥammad made his ascension to God from the *masjid al-aqṣā* and negotiated a reduction in the number of prayers his followers were required to perform each day to five."[42]

The *masjid al-aqṣā* mentioned in the Qur'ān is not a reference to a particular building but rather to the entire site of the Temple

Mount or Mount Moriah on which the ancient Temple of the Jews had once stood. While Christians had avoided the site on the basis of Christ's condemnation and built a place of worship at Golgotha (close by the original site), instead, transferring the mythology that had accrued around the Temple to their own, now privileged, church, Muslims, asserting that Islam had superseded both Judaism and Christianity, now reclaimed the site of Mount Moriah for a "temple" of their own. There was the insinuation that such a house of God built by a righteous caliph would stand the test of time.

Modern historians, with the exception of Miriam Rosen-Ayalon, have generally conceived the Dome of the Rock to be this "Muslim Temple", and in their attempts to understand the vocabulary of its architecture have therefore restricted their analyses to this building alone. The monument stands not far from the Christian Anastasis on Mount Golgotha originally built by the Emperor Constantine (d. 337 CE) and has clearly been influenced by it. Noticing the similarities between the two buildings, Henri Stierlin remarks,

> There is a deep and purposeful analogy between these two buildings; both have a central plan with a double ambulatory, topped by a cupola with an inner diameter of 20.40 meters ... both house a sacred rock underneath, where there is a grotto; in both there is a footprint—of the risen Jesus in the Holy Sepulcher and of the Messenger of God during his ascent to the heavens, in the Dome of the Rock. Such a convergence of form and function... is the result of a clear wish on the part of Caliph ᶜAbd al-Malik to appropriate the legacy of the Christians at the site sanctified by Abraham.[43]

But, as emphasized particularly by Rosen-Ayalon, the similarity of the two structures does not end there. Just as the Church of the Holy Sepulcher includes the Anastasis which forms the rotunda of the church at the eastern end continuing on to a basilica at the western end, so the Islamic application of this scheme on the Temple Mount saw the erection of the Dome of the Rock on the northern side of the platform complemented by the establishment of the al-Aqṣā mosque to its South. It leads us to believe that both the Dome of the Rock and the Masjid al-Aqṣā were planned at the same time as parts of a single complex that was to distinguish the Temple Mount.[44]

Several early historians justify this claim: The earliest extant source for the construction of al-Aqṣā by ᶜAbd al-Malik is the Jerusalemite al-Muqaddasī (d. 390/1000). Similarly, Sibṭ b. al-Jawzī (d. 655/1257) in his *Mirʾāt al-Zamān* informs us that ᶜAbd al-Malik built both the Dome of the Rock and the mosque of al-Aqṣā.[45] True, Ibn al-Athīr (d. 629/1232), Bar Hebraeus and Ibn Tiqtaqā assign the project to al-Walīd, son of ᶜAbd al-Malik (r. 86–97/705–715). But al-Muqaddasī is the earlier source and therefore probably more reliable.[46] Al-Aqṣā, then, would be the mosque in which the faithful of Jerusalem would gather for worship.[47] That the *miḥrāb* of this mosque indicated the *qibla* of Mecca suggests that the entire complex of monuments designed for the Temple Mount were established so as to indicate a Meccan focus.[48] This significant relationship between the Dome of the Rock and the Masjid al-Aqṣā is confirmed in the writings of al-Muqaddasī as well:

> [I]t was not found possible to extend the Main building of the (Aqṣā) Mosque as far as the South East angle of the area wall, lest the great *miḥrāb*, in the center place at the end of the mosque, should not then have stood opposite the rock under the Dome; and such a case was repugnant to them. [49]

The Dome of the Rock is octagonal in shape and consists of a central dome surrounded by two ambulatories. A high wooden drum rests on a rotunda just large enough to surround the rocky outcrop. The rotunda is set in an octagon, approximately twenty meters to a side, with doorways placed at the centre of the four cardinal walls. An intermediary octagon consisting of eight piers and sixteen columns, arranged such that each pier alternates with two columns, supports the roof. The rotunda has been rotated slightly within the octagon so that a view from the interior across the building is possible.[50]

The Qur'ānic inscriptions of the Dome of the Rock are situated on the outer and inner faces of the intermediary octagonal arcade which supports its roof. Despite the height of their position, both passages would have been easily accessible, given the numerous lights with which the entire space was supposedly illuminated.[51] These inscriptions declare (I believe) the defining faith of Islam as it was understood in those early years. They proclaim not only a belief in one God and His prophet Muḥammad, but also a very distinct position regarding the nature of Christ which is no longer emphasized by Muslims today.[52] Indeed, by asserting that Jesus was a Messenger of God, Islam distinguished itself from both Judaism and Christianity. Importantly, these beliefs about the nature of Christ are enshrined in verses of today's Qur'ān, dispersed in various chapters of the collected volume.

Following is a translation of the two inscriptions. The citations from the Qur'ān have been italicized.

> The Outer Inscription
>
> In the name of God the Compassionate the Merciful, there is no god but God, One, without associate. *Say: He is God, Alone, God the eternal, He does not beget nor is He begotten and there is no one like Him* (Q. 112). Muḥammad is the envoy of God, may God bless him. [rosette] In the name of God the compassionate the merciful, there is no god but God, One, without associate. Muḥammad is the envoy of God. *Indeed God and His angels bless the Prophet; O you who believe send blessings on Him with full salutation* (Q. 33:56). [rosette] In the name of God, the Compassionate the Merciful, there is no god but God, One. *Praise to God who begets no son and who has no associate in power and who has no surrogate for (protection from) humiliation, and magnify His greatness* (Q. 17:111). Muḥammad is the envoy of God, may God bless him and his angels, and peace unto him and the mercy of God. [rosette] In the name of God the Compassionate the Merciful, there is no god but God, one and without associate. *To Him is dominion and to Him is praise; He gives life or death and He has power over all things* (Q. 64:1 and 57:2). Muḥammad is the envoy of God, may God bless Him and grant his intercession on the day of resurrection for his community. [rosette] In the name of God, the compassionate the Merciful, there is no god but God. One, without associate. Muḥammad is the envoy of God. God bless him [rosette] has built this domed structure the servant of God, ᶜAbd Allāh the *imām* al-Ma'mūn, Commander of the Faithful, in the year seventy-two. May God accept it from

him and be satisfied with him. Amen. Lord of the worlds, to God is praise. [rosette] (Note: It is obvious that the name of ᶜAbd al-Malik has been replaced with that of al-Ma'mūn).

The Inscription on the Inner face

In the name of God the Compassionate the Merciful, there is no god but God. One without associate. *To Him is dominion and to Him is praise, He gives life or death and He has power over all things* [Combination of Q. 64:1 and 57:2]. Muḥammad is the servant of God and His envoy. Verily God and His angels send blessings to the Prophet. *O you who believe, send blessings on Him and salute Him with full salutation* [Q. 33:54]. May God bless him and peace upon him and the mercy of God. *O people of the book, do not go beyond the bounds of your religion and do not say about God except the truth. Indeed the Messiah Jesus son of Mary was an envoy of God and His word He bestowed on her as well as a spirit from Him. So believe in God and His envoys and do not say three; desist it is better for you. For God is one God, Glory be to Him. That He should have a son! To Him belong what is in Heaven and what is on earth and it is sufficient for Him to be a guardian. The Messiah does not disdain to be a servant of God, nor do the angels (nearest to him). Those who disdain serving Him and who are arrogant, He will gather all to Himself* [Q. 4:171–2]. Bless your envoy and your servant Jesus son of Mary, *and peace upon him on the day of his birth and the day of his death and on the day he is raised up again. This is Jesus son of Mary. It is a word of truth in which they doubt. It is not for God to take a son. Glory be to Him. When He decrees a thing He only says "be" and it is. Indeed God is my Lord and Your Lord, therefore serve Him. This is the straight path* [Q. 19:33–6]. *God bears witness that there is no God but He, as do the angels and those wise in justice. There is no God but He the almighty, the all wise. Indeed the religion of God is Islam. Those who were given the book did not dissent except after knowledge came to them (and they became) envious of each other. Whosoever disbelieves in the signs of God, indeed God is swift in reckoning* [Q. 3:18–19].[53]

Are the Inscriptions Qur'ānic?

The Qur'ān is probably our most reliable source for the message of Islam. According to Muslims, it is the word of God which He revealed to Muḥammad, the Prophet of Islam, who in turn conveyed it to his followers. Nevertheless, it is important to understand that the term Qur'ān as used today with reference to a book did not exist during the time of the Prophet, if only because such a volume had not as yet been collected together. The term *qur'ān* as used in the revelation, in fact refers simply to a portion or fragment of the revelation.

According to the most recognized of traditions from al-Bukhārī, the Qur'ān was not compiled by the Prophet himself.[54] Its many verses having first been collected after his death by his successor, the first caliph, Abū Bakr b. Abī Quḥāfa (r. 11–13/632–4), it was finally compiled during the caliphate of ᶜUthmān b. ᶜAffān (r. 23–41/644–61), under the direction of Zayd b. al-Thābit (d. 42/662) aided by ᶜAbd Allāh b. al-Zubayr (d. 72/692), Saᶜīd b. al-ᶜĀṣ (died during the caliphate of Muᶜāwiya) and ᶜAbd al-Raḥmān b. al-Ḥārith b. Ḥishām (d. 43/663). The general command given by ᶜUthmān to the latter was, "If there is divergence between you and Zayd about anything from the Qur'ān, write it down in the dialect of the Quraysh because it has been revealed in their dialect."[55] ᶜUthmān's labours did not immediately result in a unified canon. There were three basic reasons for this: 1) there were several versions (i.e., codices or *muṣḥaf*s) of the text; 2) and there was also the problem of variant readings; 3) the Arabic script had not as yet been fully developed.[56]

Several Versions: At the time of the Prophet's death there were already several collections of *qur'ān*s (here I am using the term with reference to collections of manuscripts of the revelation) kept by various Companions of the Prophet. These *qur'ān* manuscripts were inevitably different from each other as they were discrete and private collections and are identified as different codices of the revelation. Thus the Ibn Masᶜūd (d. 33/653) codex did not include *sūrat al-fātiḥa*, the first chapter of today's Qur'ān, while Ubayy b. Kaᶜb's (d. 18/639) codex included chapters no longer found in the canon;[57] together with the codex of Abū Mūsā (d. 42/662),[58] these codices had each become popular in their own right and were used in Kufa, Damascus and Basra respectively. It was in such a context, tradition informs us, that in 30/651 the general Ḥudhayfa while leading his troops in an expedition to Armenia and Azerbaijan became irritated by the quarreling among his troops regarding the vocalization of the *qur'ān*, and therefore urged ᶜUthmān to establish a unified canon.[59] Despite the unified ᶜUthmānic compilation being sent out to the central mosques of the large cities, the more popular codices continued to be used by the different populations.

Variant readings: The occurrence of variant readings was clearly unavoidable due to the significance of orality in the process of communication. Such variants involved vocalization, pronunciation, and the substitution of synonyms for the words of the text. Variants gradually accumulated in the ᶜUthmānic codex as well, so that it was no longer possible to determine the original version established by Zayd.[60] Thus a period of choice, *ikhtiyār*, was established when scholars were permitted to choose their own reading, while being guided by their knowledge of grammar, oral tradition, and the ᶜUthmānic consonantal text.[61]

Arabic script: The most obvious reason for the inability to establish a unified canon, however, was the defective nature of the Arabic script during the Prophet's lifetime and for several years after. The *qur'ān* manuscripts collected together by Zayd thus lacked the markings which help one differentiate the grammatical subject from the object, or, differentiate between two similarly formed consonants because the diacritical markings needed to distinguish one from the other were not indicated. Whether a particular letter was *fā'* or *qāf,* for instance, thus depended to a large extent on what the reader already knew, because he had already memorized it orally.

By 22/643 considerable progress had been made in developing diacritical markings as witnessed by the document known as Perf. 558.[62] But these markings had not been used in the *qur'ān*s. The emphasis on oral tradition combined, possibly, with the desire to be faithful to the original manuscripts Zayd had collected together, and the need to accommodate existing variant readings, seem to have led to a reluctance to introduce diacritical markings into the ᶜUthmānic recensions. It was with essentially a consonantal script, therefore, that the new "canon" was established; this is why scholars challenge Muslim traditions that claim that Zayd was commissioned to write down the Qur'ān in the dialect of the Quraysh. Indeed, it is reported that once, when a mistake in writing was shown to ᶜĀ'isha, the Prophet's wife, she remarked that the Arabs would correct it with their tongues.[63] However, Zayd's achievement should not be underestimated. In establishing the consonantal outline of the text, he inevitably fixed both the contents of each chapter and determined the order of the chapters as well.[64]

The development of a *scriptio plena* took several more years to evolve. There are accounts which suggest that scholars such as Abū 'l-Aswad al Du'ālī (d. 69/688), Naṣr b. ᶜĀṣim (d. 89/707) and Yaḥyā b. Yaᶜmar (d. before 90/688) found the oral tradition to be an unreliable guide for the reading of the *muṣḥaf* and they began to use dots and strokes to fix the reading of the text.[65] It is plausible, given the caliphal ambitions of ᶜAbd al-Malik and his knowledge and interest in the Qur'ān, that he took a personal interest in establishing a more thoroughly unified text, and that he encouraged al-Ḥajjāj (who had earlier been a school teacher) to work towards it. Ibn Abī Dā'ūd narrates a tradition according to which al-Ḥajjāj was responsible for eleven changes in the consonantal text.[66]

It is in this context of a lack of uniformity among the *qur'āns* that I would like to place the inscription of the Dome of the Rock, and suggest that its *qur'ānic* origins need to be recognized. Much of what is in the inscription, particularly the inner inscription, is found in today's canonized Qur'ān, scattered in various parts of its 114 chapters, in part due to the nature of the Qur'ānic compilation, which appears to be haphazardly put together.[67] The claim that Muḥammad would intercede on behalf of his followers as indicated in the outer inscription (a characteristic which follows closely on that attributed to Jesus by Christians) though it is repeated particularly in Ṣūfī traditions, is not found in today's Qur'ān. This justifies Tilman Nagel's claim that the inscriptions were derived from traditions of the community rather than the revelation—although it must also be explained that the community was far more hesitant regarding the writing down of traditions than it was about compiling the Qur'ān.[68] On the other hand, it is possible that a codex which included such a sentiment—later dropped out of the canon because it could have led to an undesired deification of the Prophet—existed in the late seventh century, and that it was from such a *qur'an* manuscript that ᶜAbd al-Malik chose to select the citations for his inscription.[69]

Finally, to attribute such a religiously focused *qur'ānic* inscription to ᶜAbd al-Malik b. Marwān is entirely reasonable. Importantly, ᶜAbd al-Malik was an Arab Muslim nationalist at heart: it was during his regime that the language of administration was established as Arabic, and the coinage was given an Arab-Muslim format and stamped with the assertion that "There is but one God and Muḥammad is his prophet." He was also known for his piety as *ḥamāmat al-masjid*.[70] Nabia Abbott, citing Khaṭīb al-Baghdādī (d. 463/1071) and Ibn Kathīr (d. 774/1373), informs us that, "ᶜAbd al-Malik applied himself so assiduously to the study of Qur'ān, *ḥadīth* and *fiqh* that he came to be ranked with such leading Medinan scholars as ᶜUrwa b. al-Zubayr, Saᶜīd b. al-Musayyib and Qabīṣah b. Dhū'ayb."[71] Wellhausen opines that he may have even ranked as a *ḥāfiẓ* of the Qur'ān.[72]

A Closer Look

The inscriptions were clearly designed for the Dome of the Rock even as the building was being planned. The tradition of using inscriptions in the classical world was continued by the Romans who recognized its artistic possibilities to underscore the authority and dignity of monuments built for propagandistic purposes. Examples are viewed in the triumphal arch in Rome built in the name of Titus (d. 81 CE), and the most famous monumental inscription in Iran established by Darius I (522–486 BCE).[73] But whereas the medieval West soon replaced the writing used in classical times with images, the Muslims who had an iconoclastic faith, continued to use inscriptions, particularly in their religious buildings, citing passages from the Qur'ān to proclaim their faith.

The inscriptions executed in mosaic on the inner and outer faces of the octagonal arcade of the Dome of the Rock are written in gold against a deep blue background. The similarity in the artistry displayed by the inscription in the Dome of the Rock to that which was later established in the mosque of Medina by Walīd I, son and successor of ᶜAbd al-Malik, is commented on by al-Ṭabarī.[74] According to Ibn al-Nadīm, the inscription at the Mosque of Medina was executed by one Khālid b. Abī Hayyāj, ṣāḥib ᶜAlī, who was recruited by Saᶜd, a scribe employed by al-Walīd. It appears that Khālid was from a district in Medina known for the copying and selling of *qur'ān* manuscripts.[75] It seems plausible that ᶜAbd al-Malik, who was a Medinan by birth and new the city well, appealed to the Medinan *qur'ān* copyists to design the inscriptions for the Dome of the Rock.[76]

Although the epigraphy of the Dome of the Rock inscriptions is similar in style and technique, the layout of the inner band is different from that on the outside. The band on the outer face is divided into six sections by the use of decorative rosettes. The first five sections consist of Qur'ānic verses and pious phrases concerning God and His messenger, Muḥammad. The sixth is essentially a historical statement providing the name of the patron and the date the construction was begun.[77]

On the inner face the text is continuous, beginning in the southwest corner and running counter-clockwise around the central, lower chamber. Following an invocation to God the text asserts His omnipotence, and extols Muḥammad as His prophet; then follow Qur'ānic verses which admonish the People of the Book, denounce the idea of the trinity which was viewed as a deviation from monotheism, and expound the proper view of Jesus as spirit of God, His word, conveyed to Mary, and as nothing other than a true servant of God and His messenger, and not His son.

The dominant presence of diacriticals in the inner rather than the outer inscription suggests that it is the inner statement that is more important, and this is further borne out by the rhetorical and polemical nature of this statement.[78] Since importance seems to have been attached to the message, it seems likely that the desire to include diacriticals which would facilitate the communication of the message would have originated from the caliph, aided by the scholar, who selected and designed the inscription for the monument. Interestingly, the only other inscription with similar marking is the milestone eight miles from Jerusalem also believed to have been established by ᶜAbd al-Malik.[79]

Blair observes that just as the representational motifs were adapted to fit the upper sections of the walls, the inscription bands were also carefully designed to fit the circumference of the two ambulatories.

> Both bands of writing fill the space exactly and are aligned with the architecture. Both begin in a corner of the building just above the edge of a mosaic panel… the beginning of a new thought is often aligned with the edge of a representational panel… The inscriptions were laid out to achieve symmetry. A single letter falls in the center of the concave pier.[80]

Referring to the inner inscription in particular, she explains that these letters are wider so that its decoration is more visible. Clearly, the inscriptions with their diacritical markings were conceived as part of the design which was to cover the walls of the arcades, and thus must surely have been intended by the man who planned the building.

What is special about the layout of the Dome of the Rock inscriptions is that the southern or *qibla* wall in particular is emphasized. In the case of the inner inscription, the emphasis is located where one sees the coherent phrase consisting of the invocation followed by a conflation of Q. 64:1 and 57:2 flanked by parts of the profession of faith. Blair recognizes an emphasis given to the outer inscription (where the southern wall displays the text of Q. 112 about God's omnipotence) as well. However, if it is the direction of Mecca that was intended, then one must recognize that one would have to face North (i.e., away from the *qibla*) to be able to read this inscription.[81] It therefore appears that it was the southern inner inscription that was specifically highlighted, which indeed it was, given that its letters were larger and marked with more diacriticals. As Blair explains, the decoration of the inner face of the octagon "cues the pilgrim that the south is the *qibla* facade."[82]

More important, however, as observed by Raya Shani, is that a visitor to the Dome was expected to enter the building from the north. This is indicated by al-Wāsiṭī (d. 5th/11th C.), who transmits an early tradition from Wahb b. Munabbih (d. 114/732), that a pilgrim who wished to visit the *sakhra* should do so from the northern gate.[83] As Shani observes,

> [T]he overall vista facing a person standing at the northern entrance and looking towards the south creates a sensual progress in this direction… ᶜAbd al-Malik had employed all possible means to impress the raison d'etre of his ambitious monument upon the viewer immediately from the northern entrance. This may indicate that the visitor was due to start his tour from here, where it is readily declared to him that Resurrection and After-Life is promised to the true believers only.[84]

The Significance of the Inscription

The Dome of the Rock inscription established by ᶜAbd al-Malik b. Marwān is essentially a statement of the basic beliefs of Islam, its two-fold creed, namely, that there is but one God, and that Muḥammad is His prophet. The most significant polemic in the Qur'ān concerns Christianity, and interestingly, this polemic which concerns the nature of Christ has been carefully selected to be demonstrated on the walls of the monument, particularly its inner walls. The purpose was surely to stress the prophethood of Jesus, which I suggest was originally, and especially in Umayyad times, as much a part of the creed as was the belief in one God and His prophet, Muḥammad. It may well explain why Muᶜāwiya chose to visit Christian holy sites soon after his "coronation."

Clearly Islam's perception of the significance of Christ is different from that of Christianity, but there are important similarities which the inscription records: that the Messiah, Jesus, was the son of Mary; that he was a "Spirit proceeding from Him [God]" committed to Mary. However this does not mean that Jesus was/is God's son, for God merely says "be" and it is. It would seem therefore that according to Islamic understanding, it is the particular notion of "son" that is unacceptable because it implies a sexual relationship which is anathema to a monotheist's conception of God. Nevertheless, Jesus **is** born because of a direct act of God—God wills the birth of Christ—and Jesus is the son of a virgin: Jesus was surely born of a miracle!

Just as significant is the statement, "Peace be upon him the day he was born, the day he dies, and the day he is raised up alive." The insinuations made here that Jesus did not die on the cross (Q. 4:157), and that he will reappear at the end of time (Q. 43:61) are clarified in the verses of the Qur'ān as indicated.[85] As important is the adjective used to describe him, namely "Messiah," which to Jews and Christians meant a savior who would arrive/reappear at the end of time. What exactly it meant to the Muslims of ᶜAbd al-Malik's era is not clear, but the chances are that they had a similar understanding. It is interesting, however, that al-Ṭabarī should explain the term as "one who wipes away sickness," referring to Jesus' powers of healing, instead.[86]

The notion of "three" asserted in the inscription is explained in Q. 5:116, "And behold! Allah will say: 'O Jesus the son of Mary! Didst thou say unto men, take me and my mother for two gods beside Allah?'" Here there is clearly a misunderstanding of the concept of the trinity which must certainly have been confusing in those early years of the seventh century (when Muḥammad probably heard of the controversies in the church), for there was much debate about the nature and will of Christ, and when there also existed a tendency to venerate, if not worship, Mary who as mother of Christ/God was given a very special place.

It must be understood that the Orthodox church of the Byzantines had segregated itself from Monophysite (Egypt, Syria) and Nestorian (Iraq, Syria) tendencies by declaring their interpretations to be heretical. It is probable that the Arab Christians for their part cast aspersions against the Byzantines, maybe even calling them worshipers of Mary. The Nestorians refused to define Mary as Mother of God, and there does, at a superficial glance, seem to be an association between the two notions however incorrect it may be. Significantly the Jewish-Christian Ebionites, according to Eusebius, also combined a belief in the virgin birth with a denial of Jesus' "pre-existence as God" as well as of his being "the Logos and the Wisdom".[87] On the other hand, Ibn Kathīr (d. 774/1373) explains that the followers of Jesus divided into three sects: Jacobites who believed that Jesus was God; Nestorians who claimed he was the son of God; and Muslims who said that Jesus was a messenger of God.

Though on one level Muḥammad seems to be equated with Jesus, son of Mary, the inscription clearly gives a more special place to Jesus. Thus, while Muḥammad is described as a prophet and recognized as one who could intercede on behalf of his followers on the day of judgment, a role not given to Muḥammad in the Qur'ān, nevertheless Muḥammad is not, as was Jesus, especially created by God, nor was he understood as someone who had been kept from death by, again, the very special powers evoked by God.

Also important is the fact that these particular inscriptions are established in a building which stood right in the midst of places of Christian worship which denied Islam's claims. The Islamic authorities did not think, however, to demolish the Church of the Holy Sepulcher, as had the Romans, who demolished the Jewish temple—or to remove the Christians, who not only prevented Jews from settling in Jerusalem, but as already mentioned, actually desecrated the ground they had held holy. Critical as it was of the way Christians practiced their faith,[88] it nevertheless permitted them to do so.

As already indicated, it was only after the Islamic conquest of Jerusalem that Jews were once again permitted to reside in that city. It would seem, therefore, that tolerance of other, particularly monotheistic, faiths was also an essential aspect of early Islam, demanded not only by the Qur'ān, but necessitated as well by the fact that Muslims were a numerical minority. Significantly, outside of Arabia, the Muslims, though still politically dominant, remained a numerical minority until the ninth century CE.

The inscriptions cited are essentially Qur'ānic. True, the passages have been established in different chapters of the volume, and, in parts, rendered more meaningful by the addition of words not included in the passage being recalled. Nevertheless, much of the inscription is available in the Qur'ān as we know it today, and, inevitably, one understands that it is the revelation that the architect of the building desired to recall for the believer when he placed these passages on its walls. The question then arises as to why ᶜAbd al-Malik would choose to build the Dome of the Rock, as he did, on the Temple Mount?

The Purpose of the Dome of the Rock

Nineteenth-century scholars such as Goldziher and Wellhausen explain that the Dome of the Rock was built as an alternative to the Kaᶜba.[89] Despite Goitein's rejection of the view as based on Shīᶜite prejudice,[90] Amikam Elad has recently resurrected the thesis with a citation from *Mirᶜāt al-Zamān* by Sibṭ b. al-Jawzī (d. 654/1256), which claims, on the authority of al-Wāqidī from al-Kalbī (d. 204/819) from his father Muḥammad b. al-Sā'ib (d. 146/763), that ᶜAbd al-Malik built the Dome of the Rock because "Ibn al-Zubayr had already taken control of Mecca and during the seasons of the *ḥajj* used to mention the vices of the Marwanids and summon the people to pay homage to him (as caliph)."[91] At the same time, recognizing the decoration within the Dome as evoking an association with the Last Days, Elad opines that ᶜAbd al-Malik was concerned to emphasize the religious significance of Jerusalem for Islam as the site of the Temple of Solomon and the symbol of the Last Days.[92]

To grasp the intentions behind the Dome of the Rock and its decoration, however, it is necessary to understand the religio-political milieu of the caliph ᶜAbd al-Malik.

It is significant that when ᶜUthmān was killed, Muᶜāwiya was the Governor of Syria and it was from there that he protested the caliph's murder and demanded an investigation. Once appointed caliph, however, he had found it convenient to remain in Syria and establish his capital in Damascus, rather than move to Medina.

Syria had been captured from the Byzantines with relative ease because of the internal conflicts within Christianity—the Monophysite and Nestorian communities having been rejected by the Byzantine church as heretical. Moreover, the Monophysite Christians were largely Arabs employed by Byzantium to protect their marches. Once declared heretics, however, their loyalty to Byzantium ended.[93] Cities such as Emessa, Yarmuk, Damascus and Jerusalem had voluntarily surrendered, agreeing to pay taxes to their new Muslim rulers on condition that they be protected and permitted to cultivate their lands and worship in their churches.[94]

The rationale for Muslim behavior towards their subordinates came from the Qur'ān which commanded that Peoples of the Book such as Jews and Christians be granted protection and permitted to practice their faith on the payment of a tax. Given the economic and social conditions which had seen the maintenance of Greek and Persian as the languages of governance, the Muslims also found it advisable to liaison with the Christians. Indeed, the Kalb, who were largely Monophysite by faith, constituted a considerable force in the northern regions of Syria. Interestingly, Muᶜāwiya had a Christian-Kalbī wife, Maysūm—the mother of his son Yazīd—a Christian court poet, al-Akhṭal, and was cared for by a Christian physician.[95] Indeed, several caliphs were to have Christian mothers, and/or Christian wives.[96]

Ironically, Kalbite allegiance-became more desirable when the community fractured. Thus, when Marwān b. al-Ḥakam claimed the caliphal title as leader of the Umayyads, he was forced to liaison with the Christian Kalb and marry the widow of Yazīd I, in order to defeat ᶜAbd Allah b. al-Zubayr who challenged him from Mecca.

Fortunately for ᶜAbd al-Malik, everything changed when his father was murdered by his new Kalbī bride. ᶜAbd al-Malik, who assumed the caliphal position, immediately negotiated with the Qays and thus rose above tribal politics. In 72/691, it was with the help of the Qays that he was able to defeat Musᶜab b. al-Zubayr, in Iraq. Having taken Iraq, he then ordered his Qaysī general al-Ḥajjāj to attack ᶜAbd Allāh, his rival caliph, in Mecca.[97]

When ᶜAbd al-Malik gave the orders for the building of the Dome of the Rock, he already had Egypt, Syria and Iraq, that is, two thirds of the Islamic lands, in his hands. That his defeat of Ibn al-Zubayr was only a matter of time seemed clear. Moreover, ᶜAbd al-Malik b. Marwān was not only an Umayyad but a Qurayshī as well, and linked, as a descendant of ᶜAbd Manāf, to the family of the Prophet. In terms of his socio-political status in Meccan society, he was, therefore, equally, if not better, qualified to rule the Hijāz, than was Ibn al-Zubayr, who was from of the clan of ᶜAbd al-Uzza.[98] Given these circumstances it does not seem plausible that he would seek to wean the Muslim pilgrims away from Mecca.

As to the claims of such as al-Wāqidī, and Sibṭ b. al-Jawzī, it was probably Mecca's and Medina's previous political centrality restored by Ibn al-Zubayr that ᶜAbd al-Malik, in fact, hoped to destroy. It was from Syria, the region in which he felt most secure, that ᶜAbd al-Malik hoped to rule. According to Elad, "Although there is no written testimony that the [Marwanids] considered Jerusalem their capital, their extraordinary investment of human and material resources in the city leaves no doubt that this was so."[99]

That ᶜAbd al-Malik did not seek to divert the pilgrimage from Mecca to Jerusalem is demonstrated by the very structure and design of the Dome of the Rock as well. Thus, Rosen-Ayalon establishes that the Dome of the Rock was built as a companion to the al-Aqṣā mosque, and that the reliquary's lack of a *miḥrāb* indicating the direction of prayer was amply compensated for by the seven *maḥārib* located on the southern wall of the Mosque of Aqṣā.[100] Raya Shani, who focuses on the architectural and artistic manifestations of the monument, claims that by dint of its southerly focus, expressed through its Northern point of entry and its suggestive decorations, the Dome of the Rock symbolically affirmed the sanctity of the Ka ᶜba in Mecca.[101] Furthermore, though there may not have been a "canonized" Qur'ān, nevertheless it was with citations from *qur'ān* manuscripts that the essential inspiration for the building, in terms of both its decoration and its major inscriptions, had been taken. ᶜAbd al-Malik's Islam clearly included an association of monotheism and the Qur'ān, with Muḥammad and Mecca, as well as with Jesus.

That ᶜAbd al-Malik chose to depict Islam's understanding of the nature of Christ on the interior walls of the Dome of the Rock is thought provoking. Why not, for instance, the well known passage that tells of the Prophet's journey from the *masjid al-ḥarām* to the *masjid al-aqṣa*? Surely that would have been more appropriate, especially considering the fact that this monument was being established on the much revered site of the Jewish temple, the *masjid al-aqṣā*.

The most plausible answer to this question is to be found in the environment of Syria and especially Jerusalem which was largely Christian. ᶜAbd al-Malik and his fellow Muslims found themselves to be a numerical minority not merely surrounded by Christians but, sometimes, even married to one, and having to justify their faith in the face of Christian practices.

The situation—despite the many years that had elapsed since the death of the Prophet—inevitably brings to mind Richard Bell's analysis of Islam as a religion that was born in a Christian environment. Significantly, there are traditions that recall the existence of a painting of Mary and Jesus on the walls of the Kaᶜba of the Prophet's time;[102] combined with the tradition that tells us that Waraqa b. Nawfal, the cousin of the Prophet's wife, Khadīja, was a Christian, they suggest that Christians were either visiting or living in Mecca during Muḥammad's lifetime.[103]

Indeed, the verses concerned indicate that Islam was keen to provide a definition of the nature of Christ, creating the impression that early Muslims might well have been sectarian Christians. This would explain the vigorous rhetoric against Christianity found in the Qur'ān. The conditions of Christian-Muslim interaction that led ᶜAbd al-Malik to inscribe those *qur'ānic* passages on the walls of the reliquary probably existed in the time of the Prophet, as well, inspiring him to proclaim those very passages.

Aggressive as these passages may seem, Islam's recognition of the birth of Jesus as the result of a special act of God, its respect for the Virgin Mary, and most of all, its insistence that both Christianity and Judaism be tolerated, must, at the same time, have facilitated Christian acceptance of Muslim political dominance.

Recognizing the existence of these religious tensions, Grabar interprets the Dome of the Rock and its inscriptions as endorsing the superiority and strength of Islam as a political force and a system of beliefs in a largely Christian city.[104] This, I believe, is an inadequate analysis. If what was intended was a challenge to Christianity, surely it would have made more sense to display the inscriptions on the outer walls of the building for all to see.

Rosen-Ayalon, on the other hand, explains the decoration of the Dome of the Rock as a recreation of Paradise, associated with the end of time, as described in the Qur'ān. She views the inscriptions as evoking the theme of resurrection.[105] Shani, meanwhile, in keeping with the explanation of the symbolism of the monument as related to both a restored Solomonic Temple and the end of time, regards the inscription as recalling for the viewer the prophetic sequence connected with the sacred site (i.e., the Temple moving from the hands of the Jews, to the Christians and finally to the Muslims), as well as a reference to eschatology.[106]

My inclination, however, is to emphasize the religious and political ambitions of ᶜAbd al-Malik, while giving considerable weight to the fact that the Dome of the Rock was but a part of a large complex in which the al-Aqṣā-congregational mosque surely had a more significant role. This is not to deny the Dome its significance as the reliquary that houses the celebrated "lapis pertusus" of the ancient Jewish Temple; but rather, by recognizing its "*qur'ānic*" setting, to appreciate its return—it had suffered years of neglect under Christian rule—to the fold of (Islamic) monotheism.

Essentially, the outer inscription is a typical foundation statement. The more significant inner inscription is almost entirely from the sacred text and distinguished by several diacritical markings. Established as one continuous inscription that encircles the inner sanctum of the reliquary, its circular manifestation suggests a ritual of repetition similar to that of *dhikr*. Thus the believer, as he paces the ambulatories of the Dome of the Rock, not only affirms his belief in the oneness of God, and the prophethood of Muḥammad, but the prophethood of Jesus as well. There is the insinuation that both the Jews and the Christians were wrong to deny Jesus his prophetic status.

Importantly, the positioning of these passages on the walls of the Dome of the Rock, despite their prominence, does not detract from the larger purpose of the site, namely, to establish Mecca as the primary sanctuary of Islam. The inscriptions of the Dome are established with an emphasis on the southern walls, tying in with the larger focus of the entire complex of buildings which was designed to face South, towards the Kaᶜba, the Muslim House of God.

That ᶜAbd al-Malik chose to have these citations depicted on the walls of a chamber whose essential decor recreates Paradise as described in the Qur'ān is also thought provoking. Given that it was a chamber which only Muslims would enter, it was clearly a statement through which the caliph was professing a bond with his followers to whom he was indicating that it was the essential creed of Islam that provided the gateway to paradise. It was a bond that confirmed his legitimacy as the rightful leader of the Muslim peoples. It would seem his motivation was both political and religious.

NOTES

1. I am grateful to Professors Michael Cook, Nalini Devdas, and Andrew Rippin for their comments on previous drafts of this paper.

2. Throughout this article I have attempted to differentiate between the canonized scripture of Islam which I have designated Qur'ān, and the pre-canonical manuscripts of the revelation which I have termed *qur'ān*.

3. See Adrian Brockett, "Value of Ḥafs and Warsh Transmissions for the Textual History of the Qur'ān," in *Approaches to the History of the Interpretation of the Qur'ān,* ed. A. Rippin (Oxford: Oxford University Press, 1988), 32, n. 5; and Estelle Whelan, "Forgotten Witness: Evidence for the Early Codification of the Qur'ān," *JAOS* 118 (1998): 1–14.

4. Oleg Grabar, grappling with the problem, while agreeing that the inscriptions are probably Qur'ānic also admits that "It is possible to consider intermediary solutions. The two passages dealing with Jesus... and the final proclamation may indeed be quotations, while the other[s] are simply parallel statements of a religious nature that would have been part and parcel of a collective expression of beliefs." *The Shape of the Holy: Early Islamic Jerusalem* (Princeton: Princeton University Press, 1996), 63. See also Tilman Nagel who argues that the citations are probably taken from the traditions that were in circulation at the time, in "Die Inschriften im Felsendom und das Islamische Glaubensbekenntnis. Der Koran und die Anfänge des Ḥadīt," *Arabica* 47 (2000): 350–65. I would like to take this opportunity to thank Johanna and Georg Feilotter for so kindly providing me with an English translation of Nagel's article.

5. Wansbrough argues that since, as indicated by Schacht, Muslim derivation of law from scripture was a phenomenon of the ninth century, and since there is no reference to the Qur'ān in the *Fiqh Akbar 1* which Wensinck places in the middle of the eighth century, it is unlikely that an ʿUthmānic recension existed before the ninth century. See *Quranic Studies: Sources and Methods of Scriptural Interpretation* (Oxford: Oxford University Press, 1977) 44.

6. Richard Bell, The Origins of Islam in a Christian Environment (London: Macmillan, 1926).

7. A. Guillaume, The Life of Muhammad: a Translation of Ibn Isḥāq's Sīrat Rasūl Allah (Oxford: Oxford University Press, 1955), 289.

8. See A. Neuwirth, "The Spiritual Meaning of Jerusalem in Islam," in *City of the Great King: Jerusalem from David to the present*, ed. Nitza Rosovsky (Cambridge: Harvard University Press, 1996), 487, n. 45.

9. Al-Wāqidī, *Kitāb al-maghāzī,* ed. J. M. B. Jones (London: Oxford University Press, 1966), 866.

10. The words are: "O God I am ready to serve you in what you love most." See al-Ṭabarī, *The History of Prophets and Kings,* vol. XII, *The Battle of al-Qādisiyya and the Conquest of Syria and Palestine,* trans. Yohannan Friedmann (Albany NY: SUNY Press, 1992), 194.

11. This tendency to equate the pilgrimage to Mecca with the pilgrimage to Jerusalem is also reflected in a verse by Farazdaq (d. 110/728): "(To us belong) two Houses: the House of God of which we are the Governors and the revered House in Upper Īliya." See Al-Farazdaq, *Dīwān,* ed. al-Sāwī (Cairo, 1936), 566, cited in M. J. Kister, "You Shall Only Set Out For Three Mosques: A Study of an Early Tradition," *Le Muséon* 82 (1969): 182.

12. Al-Ṭabarī, *History,* XII, 93–94. For a discussion of the several traditions recounting the taking of Jerusalem by ᶜUmar see Heribert Busse, "ᶜOmar's Image as the Conqueror of Jerusalem," *JSAI* 8 (1986): 149–68.

13. In 135 CE the Emperor Hadrian, who rebuilt Jerusalem renaming it Aelia Capitolina, banned Jews from living there. However Jewish pilgrimage to the city, though rare, did occur. See Mark Friedman, "Jewish Pilgrimage after the Destruction of the Second Temple," in *City of the Great King,* 137. See also Moshe Gil, *A History of Palestine 634–1099*, trans. Ethel Broido (Cambridge: Cambridge University Press, 1992), 69.

14. "Not a stone shall stand upon stone," were the angry words with which Jesus is supposed to have condemned the site. See Eutychius' explanation of why the site had been desecrated cited in F. E. Peters, *Jerusalem* (Princeton: Princeton University Press, 1985), 189–90.

15. Gil, A History of Palestine, 67.

16. See the account of the historian and later patriarch of Alexandria, Eutechius, written in around 876 CE for instance, cited in Peters, *Jerusalem,* 189–90.

17. Jamāl al-Dīn Aḥmad, *Muthīr al-ghirām,* chapter 5, cited in G. Le Strange, *Palestine Under the Moslems* (Beirut: Khayyat, 1965, 14th edition), 142–3.

18. See Philip Hitti, *History of the Arabs* (London: Macmillan, 1967), 220.

19. According to the Christian chronicler Saᶜīd b. Biṭriq, "there were people who said: let us fix it (the prayer site) thus, that the rock should be the *qibla*, but ᶜUmar refused and said: we shall fix the prayer site so that the rock will be behind it." Cited in Gil, *A History of Palestine,* 67.

20. N. J. Johnson, "Aqṣā Mosque," in *Encyclopaedia of the Qur'ān,* ed. J. D. McAuliffe (Leiden: Brill, 2001), I, 125.

21. Amikam Elad, *Medieval Jerusalem and Islamic Worship* (Leiden: E.J. Brill, 1995), 33.

22. Gil, *A History of Palestine,* 78.

23. S. D. Goitein, "al-Ḳuds," *EI2*, V, 324; also see Theodore Nöldeke, "Zur Geschichte der Araber im I Jahr-h.d. H. aus Syrischen Quellen," *ZDMG* 29(1876): 95.

24. Gil, *A History of Palestine*, 78. Also see Elad, *Medieval Jerusalem*, 33.

25. Gerald Hawting, *The First Dynasty of Islam* (London: Croom Helm, 1986), 48.

26. Tilman Nagel, "Die Inschriften im Felsendom," 343.

27. Wilferd Madelung, *The Succession to Muḥammad* (Cambridge: Cambridge University Press, 1997), 344.

28. G. R. Hawting, *The First Dynasty of Islam* (London: Croom Helm, 1986), 26.

29. Madelung, *Succession*, 137.

30. K. V. Zettersteen, "ᶜAbd al-Malik," *EI1*, I, 48.

31. Al-Ṭabarī, *The History of Prophets and Kings,* vol. XX, *The Collapse of the Sufyānid Authority and the coming of the Marwānids,* trans. G. R. Hawting (Albany NY: SUNY Press, 1989), 160–1. The story of how Marwān was smothered to death is told with much relish in Madelung, *Succession,* 350–1.

32. ᶜAbd al-Ameer Dixon, The Umayyad Caliphate 65–86/684–705: (a political study) (London: Luzac, 1971), 65–6.

33. Sheila Blair, "What is the Date of the Dome of the Rock," in *Bayt al-Maqdis: ᶜAbd al-Malik's Jerusalem*, ed. J. Raby and J. Johns (Oxford: Oxford University Press, 1993), 69.

34. Ibid. For a brief analysis of the significance of the Dome of the Rock, see Andrew Rippin, *Muslims: their Religious Beliefs and Practices* (London: Routledge, 1990), 51–6.

35. Mujīr al-Dīn al-ᶜUlaymī, *Al-Uns al-jalīl fī ta'rīkh al-Quds wa'l-Khalīl* (Cairo n.d.), I, 241, cited by S. D. Goitein in "The Sanctity of Jerusalem and Palestine in Early Islam," in his *Studies in Islamic History and Institutions* (Leiden: E. J. Brill, 1968), 138. See also Amikam Elad, citing Sibt b. al-Jawzī in "Why Did ᶜAbd al-Malik Build the Dome of the Rock?" in *Bayt al-Maqdis: ᶜAbd al-Malik's Jerusalem*, 35.

36. Nagel, "Die Inschriften im Felsendom," 335–38.

37. Christel Kessler, "ᶜAbd al-Malik's Inscription in the Dome of the Rock: A Reconsideration," *JRAS* (1970): 11, n. 20.

38. Van Ess, "ᶜAbd al-Malik and the Dome of the Rock," in *Bayt al-Maqdis: ᶜAbd al-Malik's Jerusalem*, 93.

39. Ibid., 90.

40. See "Mujīr al-Din al-ᶜUlaymī's Vision of Jerusalem," translated by D. Little, *JAOS* 115(1995): 241.

41. See Peters, *Jerusalem*, 189–90.

42. According to Ibn Isḥāq, it was from the *masjid al-aqṣā* that Muḥammad made his *miᶜrāj* or ascension to God and there negotiated a reduction in the number of prayers that his followers would have to pray each day to five. See Ibn Isḥāq, trans. A. Guillaume, *Life*, 186. On the other hand, Ibn Saᶜd informs us that Muḥammad was commanded by God to ask his community to pray five times a day when he ascended to the heavens from Mecca; see Ibn Saᶜd, *Kitāb al-Tabaqāt al-Kabīr*, trans. S. Moinul Haq (Karachi: Pakistan Historical Society, 1967), 246.

43. H. Stierlin, *Islam: Early Architecture from Baghdad to Cordoba* (Köln: Taschen Verlag, 1996), 38.

44. Myriam Rosen-Ayalon, *The Early Islamic Monuments of al-Ḥaram al-Sharīf: an iconographic study* (Jerusalem: Hebrew University, 1989), 7.

45. Elad, *Medieval Jerusalem*, citing Ibn Kathīr who quotes from *Mirᵓāt al-Zamān*. See Ibn Kathīr, *al-Bidāya* (Cairo n.d.) VIII, 280.

46. Rosen-Ayalon, *Early Islamic Monuments*, 5.

47. According to Johnson, the most recent evaluation of the mosque provided by R. W. Hamilton claims that it was built by ᶜAbd al-Malik; see "Aqṣā Mosque," *Encyclopaedia of the Qur'ān*, I, 126.

48. Elad, "Why Did ᶜAbd al-Malik Build the Dome of the Rock?" in *Bayt al-Maqdis: ᶜAbd al-Malik's Jerusalem*, 34.

49. Al-Muqaddasī, *Aḥsān al-taqāsīm fī maᶜrifat al-aqālīm,* III, 168-71, cited in Le Strange, *Palestine Under the Moslems*, 99. Also see Rosen Ayalon, *Early Islamic Monuments*, 7.

50. Blair, "What is the Date of the Dome of the Rock," in *Bayt al-Maqdis: ᶜAbd al-Malik's Jerusalem*, 60–2.

51. According to Sibṭ b. al-Jawzī there were five thousand lamps in the Dome of the Rock … each night one hundred lamps were lit in the *Ṣakhra,* and the same number were lit in the al-Aqṣā mosque. See Elad, "Why Did ᶜAbd al-Malik Build the Dome of the Rock?" in *Bayt al-Maqdis: ᶜAbd al-Malik's Jerusalem*, 36.

52. Thus today the Muslim declaration of belief includes God, His angels, His books, His prophets, and the Day of Judgment.

53. The translations are cited from Grabar, *The Shape of the Holy,* 59–61. See Christel Kessler, "ᶜAbd al-Malik's Inscription in the Dome of the Rock: A Reconsideration," *JRAS* (1970): 2–14, for a careful reproduction of the inscriptions as actually inscribed in the Dome of the Rock.

54. See al-Bukhāri, *Al-Jāmiᶜ al-ṣaḥīḥ*, eds. Ludolf Krehl and Th. W. Juynboll (Leiden: E. J. Brill, 1862–1908), III, 397, trans. Muhammad Muhsin Khan, *The English Translation of Ṣaḥīḥ al-Bukhārī with the Arabic Text* (Darrussalam 1997) IV, book 56, no. 709. Though this particular tradition, which claims that ᶜUthmān was largely responsible for the collection of the Qur'ān, has found favour among both Muslims and Orientalists, there are, in fact, several traditions concerning the compilation of the Qur'ān. Indeed, both Bukhārī and Ibn Saᶜd, transmit traditions according to which several companions had collected the Qur'ān during the time of the Prophet. See Ibid., and Ibn Saᶜd, *Ṭabaqāt al-kubrā* (Beirut 1957), 355–6.

55. Khan, *English Translation of Ṣaḥīḥ al-Bukhārī,* VI, book 61, no. 709, and Alphonse Mingana, "The Transmission of the Ḳur'ān," *Journal of Manchester Egyptian and Oriental Society,* (1915–16): 29.

56. Mahmoud Ayoub, "Qur'ān," in *Encyclopaedia of Religion,* ed. Mircea Eliade (New York: Macmillan, 1987), XII, 163.

57. Ubayy's collection, for instance, included two *sūras* not in the ᶜUthmānic codex: *sūrat al-khalᶜ* with three verses, and *sūrat al-ḥafd* with six. See A. Welch, "Al-Ḳur'ān," *EI2*, V, 407, citing A. Jeffery, *Materials for the History of the Text of the Qur'ān* (Leiden: E. J. Brill, 1937), 180 f.

58. See "Al-Ḳur'ān," *EI2*, V, 406.

59. Ibid., 408–9.

60. It was only in the tenth century that it was finally reduced to seven by Ibn Mujāhid (d. 323/935), at which time a tradition developed claiming that the Qur'ān had been revealed in seven *aḥruf*. But the transmissions could not be limited to seven either, and soon the community was forced to accommodate the numerous variations by preferring diversity to uniformity. See Ayoub, "Qur'ān," in *Encyclopaedia of Religion,* XII, 163–66.

61. Allan Jones, "The Qur'ān – II," in *Arabic Literature to the End of the Umayyad Period*, 243.

62. The document, Perf. 558 from the Catalogue of the Erzherzog Rainer Papyrus Collection by J. von Karabacek in Vienna in 1894, indicates that dots for six letters (*jīm, khā', dhāl, zā', shīn* and *nūn*) were already being used by the year 22/643. See Alan Jones, "The Dotting of a Script and the Dating of an Era: The Strange Neglect of Perf 558," *Islamic Culture,* October 1998: 95–101. Nevertheless, it is possible that such diacritical markings had not as yet been regulated: perhaps different people used different signs. It is significant that in the inscriptions of the Dome strokes are used instead of dots. A stroke below indicates the *qāf* while the *fā'* was left unmarked. Three strokes placed one above the other marked a *thā'*, two a *tay*, and one a *nūn*.

63. Ayoub, "Qur'ān," in *Encyclopaedia of Religion*, XII, 163–6.

64. According to A. Jones, once the consonantal outline was fixed, only forty variations of the consonantal text subsequently appeared of which 38 concerned the addition of a *wāw* and the others were *min* and *huwa*.

65. Jones, "The Qur'ān – II," in *Arabic Literature to the End of the Umayyad Period*, 243.

66. Popular tradition records that al-Ḥajjāj ordered Naṣr b. ᶜĀṣim to introduce markings to establish the pronunciation of the text, and it is possible that it was such a sentiment that led ᶜAbd al-Malik to add diacritical markings to the inscriptions within the Dome of the Rock, as well. See Jones, "The Qur'ān – II," in *Arabic Literature to the End of the Umayyad Period*, 243.

67. According to the believer, such apparent lack of organization is consistent with a meditative pulse which directs and guides his sojourn in this world. For the non-believing scholar it is an amorphous mix, the result of manipulative, even destructive, editing—as is claimed by Casanova and Burton, and as an organic development resulting from the process of time, as explained by Wansbrough.

68. According to Nabia Abbott, ᶜUmar b. al-Khaṭṭāb rejected the idea of compiling traditions on the basis that these sayings would compete with those of the Qur'ān. *Studies in Arabic Literary* Papyri, vol. II, *Qur'ānic Commentary and Tradition* (Chicago: University of Chicago Press, 1967), 7.

69. In fact, Jeffery treats twelve more "primary" codices, compiled by such as Umar b. al-Khaṭṭāb, Alī b. Abī Ṭālib, Ḥafsa bt. Umar, Ā'isha bt. Abī Bakr, and Umm Salama. See "Al-Ḳur'ān," *EI2*, V, 406.

70. Ibn Saᶜd, *Ṭabaqāt al-kabīr,* ed. Sachau (Leiden: E. J. Brill, 1904) III, i, 207.

71. Abbott, *Studies in Arabic Literary Papyri,* vol. II, *Qur'ānic Commentary and Tradition*, 20.

72. According to Wellhausen, ᶜAbd al-Malik's relations to Islam were different from those of his predecessors. "He was born and bred in it, nay more, he was brought up in the very town of the Prophet." See *The Arab Kingdom and its Fall* (Beirut: Khayyat, 1963, 6th edition), 215.

73. Sheila Blair, *Islamic Inscriptions* (Edinburgh: Edinburgh University Press, 1988), 3–5.

74. Al-Ṭabarī, *The History of Prophets and Kings,* vol. XXIX, *Al-Manṣūr and al-Mahdī: A. D. 763–786,* trans. H. Kennedy (Albany NY: SUNY Press, 1990), 254.

75. E. Whelan, "Forgotten Witness," 10–12.

76. Kessler, "ᶜAbd al-Malik's Inscription," 10.

77. Blair, "What is the Date of the Dome of the Rock," in *Bayt al-Maqdis: ᶜAbd al-Malik's Jerusalem*, 84.

78. Kessler, "ᶜAbd al-Malik's Inscription," 12.

79. Kessler, "ᶜAbd al-Malik's Inscription,"12–13.

80. Blair, "What is the date of the Dome of the Rock?" in *Bayt al-Maqdis: ᶜAbd al-Malik's Jerusalem*, 74–77.

81. I thank Profs Cook and Rippin for pointing this out to me.

82. Blair, "What is the Date of the Dome of the Rock?" in *Bayt al-Maqdis: ᶜAbd al-Malik's Jerusalem*, 77.

83. Al-Wāsiṭī, *Faḍā'il al-Bayt al-Muqaddas,* ed. I. Hasson (Jerusalem 1979), 89–90; also Elad, *Medieval Jerusalem*, 79. Also see Raya Shani, "The Iconography of the Dome of the Rock," *JSAI* 23 (1999): 180.

84. Shani, "Iconography of the Dome of the Rock," 179–80.

85. Mahmoud M. Ayoub, "Towards an Islamic Christology, II: The Death of Jesus, Reality or Delusion," *The Muslim World* 70 (1980): 91–121.

86. See *Tafsīr al-Ṭabarī* (Cairo 1374 AH), IX, 417 (commentary on Q. 4:156).

87. Heike Räisäinen, "The Portrait of Jesus in the Qur'ān: Reflections of a Biblical Scholar," *The Muslim World* 70 (1980): 126.

88. See Q. 9:29.

89. Wellhausen, *Arab Kingdom*, 214–5; I. Goldziher, *Muslim Studies* trans. I. Stern (London: George Allen and Unwin, 1971), II, 46. Also see Elad, *Medieval Jerusalem*, 148, and Shani, "Iconography," 158.

90. S. D. Goitein, "The Sanctity of Jerusalem and Palestine in Early Islam," in his *Studies in Islamic History and Institutions* (Leiden: E. J. Brill, 1968), 135–48.

91. Elad, *Medieval Jerusalem*, 52–61.

92. Ibid., 147–63

93. Hugh Kennedy, "Islam," in *Late Antiquity*, ed. G. W. Bowersock, P. Brown and O. Grabar (Cambridge, MA: Belknap Press, 1999), 227–8.

94. The typical *dhimma* agreement is that of the Pact of ᶜUmar. For an important explanation of the pact, see Mark Cohen, "What was the Pact of ᶜUmar? A Literary Historical Study," *JSAI* 23 (1999), 100–57.

95. Kenneth Cragg, *Arab Christianity: A History in the Middle East* (Louisville KT: John Knox Press, 1991), 72.

96. The trend seems to have been started by the caliph ᶜUthman who married Nā'ila daughter of Farāfis b. al-Aḥwās, a Christian Kalbī chief, seven years before his death. After his death, Muᶜāwiya sought her out but was rejected; Nā'ila is supposed to have removed her two front teeth to keep him away. See Madelung, *Succession,* 367.

97. According to al-Ṭabarī, "When Muṣᶜab b. al-Zubayr was killed, ᶜAbd al-Malik b. Marwān sent al-Ḥallāj against ibn al-Zubayr in Mecca." Later that year, al-Ḥallāj led the pilgrimage since Ibn al-Zubayr was besieged. See *The History of al-Ṭabarī*, vol. XXI, *The Victory of the Marwanids,* trans. M. Fishbein (Albany NY: SUNY Press, 1990), 207–9. See also Blair, "What is the Date," 69.

98. H. A. R. Gibb, "ᶜAbd Allāh b. al-Zubayr," *EI2*, I, 54–5.

99. Elad, *Medieval Jerusalem*, 160.

100. Rosen-Ayalon, *Early Islamic Monuments*, 4–7.

101. Raya Shani, "The Iconography of the Dome of the Rock," *JSAI*, 23 (1999): 179.

102. See Guillaume, *Life*, 552; al-Wāqidī, *Kitāb al-maghāzī*, 834.

103. Guillaume, *Life*, 107.

104. Oleg Grabar, "The Haram al-Sharif: An Essay in Interpretation," *Bulletin of the Royal Institute for Inter-Faith Studies* 2 (2000): 12

105. Rosen-Ayalon, *Early Islamic Monuments*, 72–3.

106. Shani, "Iconography," 187–9.

Sunnī-Shīʿī Dialectics and the Qur'ān

Asma Afsaruddin

This article will focus on two specific Qur'ānic verses that are frequently invoked in Sunnī-Shīʿī dialectics to establish the superiority of Abū Bakr's qualifications for the caliphate in the case of the *ahl al-Sunna* and to establish the uniqueness of ʿAlī's candidacy for the imamate in the case of the Shīʿa. The first verse, Q. 9:40, is known as the *āyat al-ghār* ("the verse of the cave") which is practically universally understood by Sunnī scholars to refer to a significant event in the Prophet Muḥammad's life which involved Abū Bakr. The second verse, Q. 2:207, is invoked by the Shīʿa in particular to point to another significant event in the Prophet's life which specifically involved ʿAlī. Both events occurred during the *hijra* ("emigration") to Medina in 1/622 and each event is understood to highlight the exceptional courage of the Companion involved and his exemplary fidelity to Muḥammad. These events find particular mention in the *manāqib* literature (literature that praises, in this case, the excellences of the Ṣaḥāba, the Companions of the Prophet), as well as in historical and exegetical works. The events will be briefly discussed below and a sampling of the views expressed by some major Sunnī and Shīʿī authorities with regard to their significance will be provided. These views will then be analyzed to discern what they might tell us about how the Companions came to be perceived by the succeeding generations and what their role was determined to be in conceptualizing legitimate leadership.

Al-Ghār vs. al-Mabīt

The *āyat al-ghār* refers to the following verse from *sūrat al-tawba* (Q. 9:40):

> If you do not support him, yet God has already supported him when those who disbelieved expelled him as the second of two (*thānī ithnayn)*, when they were both in the

> Cave, and he told his companion: "Do not grieve, for God is with us."

The second of two and the Companion in this case is practically unanimously understood by Sunnī scholars to be Abū Bakr, who accompanied the Prophet during his escape from Mecca to Medina.[1] In brief, the incident of the *ghār* refers to the time when Muḥammad and Abū Bakr on their way to Medina are said to have taken refuge in a cave in Mt. Thawr while being pursued by the pagan Meccans. They stayed in the cave for three nights to avoid detection by their pursuers. This event would become a paradigmatic one in the *manāqib* literature on Abū Bakr, pointing to his exceptionally close relationship with Muḥammad.

The incident of the *mabīt* centers around ᶜAlī's serving as the Prophet's decoy by sleeping in the latter's bed in order to fool the pagan Meccans into thinking that Muḥammad had not yet departed for Medina. The Meccans discovered the ruse only the following morning after the Prophet and Abū Bakr had safely escaped. For the standard (Sunnī) depiction of these events, one can refer, for example, to Ibn Hishām's *al-Sīra al-nabawiyya*.[2] In Shīᶜī *manāqib* literature, and, to a lesser extent, in Sunnī *manāqib* literature on ᶜAlī, the *mabīt* incident would be deployed as proof of ᶜAlī's unquestioning fidelity to the Prophet and exceptional courage in exposing himself to great danger.

The Event of the *Ghār* in Sunnī Literature

Sunnī *manāqib* literature in particular underscores Abū Bakr's companionship with the Prophet in the *ghār* as confirming his unassailable position as the most excellent Companion. A report given by al-Muḥibb al-Ṭabarī (d. 694/1295) relates that an unnamed man once stood before ᶜAlī and remonstrated,

> What is the matter with the Emigrants and the Helpers that they advance Abū Bakr [as their leader] while you are more illustrious with regard to excellence (*manqaba*), are the foremost in accepting Islam, and have preceded with regard to precedence (*asbaq sābiqa*)?"

ᶜAlī is said to have replied in anger,

> Woe be to you! Indeed Abū Bakr has preceded me in four [matters] which I have not been given nor have been given their equivalents. He has preceded me to the imamate (or advanced to the imamate), to the emigration, to the cave, and in openly proclaiming his submission.

The report continues with ᶜAlī threatening to whip "anyone who prefers me over Abū Bakr" for lying.[3]

Numerous accounts of the episode known as the Saqīfa mention that ᶜUmar cited the *ghār* verse to underscore Abū Bakr's uniquely close relationship with the Prophet and thus his singular qualification to become the caliph. One such report recorded by al-Nasā'ī (d. 302/914) is from the Companion Sālim b. ᶜUbayd,[4] who relates that during the Saqīfa, the Anṣār stated that there should be one leader (*amīr*) from among them and another from among the Muhājirūn, to which ᶜUmar replied, "Two swords in one scabbard, that will never do!" Then he took Abū Bakr by the hand and asked the crowd the following questions regarding the *āyat al-ghār*:

> To whom do these three belong? *When he said to his companion*—who was his companion? *When the two were in the cave*—who were the two? *Indeed God is with us*—with whom?

ᶜUmar then gave his allegiance to him [sc. Abū Bakr] and told the people gathered to do the same, upon which "the people proclaimed their allegiance in a most seemly and decorous manner."[5]

Frequent iteration of Abū Bakr's "secondness" to the Prophet in several major events in the *manāqib* literature establishes his unique claim to greater excellence over other Companions. One laudatory account from Saᶜīd b. al-Musayyab states:

> Abū Bakr al-Ṣiddīq, may God be pleased with him, was with regard to the Messenger of God, peace and blessings be upon him and his family, in the position of a deputy for he would consult with him in all matters. He was, with regard to him, the second in Islam, second in the cave, second in the

> booth on the day of Badr, and second in the grave. And the Messenger of God, peace and blessings be upon him and his family, did not give precedence to anyone else over him.[6]

According to one source, a certain Ibn Abī Ḥadhara during a debate about the respective merits of Abū Bakr and ᶜAlī asserted the following four unparalleled *manāqib* of Abū Bakr before Abū Jaᶜfar Muḥammad b. al-Nuᶜmān Mu'min (or according to his adversaries Shayṭān) al-Ṭāq (d. ca. 180/796):

> He was the second to be buried with the Prophet in his house, the second of two with him in the cave; the second of two to pray before the people the last prayer after which the Messenger of God, peace and blessings be upon him, passed away; and the second of the two al-Ṣiddīqs of this community.[7]

On account of the *ghār* episode in particular, Abū Bakr's *suḥba* ("companionship") with the Prophet is eulogized in Sunnī *manāqib* and historical literature as being of a special and unrivalled character and is a frequent leitmotif in the depiction of events in Muḥammad's life. Some of the earliest *ḥadīth*s highlight the notion of *al-ṣuḥba* (or *al-ṣaḥāba*) as the paramount theme of the *hijra*. The *Muṣannaf* of ᶜAbd al-Razzāq (d. 211/827) contains one such tradition from al-Zuhrī reporting from ᶜUrwa who said that ᶜĀ'isha related,

> One day while we were sitting in our house during the mid-day heat, someone said to Abū Bakr, "There is the Messenger of God, peace and blessings be upon him, approaching with his head covered at an hour when he does not come to visit us." Abū Bakr replied, "May my father and mother be given in ransom for him! He could only have come at this hour for a [grave] matter!" She said that the Messenger of God, peace and blessings be upon him, came and asked for permission [to enter]; it was granted him and he entered. Then Abū Bakr said, "They are your family and you are like my father, O Messenger of God!" The Prophet, peace and blessings be upon him, said, "I have been granted permission to leave." Abū Bakr responded, "And companionship

> (*al-ṣaḥāba*)? You are like my father, O Messenger of God!" The Prophet, peace and blessings be upon him, said, "Yes."[8]

Abū Bakr then offered the fastest two of his mounts which were prepared for the journey to Mecca.[9]

Belief in Abū Bakr's companionship with the Prophet in the cave, and, subsequently, throughout the Prophet's life, thus became axiomatic on account of scriptural reference to it. Ibn al-Athīr (d. 630/1232–33), for example, reports that on account of the *ghār* tradition some scholars (*baᶜḍ al-ᶜulamā'*) had stated the following:

> If someone were to say that all the Companions except Abū Bakr did not have companionship [with the Prophet], he would not be guilty of unbelief. But if someone were to say that Abū Bakr was not the Companion of the Messenger of God, peace and blessings be upon him, he would be guilty of unbelief for the Glorious Qur'ān has mentioned that he was his Companion.[10]

ᶜAbd al-Ra'ūf al-Munāwī (d. 1031/1621) similarly states that "whoever denies the companionship of al-Ṣiddīq has disbelieved due to his disavowal of the clear text (*al-naṣṣ al-jalī*)."[11] Another account states that "Muslims agree that the one indicated as the companion here is Abū Bakr; thus whoever denies his companionship has disbelieved in [this] consensus" (*kafara ijmāᶜ*)."[12] Aḥmad al-Nuwayrī (d. 733/1332) mentions that Sufyān b. ᶜUyayna had maintained that God had reprimanded all Muslims through the Prophet except Abū Bakr, "for he [sc. Abū Bakr] had escaped censure" (*kharaja min al-muᶜātaba*) on account of the divine approbation of him expressed in the *ghār* verse.[13] Ibn Taymiyya (d. 728/1328) emphasizes that the *ghār* verse establishes the exceptional nature of Abū Bakr's companionship and his unparalleled superiority (*al-afḍaliyya*) over the other Companions on account of the role he played during the *hijra* in having protected Muḥammad with his own life. This is further proof that Abū Bakr's excellences were unique to him (*khaṣā'iṣ lahu*) while the excellences attributed to ᶜAlī were shared (*mushtaraka*) by the other Companions.[14]

In his *tafsīr* work, *Mafātīḥ al-ghayb*, the Ashʿarī scholar Fakhr al-Dīn al-Rāzī (d. 606/1209) offers a detailed refutation of the standard Shīʿī views on the relative valences of the *ghār* and *mabīt* episodes. He takes particular care to establish the superior merits of Abū Bakr on account of his companionship (*li-muṣāhabatihi*) with Muḥammad in the cave in opposition to ʿAlī's solitary vigil in the Prophet's home. Firstly, he states,

> We do not deny that ʿAlī b. Abī Ṭālib's laying down that dark night on the bed of the Messenger of God was [an act of] great obedience (*ṭāʿa ʿaẓima*) and [indicative of] elevated status (*manṣib rafʿī*), except that we assert that Abū Bakr, due to his companionship, was physically present (*kāna ḥādiran*) in service to the Messenger, peace and blessings be upon him, while ʿAlī was absent (*kāna ghā'iban*). And one who is present is of a more elevated status (*aʿlā hālan*) than the one who is absent.

Secondly, al-Rāzī states that ʿAlī was subjected to such a severe trial only for that night, for once the Meccan enemies discovered the ruse, they left him alone. In contrast, Abū Bakr resided in the cave for three days with Muḥammad and, therefore, the tribulations he faced were greater (*balā'uhu ashaddu*). The third reason he advances in favor of Abū Bakr's greater excellence is that ʿAlī's minority and obscure status before the emigration shielded him from further persecution by the pagan Meccans after the night of the *mabīt* and in general; in other words, ʿAlī himself must have been aware that in serving as the Prophet's decoy as a young, relatively inconsequential youth, the personal repercussions from the incident would be slight and this would have alleviated his terror that night. On the contrary, since Abū Bakr was a powerful and influential adult Muslim who had advanced the cause of Islam through his wealth and winning ways, he could expect severe reprisals from the Meccan enemies on discovery; thus "we realize that Abū Bakr's fear for himself in service to Muḥammad, peace and blessings be upon him, was greater than the fear of ʿAlī, may God grant him an honored position, and thus the status (*daraja*) [of Abū Bakr] is more meritorious (*afḍal*) and more complete (*akmal*)."[15] Al-Rāzi also emphasizes that it was Abū Bakr who was selected with divine approbation to accompany Muḥammad to Medina, in spite of the presence of other sincere Muslims (*jamāʿa min al-mukhliṣīn*) who were genealogically closer to the Prophet. Thus, "God's selection of him (*takhṣīṣ Allāh iyyāhu*)," he states, "indicates his elevated status in religion."[16] Clearly in al-Rāzi's hermeneutical exposition of the event of the *ghār*, blood-kinship to the Prophet is easily trumped by exceptional emotional and physical propinquity to him, to which latter only Abū Bakr was privy.

In his *Risālat al-ʿUthmāniyya*, the 3rd/9th century belle-lettrist ʿAmr b. Baḥr al-Jāḥiẓ (d. 255/869) highlights the *suḥba* ("companionship") of Abū Bakr with the Prophet as the central theme of the *ghār* episode. In al-Jāḥiẓ's opinion, the role of Abū Bakr in this crucial episode confirms his status as the closest and most excellent Companion of the Prophet, for it was "God who called him [sc. Abū Bakr] a companion (*ṣāḥiban*) in His book."[17] Al-Jāḥiẓ emphasizes that this is an important distinction between the events of the *ghār* and the *mabīt*. Since the Qur'ān mentions the incident of the *ghār* and its reality is affirmed by communal consensus (*ṣaḥḥa bihi 'l-ijmāʿ*), it is transformed into an event that all must believe in just as one believes in the performance of the five prayers, the offering of the *zakāt*, and bathing after a major impurity as canonical obligations. One who denies the occurrence of this event is thus regarded as "a mad man or an unbeliever by the *umma*."[18]

Al-Jāḥiẓ replies to those (it is understood from among the Shīʿa) who maintain that the object pronoun in the verse, "Then God caused His *sakīna* to come down on him," is a reference to Muḥammad and not to Abū Bakr. He dismisses this possibility for "it was the Prophet, blessings be upon him, who was fearless, stalwart of purpose, and possessed of equanimity; it was he who consoled Abū Bakr, alleviating his deep stress, uplifting his spirit, and calming his palpitating heart." The *ghār* episode, furthermore, testifies to Abū Bakr's status as "his [sc. the Prophet's] *khalīfa*" for having shared in Muḥammad's dire predicament and for having derived strength from the Prophet's unwavering resoluteness. As the next sentence informs us, al-Jāḥiẓ is using the term *khalīfa* here vis-à-vis the Prophet as the equivalent of "the heir-apparent" (*walī al-ʿahd*) of a ruling caliph. Abū Bakr's residing in Mecca with the Prophet after the departure of ᶜUmar and the other Emigrants confirms his greater excellence over all those who had preceded them in emigrating to Medina; the implication being that Abū Bakr was then privileged to accompany the Prophet to Medina and to be his companion in the cave. Al-Jāḥiẓ continues that the complete verse in question states, "When he said to his companion, do not grieve for God is with us; then God caused His *sakīna* to come down on him." It is clear from the complete verse, he comments, that the *sakīna* must have descended on "his companion" and that the enclitic pronoun in *ᶜalayhi* ("upon him") must be a referent to "his companion." The *sakīna* after all cannot descend on someone [sc. the Prophet] who already possessed it and who is depicted as consoling his companion.[19]

Al-Jaḥiẓ couples another incident in the life of the Prophet known as the incident of the booth (*al-ᶜarīsh*) with the event of the *ghār* to categorically establish Abū Bakr's higher status with the Prophet relative to ᶜAlī's.[20] On the day of Badr, when Muḥammad resolved to engage the Quraysh in battle, Saᶜd b. Muᶜādh addressed him, "O Prophet of God, let us build for you a booth in which you will stay and we will fight before you." The Prophet granted them permission to do so. After its construction, the Prophet mobilized his army for battle, then repaired to the booth. The only other person invited into the booth was Abū Bakr.[21] Al-Jāḥiẓ describes the honor that accrues to Abū Bakr from this incident:

> Who among them could most resemble the Messenger of God, may God grant him peace and blessings, in [undergoing] great trials and in enduring hardships, and in exalted status than the one who was the second of two (*thānī ithnayn*) to advance towards Islam, the second of two to summon to God and to His Messenger, the second of two to have numerous adherents and followers, the second of two in the cave, the second of two to emigrate, and the second of two in the booth. There are many other examples similar to these.[22]

For al-Jāḥiẓ, and other Sunnī scholars as well, the incident of the *ghār*, therefore, represents one of the events in which Abū Bakr was the "second of two," sc. second only to Muḥammad in station in Islam. The Qur'ānic phrase "*thānī ithnayn*" became a common refrain in the literature of praise concerning Abū Bakr and was understood to clearly establish his superior credentials for the caliphate.

In contrast to the *ghār* episode, the *mabīt*, al-Jāḥiẓ stresses, is reported only in the *ḥadīth* literature, biographical narratives, and in poetry. The two events are, therefore, not equal in importance; this is obvious to one who is learned for such a person "knows what is objectionable and what is acceptable, and what is inferior and what is equal."[23] Another crucial difference between these two incidents is that the Companion involved does not display the same degree and kind of courage. Al-Jāḥiẓ states that even if the incident of the *mabīt* was as impeccably documented as the incident of the *ghār*, ᶜAlī cannot be said to have shown unusual merit in complying with the Prophet's request to be his decoy on the night he left for Mecca,

> because those who relate—whether truthfully or mendaciously—that the Prophet, may God bless him and grant him peace, made ᶜAlī his decoy at night are the ones who also relate that the Prophet, peace be upon him, said [to ᶜAli], "Cover yourself with my mantle, and sleep in my bed, and no harm will come to you."[24]

The words of the above tradition are well known and beyond doubt. According to this account, ᶜAlī cannot be said to have exhibited remarkable courage in exposing himself to assassination for he had been granted immunity from danger by the Prophet's assurance. In contrast, no one has reported that the Prophet ever told Abū Bakr, "spend and endure and you will not be molested or harmed." Thus, Abū Bakr's intrepidity is greater, al-Jāḥiẓ concludes, for he had exposed himself to danger without prophetic guarantees for his safety.[25]

The *Mabīt* in Shīᶜī *Manāqib* Literature

Shīᶜī authors without exception depict the *mabīt* as an epochal event in the history of nascent Islam. The Imāmī theologian Radī al-Dīn Ibn Ṭāwūs (d. 664/1266), for example, says that the *mabīt* was more wondrous than Ismāᶜīl's submission to possible death at his father Abraham's hands.[26] Al-ᶜAllāma al-Ḥillī (d. 726/1325) in his *Minhāj al-karāma* refers to an account given by the Sunnī exegete Abū Isḥāq al-Thaʿlabī (d. 427/1035) in his exegesis of Q. 2:207. According to this account, at the time when Muḥammad was preparing to undertake the emigration to Medina and had told ʿAlī to sleep in his bed that night wrapped in his green, Ḥaḍramī mantle, God sent for Michael and Gabriel. He told the two angels, "I have made you two brothers of one another and made the life-span of one of you longer than the other. Who between the two of you would choose his companion over his life?" Each of them chose life over his companion. At that God addressed them, "Could you not be like ʿAlī b. Abī Ṭālib whom I made the brother of Muḥammad and who slept in his bed and chose his companion over his life?" Then He commanded the two angels to descend to earth and guard ʿAlī against his enemies; so Gabriel stood guard by his head and Michael by his feet. And Gabriel commended ʿAlī for his exemplary behavior and commented that God had pointed to his choice with pride before the angels and caused this verse to come down as the Prophet headed for Medina. Al-Ḥillī further refers to Ibn ʿAbbās who is said to have remarked that this event points to ʿAlī's greater excellence (*ʿalā afḍaliyyatihi*) over all the Companions and, in al-Ḥillī's view, confirms that he was the Imām.[27]

Shīʿī scholars in general undermine the significance of the *ghār* episode by devaluing the importance of companionship or by suggesting that the episode in fact reflects negatively on Abū Bakr. For example, Muḥammad b. al-Ḥasan al-Ṭūsī (d. 460/1067) remarks that there is no merit inherent in mere companionship (*al-ṣuḥba*) for that can exist between "the friend and the enemy, the believer and the infidel." Furthermore, he states that the *āyat al-ghār* actually reflects negatively on Abū Bakr because it contains an interdiction directed at him, "Do not grieve!" and the Prophet only interdicts what is reprehensible (*wa'l-nabī lā yanhā illā ʿan qabīḥ*).[28] According to another report contained in the *Biḥār al-anwār*, a man from among the Imāmiyya came to solicit the opinion of a certain Abū 'l-Ḥusayn al-Khayyāṭ regarding the Prophet's command to Abū Bakr, "Do not grieve." His question was, "Was Abū Bakr's fear [an act of] obedience or disobedience?" Al-Khayyāṭ replied, "If it were [an act of] obedience then indeed he [sc. the Prophet] prohibited him [sc. Abū Bakr] from obedience and if it were [an act of] disobedience, then indeed Abū Bakr had disobeyed."[29]

Some Shīʿī exegetes tend to emphasize that the *sakīna* referred to in the *ghār* verse descended only on the Prophet to the exclusion of Abū Bakr and indicate variant readings of this verse.[30] Al-Ṭūsī, for example, articulates one of the main Shīʿī arguments against understanding the *sakīna* to have descended both on the Prophet and Abū Bakr in the cave. He points out that the object suffix of the verb is in the singular while another verse of the same chapter, Q 9:25–6, states "then God caused his *sakīna* to come down on His messenger and the believers," where the recipients other than the Messenger are clearly mentioned.[31] Al-Ṭūsī further states that in Q. 9:40, the statement "God is with us (*Allāh maʿanā*)" is still a reference to the Prophet alone, where the first person plural enclitic serves to aggrandize his status.[32]

The Shīʿī scholar Jamāl al-Dīn Aḥmad ibn Ṭāwūs (d. 673/1274–75), who wrote a refutation of al-Jāḥiẓ's *Risālat al-ʿUthmāniyya*, considers ʿAlī's role in the *mabīt* to eclipse every other achievement attributed to other Companions. If ʿAlī had not been ready and willing to lay down his life for the Prophet, the entire future of Islam would have been imperiled. On this account, Ibn Ṭāwūs comments, "There is no Muslim on the face of the earth over whom the Amīr al-Mu'minīn does not exercise the right of a benevolent master over his slave."[33]

Ibn Ṭāwūs further registers strong objection to al-Jāḥiẓ's comments that the incident of the *ghār* was a certain event (*yaqīn*) while the *mabīt* was doubtful (*ẓannī*). He responds to this claim by simply contradicting al-Jāḥiẓ and asserting that the *mabīt* is *yaqīn* while the authenticity of the event of the *ghār* is open to debate. Such an assertion does not contradict the Qur'ān for, according to Ibn Ṭāwūs, the Qur'ān does not explicitly refer to the event of the *ghār*. It is rather based upon transmission, *riwāya*, just as the *mabīt* is based upon *riwāya*. The Imāmiyya claim that the *mabīt* tradition is universally transmitted, *mutawātir*, just as others claim that the *ghār* tradition is *mutawātir*.[34] Even if the *tawātur* of both traditions is acknowledged, the Imāmiyya insist that greater excellence accrues to ʿAlī for having agreed to spend the night in the Prophet's house as his decoy, whereas there is no merit inherent in taking refuge inside a cave out of fear, nor does such an action indicate bravery or knowledge, eloquence or piety, magnanimity, or kinship. The only conclusion one can derive from the relevant Qur'ānic verse is that the person indicated was afraid and that God-inspired calmness (*sakīna*) descended upon the Prophet. As for the verse alluding to Abū Bakr as the companion of the Prophet, it does not allude to anything more than companionship and companionship alone is not deserving of either praise or blame.[35]

Next, Ibn Ṭawūs responds to al-Jāḥiẓ's argument that ᶜAlī cannot be deemed to have displayed unusual courage during the *mabīt* because of the Prophet's assurance that no harm would come to him. He says this allegation is totally without foundation; one who narrates such a tradition is highly suspect (*muttaham jiddan*) in his motives, inspired as he is by "sheer enmity" towards ᶜAlī.[36] However, if Ibn Ṭawūs were to accept this report as true, that would not reflect negatively on ᶜAlī but rather magnify his status for having readily believed in Muḥammad's assurance of safety, and for having acted without hesitation according to the latter's directive.[37]

In Shīᶜī exegetical works, Q. 2:207 is understood by practically all Shīᶜī commentators, such as Muḥammad al-ᶜAyyāshī (fl. late 3rd/9th century),[38] Faḍl b. al-Ḥasan al-Ṭabarsī (d. 548/1153)[39] and Muḥammad b. al-Ḥasan al-Ṭūsī (d. 460/1067)[40] to refer to the *mabīt* incident. One exception is the early Shīᶜī exegete ᶜAlī b. Ibrāhīm al-Qummī (d. after 307/919) who says, however, that this verse refers to Alī for his "exertion" but does not refer to the *mabīt* as such.[41] The *Biḥār al-anwār* records a report according to which ᶜAlī b. al-Ḥusayn says that the people referred to in this verse are the best of the Companions of the Prophet (*khiyār min aṣḥāb rasūl Allāh*) for they resisted being enticed away from Islam by the pagan Meccans. Among this select group are Bilāl, Ṣuhayb, Khabbāb, ᶜAmmār b. Yāsir, and his parents, with no mention of ᶜAlī.[42]

Sunnī commentators, by and large, with a few notable exceptions, do not understand this verse to have been revealed concerning ᶜAlī in the *mabīt* incident. Al-Ṭabarī in his *tafsīr*[43] says this verse refers to the Muhājirūn and the Anṣār in general. One account on the authority of ᶜIkrima links this verse to Ṣuhayb b. Sinān[44] and Abū Dharr al-Ghifārī. Fakhr al-Dīn al-Rāzī (d. 607/1210) reports a tradition from Ibn ᶜAbbās which relates that this verse was revealed concerning, in addition to Ṣuhayb and Abū Dharr, ᶜAmmār b. Yāsir, Sumayya, his mother and his father Yāsir, Bilāl, Khabbāb b. al-Aratt, and ᶜAbis, the freedman of Ḥuwaytib.[45] Ibn Taymiyya remarks that the majority of the commentators regard this verse as Medinan, that is, revealed after the Prophet's emigration to Medina, and, therefore, it cannot be understood to be a reference to the *mabīt* incident. The verse is rather a reference to Ṣuhayb, who, at the time of his emigration to Medina, had to surrender his wealth to the Meccans who were in pursuit of him.[46] Other accounts report that this verse is in reference to Muslims in general who enjoin good and prohibit evil.[47]

Among Sunnī exegetes who refer to the *mabīt* incident in connection with this verse are al-Rāzī[48] and Abū Isḥāq al-Thaᶜlabī, as already mentioned. In his *al-Kashf wa'l-bayān fī tafsīr al-Qur'ān*, al-Thaᶜlabī states that this verse was revealed in reference to the *mabīt bi'l-firāsh* incident in which ᶜAlī had consciously chosen the Prophet over his life.[49] Al-Thaᶜlabī, however, does not deem ᶜAlī as the only possible referent in this verse. He refers to additional reports from Ibn ᶜAbbās and al-Ḍaḥḥāk, who related that this verse was revealed in reference to al-Zubayr and al-Miqdād. Al-Thaᶜlabī, like al-Ṭabarī, mentions in addition that, according to most commentators, this verse had to do with Ṣuhayb b. Sinān who was tortured by a group of polytheists.[50]

Conclusion

In Sunnī- Shīᶜī dialectics regarding legitimate leadership of the Muslim polity, Qur'ānic warrants, in addition to *ḥadīth*, were important proof-texts. In the extensive discourse that grew up around this crucial topic, the two verses, Q. 9:40 and 2:207, came to be frequently invoked as establishing the superior qualifications of Abū Bakr and ᶜAlī respectively. Sunnī historical and exegetical literature offer evidence that Qur'ān 9:40 was invoked by ᶜUmar as early as the Saqīfa episode to categorically establish Abū Bakr's most excellent status among all of the Companions and, thus, his unparalleled claim to the office of the caliph. The undergirding themes of this discourse are the two key Qur'ānic concepts of *sābiqa* and *faḍl/faḍīla*, which, as I have discussed in detail elsewhere, were the hallmarks of the Prophet's successors.[51] Those Companions who possessed these traits to a greater extent came to be recognized by the community as possessing a greater claim to leadership of the polity.

By the third/ninth century, Islam's great period of consolidation and efflorescence, the moral excellence and precedence of the Companions had become axiomatic for Sunnīs, backed as they were by Qur'ānic and *ḥadīth loci probantes*. The influence of this early discourse on leadership has been wide-ranging, becoming most evident, for instance, in the arrangement of the major biographical works composed on the Ṣaḥāba from the third/ninth century on. Muḥammad b. Saᶜd (d. 230/844–45), for example, in his magisterial biographical dictionary *al-Ṭabaqāt al-kubrā* starts his entries with the first tier of Muslims, drawn from the ranks of those who were among the first to accept Islam (*al-sābiqūn al-awwalūn*, cf. Q. 9:100; *al-sābiqūn al-sābiqūn*, cf. Q. 56:10–12).[52] Medieval historiography was also greatly affected by the development of this paradigm of leadership. Al-Ṭabarī and al-Suyūṭī, as we have seen, were among those historians whose historical vision of the formation of the polity is predicated on this paradigm.

The Shīᶜa, on the other hand, came to insist by the third/ninth century that only ᶜAlī possessed the combination of *sābiqa* and *faḍl/faḍīla* among the Companions and, after him, his progeny, although there is evidence that in the first two centuries, their predecessors recognized the general excellence and precedence of all or most of the Companions.[53] To this constellation of attributes, the Shīᶜa of the second/eighth century would also add *naṣṣ*, the explicit designation of the imām who was descended from the family of the Prophet. Once this soteriological principle had become firmly established among the Shīᶜa by the third/ninth century, it became the cornerstone of their doctrine and the hallmark of legitimate leadership. However, in their conversations with one another, whether dialogic or polemical, both the Sunnīs and the Shīᶜa would continue to emphasize the centrality of the concepts of *sābiqa* and *faḍl/faḍīla* in defining the paradigm of legitimate leadership.

NOTES

1. See, for example, al-Ṭabarī, *Jāmiᶜ al-bayān ᶜan ta'wīl āy al-Qur'ān*, eds. Maḥmūd Muḥammad Shākir and Aḥmad Muḥammad Shākir (Cairo 1373-/1954-on), XIV, 257–60; al-Zamakhsharī, *al-Kashshāf ᶜan ḥaqā'iq al-tanzīl* (Calcutta 1273/1856), I, 542–3; Muslim,

Ṣaḥīḥ, 4:1478. Ibn Sa^{c}d, *al-Ṭabaqāt al-kubrā*, ed. Muḥammad ^{c}Abd al-Qādir ^{c}Atā' (Beirut 1418/1997), III, 181, mentions that when the caliphate was first offered to Abū ^{c}Ubayda, he declined by saying that he could not accept it on account of the second of two being present among them. A variant account has Abū ^{c}Ubayda referring to Abū Bakr as *thālith al-thalātha* ("the third of the three"), indicating that Abū Bakr was present in the cave as the third besides God and His Prophet.

2. Ibn Hishām, *al-Sīra al-nabawiyya*, ed. Suhayl Zakkār (Beirut 1412/1992), I, 332–5, for the *mabīt*; and 1:335–9, for the *ghār*.

3. Al-Muḥibb al-Ṭabarī, *al-Riyāḍ al-naḍira fī manāqib al-^{c}ashara*, ed. Muḥammad Muṣṭafā Abū 'l-^{c}Alā' (Cairo n.d.), I, 103.

4. He is one of the *ahl al-ṣuffa* ("people of the bench"); for whom see Ibn Ḥajar al-^{c}Asqalānī, *al-Iṣāba fī tamyīz al-ṣaḥāba* (Beirut n.d.), III, 54–5, no. 3039; idem, *Tahdhīb al-tahdhīb*, ed. Khalīl Ma'mūn Shīḥā (Beirut 1417/1996), II, 262. For the *ahl al-ṣuffa*, see *EI2*, I, 266–7.

5. Al-Nasā'ī, *Faḍā'il al-ṣaḥāba*, ed. Fārūq Ḥamūda (Casablanca 1404/1984), 55–6.

6. See al-Ḥākim al-Naysābūrī, *al-Mustadrak ^{c}alā 'l-ṣaḥīḥayn fī 'l-ḥadīth* (Riyadh n.d.), III, 63, and al-Suyūṭī, *Ta'rīkh al-khulafā'* (Beirut 1389/1969), 56. Similar sentiments are expressed by al-Rāzī, *Mafātiḥ al-ghayb* (Cairo 1889), IV, 434.

7. See Aḥmad al-Ṭabarsī, *Kitāb al-Iḥtijāj*, ed. Muḥammad Bāqir al-Khurasānī (Najaf 1386/1966), II, 144. For Mu'min al-Ṭāq's spirited refutation based on "Qur'ānic account, clear prophetic *ḥadīth*, and rational proof," see *ibid*.

8. ^{c}Abd al-Razzāq, *al-Muṣannaf*, ed. Ḥabīb al-Raḥmān al-A^{c}ẓam (Beirut 1970–72), V, 388.

9. Similar accounts, also from ^{c}Urwa, are contained in al-Bukhārī, *al-Ṣaḥīḥ* (Cairo 1379/1959), VI, 206–13, no. 3457; Ibn Sa^{c}d, *Ṭabaqāt*, I, 176; Ibn Hishām, *Sīra*, I, 336. For similar and variant accounts, see also Ibn Kathīr, *al-Bidāya wa'l-nihāya* (Beirut and Riyadh 1966), III, 178–82.

10. Ibn al-Athīr, *Usd al-ghāba fī ma^{c}rifat al-ṣaḥāba*, ed. Shihāb al-Dīn al-Najaf (Tehran n.d.), III, 209.

11. Al-Munāwī, *Fayḍ al-qadīr*, ed. Aḥmad ^{c}Abd al-Salīm (Beirut 1415/1994), I, 120.

12. Al-^{c}Iṣāmī, Simṭ al-nujūm al-^{c}awāl fī anbā' al-awā'il wa'l-ta'wīl (Cairo 1380/1960), II, 317.

13. See his *Nihāyat al-^{c}arab fī funūn al-adab*, ed. Muḥammad Abū 'l-Faḍl Ibrāhīm (Cairo 1395/1975), XIX, 15.

14. Ibn Taymiyya, *Minhāj al-sunna al-nabawiyya*, ed. Muḥammad Rashīd Sālim (Saudi Arabia 1406/1986), VII, 120–1.

15. Al-Rāzī, *Mafātīḥ*, IV, 437. Similar sentiments are expressed by Ibn Taymiyya in his *Minhāj al-sunna*, VII, 110ff.

16. Ibid., IV, 434.

17. Al-Jāḥiẓ, *al-^{c}Uthmāniyya*, ed. ^{c}Abd al-Salām Hārūn (Cairo 1474/1955), 51.

18. Ibid., 43–4.

19. Ibid., 107–8.

20. Ibid., 53 ff.

21. See, for example, Ibn Hishām, *Sīra*, I, 458.

22. Al-Jāḥiẓ, *al-^{c}Uthmāniyya*, 54.

23. Ibid., 44.

24. Ibid., 45.

25. Ibid. Cf. al-Muḥibb al-Ṭabarī, *Riyāḍ*, I, 291, where ᶜAlī reports that the Prophet had promised him that he would not die until he came to power (*amira*) and until he came to dye his beard and his hair. See also Ibn Abī 'l-Ḥadīd, *Sharḥ nahj al-balāgha*, ed. Ḥasan Tamīm (Beirut 1963), I, 812, where in a report from Abū Jaᶜfar Muḥammad b. ᶜAlī (the fifth Shīᶜī Imam), the Prophet tells Abū Bakr and ᶜUmar to console ᶜAlī that he would not die "until treachery and corruption had become widespread and he had become an exemplar for the people after him."

26. See his *Kitāb ṭarā'if fī maᶜrifat madhāhib al-ṭawā'if* (Qumm 1400/1979), 33–5.

27. Al-ᶜAllāma al-Ḥillī, *Minhāj al-karāma*, 153–4, contained in Ibn Taymiyya's *Minhāj al-sunna al-nabawiyya fī naqḍ kalām al-shīᶜa al-qadariyya*, ed. Muḥammad Rashād Sālim (Cairo 1382/1962), vol. I. Ibn Taymiyya dismisses this report as patently false; see his *Minhāj al-sunna* (Saudi Arabian edition), VII, 116.

28. See his *Talkhīṣ al-shāfī*, ed. al-Sayyid Ḥusayn Baḥr al-ᶜUlūm (Najaf 1383/1963), III, 212–3. Al-Iskāfī expresses a similar opinion; cf. Appendix to the *ᶜUthmāniyya*, 341–2.

29. Al-Majlisī, Muḥammad Bāqir, *Biḥār al-anwār* (Beirut 1403–1983), X, 418, 410; cf. al-ᶜAllāma al-Ḥillī, *Minhāj al-karāma*, 199.

30. See al-ᶜAyyāshī, *Kitāb al-tafsīr*, ed. Hāshim al-Rasā'il al-Maḥallātī (Qumm 1380/1960), II, 88–9; al-Majlisī, *Biḥār*, XIX, 71, 80, 88. See also the account of debates between Sunnī and Shīᶜī commentators regarding the interpretation of this verse in the *Biḥār*, X, 419–24.

31. Al-Ṭūsi, *Talkhīṣ*, III, 213–4.

32. In contrast, see al-Suyūṭī, *Ta'rīkh al-khulafā'*, 44, where he records a report from Ibn Abī Ḥātim relating from Ibn ᶜAbbās that the *sakīna* had descended on Abū Bakr and not on the Prophet; see also al-Muḥibb al-Ṭabarī, *Riyāḍ*, I, 124, where a report defines the *sakīna* in this context as the assurance given to Abū Bakr.

33. See his *Binā' al-maqāla fī naqd al-risāla al-ᶜuthmāniyya*, ed. ᶜAlī al-ᶜAdnānī al-Ghurayfī (Qumm 1990), 91–2. See also Radī al-Dīn ibn Ṭāwūs, *Ṭarā'if*, 33–5, where the author expresses similar sentiments.

34. Ibn Ṭāwūs, *Binā' al-maqāla*, 113.

35. *BA*, 48; *BQ*, 113.

36. See Raḍī al-Dīn ibn Ṭāwūs, *Saᶜd al-suᶜd* (Najaf 1369/1950), 216–17, where he remonstrates that the statement *lā yasil ilayka minhum makrūh* must be a later addition (*ziyāda*) to the tradition, for why else would it be said that ᶜAlī had earned divine approbation by choosing the Prophet over his life?

37. During the incident of al-Ḥudaybiyya in 6/628, Muḥammad decided to make the *ᶜumra* or the lesser pilgrimage to Mecca. The Prophet feared that the Quraysh might prevent him from visiting the Kaᶜba and, therefore, invited all "the Arabs and neighboring Bedouin to march with him." Many of the Bedouin Arabs are said to have demurred and the Quraysh did in fact prevent him from entering Mecca, so Muḥammad encamped at Ḥudaybiyya, a small town on the outskirts of Mecca; see Ibn Hishām, *Sīra*, I, 499f. Ibn Ṭāwūs is thus contrasting the ready compliance of ᶜAlī with the Prophet's directives to the refusal of some of the Arabs to respond to the Prophet's invitation in the year of the Ḥudaybiyya. For the terms of the treaty, see "al-Ḥudaybiya," *EI2*, III, 539.

38. *Tafsīr*, I, 101.

39. *Majmaᶜ al-bayān fī tafsīr al-Qur'ān* (Beirut 1380/1961), II, 174.

40. *Tafsīr al-tibyān*, ed. Aḥmad Shawqī al-Amīn and Aḥmad Ḥabīb Qaṣīr (Najaf n.d.), II, 183.

41. Al-Qumm, *Tafsīr*, II, 71.

42. Al-Majlisī, *Biḥār*, XXII, 338.

43. *Jāmiʿ al-bayān*, IV, 247.

44. See also al-Zamakhsharī, *Kashshāf*, I, 352–3; al-Ḥākim, *Mustadrak*, III, 398; Ibn Taymiyya, *Minhāj al-sunna*, VII, 118–20.

45. Al-Ṭabarī, *Jāmiʿ al-bayān*, V, 223; for this interpretation, see also al-Ṭabarsī, *Majmaʿ*, II, 184–5, and al-Ṭūsī, *Tafsīr al-tibyān*, II, 183.

46. *Minhāj al-sunna*, VII, 118–19.

47. See al-Ṭabarī, *Jāmiʿ al-bayān*, IV, 249–50; al-Zamakhsharī, *Kashshāf*, I, 352.

48. See his *Mafātīḥ al-ghayb* (Cairo 1889), V, 223.

49. *Al-Kashf wa'l-bayān ʿan tafsīr al-Qur'ān*, Ms. Istanbul Universitesi Kütüphanesi, catalog no. A1731, fol. 99b; cf. ʿAllama al-Ḥillī, *Minhāj al-karāma*, I, 153.

50. *Al-Kashf wa'l-bayān*, fol. 99a. These various interpretations are also given by al-Qurṭubī in his *Jāmiʿ*, II, 21.

51. For this discussion, see my *Excellence and Precedence: Medieval Islamic Discourse on Legitimate Leadership* (Leiden: E. J. Brill, 2002), esp. 36–51.

52. Cf. Wadād al-Qāḍī, "Biographical Dictionaries: Inner Structure and Cultural Significance," in *The Book in the Islamic World: The Written Word and Communication in the Middle East*, ed. George N. Atiyeh (Albany NY: SUNY Press, 1995), 97–9, where she discusses the arrangement of Ibn Saʿd's *ṭabaqat* work according to the critical criterion of *sābiqa*.

53. See *Excellence and Precedence*, 44–5.

Chapter 7

The Hermeneutics of Fakhr al-Dīn al-Rāzī

Carl Sharif El-Tobgui

Verse 7 of *Āl ᶜImrān*, the third *sūra* of the Qur'ān, reads:

> He it is Who has sent down to thee the Book. In it are verses basic or fundamental, of established meaning (*āyāt muḥkamāt*); they are the foundation, or "mother," of the Book. Others are allegorical (*wa-ukhar mutashābihāt*). But those in whose hearts is perversity follow the part thereof that is allegorical, seeking discord, and searching for its hidden meanings, but no one knows its hidden meanings except God. And those who are firmly grounded in knowledge say: "We believe in the Book; the whole of it is from our Lord;" and none will grasp the message except men of understanding.[1]

This verse is the most important of several Qur'ānic passages that deal not with questions of theology, eschatology, spirituality, ethics or law, but rather with the very nature and characteristics of the 6,236 verses that compose the Holy Book. In Q. 3:7, we read that the revelation is made up of two, mutually exclusive categories of verses: those that are *muḥkam*, or "of established meaning," and those that are *mutashābih*, or "allegorical." In addition to the verse cited above, two further passages describe the entire Qur'ān as being *muḥkam*,[2] while a third verse qualifies the whole of it as *mutashābih*.[3] It is clear that the terms *muḥkam* and *mutashābih* have different meanings across these four verses, such that all verses of the Qur'ān can, without contradiction, be simultaneously *muḥkam* and *mutashābih* as complementary categories in one sense, while still dividing into the separate, mutually exclusive categories of *muḥkam* and *mutashābih* in another sense, as indicated in Q. 3:7.

The ability to determine which verses are *muḥkam* and which are *mutashābih* is critical, since the Qur'ān itself describes the former as the "mother of the Book,"—that is, verses that make up the core of the revelation and whose precise meaning can be determined in a definitive manner—while the latter are declared to be of an allegorical nature whose true signification is known only to God. The division of verses into the categories of *muḥkam* and *mutashābih* has crucial epistemological implications, for definitive knowledge—be it knowledge of God, revelation, prophets and prophecy, the origins and nature of the cosmos, eschatological information concerning man's destiny after death, ethics, law, social, economic and political precepts, etc.—may be derived only from conclusive verses whose exact significance can be established with certitude. Verses of allegorical import, on the other hand, may very well further the general edification of human beings, or perhaps intimate certain verities that lie beyond the realm of strict discursive reasoning, but truth, as such, may not be identified with the literal denotation of such verses. Confusing a literal with an allegorical verse, or vice versa, could lead to a serious distortion of the meaning of revelation, whereby one erroneously construes in a literal sense a verse meant symbolically, or conversely, mistakes for allegory a passage whose truth value is, in fact, embedded precisely in its literal signification. Such misguided allegorization may, in some instances, be tantamount to canceling out the verse's intended meaning altogether, thereby obfuscating a part of that ultimate truth whose conveyance to mankind is the very essence and *raison d'être* of revelation.[4]

This article aims to present a detailed, commentated exposition of the understanding of Fakhr al-Dīn al-Rāzī (d. 606/1209) regarding the notion of *muḥkam* and *mutashābih* verses in the Holy Qur'ān as evidenced in his titanic, thirty-two volume exegetical work, *Mafātīḥ al-ghayb* ("Keys to the Unseen"),[5] also known as *al-Tafsīr al-kabīr* ("The Great Exegesis"). Of the four verses mentioned above that address the topic at hand, only Q. 3:7 has as its main subject the categories of *muḥkam* and *mutashābih* verses, while the other three passages make mention of the topic rather incidentally. For this reason, Q. 3:7 has widely been considered to be "the" verse on the subject of *muḥkam* and *mutashābih*. This fact may likely explain why our exegete wrote no fewer than fourteen pages on Q. 3:7 alone, whereas each of the other three verses merited less than one page each. Due to the centrality of Q. 3:7 in understanding the concept of "clear" and "ambiguous" verses and to avoid overcomplicating an already intricate subject, we will present here only al-Rāzī's commentary on the verse cited above. In any case, al-Rāzī added to what he said about Q. 3:7 only relatively small details in his commentary on the remaining three verses. In fact, at several points in his treatment of theses verses, our author refers the reader back to his explication of Q. 3:7 to orient the reader and to ground his argument.

My goal here is to provide as accurate and detailed a presentation of al-Rāzī's thought and argumentation as possible. Nevertheless, the prodigious thoroughness with which our author covers his topic has obliged me in many instances to paraphrase very generally, and in some cases, to pass over altogether certain tangential arguments and lines of reasoning which do not have a direct bearing on the topic at hand. In order to render al-Rāzī's thought more transparent to the non-specialist, I have in most cases replaced his original Arabic terminology with what I have attempted to identify as the most suitable English equivalents, while recognizing the difficulties this can create.

Al-Rāzī's Life and Thought: a Biographical and Intellectual Profile

Abū ᶜAbd Allāh Abū 'l-Faḍl Muḥammad ibn ᶜUmar ibn al-Ḥusayn ibn al-Ḥasan ibn ᶜAlī al-Tamīmī al-Bakrī al-Rāzī—known more succinctly by the honorific Fakhr al-Dīn ("Glory, or Honor, of the Faith") al-Rāzī—was born on 25 Ramaḍān, 543 or 544 AH (1149 or 1150 CE) in the city of Rayy in northern Persia, just south of present-day Tehran. Al-Rāzī belonged to a family of religious scholars who originally hailed from Ṭabaristān, and his father, Ḍiyā' al-Dīn ᶜUmar al-Rāzī, was himself an influential scholar popularly known as Khaṭīb al-Rayy, or the preacher of Rayy. The young al-Rāzī began his religious studies under the tutelage of his father, through whom he entered a chain of scholars that can be traced back, in theology, to the famous Abū 'l-Ḥasan al-Ashᶜarī (d. 324/935–6), founder of the Ashᶜarite school of theology eventually acknowledged by a great many Sunnī scholars as the fittest expression of Islamic belief in theological terms, and, in law, to the celebrated Muḥammad ibn

Idrīs al-Shāfiʿī (d. 204/820), founder of one of the four universally accepted legal rites of Sunnī Islam. After his father's death, al-Rāzī continued his studies in Rayy, Maragheh and Khurasan, primarily in the fields of philosophy and theology, though he did gain a mastery of the mathematical, medical and natural sciences as well. After completing his formal education, al-Rāzī traveled eastwards to Khwarazm in order to combat the considerable influence of the rationalistic Muʿtazilite school of speculative theology influential in that area. After bitter controversies, he was forced to leave for Transoxania, where he likewise managed to arouse the opposition of certain scholars and courtiers, especially among the Bāṭinites (i.e., Ismāʿīlīs) and a rigorously literalistic, anthropomorphist sect known as the Karrāmites. Eventually compelled to quit Transoxania, al-Rāzī held discussions and debates of a juridical, philosophical and theological nature with scholars in Bukhara and Samarqand, taught for a short while in Ghazna, then settled at length in the city of Herat, where he enjoyed the patronage and support of the local rulers. In time, a special *madrasa*, or religious college, was founded for him, where he taught and preached for the remainder of his days. Al-Rāzī was known throughout his life for his outstanding eloquence, finely honed rhetorical skills and daunting force of argumentation in both Arabic and Persian. Such was his popularity and intellectual authority that, during his days in Herat, it is reported that he never moved about without a following of 300 disciples. Al-Rāzī died in Herat at the height of honor and fame in the year 606/1209, around the age of sixty, shortly before the Tatar invasion of that region.[6]

The classical Muslim biographer and historian, Ibn Khallikān (d. 680/1282), describes Fakhr al-Dīn al-Rāzī as the greatest authority of his time in the Greek sciences,[7] and contemporary Western scholars have characterized him as "the most outstanding figure of speculative theology in post-Ghazalian Islam"[8] and as a "subtle dialectician, possessor of a vast philosophical and theological culture as well as of an intellectual courage rare in his time, [who] is among the leading representatives of Sunnite Islam."[9] More than 70 treatises have been attributed to al-Rāzī, covering the fields of history, law and jurisprudence, Qur'ānic exegesis, theology, philosophy, Ṣūfism, the sciences of grammar and rhetoric as regards the miraculously inimitable nature (*iᶜjāz*) of the Qur'ān, and the natural sciences, including medicine and mineralogy.[10] Among his many compositions is a scientific encyclopedia entitled *Jāmiᶜ al-ᶜUlūm*, which includes the definitions, scope and major principles of the various sciences cultivated in the classical Muslim world. Concerning al-Rāzī's degree of mastery of such diversified fields of knowledge, we know, for instance, that his familiarity with medicine was much greater than that of a mere dabbler, for among his works is a commentary on the *Qānūn* of Ibn Sīnā (Avicenna) (d. 429/1037), which he often critiques from a standpoint that bespeaks familiarity with the works of the Hellenistic arch-physician Galen as well as those of the Muslim medical masters, especially Muḥammad ibn Zakariyyā al-Rāzī.[11] Indeed, Seyyed Hossein Nasr remarks that "there have been very few Muslim theologians who have had so much knowledge of the mathematical and natural sciences as Imam al-Razi."[12] Notwithstanding the depth of al-Rāzī's competence in such a variegated range of disciplines, however, he is most famously known for his theological and philosophical works, in addition to his amplitudinous commentary on the Qur'ān, whose verses provide him the most fertile of ground for the playing out of his metaphysical and doctrinal premises.

Al-Rāzī has been characterized by one modern analyst as a "theologian with philosophical tendencies, or, if one prefers Arabic terminology, a *mutakallim* very attracted to *falsafa*."[13] Most of his theological work proposes to combat the Muᶜtazilite sect from a vantage point clearly committed to Ashᶜarite theological doctrine. Al-Rāzī likewise takes issue with the *falāsifa* (Muslim philosophers) on a number of points, attempting to undermine the relevance of their arguments with regard to, say, the resurrection of the body or God's knowledge of particulars, both of which the philosophers roundly denied. Although al-Rāzī's commitment to the defense of Ashᶜarism is beyond question, an outstanding feature of his thought—as we shall discover—is its bold, sometimes striking, independence. Indeed, he is ready to concede to and concur with his opponents on discrete points where he recognizes some truth in what they propound, as well as to criticize Ashᶜarite doctrine—and even al-Ashᶜarī himself—where he deems fit to do so.[14] P. Kraus characterizes al-Rāzī's doctrine as a "curious and original attempt to reconcile philosophy with religious tradition," further remarking that "his rationalism, which led him to accept all the dictates of reason, gave him the courage to venture where none of his precursors had dared."[15] Among the various influences that left their mark on al-Rāzī's formidable intellect—and which he seems to have accepted in full conscience—we may cite Abū Naṣr al-Fārābī (d. 339/950) and especially Ibn Sīnā among the earlier *falāsifa*, Abū Ḥāmid al-Ghazālī (d. 505/1111), and the Jewish philosopher and convert to Islam Abū 'l-Barakāt al-Baghdādī (d. 547/1152), along with the Ashᶜarite theological school, the Shāfiᶜite legal rite, the scientists, the grammarians and rhetoricians, and even, as already mentioned, his primary adversaries, the Muᶜtazilites.[16] Given the eclectic character of al-Rāzī's scholastic background and intellectual makeup, one may wonder to what degree, in the final analysis, our author can simply be said to be an Ashᶜarite *tout court*. Alternatively, we might ask what precisely, despite al-Rāzī's multi-faceted and colorful intellectual composition, may have assured the pledging of his ultimate allegiance to the Ashᶜarī school of thought.

An answer to these questions is suggested by R. Arnaldez, who argues that al-Rāzī was attempting to tie different strands of Islam together and synthesize them. Whereas both the Muᶜtazilites and the *falāsifa* were most commonly seen as sects, unrepresentative of the Muslim mainstream, Ashᶜarism by al-Rāzī's time had come to be accepted as orthodox theology by a great many religious scholars. Furthermore, the Ashᶜarite formulation of the creed had shown "great possibilities for development, a remarkable power of assimilation and a favorable adaptability"[17] at the hands of al-Juwaynī and al-Ghazālī. Indeed, Ashᶜarism, pursues Arnaldez, had defined itself as a "middle position, seeking to reconcile extreme sects, opening the door to speculation, yet remaining very attached to the text of the Qur'ān and *ḥadīth*; admitting a theology, somewhat reluctantly, most especially for the sake of having a defensive weapon against heretics and innovators."[18]

As a complement to these intellectual factors, Arnaldez suggests a parallelism between al-Rāzī's work and thought, on the one hand, and the larger politico-historical context in which he found himself, on the other. Al-Rāzī lived in turbulent times, at a period when the broad political unity of the first two centuries of ᶜAbbāsid rule had long given way to widespread disunity and fragmentation. His was a time in which the dynasty of Seljuk sultans had, for already more than a century, deployed considerable efforts to reestablish Sunnism after an extended period of Shīᶜī/Ismāᶜīlī rule from the late 4th/10th until the 6th/12th centuries and was now being challenged by efforts from the ᶜAbbāsid caliphs—themselves, significantly, quintessentially Sunnī—to regain their power and influence vis-à-vis the Seljuks. The fall of the Ismāᶜīlī Fāṭimid dynasty in Egypt at the hands of the legendary Ṣalāḥ al-Dīn al-Ayyūbī (Saladin) in 566/1171 was followed by nominal recognition of the ᶜAbbāsid caliph al-Mustaḍī' (r. 566–575/1170–1180), only to be undermined by the rise of the Ayyūbids in Egypt and growing dominance of the Turks (also committed to Sunnī Islam) in the eastern provinces, likewise at the expense of the ᶜAbbāsids. Despite these myriad political quarrels and battles, added to the ongoing combat against Muᶜtazilism, Arnaldez remarks that, nonetheless, "we see an overall idea taking shape,"—namely, to reunite the Muslim world at least religiously and intellectually, if not politically, through a concerted effort to reestablish and reassure the foundations of Sunnism in the face of myriad competing doctrines and allegiances—an idea "to which al-Rāzī cannot have been insensitive."[19]

Qur'ānic Exegesis and al-Rāzī's Place therein

Al-Rāzī's Qur'ān commentary, *Mafātīḥ al-ghayb*, has been described as "the most important theological commentary ever written on the Qur'ān."[20] The colossal work belongs to the later period of al-Rāzī's life and may have been initiated under the impulsion of a profound internal experience, akin to a mystical enlightenment or spiritual epiphany.[21] Unfinished at the time of our author's death, the commentary was eventually completed by two of his students.[22] The *Mafātīḥ* has been seen as a commentary whose primary goal is the refutation of Muᶜtazilite theology, perhaps conceived particularly as a response to the influential exegetical work, *al-Kashshāf*, composed by the well-known Muᶜtazilite philologist, rhetorician and Qur'ān commentator Abū 'l-Qāsim Maḥmūd b. ᶜUmar al-Zamakhsharī (d. 538/1143).[23] Yet more than simply a response to staunchly Muᶜtazilite exegetes like al-Zamakhsharī, Kraus points out that, upon going through the commentary, one perceives that "its author, under the pretence of having adopted the thesis that the Qur'ān contains every science, discusses the most difficult problems of philosophy."[24] So encompassing, in fact, is the embrace of al-Rāzī's work that the famous theologian Ibn Taymiyya (d. 728/1328), known for his avid dislike of rational speculation in theological matters, complained that the *Mafātīḥ* "contains everything except *tafsīr*." To this it was responded that the work, in fact, "contains everything together with *tafsīr*."[25]

The exegetical style of the *Mafātīḥ* may be characterized as essentially philosophical, or perhaps more accurately, theo-philosophical. Such a style is to be distinguished from other types of commentaries, such as those dealing primarily with grammatical or rhetorical concerns, juridically-based commentaries, commentaries founded primarily on the narration of Prophetic *ḥadīth*, or mystically oriented, Ṣūfī commentaries. Like other exegetes, al-Rāzī draws significantly on the accomplishments of previous commentators and, especially, on the resources provided by scholars specialized in various auxiliary disciplines essential to the systematic explication of the Qur'ānic text. Thus, al-Rāzī calls to witness scholars hailing from a plethora of sundry disciplines for enlightenment on a host of relevant topics. Such topics include, for instance, information regarding the seven canonical readings (or *qirā'āt*) of the Holy Text, clarification on delicate points of Arabic grammar or rhetorical usage, reports concerning the historical circumstances in which a particular verse was revealed (known as the science of *asbāb al-nuzūl*), rulings of major jurists regarding the legal implications of a given passage, Prophetic *ḥadīth* essential for rounding out or providing details on topics receiving only perfunctory treatment in the Qur'ān, and so forth.[26]

One issue of particular importance to our study of Q. 3:7, dealing with the categories of *muḥkam* and *mutashābih*, is the question of *ta'wīl*, or "interpretation"—that is, of construing a verse according to other than its most obvious, literal connotation. As we shall see below, the issue of if and when it is legitimate to make *ta'wīl* and of what conditions regulate the use of *ta'wīl* as a hermeneutical tool forms a major part of al-Rāzī's concern in explicating Q.

3:7 and will, consequently, be treated in considerable detail in the following section. Nevertheless, a few preliminary comments are necessary in order to contextualize the question of *ta'wīl* within Muslim exegetical and theological discourse, as a prerequisite for better appreciating and analyzing al-Rāzī's own stance on this contentious point of creed.

The debate over the legitimacy of interpreting Qur'ānic verses metaphorically arose initially with respect to certain passages of the Holy Book which, if taken literally, would seem to ascribe to God attributes distinctive of created beings, especially the possession of a body analogous to that of a man.[27] While early theologians of most tendencies readily rejected such crass anthropomorphism—understanding intuitively that God's immateriality precludes His having a body of any sort and bolstered by the unambiguous proclamation in Q. 42:11 that "nothing is like unto Him" (*laysa ka-mithlihi shay'*)—there nevertheless arose disagreement as to how, precisely, such verses were to be apprehended. While a handful of inveterate anthropomorphists—referred to collectively as the *mujassima* (lit: "those who ascribe a body to God") or the *mushabbiha* (lit: "those who liken God [to His creation]")—insisted on maintaining that God possessed eyes, ears, hands, etc. in a literal sense, the majority of scholars and theologians took one of two decidedly non-anthropomorphist positions. Rationalistically inclined thinkers—notably the Muᶜtazilites and, especially, the *falāsifa*—not merely denied the admissibility of construing such verses literally, but went beyond this to assign such phrases a precisely defined metaphorical meaning which they maintained to be the true intended significance of the verses in question. What may be considered the mainstream of early scholars, however, largely mistrusted the methods employed by the speculative thinkers and, in fact, harbored deep misgivings towards any kind of rational hypothesizing whatsoever in the realm of theology. While still upholding the rejection of pure literalism with regard to verses of seemingly anthropomorphic implication, such scholars simultaneously denied the permissibility of engaging in conjecture as to what precise metaphorical interpretation might concur with God's purport. One was to affirm such verses as part of revelation, understanding that while they must not be construed literally, their actual import is known to God alone. Rather than venturing down the slippery slope of hazardous presumption, Muslims are called upon to accept such verses *bi-lā kayf*, that is, without undue inquiry after their precise modalities.

With time and the increasing sophistication of rationalist theological discourse, there developed an attempt to defend the (non-rationalistic) theses upheld by the scholarly mainstream precisely by using the methods of (rational) argumentation that had developed in the science of *kalām*—a way of beating the Devil at his own game, if you will. The primary inaugurator of this endeavor was the aforementioned Abū 'l-Ḥasan al-Ashʿarī, erstwhile student of the famed Muʿtazilite theologian, Abū ʿAlī Muḥammad al-Jubbā'ī (d. 303/915–16), from whom al-Ashʿarī eventually broke off. As a defender of what came to be considered orthodox theological doctrines, it is not surprising that al-Ashʿarī rejected the metaphorical interpretation (*ta'wīl*) of outwardly anthropomorphic verses, or at least tolerated such only to a very limited degree.[28] This attitude seems also to have been maintained by al-Bāqillānī (d. 403/1013), the first important figure in the Ashʿarite school after al-Ashʿarī himself, as well as by al-Bayhaqī (d. 458/1066), "the most noteworthy representative among the Ashʿarites of this non-speculative line."[29] Nevertheless, a student of al-Ashʿarī himself by the name of ʿAlī ibn Muḥammad Abū 'l-Ḥasan al-Ṭabarī is reported by the famous biographer, Tāj al-Dīn ibn Taqī al-Dīn al-Subkī (d. 769/1368), to have composed a work entitled *Ta'wīl al-Aḥādīth al-Mushkilāt al-Wāridāt fī'l-Ṣifāt* ("Metaphorical Interpretation of Ambiguous *Ḥadīth* Reports Concerning the Divine Attributes").[30] Other Ashʿarite scholars, such as Ibn Fūrak (d. 406/1015) and al-Baghdādī (d. 429/1037), likewise seem to have gone beyond al-Ashʿarī's views by arguing that anthropomorphic terms applied to God should be interpreted (metaphorically) in a manner consistent with the transcendence of the Almighty, rather than risk compromising this transcendence through the literal interpretation of texts whose true meaning may not have been adequately grasped by the intellect. Imām al-Ḥaramayn al-Juwaynī (d. 478/1085), one of the most outstanding representatives of the Ashʿarite school, had also moved away from al-Ashʿarī, like his predecessors Ibn Fūrak and al-Baghdādī, by admitting *ta'wīl* with respect to certain would-be anthropomorphic terms applied to God in the Qur'ān and *ḥadīth*.

Thus, rather than arguing, in the way of al-Ashᶜarī or the Ḥanbalites, that a phrase like "God's hand" should be understood neither literally nor metaphorically—that is, *bi-lā kayf*—al-Juwaynī insists that since the word "hand" cannot be understood literally (that is, corporeally) in the case of God, it must be interpreted to mean "power."[31]

Al-Rāzī, as we shall see below, follows the bulk of his post-Ashᶜarī forerunners in as far as he admits that certain verses and expressions—precisely those determined to be *mutashābih*—cannot be construed in their literal sense. Indeed, Goldziher goes as far as to claim that out of the Ashᶜarites, "al-Rāzī did the most for the methodological grounding of *ta'wīl*."[32] Establishing the legitimacy and indispensability of *ta'wīl* is, in fact, the primary object of al-Rāzī's important theological tract, *Asās al-Taqdīs* ("The Foundation of Reverence"). Nevertheless, as we shall presently discover, al-Rāzī turns out to be rather conservative when it comes to allowing specific, precisely defined metaphorical meanings to be fixed in the case of *mutashābih* verses. Indeed, while the broad legitimation claimed for *ta'wīl* as a hermeneutical principle may seem to be an all-out concession to Muᶜtazilite doctrine on the part of the Ashᶜarites, al-Rāzī is careful to underscore the differences which mark his conception of *ta'wīl* from that proffered by the most notable representative of the rival (i.e., Muᶜtazilite) camp, al-Zamakhsharī. Whereas this latter takes rhetorical considerations to be the most relevant in determining when a verse should be interpreted metaphorically—whereby he, in fact, freely allegorizes any verse whose apparent meaning contradicts his theological commitments, thereby obviating from the outset any difficulties with which such verses may surprise him,—al-Rāzī stridently rejects simple rhetoric as a legitimate basis for *ta'wīl*. Such a principle, he contends, would leave the door wide open to the sort of gratuitous allegorizations of other-worldly realities wantonly peddled by the philosophers, such that a Qur'ānic phrase like: "Gardens beneath which rivers flow"[33] is taken to denote neither the presence of gardens nor of rivers in the Hereafter, but rather is reduced to a mere allegory for spiritual bliss and beatitude. Such an approach, warns al-Rāzī, would lead to the abrogation of Sacred Law and, indeed, to the rescinding of religion altogether.[34] In place of rhetoric, al-Rāzī—significantly—declares reason and "rational indicators" to be the only factor that can justify the abandonment of a verse's literal significance. It is to the details of al-Rāzī's discussion concerning rational indicators that the remainder of this essay is dedicated.

Al-Rāzī and Rational Indicators in Exegesis

At the beginning of his commentary on Q. 3:7, al-Rāzī explains that the Holy Book indicates three different things with regard to its being composed of *muḥkam* and *mutashābih* verses. As mentioned above, Q. 11:1 declares the Qur'ān to be *muḥkam* in its entirety: "*Alif. Lām. Rā'*. (This is) a book, with verses basic or fundamental (of established meaning), further explained in detail,—from One Who is Wise and Well-Acquainted (with all things)." The Qur'ān, according to al-Rāzī, is *muḥkam* in its entirety in the sense that it is "true speech (*kalām ḥaqq*), of sound meaning conveyed by eloquent words, such that it surpasses any speech or utterance both in eloquence of wording and in forcefulness of meaning."[35] This interpretation of *muḥkam*, al-Rāzī tells us, conforms to conventional Arabic usage, in which the same word can be used in reference to a sturdy building or a tight, insoluble knot. Secondly, however, the Qur'ān also indicates that it is *mutashābih* in its entirety, as in Q. 39:23: "God has revealed (from time to time) the most beautiful message in the form of a book, consistent with itself (*mutashābihan*), (yet) repeating (its teaching in various aspects)." Al-Rāzī explains *mutashābih* here to mean that each part of the Qur'ān resembles every other part of it in beauty and that each part of it confirms and verifies every other part, a notion which is also alluded to in Q. 4:82, "Do they not consider the Qur'ān (with care)? Had it been from other than God, they would surely have found therein much discrepancy (*ikhtilāfan kathīran*)."[36] Were the Qur'ān not, in its entirety, *mutashābih* in the sense just mentioned, it would be self-contradictory and its verses would be of unequal literary merit, some exquisitely eloquent while others merely run-of-the-mill. Thirdly, there is evidence within the Qur'ān to suggest that some parts of the Book are *muḥkam* while other parts are *mutashābih*, as indicated by Q. 3:7, the exegesis of which forms the topic of this essay.

As a first step in reaching a proper understanding of this critical verse, al-Rāzī adopts the customary methodology observed in

Islamic scholarship, which consists first of indicating the literal, etymological meaning of a word, then of giving a more restricted definition of the word used as a technical term belonging to a given discipline. According to al-Rāzī, the linguistic meaning of the word *muḥkam* is "to prevent, stop, avert, obviate" (*manaᶜa*). In support of this meaning, he cites the following *ḥadīth* reported by the early Kūfan legist Ibrāhīm al-Nakhaᶜī (d. 95/713): *uḥkum al-yatīma kamā taḥkumu waladak*, which al-Rāzī understands to mean *imnaᶜhu ᶜan al-fasād*, or "prevent him from [doing] evil." Similarly, a building or a structure may be described as *muḥkam* in Arabic if the solidity of the structure is such that it forcefully withstands attempts to undermine or weaken it. Further, wisdom in Arabic is called *ḥikma*, derived from the same root, precisely because it averts, or guards against, that which is incorrect and undesirable—presumably ignorance and false judgment. As for the term *mutashābih*, al-Rāzī maintains that it denotes an almost identical resemblance, whereby one thing is so similar to another that the mind is incapable of distinguishing between them. This meaning is clear in verses such as Q. 2:70, "To us are all heifers alike," *inna 'l-baqara tashābaha ᶜalaynā*, and Q. 2:118, "Their hearts are alike," *tashābahat qulūbuhum*.

Concerning the meaning of *muḥkam* and *mutashābih* as technical terms in the fields of law, theology and Qur'ānic exegesis, al-Rāzī explains the following: If a word is capable of signifying only one meaning, then this word is classified as "univocal" (*naṣṣ*).[37] If, however, it is possible for the word to have more than one meaning, then two further possibilities arise: (1) either one of the meanings is more primary and immediate than—and is therefore preponderant (*rājiḥ*) over—the other; or (2) neither meaning is considered more primary than the other. In the first case, the word in question is considered "apparent" (*ẓāhir*) with regard to the preponderant meaning and "non-apparent" (*mu'awwal*) with regard to the less obvious, secondary meaning.[38] If, however, neither meaning takes clear priority over the other, then the word is considered "equivocal" (*mushtarak*) with regard to the two meanings taken together and "non-specified" (*mujmal*) with regard to each of its meanings considered separately.[39] By way of summary, therefore, it may be said that any given word is either univocal, having only one meaning and allowing of only one definitive interpretation, or it is not univocal. If it is not univocal, then either: (1) the word has two meanings of unequal semantic preponderance and is considered "apparent" with respect to the preponderant meaning and "non-apparent" with respect to the non-preponderant meaning, or (2) the word is equivocal with respect to two equally likely meanings, in relation to each of which it is considered "non-specified."

Based on what, one may ask, is a word's putative preponderancy to be established? By way of responding to this question, al-Rāzī here speaks of the meaning(s) of words *bi-aṣl al-waḍ*ᶜ, that is, with regard to what is taken by Muslim jurists and theologians to be the primordial semantic denotation of words considered in isolation and *before* they enter into any actual linguistic context. It is at this stage that a word's meanings may be identified as "apparent" (*ẓāhir*) and "non-apparent" (*mu'awwal*), "preponderant" (*rājiḥ*) and "non-preponderant" (*marjūḥ*). Thereafter, it is only when a word appears in a given context, such as a Qur'ānic verse, that one may determine—based on criteria to be discussed at length further on—whether the word is to be interpreted *in that context* according to its apparent, preponderant meaning, making the verse in question *muḥkam*, or according to its non-apparent, non-preponderant significance, rendering the verse *mutashābih*.

Words characterized by univocalness or by apparentness share in the fact that they both enjoy preponderancy (*tarjīḥ*), albeit a univocal word does so exclusively due to the presence of only one possible meaning to begin with, while an "apparent" text does so by virtue of the fact that one of its several meanings is found to preponderate over the others. It is this shared quality of preponderance by which a text whose operative words are either univocal or "apparent" is rendered *muḥkam*. As for the categories of "non-specified" and "non-apparent," these have in common the fact that their assigned meaning does not enjoy preponderance (*dalālat al-lafẓ ᶜalayhi ghayr rājiḥa*), with the difference that a meaning which is "non-apparent" is actually considered to be "preponderated over" (*marjūḥ*) by the primary meaning, whereas a meaning classified as non-specified neither preponderates nor is preponderated over, due to its co-existence with another, equally likely meaning. In any case, the presence of non-apparentness or non-specificity in a verse both render that verse *mutashābih*, since neither category permits the verse's meaning to be established in a definitive manner free of all ambiguity. Thus, the term *mutashābih* may be said to apply to any verse which, due to the ambiguity of the terms in which it is expressed (as discussed above), cannot in any way be known with absolute certainty (*lā yuᶜlamu iṭlāqan*).[40]

But now, how are we to go about determining whether a particular verse is *muḥkam* or *mutashābih*? This is a methodological question of critical importance to which al-Rāzī devotes much of the rest of his exegesis of Q. 3:7. Defining a neat, compelling and, most importantly, objective methodology is indispensable for al-Rāzī, who bemoans the fact that proponents of various schools of thought tend to define those verses that bolster their position as *muḥkam* and those that contradict their views as *mutashābih*. The Muᶜtazilite, for example, declares Q. 18:29, "So whosoever wills, let him believe, and whosoever wills, let him disbelieve" to be *muḥkam* and Q. 81:29, "(But) ye shall not will except that God wills, the Cherisher of the Worlds" to be *mutashābih*, whereas the Sunnite does exactly the opposite. In order to transcend this partisan basis on which verses are classified as either *muḥkam* or *mutashābih*, al-Rāzī proposes a universal rule. If a word has two meanings, one "apparent" and the other "non-apparent," and we in fact construe the word in a given context according to its apparent meaning, then the verse is *muḥkam*. If, however, the word is construed according to its "non-apparent" meaning, then the verse is *mutashābih*. But—and this is crucial—the non-apparent meaning can be preferred over the obvious meaning solely by virtue of an independent proof or indicator (*dalīl munfaṣil*) requiring that the normally non-preponderant meaning be given preference over the preponderant meaning in the context of a given verse.

Such indicators, according to al-Rāzī, are theoretically of two kinds: lexical (*lafẓī*) and rational (*ᶜaqlī*).[41] As it turns out, however, corroborative lexical evidence is an unreliable guide to the definitive establishment of a verse's meaning. The reason for this is that when a word has two opposing[42] meanings, explains al-Rāzī, one may advance two possible reasons for preferring one meaning over the other: (1) that one meaning is conclusive in its lexical signification (*qāṭiᶜ fī dalālatih*) while the other is inconclusive (*ghayr qāṭiᶜ*), causing the former to be preferred over the latter; or (2) that both meanings are preponderant (*rājiḥ*), albeit one is more preponderant (*arjaḥ*) than, and therefore preferred over, the other. Al-Rāzī declares the first position invalid by arguing that lexical proofs can never be fully conclusive, since they depend on various presumptive and inconclusive factors, such as the transmission of the language over time, the transmission of the language's grammar and morphology, assumption of the absence of figurative usage, assumption of the absence of equivocalness, and the lack of a contradicting factor based in revelation or reason (*ᶜadam al-muᶜāriḍ al-naqlī wa'l-ᶜaqlī*),[43] among other things. Naturally, concludes al-Rāzī, that which relies on presumptive, inconclusive evidence can itself be no more than presumptive and inconclusive, and cannot therefore be held to be of definitive, incontrovertible proof value.

But here, the question may arise: if these factors are inconclusive and engender merely weak supposition (*al-ẓann al-ḍaᶜīf*), and the identification even of univocal and apparent meaning is dependent upon them, then how can *any* verse be considered *muḥkam*? That is, how can we ever know the meaning of a verse conclusively when the meanings of the words which make up the verse cannot be established in an absolutely definitive manner—i.e., if the very means of transmission of the language over time, knowledge of its grammar and morphology, etc. are considered merely presumptive? The answer to this difficulty seems to lie in the assumption that the factors mentioned are relevant only when trying to decide between or among various non-apparent meanings. The knowledge that a given meaning is apparent/preponderant does not seem, for al-Rāzī, to depend on investigation based on the factors enumerated above. Rather, it seems that no investigation is required whatsoever in such cases, which is precisely why, one may suppose, that particular meaning is considered to be—or rather, is known to be—preponderant. Although al-Rāzī does not state any of these principles explicitly, they appear to constitute an essential part of the underlying assumptions on the basis of which he builds his argument. This inference seems, moreover, to be justified by the fact that no communication would be possible if words were not merely presumed, but rather somehow known, to have certain basic, primary meanings. This, after all, is precisely what it is to know what a word means.[44]

As for the second kind of indicator that theoretically may necessitate a preference of non-primary meaning—that is, one of two preponderant meanings being considered more preponderant than the other—al-Rāzī considers it valid, in a case where both meanings of a given word are considered likely (albeit not totally conclusive), to posit that one meaning is *more* likely or stronger than the other. In this case, however, the preference of the less preponderant over the more preponderant meaning based only on lexical or semantic indicators is still in itself presumptive (*ẓannī*), and as such cannot be relied upon as evidence in definitive (*qaṭʿī*) matters. Such matters include what al-Rāzī refers to as "fundamental issues" (*masā'il uṣūliyya*), by which he seems to understand the fundamentals of religion and creedal matters—that which is technically referred to as *uṣūl al-dīn*, literally, "the foundations of religion." Relying on such evidence appears to be valid, however, in matters of Sacred Law (*masā'il fiqhiyya*), which al-Rāzī seems to consider non-definitive (*ẓanniyya, ghayr qaṭʿiyya*).[45]

In definitive, creedal matters (i.e., *uṣūl al-dīn*), however, the non-apparent meaning of a word can be preferred over its obvious meaning only with the establishment of a definitive rational proof (*dalīl qaṭʿī ʿaqlī*) indicating that the literal implication of the word is rationally impossible (*muḥāl ʿaqlan*) in a given context. In such a case, *ta'wīl*, or the preference of the secondary, non-preponderant meaning over the preponderant one, becomes incumbent. Once again, it must be stressed that the existence of conclusive rational evidence is the *only means*, according to al-Rāzī, by which the non-apparent meaning of a word can supersede—or, more precisely, must supersede—its apparent meaning. In other words, the existence of such a rational proof or indicator is both a necessary and a sufficient condition for making *ta'wīl*, obligating the exegete to abandon the word's literal signification in favor of its secondary, non-apparent meaning.[46]

At this juncture in his argument, the very pith of al-Rāzī's understanding of the issue of *muḥkam* versus *mutashābih* begins to unfold. Al-Rāzī's granting of paramount status to *ʿaql*, or reason, above all other modes of knowing—such as religious knowledge apprehended through transmission (*naql*), for example, which he does not mention at all in this connection[47]—is confirmed by the fact that he makes reason the sole criterion of judgment in what he considers to be the most crucial and sensitive issues (i.e., the *masā'il uṣūliyya*), those issues in which nothing less than definitive, non-speculative—and therefore fully reliable—knowledge may be countenanced.

As we have seen, then, a verse is considered *mutashābih* whenever a word has two possible meanings, one of which is "apparent" and the other "non-apparent," *and* the usage in a given context necessitates the preference of the non-apparent meaning over the apparent meaning. An example of such a *mutashābih* verse is Q. 9:67, where God says: *nasū 'llāha fa-nasiyahum*, i.e., "They have forgotten God, so He hath forgotten them." In this case, the apparent meaning of *nasiya*, "to forget," entails an imperfection in knowledge, which cannot rationally be posited of God, Whose knowledge is necessarily perfect and encompassing of all things. Consequently, this situation necessitates a deferral to the "non-apparent" meaning of *nasiya*, which, according to al-Rāzī, is "to leave alone" or "to abandon." This verse, therefore, is considered *mutashābih* precisely because the non-apparent meaning must be preferred over the literal meaning, as opposed to *muḥkam* verses containing the same root word, such as Q. 19:64, *wa-mā kāna rabbuka nasiyyan*, "and thy Lord never doth forget," and Q. 20:52, *lā yaḍillu rabbī wa-lā yansā*, "My Lord neither errs, nor does He forget." In these two cases, there is no reason[48] not to interpret these verses in function of the literal, apparent meaning of the root *nasiya,* i.e., "to forget."[49]

It is to be noted that throughout this discussion, the categories of "apparent" and "non-apparent" appear to be strictly semantic categories, that is, they pertain exclusively to the primary versus the secondary meaning of a polysemantic word taken as a lexical item *in abstractum*, regardless of the context in which the word may appear in an actual text. In other words, when the word *nasiya* in *nasū 'llāha fa-nasiyahum* ("They have forgotten God, so He hath forgotten them") is taken to mean "left alone, abandoned" rather than "forgot," this does not mean that "left alone, abandoned" happens to be the apparent meaning in this particular instance only, since "to forget" is always the apparent meaning of the phonetic compound *nasiya*. Rather, this instance is properly described, quite simply, as one in which the non-apparent meaning, "to leave, abandon," has been preferred over the apparent meaning based on the decisive rational impossibility of ascribing forgetfulness, in the proper sense, to God.

Be that as it may, pursues al-Rāzī, once it has become clear, based on an incontrovertible rational proof, that God could not have meant a particular word in a given context to be interpreted according to its preponderant meaning, it is not then valid to speculate as to what non-apparent meaning of the word actually applies in the given context. This is especially true in the case of "decisive issues" regarding creed (*masā'il uṣūliyya*), since attempting to establish specific non-apparent meanings for the relevant verses can only lead to presumptive, inconclusive results. This is so, according to al-Rāzī, because any speculation in an attempt to fix the non-apparent meaning would entail either giving preference to one metaphorical meaning over another metaphorical meaning (*tarjīḥ majāz ᶜalā majāz*), or preferring one non-apparent meaning over another.[50] Now, neither of these interpretive processes can obtain except by means of lexical or semantic indicators, which al-Rāzī has already argued to be merely presumptive and, therefore, inconclusive. It is for this reason that al-Rāzī declares it impermissible to speculate in creedal matters regarding the specific non-apparent meaning intended in a given context.[51]

Now, while al-Rāzī's argument here is cohesive enough, he seems to be somewhat inconsistent with himself in practice, since with regard to the verse *nasū 'llāha fa-nasiyahum* ("They have forgotten God, so He hath forgotten them"), he *does* specify the non-apparent meaning of *nasiya* as "leaving, abandoning" (*tark*), as we have seen. It may simply be, however, that al-Rāzī considers this issue to be non-definitive (*ghayr qaṭᶜī*), in which case it would seemingly be permissible to entertain speculation as to the specific, non-apparent import of the word *nasiya*. Alternatively, it may be that al-Rāzī considers the word *nasiya* to have only one, rather than numerous, non-apparent meanings, such that no actual speculation would be involved as to the meaning of the verse once a definitive rational indicator has established the inadmissibility of interpreting the word in question according to its apparent meaning.

The implication of al-Rāzī's argument here seems to be that although reason is capable of determining that the apparent meaning of a given word could not have been intended in a particular context, it is never capable of determining positively which of various contending non-apparent meanings is, in fact, meant in the case specified. We may infer from this, however, that when the apparent meaning is clearly inadmissible and there is only one non-apparent meaning, there is no harm in specifying the meaning of the verse in accordance with this (non-apparent) meaning. Not allowing this would imply that the verse in question simply has no knowable meaning at all. This is so, of course, because if a word has exactly two meanings, one apparent and the other non-apparent, and reason has established the impossibility of interpreting the passage according to the apparent meaning, then we have, in fact, no choice but to interpret the verse in accordance with this (one and only) non-apparent meaning of the word. Yet if this is the case, then are we not in a position to claim to know exactly what the verse means? And if so, then what does it mean for the verse still to be considered *mutashābih*?

After presenting in some detail various other views that have been held regarding the *muḥkam–mutashābih* dichotomy, as well as the manifold benefits of having ambiguous verses in the Qur'ān,[52] al-Rāzī proceeds to tackle the next segment of Q. 3:7, which reads: *hunna umm al-kitāb*, i.e., "they [the *muḥkam* verses] are the foundation, or 'mother,' of the Book." In explicating this verse, al-Rāzī points out that from a semantic perspective, the word *umm* signifies the root (*aṣl*) from which something derives. *Muḥkam*, or "clear," verses are the "root" of *mutashābih*, or "ambiguous," verses in the sense that the former are understood immediately in and of themselves (*bi-dhawātihā*),[53] while the latter can be understood only with recourse to the former to clarify them.[54]

Judging from al-Rāzī's previous arguments, however, one would have presumed that ambiguous verses could not be clarified *per se*, but only "clarified" as being ambiguous. One may ask, therefore, what precisely it means to clarify ambiguous verses by referring them back to unambiguous ones. Alternatively, perhaps what al-Rāzī means to say is that we must refer to the *muḥkam* verses for clarification on the overall subject dealt with in both the ambiguous verse as well as in the clear verse purported to be its *umm*, without, however, attempting to fix the precise meaning of the ambiguous verse in question. Is, therefore, the *umm* of a verse like *al-Raḥmānu ᶜalā 'l-ᶜarshi 'stawā*, literally "the Merciful has settled upon the throne," a verse like *laysa ka-mithlihi shay'*, "there is nothing like unto Him"? Are the *umm*s of a verse like *nasū 'llāha fa-nasiyahum* ("They have forgotten God, so He hath forgotten them") verses like *lā yaḍillu rabbī wa-lā yansā*, ("My Lord neither errs, nor does He forget") and *wa-mā kāna rabbuka nasiyyan* ("and thy Lord never doth forget")? This would indeed appear to be the case, especially since al-Rāzī has earlier identified the latter verse(s) in each of these instances as the *muḥkam* of the former, *mutashābih* verse.

Having firmly established the meaning of *muḥkam* and *mutashābih*, al-Rāzī then moves on to the following part of the verse, which reads: "But those in whose hearts is perversity (*zaygh*) follow the part thereof that is allegorical, seeking discord, and searching for its hidden meanings." Al-Rāzī clarifies that the word *zaygh* here signifies a "leaning away from the truth," then cites several opinions of past scholars regarding the possible identification of those who may have occasioned the revelation of this verse. In one opinion, for instance, this group is to be identified with the delegation from Najran whose members argued with the Prophet regarding Jesus. On another view, it refers to the Jews in Medina, who tried to calculate how long the Islamic community would last on the basis of the detached letters (*al-ḥurūf al-muqaṭṭaᶜa*) found at the beginning of certain chapters of the Qur'ān. According to yet another position, the reference here is to the unbelievers in general, who deny the final resurrection. Regardless of who may have been the immediate cause for the revelation of this verse, however, al-Rāzī asserts that the *import* thereof is nonetheless of general application regarding any and all who seek to support invalid opinions or positions by clinging to ambiguous verses. Al-Rāzī grounds this assertion by appealing to the well-known juridical principle according to which *khuṣūṣ al-sabab lā yamnaᶜu ᶜumūm al-lafẓ*,[55] that is, the fact that the revelation of a verse was occasioned by a specific cause neither negates nor restricts the general applicability of the verse's import. Al-Rāzī then states that among that which is ambiguous in the Qur'ān is anything that contains obscurity, uncertainty or abstruseness (*labs*) on the one hand or dubiousness (*ishtibāh*) on the other, including such things as the victory God has promised to the Prophet and the retribution He has promised to the unbelievers.[56]

Al-Rāzī then gives two concrete examples of groups that have appealed to what he views as clearly ambiguous verses to uphold their errant positions. The first is with regard to the anthropomorphists and their literal interpretation of Q. 5:20, *al-Raḥmānu ᶜalā 'l-ᶜarshi 'stawā* ("The Merciful has settled upon the throne"), despite the fact that this verse is, according to al-Rāzī, undisputedly "ambiguous," or *mutashābih*. This is made clear by the obvious dictates of reason (*ṣarīḥ al-ᶜaql*), according to which any entity contained in a space (*mukhtaṣṣ bi'l-ḥayyiz*) must either exist as a small, inseparable particle of a larger whole (i.e., it must be an atom), or else be larger than that, in which case it is composite and, consequently, divisible. As all composites are ontologically contingent (*mumkin*) and originated in time (*muḥdath*), says al-Rāzī, it is clear that God—Whose existence is both necessary and sempiternal—cannot be contained in a space, which confirms the rational necessity of classifying the verse in question as *mutashābih*. This particular instance, we may note in passing, appears to exemplify precisely one of those cases where a decisive rational indicator necessitates a transfer to non-apparent meaning.

Al-Rāzī's second example of the partisan abuse of *mutashābih* verses concerns the Muᶜtazilites, who attribute the production of acts in their totality to human beings (*tafwīḍ al-fiᶜl bi'l-kulliyya ilā al-ᶜabd*)[57] by maintaining the apparent meaning of verses which imply this.[58] Nevertheless, argues al-Rāzī, the proof of reason makes it clear that the actualization of an act depends on the occurrence of an occasioning factor (*ḥuṣūl al-dāᶜī*) external to the agent. Now, it has further been established that the occurrence of such a factor stems from God alone, and that whenever God causes the occasioning factor to be present, the act *must* necessarily follow. Conversely, whenever the occasioning factor is absent, the act must also of necessity *not* occur. The notion of *tafwīḍ* having thus been disproved, it becomes clear that all acts occur solely as a result of the will and decree (*qaḍā'*, *qadar* and *mashī'a*) of God—a position central to Ashᶜarism and the Ashᶜarites. The contrary conclusions of the Muᶜtazilites based on the literal meaning of selected verses constitute, therefore, nothing more than specious deductions based on passages that, for al-Rāzī, are clearly *mutashābih*. Such verses as exploited by the Muᶜtazilites, as well as Q. 5:20 (discussed in the previous paragraph), must, according to al-Rāzī, be taken as *mutashābih*, with the result that they also must be construed according to their non-apparent meaning,[59] as reason itself has ruled out any possibility of the preponderance of their literal signification.[60]

Al-Rāzī then laments once again the fact that most people classify verses as *muḥkam* or *mutashābih* merely so as to concur with their own parochial point of view. The impartial investigator, however, classifies verses into three categories. First are those verses whose apparent meaning is confirmed by rational evidence; this, according to al-Rāzī, is true non-ambiguity (*al-muḥkam ḥaqqan*).[61] Second are those verses whose interpretation based on apparent meaning has been precluded by conclusive (rational) indicants (*dalā'il qāṭᶜiyya*). This is the category in which a judgment is made, based on rational indicators, that the meaning intended by God is, of necessity, other than the apparent meaning; such verses are of definitive ambiguity. The third category comprises those verses for which no clear evidence exists either in favor of making the apparent meaning preponderate over the non-apparent meaning, or vice versa. Such verses are *mutashābih* by virtue of the fact that neither of the first two possibilities clearly outweighs the other. In such cases, according to al-Rāzī, it would most likely be closest to the intended meaning to interpret such verses according to their apparent meaning.[62] But this, al-Rāzī seems to imply, still does not make the verses unambiguous. In other words, if we favor a verse's literal meaning as a way of erring on the side of caution without it being clear that the literal meaning *must* apply, then the verse must still be considered *mutashābih*.[63] Admittedly, it is not entirely clear what is meant here by apparent meanings being positively confirmed by rational evidence. Thus far in his exegesis of Q. 3:7, as we have seen, al-Rāzī has laid down the principle that verses are to be interpreted literally according to their apparent meaning as a matter of course, unless a rational indicator proves this to be impossible. He has not, however, set down any criteria for when reason can—or should—positively confirm the appropriateness of deferring to literal meaning. Further, it is unclear from the relevant passage as to whether the confirmatory rational evidence alluded to—whatever it may consist in—is *necessary* for establishing literal meaning, or merely corroborative.

At this point in his commentary, al-Rāzī returns to the segment of Q. 3:7 with which he was last dealing, namely: "But those in whose hearts is perversity follow the part thereof that is allegorical, seeking discord, and searching for its hidden meanings." This segment of the verse, asserts al-Rāzī, confirms the existence of a group of people whose hearts are afflicted by an inclination away from the truth (*zaygh*) and who cleave to the ambiguous verses of the Qur'ān to the exclusion of those of univocal import. Two explicit objectives of such people are given in the verse itself, namely: (1) the desire to incite discord (*fitna*), and (2) the desire to make *ta'wīl*, or interpretation, of these verses. We shall present only al-Rāzī's treatment of the second of these two motives, since it is the question of *ta'wīl* that is directly relevant to our discussion.

Al-Rāzī explains that the word *ta'wīl* in this verse means *tafsīr* ("explication," "exegesis"), and that it is semantically related to the words *marji*ᶜ and *maṣīr*, roughly "a place of return," or "an original place to which someone or something goes back." Al-Rāzī shows that *tafsīr* is referred to as *ta'wīl* in the Qur'ān itself, such as in Q. 18:78, *sa-unabbi'uka bi-ta'wīli mā lam tastaṭi*ᶜ *ᶜalayhi ṣabran*, "Now will I tell you the interpretation (*ta'wīl*) of (those things) over which you were unable to hold patience." With respect to the specific passage regarding *muḥkam* and *mutashābih* verses which forms the subject of this article, al-Rāzī explains that what is meant by those who seek *ta'wīl* is that such people demand the explanation of things for whose details there are no proofs or explicit indications to be found in the Book of God. Such questions include, for instance, precisely when the Last Hour is to be established, what the exact amount of reward and punishment on the Day of Judgment shall be, and other such matters. It is important to point out that the *ta'wīl* referred to here is of a different nature from the *ta'wīl* discussed up until now with regard to the preference of non-apparent over apparent meaning. Whereas that *ta'wīl* was a neutral, factual category relating simply to the non-preponderant, or secondary, meanings of words having more than one signification, al-Rāzī makes it clear that *ta'wīl* as alluded to in this segment of the verse amounts to an unjustified, reprovable presumptuousness in hazarding to identify specifically the precise meaning or nature of things known only to God.[64]

Al-Rāzī then proceeds to explicate the subsequent segment of the verse, which reads: "But no one knows its hidden meanings except God; and those who are firmly grounded in knowledge say: 'We believe in the Book'." As al-Rāzī explains, people have differed in their understanding of this part of the verse. Some, for instance, are of the view that there is an obligatory pause after "But no one knows its hidden meanings except God" and that the conjunctive particle *wa* ("and") in the phrase "and those who are firmly grounded in knowledge" is a case of what is known in Arabic grammar as *wāw al-ibtidā'*, or "the *wāw* of beginning," which serves to introduce a new sentence or phrase. According to this interpretation, God alone knows the real meaning of the ambiguous verses. This position, al-Rāzī reports, was held by such early figures of authority as Ibn ᶜAbbās (d. 68/687–8), ᶜĀ'isha (d. 58/678), al-Ḥasan al-Baṣrī (d. 110/728), Mālik ibn Anas (d. 179/795), al-Kisā'ī (d. ca. 189/805), al-Farrā' (d. 207/822) and the Muᶜtazilite al-Jubbā'ī (d. 303/915–16), and happens to be the opinion that he himself favors as well. Adherents of a contrasting position contend that the pause comes after "and those who are firmly grounded in knowledge," in which case not only God, but also "those firmly grounded in knowledge,"—whoever they may be—know the real meaning of the ambiguous verses. Al-Rāzī states that this opinion was also reported of Ibn ᶜAbbās, as well as of Mujāhid (d. between 100/718 and 104/722), al-Rabīᶜ ibn Anas (d. during the rule of the ᶜAbbāsid caliph al-Manṣūr, r. 136–58 / 754–75) and "most of the *mutakallimūn*," or dialectical theologians.[65] Nevertheless, asserts al-Rāzī, the arguments which recommend the first position are numerous. In support of this position, al-Rāzī himself advances six arguments, some in great detail, of which we shall present only the two most relevant ones. The remaining four arguments entail mostly grammatical and stylistic issues which, though not inherently uninteresting, do not bear immediate relevance to our topic of concern.

According to the first argument, then, if a word has a preponderant meaning and, simultaneously, a strong indicator (*dalīl*) denotes that the apparent meaning is not what was meant by God, then the intended meaning must consist in some metaphorical interpretation of the obvious, outer meaning of the text. Now, metaphorical meanings of a given word are often numerous, and the preference of one metaphorical meaning over another could only come about through linguistic indicators, which, as al-Rāzī has previously argued, yield no more than presumptive, and hence inconclusive, knowledge. Now if the issue at hand is one of those definitive matters concerning fundamentals of the creed, which can brook nothing short of absolute certainty (*masā'il qaṭᶜiyya yaqīniyya*), then it is invalid to attempt to specify the exact meaning through such inconclusive evidence. An example of such a verse is Q. 2:286, *lā yukallifu 'llāhu nafsan illā wusᶜahā*,[66] "God does not lay on any soul a burden greater than it can bear." The issue addressed in this verse, according to al-Rāzī, counts as one of those definitive matters concerning fundamentals, presumably because it deals with creedal issues such as the nature of God's actions and the nature of His relationship to and interaction with His creation. Now, al-Rāzī refers us to five arguments which he has elaborated in his explication of the verse mentioned above which together form conclusive proof that such *taklīf* (i.e., God's laying upon a soul more than it can bear) has indeed taken place, with the consequence that this particular verse must have been meant to be taken metaphorically and not literally. However, since metaphorical meanings are many and can be preferentially ordered only on the basis of inconclusive linguistic indicators, and furthermore, since this verse treats of a definitive creedal matter, it is entirely invalid to attempt to specify precisely which of the possible metaphorical meanings may have been intended by God. It follows, once again, that only God Himself can know the real meaning of *mutashābih* verses such as this one.[67]

Furthermore, we may note as well that although it is permissible to speculate concerning the non-apparent meaning which may have been intended in a verse dealing with non-definitive matters (*masā'il ẓanniyya*), this does not imply that the real meaning of such verses can thereby be uncovered, but only that speculation with regard to their meaning is not prohibited as it is with definitive issues. The conclusions reached, however, are still every bit as presumptive. Consistent application of this principle would seem to imply that al-Rāzī, if he is not in contradiction with himself, must view a verse such as *nasū 'llāha fa-nasiyahum* ("They have forgotten God, so He hath forgotten them")—discussed earlier on—as one pertaining merely to a non-definitive matter, since he takes the liberty to speculate as to the intended meaning of the verb *nasiya* when applied to God, namely, that it metaphorically signifies an abandonment or a leaving alone (*tark*). An alternative explanation might be that al-Rāzī does in fact consider this to be a definitive matter (*mas'ala qaṭʿiyya*), but that *tark* is the one and only non-apparent meaning of the word *nasiya*, such that the meaning of the verse can still be determined with precision.

The second argument adduced by al-Rāzī concerning where the obligatory pause in reading the verse should occur[68] draws attention to the fact that in the preceding section of the verse, God has censured those who seek out the meaning of ambiguous verses. If pursuing their meaning were a legitimate activity from which human beings—those "firmly grounded in knowledge" among them—could legitimately derive knowledge, God would not have declared it reproachable. Al-Rāzī here raises, and subsequently responds to, a potential objection to this line of argument. Perhaps, the objection goes, God's criticism in this instance is directed specifically and exclusively to those who ask about eschatological issues, such as the coming of the Last Hour, precise details concerning otherworldly reward and punishment, and so forth. Al-Rāzī's response to this objection is that if God has stated that He has divided the Qur'ān into two kinds of verses—clear (*muḥkam*) and ambiguous (*mutashābih*)—and then imputed those who seek to specify the exact meaning of the ambiguous verses, it follows that our subsequent restriction, without solid evidence, of the universality of God's reproof such that it would refer only to some ambiguous verses to the exclusion of others, would itself entail an abandonment of the obvious, apparent meaning of the verse in question. In other words, we would be making *ta'wīl* of Q. 3:7 itself, which is clearly preposterous. That is, since Q. 3:7 is the very verse which establishes the categories of *muḥkam* and *mutashābih* in the Qur'ān, it must *a priori* be considered *muḥkam*, for it would be quite paradoxical indeed if the very passage delineating the categories of clear and ambiguous verses within the Holy Book were itself of equivocal import![69]

Al-Rāzī concludes this section on the possibility of ascertaining specifically the meanings of *mutashābih* verses by referring to the response of the great jurist and early religious authority Mālik ibn Anas (d. 179/795) when asked about God's act of settling (*istiwā'*) upon His throne—namely, that the fact of God's settling is known; that the modality, or the "how" of it, however, is unknown; that belief in it is mandatory for the Muslim; and that inquiring into it—i.e., into its inherently unfathomable aspects—is *bidᶜa*, a reprehensible innovation in matters of religion. This instance seems to reflect quite accurately al-Rāzī's own position regarding what he views as sheer presumption, manifested in the illegitimate attempt to specify the exact meaning of *mutashābih* verses that deal with fundamental creedal matters whose details, in some instances, remain known exclusively to God—a remarkably cautious position, at the end of the day, for a thinker as philosophically inclined as al-Rāzī. This more than anything, perhaps, confirms that al-Rāzī—notwithstanding his recurrent forays into the outer bounds of philosophical speculation—remains, when all is said and done, firmly implanted in the worldview of the classical Ashᶜarite theologians.

•

At length we come to the end of Q. 3:7, where al-Rāzī comments on the verse's very final segment: "and none will grasp the message except men of understanding." According to our author, this statement means that only those who have complete, perfected minds (*dhawū 'l-ᶜuqūl al-kāmila*) receive admonition from what is in the Qur'ān. Al-Rāzī interprets this portion of the verse as affirming that such people as use their minds and intellects in understanding the Qur'ān are considered particularly worthy of praise. Such men know God's essence and attributes by means of definitive rational indicators and likewise know, on account of similarly conclusive evidence, that the Qur'ān is the Word of God. They distinguish clearly those verses whose outer, apparent meaning conforms to the dictates of reason (*dalā'il al-ᶜuqūl*) and recognize them to be "clear verses of established meaning," i.e., *muḥkam*. Likewise, they are able to identify those verses whose outer meaning contradicts the evidence of reason—or which contain words of equivocal signification—and recognize these as ambiguous, or *mutashābih*. Since they are assured that all of the Qur'ān comes from God, in Whose Book no contradiction or falsehood is in evidence, they comprehend that the ambiguous verses necessarily have a correct, definitive interpretation which, nonetheless, is known only unto their Author. They believe in all of the revelation, as it is all from their Lord, and their faith is disquieted neither by their inability to fix with precision the meanings of the *mutashābih* verses nor by the very presence of such in the Holy Book.[70]

NOTES

1. The verse in Arabic reads: *Huwa 'lladhī anzala ᶜalayka 'l-kitāba minhu āyātun muḥkamātun hunna ummu 'l-kitābi wa-ukharu mutashābihātun fa-ammā 'lladhīna fī qulūbihim zayghun fa-yattabiᶜūna mā tashābaha minhu 'btighā'a 'l-fitnati wa-'btighā'a ta'wīlihi wa-mā yaᶜlamu ta'wīlahu illā 'llāhu wa-'l-rāsikhūna fī'l-ᶜilmi yaqūlūna āmannā bihi kullun min ᶜindi rabbinā wa-mā yadhdhakkaru illā ulū 'l-albāb.*

2. These are Q. 11:1, which reads: "*Alif, Lām, Rā'*. (This is) a book, with verses basic or fundamental (of established meaning) [*kitābun uḥkimat āyātuhu*], further explained in detail—from One Who is Wise and Well-Acquainted (with all things)" and Q. 47:20, which reads: "Those who believe say, 'Why is not a *sūra* sent down (for us)?' But when a *sūra* of basic or categorical meaning [*sūra muḥkama*] is revealed, and fighting is mentioned therein, thou wilt see those in whose hearts is a disease looking at thee with a look of one in swoon at the approach of death." The English renditions of Qur'ānic verses throughout this essay have been taken, with occasional slight modifications, from ᶜAbdullāh Yūsuf ᶜAlī, *The Holy Qur'ān: Text, Translation and Commentary* (Brentwood: Amana Corporation, 1409/1989).

3. Q. 39:23: "God has revealed the most beautiful message in the form of a book, consistent with itself [*mutashābihan*], (yet) repeating (its teaching in various aspects)."

4. For an excellent, cross-section study of medieval commentaries on Q. 3:7 contrasting Sunnī, Shīᶜī, Muᶜtazilī and Ṣūfī approaches, as well as commentaries based on Prophetic *ḥadīth* vs. those based on presumptive reasoning (*ra'y*), see Leah Kinberg, "*Muḥkamāt* and *Mutashābihāt* (Koran 3/7): Implication of a Koranic Pair of Terms in Medieval Exegesis," *Arabica* 35 (1988): 143–72, the appendix of which also provides a concise survey of a number of modern studies on the topic. For a recent, in-depth study of Fakhr al-Dīn al-Rāzī in particular, both as a theologian and an exegete, see Yasin Ceylan, *Theology and Tafsīr in the Major Works of Fakhr al-Dīn al-Rāzī* (Kuala Lumpur, International Institute of Islamic Thought and Civilization: 1996), esp. chapter 2, "Approach to the Qur'ān."

5. This title seems to have been inspired by the Qur'ān itself, where we read (Q. 6:59), "With Him are the keys of the Unseen (*mafātiḥ al-ghayb*), the treasures that none knoweth but He."

6. For a brief survey of the life and times of Fakhr al-Dīn al-Rāzī, see M. Ṣaghīr Ḥasan Maᶜṣūmī, "Imām Fakhr al-Dīn al-Rāzī and his Critics," *Islamic Studies* 6 (1967): 355–74 [specifically 355–7]; Murtada A. Muhibbu-Din, "Imām Fakhr al-Dīn al-Rāzī: Philosophical Theology in *al-Tafsīr al-Kabīr*," *Hamdard Islamicus* 17, iii (1994): 55–84 [esp. 55–7]; and Paul Kraus, "The 'Controversies' of Fakhr al-Dîn Râzî," *Islamic Culture* 12 (1938): 131–53 [esp. 132 and 134]. For a more detailed discussion of the tumultuous political circumstances of al-Rāzī's time, and the positioning of his thought within the context of these circumstances, see the informative and insightful article of Roger Arnaldez, "L'œuvre de Fakhr al-Dīn al-Rāzī : commentateur du Coran et philosophe," *Cahiers de civilisation*

médiévale, Xᵉ–XIIᵉ siècles 3 (1960): 307–23 [esp. from the second full paragraph of 312 to the end of 314].

7. See Ibn Khallikān, *Wafayāt al-Aᶜyān wa-Anbā' al-Zamān* (Beirut: Dār al-Thaqāfa, n.d.), IV, 252, cited in Muhibbu-Din, "Imām Fakhr al-Dīn al-Rāzī," 55.

8. See Ignaz Goldziher, "Aus der Theologie des Fachr al-dīn al-Rāzī," *Der Islam* 3 (1912): 213–47, where he describes al-Rāzī as "die hervorragendste Erscheinung der spekulativen Theologie im Islam der nach-ġazālischen Zeit" (223).

9. Kraus, "Controversies," 131.

10. See Muhibbu-Din, "Imām Fakhr al-Dīn al-Rāzī," 58–62, for a listing, by name and subdivided by subject, of no fewer than 76 treatises attributed to al-Rāzī.

11. Muhibbu-Din, "Imām Fakhr al-Dīn al-Rāzī," 55.

12. Quoted in ibid., 61.

13. See Guy Monnot, "Le panorama religieux de Fahr al-Dīn al-Rāzī," *Revue de l'histoire des religions* 203 (1986): 263–80 [esp. 265]. A *mutakallim* is a practitioner of *kalām*, the name given in Islam to the discipline of theological speculation. *Falsafa*, the Arabized form of Greek *philosophia*, simply refers to the philosophical tradition—particularly Aristotelian and Neo-Platonic—inherited from Greece and further developed by the Muslim philosophers, or *falāsifa*.

14. See Arnaldez, "L'œuvre," 315, and especially Goldziher, "Aus der Theologie," 230–7, for a discussion of how al-Rāzī contravenes the Ashᶜarite position—and approaches that of the Muᶜtazilites—on the fundamental and very sensitive question of the authority of Prophetic *ḥadīth*, rejecting their use in credal matters but admitting them in the derivation of legal rulings. This difference between the standard of proof required in questions of creed versus that required in legal matters will be crucial, as we shall see below, in al-Rāzī's discussion of metaphorical interpretation with respect to *muḥkam* and *mutashābih* verses.

15. Kraus, "Controversies," 132–3.

16. See Goldziher, "Aus der Theologie," *passim.*, for various Muᶜtazilite influences on al-Rāzī's thought. See also, however, W. M. Watt, *Islamic Philosophy and Theology: an Extended Survey*, 2nd edition (Edinburgh: Edinburgh University Press, 1985), 95, who aptly remarks that the points of concurrence with Muᶜtazilite doctrine highlighted by Goldziher turn out, in the final analysis, to be fairly minor—with the exception, nonetheless, of al-Rāzī's position on the use of *ḥadīth* (see note 14 above). In light of this observation and of al-Rāzī's position overall, it must be admitted that Arnaldez' claim ("L'œuvre," 314) that al-Rāzī "borrowed so much from [the Muᶜtazilites] that his doctrine could often pass for a Neo-Muᶜtazilism" is certainly taking the issue too far.

17. Arnaldez, "L'œuvre," 315 (translation mine).

18. Ibid., 312 (translation mine).

19. Ibid., 313–14.

20. Cited in Muhibbu-Din, "Imām Fakhr al-Dīn al-Rāzī," 59 (but taken from M. M. Sharif, *History of Muslim Philosophy* [Wiesbaden: Harrassowitz, 1963]).

21. For an account of this experience as reported in the classical sources, see Jacques Jomier, "Les Mafatih al-Ghayb de l'Imam Fakhr al-Din al-Razi: quelques dates, lieux, manuscrits," *MIDEO* 13 (1977): 253–77 (esp. 273–4).

22. Muhibbu-Din, "Imām Fakhr al-Dīn al-Rāzī," 58. For a detailed study of precisely which parts of the commentary were written by al-Rāzī (and in what order) and which parts by others, see Jacques Jomier, "Les Mafatih al-Ghayb" and Jomier, "Qui a commenté l'ensemble des sourates al-ᶜAnkabūt à Yāsīn (29–36) dans 'le Tafsīr al-kabīr' de l'Imām Fakhr al-Dīn al-Rāzī?" *IJMES* 11 (1980): 467–85.

23. See, for example, Arnaldez, "L'œuvre," 320, Goldziher, "Aus der Theologie," 223 and Kraus, "Controversies," 133. It is relevant to note that despite the fact that Goldziher's article as a whole is dedicated to delineating the influence of Muᶜtazilite theology on al-Rāzī's thought, he nevertheless states: "Fakhr al-Dīn al-Rāzī is an Ashᶜarite by doctrine, and as such is pitched in a fervent battle with the Muᶜtazilites. Especially compelling [in this regard] is his large commentary on the Qur'ān, in which he dedicates lengthy discussions to refuting the Muᶜtazilites wherever they have taken a position [on a point of exegesis] that deviates from the conception generally accepted among the Orthodox." (Translation mine. See Goldziher, "Aus der Theologie," 223 for original text.) For more detail on al-Zamakhsharī and a brief, but informative, treatment of his famous Qur'ān commentary, *al-Kashshāf*, see Goldziher, "Aus der Theologie," 220–2.

24. Kraus, "Controversies," 133.

25. See Maᶜṣūmī, "Imām Fakhr al-Dīn al-Rāzī and his Critics," 357. The response cited is that of the Qāḍī Ḍiyā' al-Dīn Abū 'l-Ḥasan ᶜAlī al-Subkī (d. 725/1325).

26. See Jacques Jomier, "Fakhr al-Dīn al-Rāzī et les commentaires du Coran plus anciens," *MIDEO* 15 (1982): 145–72 for an exhaustive cataloguing of all previous scholars and exegetes referenced by al-Rāzī in his exegesis of *sūra* 3 (the very *sūra* in which appears the passage on *muḥkam* and *mutashābih* verses explored in this essay), with details on the specific information our author gleaned from each authority.

27. Two examples of such verses are Q. 39:67: "No just estimate have they made of God such as is due to Him; on the Day of Judgement, the whole of the earth will be but His handful and the heavens will be rolled up in His right hand. Glory be to Him!" and Q. 52:48: "Now await in patience the command of thy Lord, for verily thou art in Our eyes; and celebrate the praises of thy Lord the while thou standest forth."

28. Goldziher, "Aus der Theologie," 226.

29. Watt, *Islamic Philosophy and Theology*, 76 and 81, respectively. Their full names are Abū Bakr ibn al-Ṭayyib al-Bāqillānī and Abū Bakr Aḥmad ibn al-Ḥusayn al-Bayhaqī.

30. See Goldziher, "Aus der Theologie," 227, note 5.

31. Watt, *Islamic Philosophy and Theology*, 83.

32. Goldziher, "Aus der Theologie," 227.

33. This phrase, describing Paradise, appears a total of 35 times throughout the Qur'ān, in addition to three more occurrences of a very like phrase. See, for instance, Q. 2:25, 3:136, 5:12, 14:23, 25:10, 47:12, 58:22, 65:11, 98:8, et al.

34. See Arnaldez, "L'œuvre," 320, and also Goldziher, "Aus der Theologie," 228–9, of whose presentation the synopsis above is a rough paraphrase.

35. See Fakhr al-Dīn al-Rāzī, *al-Tafsīr al-kabīr* [*Mafātīḥ al-ghayb*] ([Cairo]: al-Maṭbaᶜa al-Bahiyya al-Miṣriyya, 1354–57 / 1935–38), XXIV, 179, lines 4–13.

36. The noun *ikhtilāf* ("discrepancy," "difference") in this verse is roughly antonymous to the noun *tashābuh* ("similarity," "resemblance"), from which the active participle "*mutashābih*" ("similar," "that which resembles") is derived.

37. Rāzī, *Tafsīr*, XXIV, 180, ll. 5–6.

38. For an excellent discussion on the "*waḍᶜ*," or "primordial institution" of the Arabic language as viewed by most Muslim jurists and theologians, see Bernard G. Weiss, "*ᶜIlm al-Waḍᶜ*: An Introductory Account of a Later Muslim Philological Science," *Arabica* 34 (1987): 339–56; Weiss, "Language and Tradition in Medieval Islam: The Question of *al-Ṭarīq ilā maᶜrifat al-lugha*," *Der Islam* 61 (1984): 91–9; Weiss, *Language in Orthodox Muslim Thought: A Study of "Waḍᶜ al-lugha" and its Development* (Ph.D. dissertation: Princeton University, 1966); and Weiss, *The Search for God's Law: Islamic Jurisprudence in the Writings of Sayf al-Dīn al-Āmidī* (Salt Lake City: University of Utah Press, 1992), 117–150.

39. Rāzī, *Tafsīr*, XXIV, 188, ll. 6–10.

40. See ibid., XXIV, 180, ll. 2–18.

41. Ibid., XXIV, 180, l. 26 – 181, l. 7.

42. It is not clear why al-Rāzī uses the word "opposing" (*taʿāruḍ*) here, which to me implies that the meanings referred to must necessarily be opposite or in direct contradiction to each other, such as in the case of the word *qur'*, which al-Rāzī cites (in a different context) as referring to both menses (*ḥayḍ*) and purity (*ṭuhr*). I take *taʿāruḍ* here to describe simply a case in which a word has two *different* meanings, regardless of whether those two meanings are in actual contradiction to each other or not.

43. This phrase is admittedly unclear, even in context (see *Tafsīr*, XXIV, 181, ll. 13–17), and it is unfortunate that al-Rāzī does not expound upon it any further.

44. This particular paragraph of al-Rāzī's commentary is, we must concede, somewhat vague. Grasping every detail of the argument, however, does not seem to be of critical importance for our purposes. In fact, it seems that al-Rāzī is simply nitpicking in his insistence that we can never claim a word to be absolutely conclusive (*qāṭiʿ*) in its signification, although, as we shall see in the next paragraph, we can say that one of the word's meanings is more primary than the other, which is really what is essential for being able to categorize a verse as *muḥkam* or *mutashābih*.

45. This interpretation of al-Rāzī's conception of definitive versus non-definitive matters is corroborated by our secondary sources. See, for instance, Goldziher, "Aus der Theologie," 230, 232 and 233, as well as Arnaldez, "L'œuvre," 315.

46. See Rāzī, *Tafsīr*, XXIV, 181, ll. 18–25.

47. For a detailed treatment of al-Rāzī's attitude towards and use of Prophetic *ḥadīth*, especially as it contrasts with those of most mainstream scholars including the Ashʿarites, see Goldziher, "Aus der Theologie," 230–7. See also Arnaldez, "L'œuvre," 309, on the position of the Muʿtazilites with respect to *ḥadīth* and why, because of their rationalism, they ended up opposing the *muḥaddithūn* (scholars of *ḥadīth*).

48. I understand "reason" here to mean "rational proof," as this is the only criterion al-Rāzī allows for preferring the non-apparent meaning over the more obvious, apparent meaning of a word.

49. See Rāzī, *Tafsīr*, XXIV, 180, ll. 24–5. See ll. 21–4 for another example of this phenomenon concerning Q. 17:16: "When We decide to destroy a population, We (first) send a definite command (*amarnā*) to those among them who are given the good things of this life and yet transgress; so that the word is proven true against them: then We destroy them utterly." The apparent meaning of this verse is that the impious inhabitants of the city are commanded by God to commit iniquities, which cannot be understood in its literal sense, as God never commands, properly speaking, the commission of evil deeds, a fact evidenced by Q. 7:28: "Nay, God never commands (*ya'mur*) what is shameful." This latter verse is, according to al-Rāzī, the *muḥkam* of the former verse, and was meant to respond to those evil-doers who have the shameless effrontery to blame their own misdeeds on God, as reflected in the first part of Q. 7:28, which reads: "When they do aught that is shameful, they say: 'We found our fathers doing so' and 'God commanded us (*amaranā*) thus.'"

50. Only in the case, presumably, where there is morе than just one non-apparent meaning, as previously explained.

51. Rāzī, *Tafsīr*, XXIV, 181, l. 25 – 182, l. 7.

52. See ibid., XXIV, 183, l. 17 – 185, l. 2, esp. 184, l. 5 ff. Also see Michel Lagarde, "De l'ambiguïté (*mutašābih*) dans le Coran: tentatives d'explication des exégètes musulmans," *Quaderni di Studi Arabi* 3 (1985): 45–62 (esp. Section 3, "Les avantages du *mutašābih*," 53–4) for an account of the various benefits of *mutashābih* verses being in the Qur'ān as enumerated by al-Rāzī, as well as other scholars, such as al-Zamakhsharī in his *Kashshāf*, Jalāl al-Dīn al-Suyūṭī (d. 911/1505) in his *Itqān fī ʿUlūm al-Qur'ān* and, more recently,

Rashīd Riḍā (d. 1354/1935) in *Al-Manār*. Among the advantages cited are, for example, that the presence of *mutashābih* verses renders apprehension of the truth more difficult and challenging, thereby resulting in greater reward for those who undertake the task of interpretation. Further benefits derive from the fact that the presence of *mutashābih* verses in the Qur'ān requires the speculative theologian to exploit the guidance of reason, thereby escaping the darkness of blind adherence to received doctrine (*taqlīd*). Furthermore, scholars' attempts to discover the meaning of *mutashābih* verses require them to be adept at various methods of weighing conflicting interpretations against each other, which in turn compels them to develop and cultivate numerous and beneficial auxiliary sciences, such as linguistics, jurisprudence, etc. Finally, the strongest reason for the Qur'ān comprising *mutashābih* verses, according to al-Rāzī, lies in the fact that their presence allows fundamental concepts not easily absorbed by the common man to be presented gradually. For instance, if a common person were told of the existence of a non-corporeal being that neither occupies space nor can be indicated by direction (i.e., God), he may easily leap to the conclusion that the being in question is merely nothingness (*ᶜadam*) and negation (*nafy*), thereby falling into the error of *taᶜṭīl*, i.e., denying God's positive attributes altogether (the cardinal sin, we might add, of the Muᶜtazilites and the *falāsifa*). *Mutashābih* verses describing God in seemingly anthropomorphic terms, therefore, serve the purpose of communicating to the simple mind at least some aspects of the nature and attributes of the Diving Being, until such a time as the understanding can absorb the concept of God's complete and utter transcendence and His lack of resemblance to anything human—fundamental truths spelled out clearly in the Qur'ān's numerous *muḥkam* verses dealing with the nature of God (particularly the previously cited verse *laysa ka-mithlihi shay'* : "There is nothing like unto Him" — Q. 42:11).

53. That is, presumably, by the same type of (linguistic) intuition by which one is able to identify the preponderant meaning of a word as such.

54. See Rāzī, *Tafsīr*, XXIV, 185, ll. 8–11. This is also true of a second example of this sort which al-Rāzī gives on XXIV, 180, l. 21–4.

55. See ibid., XXIV, 186, l. 12.

56. Ibid., XXIV, 186, ll. 3–14. This last sentence is somewhat unclear, and unfortunately al-Rāzī does not expound upon or elucidate it any further. Nevertheless, it does afford added insight into al-Rāzī's thinking on what kinds of verses are *mutashābih*, although what he means precisely still remains somewhat obscure.

57. See Rāzī, *Tafsīr*, XXIV, 186, l. 20.

58. Consider, for instance, Q. 18:29: "Say, 'The Truth is from your Lord': Let him who will, believe, and let him who will, reject (it)" or Q. 4:79: "Whatever good (O man!) happens to thee, is from God; but whatever evil happens to thee is from thy (own) soul."

59. Understood, one may ask, according to their (one) non-apparent meaning, or simply left un-interpreted once we know that the literal meaning does not apply?

60. Rāzī, *Tafsīr*, XXIV, 186, l. 15 – 187, l. 23.

61. Assuming, of course, that the word is not univocal (*naṣṣ*), in which case there is only one possible meaning to begin with.

62. See Rāzī, *Tafsīr*, XXIV, 188, l. 2.

63. Ibid., XXIV, 187, l. 23 – 188, l. 3.

64. Ibid., XXIV, 188, ll. 12–20.

65. See ibid., XXIV, 188, l. 20 – 189, l. 1.

66. Very similar to this is Q 2:233, *lā tukallafu nafsun illā wusᶜahā*, "No soul is charged with a burden greater than it can bear," as well as Q. 6:152, 7:42 and 23:62, all of which read *lā nukallifu nafsan illā wusᶜahā*, "We [God] do not lay on any soul a burden greater than it can bear."

67. Rāzī, *Tafsīr*, XXIV, 189, ll. 2–15.

68. The reader will recall that what is at issue here is whether the verse is to be read: "But no one knows its hidden meanings except God. And those who are firmly grounded in knowledge say: 'We believe in the Book; the whole of it is from our Lord'" or rather: "But no one knows its hidden meanings except God *and* those who are firmly grounded in knowledge. They [i.e., those who are firmly grounded in knowledge] say: 'We believe in the Book…'"— with the obvious implications this has for whether human beings can ever ultimately know the true meaning of *mutashābih* verses in the Qur'ān, or whether God has reserved such knowledge for Himself alone, for a wisdom known only unto Him.

69. Rāzī, *Tafsīr*, XXIV, 189, ll. 16–25.

70. Ibid., XXIV, 191, ll. 3–6 and ll. 13–17.

Chapter 8

Qur'ān and *Ḥadīth* in the School of Al-Suhrawardī

Qamar-ul Huda

The process of scriptural reasoning for Suhrawardī Ṣūfī scholars entailed a complex hermeneutical methodology consisting of theology, philosophy, linguistics, and legal studies. Unlike the disputations between the jurists, where Qur'ānic commentaries (*tafāsīr*) were tied to discovering the legal nature of the text, Ṣūfī commentaries were more connected to the inner journey of encountering the divine. Many Ṣūfī scholars were also trained as jurists, and wrote separate Qur'ānic commentaries to contribute the legal discipline. However, within Ṣūfī treatises there is an enormous wealth of scholarly exegesis of the Qur'ān and *ḥadīth* to illustrate the unity of *taṣawwuf* and Islamic scholarship. Ṣūfī scholars like Abū Ḥafṣ ᶜUmar al-Suhrawardī (lived 539/1145–632/1234), and his disciples such as Bahā' al-Dīn Zakariyyā (d. 661/1262) and Jalāl al-Dīn Tabrīzī (d. ca 642/1244), wrote treatises that employed a two-pronged methodology to prepare Sūfīs for the moment of divine presence. Firstly, their focus on the Qur'ān was through lenses that were integral to their *taṣawwuf* path. The hermeneutical process for Suhrawardī scholars went beyond an intellectual exercise of dialectical argumentation. Rather, scriptural studies focused on understanding the inner Qur'ān (*baṭn al-Qur'ān*) which contained instructional messages to reunite with God and specific spiritual exercises for Ṣūfī disciples to incorporate into their prayers. Secondly, the intensive use of *ḥadīth*s displayed their authoritative knowledge of the Prophet and his extra-Qur'anic instruction, as well as the esoteric knowledge used as a real device to remember and embody the Prophet's spiritual legacy.[1]

Al-Suhrawardī's Background

Abū Ḥafṣ ᶜUmar al-Suhrawardī was initiated into the Ṣūfī path by his uncle, Abū Najīb al-Suhrawardī (d. 563/1168), who was the original shaykh of this Ṣūfī order. Al-Suhrawardī was a trained jurist (*faqīh*) in the Baghdadi Ḥanbalī legal tradition and specialized in law (*sharīᶜa*), Qur'ānic exegesis (*tafsīr*), reasoning and ethics in *taṣawwuf*, philosophy (*falsafa*) and was a scholar on the life of Prophet Muhammad (*dirasāt al-sunnā wa sīrat rasūl Allāh*). As a student of two prominent Ṣūfī shaykhs, ᶜAbd al-Qādir al-Jilānī (d. 561/1166) and Abū Najīb al-Suhrawardī, he was influenced by a pragmatic practice that asserted the supremacy of obeying the law while bringing a rational interpretation of Sufism. As a Ḥanbalī jurist he followed the tradition of presenting evidence with passages of the Qur'ān, citing sources from the *sunna* and *ḥadīth*, and using sayings from past eminent Ṣūfī masters. In the year 596/1200, the ᶜAbbāsid caliph al-Nāṣir (r. 575/1179–622/1225) designated al-Suhrawardī as *Shaykh al-Islām*, the prestigious position that administered the religious affairs for the state, thereby moving his ideas of Ṣūfī-state co-operation and his Ṣūfī order to the forefront of Islamic religious politics.[2]

Al-Suhrawardī's writings reflected a conservative tone opposing contemporaneous views such as those of Ibn al-ᶜArabī (d. 638/1240) for the excessive reliance on philosophy as the main way of theological reflection. As a trained jurist, al-Suhrawardī was a strong proponent of obeying the law closely as well as all its related disciplines, mainly because, for him, strict observance of the law (*sharīᶜa*) was related to one's spiritual ascension. For him, the *sharīᶜa* was more than a set of divine legal codes to follow; it was rather a divine path that leads the individual back to the Creator. This opposition to philosophical speculation as the sole path of contemplating on the nature of the divine was due to the fear that an untrained person could put forth an interpretation that was totally false to the tradition and that interpretation could be misconstrued as authentic to Ṣūfī teachings. Nevertheless, although al-Suhrawardī was tolerant of all kinds of Ṣūfī beliefs and practices, his activities and texts demonstrate that he was primarily interested in advancing the particular Suhrawardīyya path of law and Sufism.

Al-Suhrawardī and Reasoning

Al-Suhrawardī's *ᶜAwārif al-Maᶜārif* ("The Benefits of the Spiritually Learned")[3] is designed for Ṣūfīs to read, memorize, study, and practice *taṣawwuf* on a regular basis.[4] The text does not supplant the primary importance of the Qur'ān and the literature surrounding the Prophet, but it acts as the spiritual interpreter of the primary religious texts.[5] The function of the text is to aid in the daily spiritual exercises of *taṣawwuf* and in the intellectual growth of the Suhrawardiyya members.[6] Al-Suhrawardī's treatise ranges from Qur'ānic hermeneutics, *ḥadīth*, *tafsīr,* rational arguments on epistemology, understanding the different levels of spirituality, proper etiquette, and criticism of Ṣūfī orders and their various interpretations of the mystic path. In many of these areas, his arguments rest upon his authority on *ḥadīth* and knowledge of the Prophet which allowed him to write a guide book on Ṣūfī theology and practices. While the use of *ḥadīth* in legal, philosophical, poetical, and religious texts have been historically used for standard argumentation, *ḥadīth* in a Ṣūfī spiritual manual are important in mirroring the model of the Prophet. Al-Suhrawardī's intensive use of *ḥadīth* is a significant feature to remembering and re-enacting the life of the Prophet Muḥammad so that members of the Ṣūfī *ṭarīqa* could move from mere imagining to embodying the Prophet's spirituality. While the *Qur'ān* is repeated and delicately memorized for the ritual prayers, al-Suhrawardī's use of *ḥadīth* was primarily committed to memory in order to cultivate a closer kinship to the Prophet and maintain his sacred presence at every moment.[7] According to al-Suhrawardī, disciples who desired access to the holy needed to adhere to a hierarchical system that consisted of proper teaching in every possible way.

One of the primary areas for concern in al-Suhrawardī's treatise is his goal of developing an internal and external discipline that sharpens the intellectual abilities to comprehend *taṣawwuf.* Al-Suhrawardī was interested in having his disciples actively practice reasoning (*ᶜaql*) in understanding their *taṣawwuf* because it was important to develop the mind in conjunction with striving toward spiritual enlightenment. For him, inner enlightenment required students to be actively engaged with examining the Qur'ān and other texts in order to intellectually understand the complexities of the tradition.[8] Since al-Suhrawardī's Ṣūfī order stressed being politically active in the affairs of the state, it is logical to assume that he wanted his disciples to be intellectually capable of meeting challenges of political activities. In addition, another reason to stress the importance of *ᶜaql* in *taṣawwuf* is to distinguish his order from the antinomian Ṣūfī's who, to him, were not intellectually inclined and were actually in violation of the *sharīᶜa* and the larger Islamic tradition. On the subject of *ᶜaql,* al-Suhrawardī wrote thus :

> Reasoning (*ᶜaql*) is the job of language. The power to think is reflected in the following *ḥadīth*: First, God made the human mind so that his creation could think. The ability to use *ᶜaql* is related to worship, as another *ḥadīth* reports that with *ᶜaql* you can know me and also praise me. [9]

The statement, "The ability to use *ᶜaql* is related to worship...with *ᶜaql* you can know me and also praise me" reflects al-Suhrawardī's central feature to his *taṣawwuf* : the act of praising the Divine requires the individual to use reasoning as a primary instrument in the path. Essentially, any *taṣawwuf* knowledge which does not incorporate the elementary practices of logic and reasoning will ultimately fail to encounter God. In other areas of his treatise, al-Suhrawardī quotes a *ḥadīth* to buttress his position: "The Prophet[10] said that *ᶜaql* is the best means to evaluate oneself. Obedience to the almighty God involves *ᶜaql*, and with more *ᶜaql* involved, then people will apply more righteous actions. They will benefit as their righteous actions increase."[11]

While there is an overwhelming emphasis for disciples to use reasoning in their *taṣawwuf* training, according to al-Suhrawardī, just as there existed a hierarchy in the Ṣūfī order, there is a hierarchy in reasoning skills. It takes a considerable amount of attention to proceed up the ranks of mastering the act of using reasoning and logic. It is important first for Ṣūfīs to understand the hierarchical structure so that they may proceed to identify what specific reasoning skills are necessary at each step of the *taṣawwuf* journey. If one neglects to do this or argues against this hierarchy as superficial, then, according to al-Suhrawardī, one will encounter faulty understandings of spirituality and the guidance provided to the Ṣūfī disciple will be incoherent. To defend his point, he quotes another *ḥadīth* that states, "The Prophet once said the truth is that almighty God gave His servants *ᶜaql* piece by piece. They learn to increase their knowledge, practice pure prayers and try to do proper fasting, but there is a great difference in their *ᶜaql*." [12] This is an example of the importance of all the various parts that comprise reasoning in Suhrawardī texts.

Al-Suhrawardī's repetitive references to *ḥadīth* on the use of reasoning is to principally link the Suhrawardiyyā *taṣawwuf* with the *sunna*. By seeking provenance in highest authority in spirituality, namely the Prophet, it demonstrated the numerous ways in which his Ṣūfī order mirrored and celebrated the example of the Prophet. Proper reasoning must be learned by teachers who understand the connection of knowledge of the Qur'ān, *ḥadīth*, *sunna*, and the Ṣūfī path.

Al-Suhrawardī on Prayers

As *Shaykh al-Islām* of the ᶜAbbāsid empire, al-Suhrawardī took a firm position on not missing any of the daily ritual prayers. On this issue he was adamant about following the *sunna* as strictly as possible and not being negligent about prayers as was common in other Ṣūfī orders. He points to a *ḥadīth* that refers to God calling prayers the "pillars of the religion."[13] Al-Suhrawardī was concerned about the behavior of Ṣūfīs reflecting a complete adherence to example of the Prophet. He stated that "God has prescribed five obligatory prayers and the holy Prophet stated that God claimed that prayers are the pillars of the religion; whoever neglects prayers becomes part of the unbelievers. With prayer, one encounters a binding testimony. One of the parts to prayer is that testimony comes with prayer." He continues to explain that "a *ḥadīth* reports that when a seeker of truth prepares to observe prayers, then almighty God places a protective veil over the seeker, and with personal greetings God places angels on the shoulders who also simultaneously pray with the believer."[14] This insistence on the critical role of disciples in the Ṣūfi order could be dismissed as statements from a staunch jurist; however, a closer examination of al-Suhrawardī's arguments shows that he was concerned with the inner dimension of prayer and the soul's quest of God's self-disclosure.

This concern is manifested by the rubrics of discussion in his *ᶜAwārif al-Maᶜārif* ; sub-headings entitled "The Excellence of

Prayers" and "The Humility of Prayers," underline his interest in ensuring that prayers are not just ritualistic performances ordered by the rules of *sharīᶜa,* but that prayers need to be understood as an integral component of the mystic path. Under the subheading "The Excellence of Prayers," al-Suhrawardī uses a *ḥadīth* to show that the power of prayer opens the heart to experience a type of humility that is tied to the experiences of heaven. In this quote, al-Suhrawardī brings the spiritual experience and prayer together as two dependent entities:

> It is the tradition of ᶜAbd Allāh ibn ᶜAbbās that the Prophet reported that almighty God created heaven and there are unique things that exist in it. It is a place where the eyes have not seen things, and the ears have not heard things, and nor has any person's heart ever experienced [it]. And God tells us in the holy Qur'ān, "The believers that will succeed are those who are humble in their prayers." [15]

For al-Suhrawardī, one of the most important features of prayer is for the Ṣūfī heart to grow in humility and that the disciple realizes the transformation that is being experienced. The purpose of al-Suhrawardī's analysis of *ḥadīths* in the prayer section is to connect the individual's prayer with the Prophet's spiritual journey and to view oneself in a relationship with the Prophet, aimed at experiencing a similar transcendental and spiritual experience. The relationship between the Ṣūfī and the Prophet is one of remembrance and celebration, but prayers ultimately bring the Ṣūfī disciple to the divine. Al- Suhrawardī states:

> Prayers are a means of establishing a relationship between the divine and the believers. Therefore it is necessary for the believer to practice the most humility in prayer and whenever God hears you pray, it is the humblest prayers that appeal to Him. Praying with humility will lead to victory.[16]

Prayers Regarding *Sūrat al-Fātiḥa*

Al-Suhrawardī's discussion of particular *sūra*s of the Qur'an is consistent with traditional Ṣūfī thought that certain chapters and verses of the Qur'ān have more "spiritual power" than others.[17] His exegesis begins with *sūrat al-fātiḥa*, after which he cites the well-known saying of the Prophet that it was his favorite *sūra* in the Qur'ān. Al-Suhrawardī's exegesis of *sūrat al-fātiḥa* gives him extended opportunity to build upon his expertise in *ḥadīth,* drawing upon the Prophetic traditions to show the connections to the spiritual experience. While it reinforces his scholarly authority in the *taṣawwuf* and *ᶜulamā'* tradition, the crucial point is that it established the Qur'ānic revelation recited by the Prophet an integral facet of the *taṣawwuf* spiritual experience. Al-Suhrawardī's interpretation of *sūrat al-fātiḥa* is as follows:

> God gave believers a special favor with the revelation of *sūrat al-fātiḥa*. With this *sūra* one's prayers are acted upon by God as quickly as possible and God has taught His believers the way to pray. *Sūrat al-fātiḥa* is recited from morning to night because it is so important that it was revealed to the holy Prophet on two separate occasions. One time it was revealed in Mecca and another time it was revealed in the holy city of Medina. Only if this *sūra* is recited at different times, can you begin to understand its deeper meanings. If you were to repeatedly recite *sūrat al-fātiḥa* a thousand times, you would learn a new meaning each time. [18]

Al-Suhrawardī applies the explanation of Abū Hurayra who believed that *sūrat al-fātiḥa* was an example of the way the Divine keeps an ongoing dialogue going with His creation. From Abū Hurāyra's analysis, the relationship between the Creator and the believer reaches a critical moment when the believer praises God and beseeches His guidance. Al-Suhrawardī's decision to cite Abū Hurāyra's discussion of the recitation of *sūrat al-fātiḥa* again reinforces the rules of Ṣūfī spiritual conduct and the need to follow the rules of the Suhrawardiyya order as closely as possible.

> Abū Hurayra's tradition [is] that the Prophet (s) reported that prayer divides the believer in between two parts. That is when the believer recites *bismi'llāh al-raḥmān al-raḥīm* [In the Name of God, the most Benevolent, ever-Merciful] then God replies, 'My servant has called upon Me.' When the believer continues to recite *al-hamdu li'llāh rabb al-ᶜālamīn* [All praise be to Allāh, Lord of the worlds] then

> God responds by stating that my believer has praised me. When the believer recites *al-raḥmān al-raḥīm*' [The most Beneficent, ever-Merciful] then God states that my believer has commended me. As the believer continues to recite *mālik yawm al-dīn* [The King of the Day of Judgment] then God replies and states that my believer has placed the responsibilities of all work onto me. Then the believer recites *iyyāka naᶜbudu wa iyyāka nastaᶜīn* [You alone we worship, and to You alone we turn for help] then God states that there is room in the believer for me. As the believer states *ihdinā 'l-ṣirāṭ al-mustaqīm ṣirāṭ alladhīna anᶜamta ᶜalayhim ghayri 'l-maghḍūb ᶜalayhim wa la ḍāllīn* [Guide us, O Lord, to the path that is straight, the path of those You have blessed, not of those who have earned Your anger nor those who have gone astray] God states that all of this is for My believer and whatever he desires it will be granted.[19]

Al-Suhrawardī quotes this *ḥadīth* to point out that there is a constant dialogue between the divine and human beings, and, more importantly, that the recitation of the Qur'ān brings about a real response from its divine author. *Sūrat al-fātiḥa* becomes the forum for this dialogue and al-Suhrawardī links the personal prayers of the faithful with divine communication. This exemplifies al-Suhrawardī as the authoritative Ṣūfī shaykh guiding his disciples toward God by using the Qur'ān primarily as a text to engage with in one's *taṣawwuf* knowledge. In addition, by remembering the customs of the Prophet he is upholding the model of *al-insān al-kāmil*, the "perfect being" as the goal to achieve.

Bahā' al-Dīn Zakariyyā

Bahā' al-Dīn Zakariyyā was al-Suhrawardī's primary disciple who was instructed to establish the Suhrawardī Ṣūfī order in Multan, an important city for Lodhi and Delhi sultanate dynasties. He was born at Kot Karor, near Multan, in about 578/1182–3. His father passed away when he was twelve years old and, at that time, he pursued Qur'ānic studies in Khurasan. About seven years later, after having memorizing the Qur'ān, he left for Bukhara. In Bukhara, he obtained a certificate in *ijtihād*. The people of Bukhara called him angel for his beauty and his sense of piety.[20] Afterwards, he left for Mecca where he studied *ḥadīth* for five years under a prominent scholar, Mawlānā Kamāl al-Dīn Muḥammad. Afterwards he went to Jerusalem, then to Baghdad, where al-Suhrawardī personally initiated him into his Ṣūfī order and made him his *khalīfa*.[21] Many of al-Suhrawardi's disciples were displeased to see Bahā' al-Dīn Zakariyyā elevated to the status of *khalīfa* after only seventeen days of spiritual training. ᶜUmar al-Suhrawardī sensed the discontent and jealousy of other disciples and immediately responded by stating that when they had first come to him they were like green wood which would not catch fire, but Bahā' al-Dīn Zakariyyā had been like dry wood which had begun to burn with a single breath.[22]

Against the criticism of Multan's *ᶜulamā'*, Zakariyyā established himself as the distinguished *khalīfa* of al-Suhrawardī by claiming religious authority in Ṣūfī theology, philosophy, *sharīᶜa*, and in the Islamic sciences. Amīr Sijzī, the famous Chishtī chronicler who wrote *Fawā'id al-Fu'ād*, explained that merchants from Iraq and Khurasan were attracted to the shaykh's teachings in large numbers and it did not take long before a wide group of travelers from all corners of the Islamic world paid a visit to Zakariyyā.[23]

Zakariyyā considered prayer as the highest form of devotion, and he credited all of his achievements to prayer; for him, a disciple's development depended on his ability to master prayer with only one shaykh.[24] Zakariyyā stated that missing prayers was an early form of death.[25] That is to say, missing prayers was like the death of spirituality and without prayers one does not know the meaning of completely surrendering to God. For Zakariyyā, both the *dhikr* (the additional prayers of contemplation) and attempts to increase the number of Ṣūfī disciples were secondary to perfecting one's daily prayer. In one incident, his disciples were in the midst of performing ablutions for prayers when he entered the room. All of his disciples rushed to pay proper respects to him except for one disciple who continued to wash himself. Zakariyyā praised the lone disciple as outstanding because he chose to complete his ablutions first, thus demonstrating greater respect to religious duties.[26]

Purifying the Heart

In Zakariyyā's treatise, *Khulāsāt al-ᶜārifīn*, an extensive commentary on the Qur'ān and the many ways Ṣūfīs should obey it in order to live a steady path of inner enlightenment are included. Like his spiritual mentor al-Suhrawardī, Zakariyyā wrote a section entitled "Interpretations of Knowledge," in which he explained ten specific ways one must act to achieve higher levels of inner knowledge (*al-ᶜilm al-majhūl*). He stated that "understanding knowledge requires a person to descend, just like water descends in a stream, there are various steps and stages for the individual to change his heart and behavior."[27] To descend is to create changes in form. Descending is symbolic of new motions of the body, both physical and spiritual. This reference to "descending as water descends in a stream" is to prepare the Ṣūfī seeker for new and unexpected challenges along the *taṣawwuf* path. For Zakariyyā, the Qur'ān contains detailed spiritual instructions for followers in order to purify their inner selves and prepare for the ultimate return to the divine. For him Qur'ānic verses entail more than ethical and daily conduct guidelines, but, rather, are themselves real invitations from the Creator.

In Zakariyyā's section of "Interpretations of Knowledge," he lists these steps for his disciples to follow:

A. The knowledge of the heart is true and comes from the heart. Untrue knowledge or false truth is obvious and is distinct.

B. The true Ṣūfī person (*zāhid*) seeks to completely connect himself to the moment of reunion with God.

C. One must control oneself from temptation and any misfortune or calamity that may occur during life. Appreciate the blessings of peace.

D. One should seek solitude for the purpose of achieving peace.

E. The individual should not seek reward for his accomplishments.

F. One needs to be humble in front of the Creator at all times.

G. Beware of your actions and do not let go of your faith.

H. Do not allow your emotions or sensations to control your directions.

I. At all times, the heart should remain pure and not be attached to anything excessive.

J. Everything that comes from truth returns to it also, and that which is not from truth will obviously be strange to it.[28]

Zakariyyā's interpretation of knowledge provides a concise model for Suhrawardī Ṣūfīs to emulate in their spiritual journey toward God. Ṣūfīs need first to identify the source of their knowledge, that is, they must conduct an epistemological inquiry into whether the knowledge is truly connected to the Ṣūfī path. In step number one, "the knowledge of the heart is true and comes from the heart" is in reference to deeper meaningful concepts that are tied to truth. Zakariyya is continuing the legacy of his spiritual teacher, al-Suhrawardī, who wrote that the "heart (*qalb*) is different from the rest of the human body although it is a part of it. The heart of a true believer (*mu'min*) is like a pure soul and is illuminated by a shining light."[29] Zakariyyā is building upon the lessons he learned from his predecessor by making the heart the main point of the Suhrawardī Ṣūfī path. For him, as for al-Suhrawardī, the heart is more than a bodily organ that pumps blood to various parts of the body; rather, it is the main organ for spiritual cleansing, inner awareness, and the primary place for Ṣūfīs to understand the Creator's presence. Zakariyyā quotes from al-Suhrawardī's text, "for those who are not believers or are hypocrites, their hearts are made from a lowly substance and shrouded in a veil.[30]

The primary reason Zakariyyā places a great deal of emphasis on the heart is reflective on the fact that Suhrawardī Ṣūfism is deeply rooted in the Qur'ān and the *ḥadīth* of the Prophet. The Suhrawardī texts, *ᶜAwārif al-maᶜārif*, *Khulasāt al-ᶜārifīn* and *al-Awārd* strongly advocate that the *taṣawwuf* path begin with proper understanding and cleansing of the heart (*ṭahārat al-qalb*). This is proven by Qur'ānic verses reminding believers that God gave humankind a heart for knowing God. Every person is given only one heart and one can either use it for or against God's wishes. Suhrawardī Ṣūfīs repeat verses from the Qur'ān that remind believers of the constant presence of God in their hearts. For example in Q. 33:51, "God knows what is in your hearts; God is All-Knowing" and Q. 8:24, "Know that God stands between a man and his heart" are common quotations in the texts. Zakariyyā believed that the problems of human weakness come when we fall to forgetfulness, but it is what is in their hearts and intentions that matter to God. He quotes from Q. 33:5, "There is no fault in you if you make mistakes, but only in what your hearts premeditate."[31] Zakariyyā chose a specific verse from the Qur'ān so that Ṣūfīs would understand that the journey of *taṣawwuf* is a long and arduous one that requires a constant struggle to purify the heart in order to encounter God. The combination of continued spiritual exercises (*dhikr*), prayers (*ṣalāt*) and pure intentions (*niyāt*) is a definite cure for the ills of the heart and puts one on a *taṣawwuf* path toward reuniting with God.[32]

Zakariyyā affirms to his audience, which is cynical about Ṣūfī religious exercises and beliefs, that if they are truly concerned with actively living the life of the true message, then they should remember that the heart is not left alone but God inspires it. He cites Q. 58:22, "As for the true believers it is they in whose hearts He has inscribed faith and whom He has strengthened with inspiration from Himself." Zakariyyā explains that verse 22 specifically mentions the ways Ṣūfīs becomes spiritually strengthened and uplifted by way of inspiration. This spiritual inspiration is not a momentary emotional stimulation that comes from intense exhilaration. This spiritual moment is the heart moving from a deep sleep and being awakened with the touch of divine illumination. When the heart is in prayer and in remembrance of God, it begins to cleanse away its worldly concerns because it opens itself up as the divine presence (*ḥaḍārat al-ḥaqq*) makes itself known to the spiritual seeker.[33] He believed that, at any given moment, the heart is like a patient lover waiting for affection from a partner who can only receive the blessings of illumination if the Ṣūfī understands the vulnerability of the heart. During these precious moments of contact, those who feel uncertain let the heart oscillate as if it is under severe duress; they then need to repeat the spiritual exercises of the heart. However, if the Ṣūfī's heart is guided toward patience, the patience that he has been practicing in daily exercises, then real guidance is guaranteed as it was stated in Q. 64:11 "Whosoever believes in God, He will guide his heart."[34]

Zakariyyā's interpretation of the Qur'ān is instructive for Ṣūfī disciples in their performance of certain religious exercises, and at the same time, it provides a degree of spiritual and temporal comfort in their Ṣūfī journey. For example, when Zakariyyā refers to the intentions of the heart, he is raising important mystical theological issues of inner and outer essences. To state that God knows the intentions of the heart could mean to the Ṣūfī that one should have a sense of fear of God's knowledge of every single aspect of one's being. Instead, Zakariyyā quotes from Q. 4:63, "God knows what is in their hearts," to paint a picture in which God is waiting for the proper time to be invited into the heart of the Ṣūfī to disclose His love to the seeker. The invitation comes from God but the Ṣūfī seeker needs to prepare for the glorious moment by specific cleansing exercises or *tahāra*. Especially in the case in which Zakariyyā makes a reference to the jugular vein, *warīd*, from Q. 50:16, "We are nearer to him than the jugular vein," is a reminder that God is present at all times around one and actively present within one's body.[35]

For Ṣūfīs following the Suhrawardī order, Zakariyyā's analysis of Qur'ānic verses connected to the heart (*qalb*) is an important reminder that they are never left alone in this world. The world is not a place for intense ascetic practices where one is alienated from the community and neglectful of the *sharīʿa*. Instead, Zakariyyā's teachings urge his disciples to study the Qur'ān closely and to adhere to the essential teachings of *sharīʿa* by embodying in themselves the *sunna* of the Prophet. The verses from the Qur'ān are considered divine illuminations given to the Prophet who then recited them to the rest of the community. These verses came from the mouth of the Prophet who simultaneously contained as many aspects of the spiritual message as humanly possible. Suhrawardī followers are reminded by these verses referring to the heart to maintain an intimate closeness to God (*uns*) and to maintain a constant sense of Ṣūfī piety in preparation for the moment of divine encounter.[36] In addition, any invitation by God to disclose Himself in the hearts of Ṣūfīs means that piety must be practiced in everyday living. The requirements of adhering to the *adab* of the order and the shaykh, following the *sunna* of the Prophet, and obeying the *sharīʿa* is the training of outer piety. All aspects of outer pietistic expressions are meant to develop gradually the inner piety of love. The "outer love is connected to the inner heart" is a common statement in al-Suhrawardī and Zakariyyā's texts.[37]

For followers of Suhrawardī the heart is the starting place to concentrate on purifying their inner essence or *nafs*.[38] The heart can be used as a weapon to be self-destructive or it can be trained to remember God (*dhikr Allāh*). When a person decides to choose evil actions (*ᶜammān*), these actions directly affect the heart's receptivity to future blessings and invitations from God. Zakariyyā expands on numerous Qur'ānic references to the heart being sealed. He treats, for example, Q. 7:101, "So God seals the hearts of the unbelievers," and Q. 2:7, "God has set a seal on their hearts and hearing." According to Zakariyyā, verses that state "God has set a seal on their hearts" are not about a predestined life fixed by God.[39] Moreover, the sealing of the heart is a consequence of one's own choosing, of one's mindful action, and of persistent violation of God's wishes. To the Suhrawardī shaykh, Q. 3:167, "Saying with their mouths that which never was in their hearts" is a Qur'ānic example of hearts that were affected from misguided actions performed by dishonest intentions.[40]

For Zakariyyā, these Qur'ānic verses do not condemn the believer to be an unbeliever with no possibility to return to God's path. On the contrary, one has the ability to contribute to the development of the heart's personality by bringing together the cognitive and spiritual dimensions of the human experience. He turns to the Q. 6:25, "We lay veils upon their hearts but they fail to understand it," to demonstrate that understanding one's heart is critical in cultivating compassion, mercy and love. A Ṣūfī seeker can not bring about a change to their *taṣawwuf* or even expect spiritual progress if s/he does not understand the reasons behind the continual fault making. The Qur'ānic verses used by both al-Suhrawardī and Zakariyyā are indicative of their own concerns that their followers are theologically grounded in God's instructions for the return. The "word of God" for them is more than a book of divine guidance given to the Prophet, but contains inner instructional messages (*baṭn al-Qur'ān*) that aids the Ṣūfī seeker in reunion. For most Muslims Qur'ānic references to the human body are metaphors for preserving an ethical and pious life. In some sections of the Qur'ān, the human anatomy is treated as a functional element for the body, such listening, hearing, weeping, and the circulation of blood. For the most part, human anatomy in the Qur'ān is cited in conjunction with the faith of its believers to ensure that there is a complete understanding of the relationship between the workings of their body and the message of the Qur'ān.[41] The Suhrawardī reading of the Qur'ān, like other Ṣūfī exegetes of the Qur'ān, takes the surface meaning as a vehicle to another area of deeper subtext. The surface text and subtext are not sitting on a separate two-tiered ladder with no connection, but they are directly related to the Ṣūfī *taṣawwuf* practice and spiritual enlightenment.

Zakariyyā's texts, *Khulasāt al-ᶜārifīn* and *al-Awārd*, continue the tradition of teaching Ṣūfī disciples proper *taṣawwuf* exercises. Replicating al-Suhrawardī's stress in *ᶜAwārif al-maᶜārif*, Zakariyyā is interested in instilling the appreciation of the spiritual components of *taṣawwuf* , the necessity of reasoning, and the fundamental connection to *sharīᶜa* of Ṣūfī practice. Truth is attained through a cleansing of the inner self in order for God's presence to be encountered.[42] For Zakariyyā, *taṣawwuf* needs to be understood in its intricate details because so many writers in the tradition have tried to explain it with little or no Ṣūfī training. Zakariyyā repeats in his texts that Ṣūfīs needs to be mindful of the premise that *taṣawwuf* aims to reach truth in the individual's life time, which means to return to the original existence with God. By centering God in life, everything else becomes insignificant. Zakariyyā is concerned to have his followers move beyond the linear pursuit of intellectual knowledge of *taṣawwuf* and its imprint on human history, even though there is great value to this knowledge, and to have them live contemplating every moment coming back to God's rightful guidance. Like al-Suhrawardī, Zakariyyā validates his *taṣawwuf* theology by using *ḥadīth*, *sunna* accounts and Qur'ānic verses; on the whole, his texts are definitive spiritual exercises for Suhrawardī Ṣūfīs.

Zakariyyā's Ṣūfī texts do not try to duplicate the theological work of al-Suhrawardī by reaffirming the historical, religious, and legal legitimacy of *taṣawwuf*. At great length al-Suhrawardī supported *taṣawwuf*'s roots in the Qur'ān, in the *sunna* of the Prophet and in the lives of the Prophet's companions. Qur'ānic phrases such as "Those firmly rooted in knowledge" (Q. 3:7 and 4:162) were clear evidence for al-Suhrawardī that enlightened Ṣūfīs were indeed the keepers of an inner knowledge rooted in divine guidance. As a Ḥanbalī jurist who used *fiqh*, *sharīᶜa*, and *falsafa* in argumentation, it is not surprising to see that al-Suhrawardī's *taṣawwuf* contains a variety of aspects from the Islamic sciences. It would be reasonable to suppose that Zakariyyā as a disciple of al-Suhrawardī and as a Ṣūfī trained in *fiqh* and *sharīᶜa* would have used similar patterns of *taṣawwuf* argumentation. This is not the case with Zakariyyā, however, given the evidence of his texts which contain less legal and religious jargon defending the legitimacy of the *taṣawwuf* tradition.[43] Zakariyyā's texts are specific and detailed spiritual practices for Suhrawardī Ṣūfīs to incorporate into their daily lives. For example, in Zakariyyā's texts, unlike his predecessor, he does not have categories that attempt to prove the validity of the *taṣawwuf* or the Suhrawardī Ṣūfī tradition. He does not have headings or subheadings entitled "the truth of *taṣawwuf*," "the excellence of *taṣawwuf*,:" or "the way of the Ṣūfī" as al-Suhrawardī wrote in his treatise. These types of headings by al-Suhrawardī were designed to make disciples internalize the theosophical legacy of *taṣawwuf* before they immersed themselves in self-examination, contemplation, and detached themselves for self-annihilation (*fanā'*) in God. He was concerned to balance the two worlds of *sharīᶜa* and *taṣawwuf* in order for the Ṣūfīs in his order to be law abiding spiritual seekers. For Zakariyyā laying down the rules of *sharīᶜa* and linking *taṣawwuf* to the law was not of primary importance because it was already established by al-Suhrawardī's works. Moreover, Zakariyyā was working to institutionalize the Ṣūfī order in Multan, which meant that he knew that historical and legal arguments were not going to affect the spirituality of Ṣūfīs; providing specific spiritual models as exercises would be much more influential.

NOTES

1. See Qamar-ul Huda, "The Remembrance of the Prophet in Suhrawardī's *ᶜAwārif al-Ma'ārif*," *Journal of Islamic Studies* 12:2 (2001): 129–50; Muhammad Hamidullah, *Le Prophete de l'Islām*, 2 vols (Paris 1959); Abū Nuᶜaym al-Iṣbahānī, *Dalā'il al-nubuwwa* (Hyderbad Deccan 1950); and, Annemarie Schimmel, "The Veneration of the Prophet Muhammad, as Reflected in Sindhi Poetry" in *The Saviour God: Comparative Studies in the Concept of Salvation*, ed. S. Brandon (Manchester: Manchester University Press, 1963), 129–43.

2. For more on the political relationship of al-Suhrawardī and the caliph al-Nāṣir see Qamar-ul Huda, *Striving for Divine Union: Spiritual Exercises for Suhrawardī Sūfīs* (London: Cur-

zon, 2003), 13–40, and Angelika Haartmann, *An-Nāṣir li-Dīn Allāh : (1180–1225): Politik, Religion, Kultur in d. späten Abbāsidenzeit* (Berlin: de Gruyter, 1975).

3. The title has been variously rendered as "Knowledge of the Gnostics" or "Manual of the Dervishes" or "The Gifts of the Spiritual Perceptions", but all of these titles are confusing because of associations to other religious traditions or the inaccuracy in appreciating the intellectual dimensions of al-Suhrawardī's *taṣawwuf.*

4. The *ᶜAwārif al-maᶜārif* is still a popular Ṣūfī manual found in many Ṣūfī bookstores in the Middle East and in South Asia.

5. On the texts see Wilfred Cantwell Smith, *The Meaning and End of Religion: A New Approach to the Religious Traditions of Mankind* (New York: Macmillan, 1962); *The Critical Study of Sacred Texts*, ed. Wendy Doniger O'Flaherty (Berkeley: University of California Press, 1979); and Harry Buck, "Saving Story and Sacred Book: Some Aspects of the Phenomenon of Religious Literature," in *Search the Scriptures: New Testament Studies in Honor of Raymond T. Stamm, Gettysburg Theological Studies*, no.3, ed. J.M. Myers, O. Reimherr, and H.N. Bream (Leiden: E. J. Brill, 1969), 79–94.

6. Seyyid Mahjub Hasan Wasti, "*Hazrat Shaikh al-Shayūkh wa Awārif al-Maᶜārif*" in *Suhrawardī Silsila Risāla* 3 (1989): 5–22, Shah Owais Sohrawardī (ed.).

7. See William Greene, "The Spoken and the Written Word," *Harvard Studies in Classical Philology* 60 (1951): 23–59; William Graham, *Beyond the Written Word: Oral Aspects of Scripture in the History of Religion* (Cambridge: Cambridge University Press, 1987); William Graham, "Qur'ān as Spoken Word: An Islamic Contribution to the Understanding of Scripture" in *Approaches to Islam in Religious Studies*, ed. Richard C. Martin (Tucson: University of Arizona Press, 1985), 23–40; André Louf, "The Word Beyond Liturgy." *Cistercian Studies* 6 (1971): 353–68; Frederick Denny, "The Adab of Qur'ān Recitation: Text and Context" in *International Congress for the Study of the Qur'ān,* ed. Anthony Johns (Canberra: Australian National University, 1981), 143–60.

8. Abū Hafs ᶜUmar al-Suhrawardī, *ᶜAwārif al-maᶜārif* (Cairo 1973), 410, hereafter cited as AM.

9. *AM*, 411.

10. When al-Suhrawardī quotes from the *Qur'ān* he usually takes sections of a verse to support his particular idea and supplies the citation. Whenever he makes a reference to the Prophet he follows the *sunna* by supplying the proper benediction of *ṣallā 'llāhu ᶜalayhi wa sallam*, and with companions to the Prophet, members of the Prophet's family, Shīᶜī Imāms, and eminent Ṣūfī shaykhs he applied *raḥmat Allāh ᶜalayhi*.

11. *AM*, 412.

12. *AM*, 412.

13. AM, 274.

14. AM, 275.

15. AM, 64.

16. AM, 273.

17. See A. J. Wensinck, *Concordance et indices de la tradition musulmane*. 8 volumes (Leiden: E. J. Brill, 1936–1971); Frederick Denny, "Exegesis and Recitation: Their Development as Classical Forms of Qur'ānic Piety" in *Transitions and Transformations in the History of Religions. Essays in Honor of Joseph M. Kitagawa,* ed. Frank Reynolds and Theodore M. Ludwig (Leiden: E. J. Brill, 1980), 91–123; and Abū 'l-Qāsim ᶜAbd al-Karīm al-Qushayrī, *Al-Risāla al-Qusharyriyya fī ᶜilm al-taṣawwuf*, 2 volumes, ed. ᶜAbd al-Ḥalīm Maḥmūd and Maḥmūd b. al-Sharīf (Cairo 1974).

18. AM, 272.

19. AM, 272–273.

20. Ḥamīd ibn Fazl Allāh Jamalī, *Siyār al-ᶜārifīn*, trans. Muhammad Ayoub Qadiri, (Lahore 1967), 144.

21. Ibid., 145–146.

22. Amīr Ḥasan Sijzī, *Fawā'id al-Fu'ād*, ed. Muhammad Latif Malik (Lahore 1966), 49, and Jamalī, *Siyār al-ᶜārifīn*, 148.

23. Amīr Ḥasan Sijzī, *Fawā'id al-Fu'ād*, 243.

24. Ibid., 240.

25. Ibid., 248.

26. Jamalī, Siyār al-ᶜĀrifīn, 121.

27. Shamīm Zaidī (ed.), *Bahā' al-Dīn Zakariyyā khulasāt al-ᶜārifīn* (Rawalpindi 1974), 99 (hereafter KA).

28. KA, 100–101.

29. AM, 267.

30. AM, 268.

31. KA, 92–93.

32. KA, 95.

33. Bahā' al-Dīn Zakariyyā, *al-Awārd* (Lahore 1987), 22–5 (hereafter AA).

34. AA, 26.

35. KA, 94.

36. For more information on mystical language see *Mysticism and Language*, ed. Steven Katz (Oxford: Oxford University Press, 1994); Annemarie Schimmel, *As Through a Veil: Mystical Poetry in Islam* (New York: Columbia University Press, 1982); *Mystical Union in Judaism, Christianity and Islam: an Ecumenical Dialogue*, ed. Moshe Idel and Bernard McGinn (New York: Continuum, 2000).

37. See AM, 280; KA, 95, and AA, 26.

38. The word *nafs* has been described by many scholars as the soul, inner life, or as the breathing life system of the body. In accordance with al-Suhrawardī's terminology, *nafs* can be used as the inner essence or the real being. This is not to be confused by the lower appetitive soul or the substance that resembles the animal spirit (*laṭīfa-yi rūh-e ḥaywānī*).

39. For more Qur'ānic verses referring to sealed hearts see Q. 6:46, 9:87, 9:93, 10:74, 16:108, 30:59, 40:35, 42:24, 45:43, 47:16, and 63:3.

40. KA, 97.

41. See Fazlur Rahman, *Health and Medicine in the Islamic Tradition: Change and Identity* (New York: Crossroad, 1997); Musa Ahmed, *Health and healing in the Qur'ān* (Sa'adu Zungur, Kano 1998); Nidāl Samīḥ ᶜĪsā, *al-Ṭibb al-wiqaᶜī bayn al-ᶜilm wa'l-dīn* (Damascus 1997); Zuhayr Muḥammad Zumaylī, *Zad al-marīd wa'l-mubtalī* (Amman 1988) and Qamar-ul Huda, "Anatomy," in *Encyclopaedia of the Qur'ān*, ed. J. D. McAuliffe (Leiden: E. J. Brill, 2001), I, 79–84.

42. KA, 100.

43. This does not mean, of course, that Zakariyyā does not incorporate Qur'ānic texts, *ḥadīths*, *sunna* accounts, and *fiqh* as evidence in his texts; there are plenty of references to all of them in the texts. However, he does not use these accounts in the way a *muḥaddith* would apply them as evidence to a legal argument.

The Qur'ān in the modern world

Chapter 9

The Qur'ān in Egypt I: Bint al-Shāṭi' on Women's Emancipation

Roxanne D. Marcotte

The return to the Qur'ān through a commentary (*tafsīr*) has always been exercised by men who, in their search for Islamic identity, have produced an impressive number of works. In modern times, however, some women have risen to prominence in the field of exegesis, predominantly adopting the methodology of making the Qur'ān relevant to the present age. ᶜĀ'isha ᶜAbd al-Raḥmān (1913–98), better known under her pen-name of Bint al-Shāṭi', was one of the first such modern woman commentators of the Qur'ān. Professor of Arabic literature and Qur'ānic studies, she wrote numerous exegetical studies and, therefore, occupies a privileged position among the commentators of the Qur'ān.[1] While she did not write an independent work of Qur'ānic exegesis on women's issues, she nonetheless strove to articulate a new Islamic discourse on women that could be more in tune with her time. In a sense, she may be considered one of the precursors to the new prevalent discourse on women in Islam.

Issa Boullata has written about Bint al-Shāṭi' for more than a quarter of a century. In 1974, he wrote, in *The Muslim World*, his "Modern Qur'ān Exegesis: A Study of Bint al-Shāṭi''s Method." Almost twenty years later, he included in his *Trends and Issues in Contemporary Arabic Thought* (1990) a section on the works and thought of a number of Arab women among whom he included Bint al-Shāṭi'. At the Institute of Islamic Studies (McGill University), he then taught a course on Bint al-Shāṭi''s Qur'ānic exegesis out of which a number of articles of his students were eventually published.[2]

In what follows, first, the life and the exegetical works of Bint al-Shāṭi' will be presented, along with her positions regarding women and Islam via the study of some of her works, such as her *Islamic*

Concept of Women's Emancipation. Written more than thirty-five years ago, the latter work offers a glimpse of what might have been Bint al-Shāṭi''s Qur'ānic exegesis regarding women's place in Islam had she written such a work. This text provides the reader with what Bint al-Shāṭi' calls an "Islamic" understanding of Muslim women's emancipation and illustrates the difficulties any interpretation of the religious tradition encounters and some of the tensions that necessarily arise out of such an exercise, especially in view of the sensitive issues of women's status and rights in Islam.

Life, Work, and Qur'ānic Exegesis

ᶜĀ'isha ᶜAbd al-Raḥmān was born in Damiet, on the Nile Delta in 1913. Her early education was quite traditional. Schooled by her father, an *ᶜālim* who studied at al-Azhar (Cairo) and who did not allow her to attend public school, she eventually attended a public institution from which she graduated as a teacher of Arabic language (in 1929). In 1936, she attended Fu'ad I University (which later became Cairo University) where she completed a PhD (1950) with a dissertation on the Arab poet, Abū ᶜAlā' al-Maᶜarrī (d. 1058). She then became a professor of Arabic literature at the ᶜAyn al-Shams University in Cairo (1951). Moreover, during her academic career, she was Visiting Professor at a number of Arab universities: Islamic University in Umm Durmān and Khartūm University (1967–70) (Sudan), al-Qarawiyyīn University and the Faculty of Theology in Fez (1970), Beirut University (1971) and Algier University.

ᶜĀ'isha ᶜAbd al-Raḥmān took the pen-name Bint al-Shāṭi' in order to conceal her literary activities from her father. During her lifetime, she wrote more than sixty books and articles: Qur'ānic studies, literary critiques, essays, novels, biographies, autobiographies, columns (in the Egyptian magazine *al-Hilāl*) and newspaper articles (*al-Ahrām*, etc.), short stories and critical editions of classical texts, receiving numerous distinctions for her literary activities. More than forty of her works are dedicated to Qur'ānic and Islamic studies.[3]

Bint al-Shāṭi' was a determined woman, unafraid of voicing her opinion. Syamsuddin notes that, on the one hand, she was receptive to the idea of some freedom of expression, having even criticized in person Anwar Sadat for his curtailment of the freedom of the press, while, on the other hand, she was receptive to the idea of some freedom of belief.[4] This assessment does not, however, take into consideration her stances against the freedom of expression allowed to the (political) left and her numerous attacks against Jews and Baha'is. Bint al-Shāṭi' did not venture in the political arena, but this did not prevent someone like Egyptian Ḥasan Ḥanafī from giving her the title of "Jurist *(faqīha)* of the Sultan," on account of her overtly anti-leftist positions and Aḥmad Hāshim Sharī (in *Ṣabāḥ al-khayr*, Sept. 1, 1977) from criticizing her refusal to recognize freedom of expression to the political left in one of her articles published in *al-Ahrām*.[5]

In her polemical work, *Jewish Sources in the Intellectual Razzia* (1975), she discards Jewish narratives (*isrāᶜīliyyāt*) as unreliable for Qur'ānic exegesis, because the sole purpose of these narratives is to attack Islam and to corrupt its message. Classical commentators such as al-Ṭabarī (d. 310/923), Ibn ᶜAsākir (d. 519/1125), and al-Dhahabī (d. 753/1352) did not, however, hesitate to use these narratives in their exegetical works.[6] Brinner convincingly demonstrates that the polemical character of the work rests on a superficial understanding of the Jewish tradition, mainly based on secondary sources. She is unable to clearly distinguish between Judaism and Zionism.[7] More instructive are the more than sixty articles (with multiple reprints) and books she wrote between 1985–87 against the Baha'i faith, accusing its adherents of collusion with the Jews to destroy Islam.[8]

A number of studies have focused more specifically on her exegesis. Some studies are very general,[9] while others tackle more specific issues such as free will,[10] her interpretation of oath (*qasam*) in sura 93,[11] the notion of "inimitability" (*iᶜjāz*) of the Qur'ān,[12] the "occasions of revelation" (*asbāb al-nuzūl*) and what she identifies as "what surrounds" the Qur'ān.[13] Other studies focus on her contemporary linguistic approach[14] or on her hermeneutics[15] and on Amīn al-Khūlī's influence on her exegesis.[16]

Bint al-Shāṭi''s Qur'ānic exegesis was greatly influenced by al-Khūlī's (d. 1966) own exegetical method, her teacher and, later, her husband (in 1945).[17] Bint al-Shāṭi' adopted al-Khūlī's chiefly literary analysis—a "rhetorical exegesis"—of the Qur'ān and applied it faithfully to her own Qur'ānic studies. Her modern interpretation further differs from the linguistic approach of classical authors such as al-Zamakhsharī (d. 539/1144) with its concise and clear style.[18]

One of the most distinctive characteristics of Bint al-Shāṭi' exegesis consists in her rejection of multiple interpretations for any given term or passage of the Qur'ān and of the possibility of any type of synonymy. Each term possesses only one interpretation that the commentator attempts to uncover. This is achieved by studying the whole Qur'ān and the different contexts in which these terms appear, without overlooking the fact that some verses have but a mere rhetorical role.[19] Syamsuddin has labeled her method a "cross-referential" approach.[20] Bint al-Shāṭi' also believes that there exists a uniformity of meaning throughout the Qur'ān.[21] One such example is the various terms used in the whole Qur'ān to designate human beings, each having a specific meaning: the biological being (*bashar*), the superior human existence (*ins* or *nās*) as opposed to *bashar*, and finally, the human being in becoming (*insān*).[22]

The exegesis of Bint al-Shāṭi' rests on, but is not limited to, her linguistic analysis.[23] She attempts to discover the meaning of the Qur'ān in accordance with what it might have meant to Muḥammad and the first Muslims. However, she emphasizes that the Qur'ān is neither a historical nor a scientific text. Bint al-Shāṭi' rejects any type of "scientific" exegesis of the Qur'ān, an idea held by people like Ṭanṭawī Jawharī (d. 1941) in his *Jawāhir fī'l-Qur'ān*. Twentieth century science is not found in a seventh century text.[24] In *The Qur'ān and Contemporary Exegesis*,[25] she criticizes and replies to the physician Muṣṭafā Maḥmūd's "modernist" and "scientific" interpretation of the Qur'ān.[26] This did not prevent her, however, from trying, paradoxically, to reject evolutionism (Darwinism) by resorting to a verse of the Qur'ān (Q. 2:30), while attempting, as Wahyudi notes, to discover in the Qur'ān elements of a theory of evolution, especially in verses where creation occurs in "successive phases" (e.g., Q. 71:14; cf. Q. 11:25–49 and Q. 23:23–30).[27] In spite of what appears to be contradictory stances, Bint al-Shāṭi' generally prefers to highlight the specificity of the Qur'ān: it provides moral and spiritual guidance for the believer. Among her major exegetical works, one must mention the following: *The Islamic Personality:*

Qur'ānic Studies (1977), *Treatise on the Human Being: Qur'ānic Studies* (1969), *The Qur'ān and the Human Condition* (1978), *Rhetorical Exegesis of the Glorious Qur'ān* (1990), *Introduction to the Method* (1971), and *Explanatory Inimitability of the Qur'ān and the Problems of Ibn al-Azraq* (1971).

The Islamic Concept of Women's Emancipation

There are only a few studies on Bint al-Shāṭi' views on women's status and rights. The studies of Zuhur[28] and Hoffman-Ladd[29] only discuss her views on women's social role. A recent translation of the third installment of the address she delivered at the Sant' Egidio Conference in Padua, Italy, in October 1997 and published in *al-Ahrām*[30] with a discussion on what she calls the "new woman," offers a glimpse of her lasting preoccupation with the role and status Islam provides women, especially in today's modern Muslim society.[31]

In *The Islamic Concept of Women's Emancipation*, the published version of a conference delivered in 1967 at the Islamic University of Umm Durmān (Khartoum, Sudan), Bint al-Shāṭi' discusses at length her views on women and Islam.[32] Apart from this short work, she did not apply her linguistic analysis of the Qur'ān to issues pertaining to women, her status, her role or the legal prescriptions applying to her. The reasons for her silence remain obscure. One can only speculate that she was cautious not to venture in an arena where the potential for controversies are enormous. Her refusal to tackle these issues is, nonetheless, indicative of conservatism—at least in the exegetical realm—if she is compared to women of her generation.[33] She was certainly not uninterested in women's issues found in the Qur'ān. Although *The Islamic Concept of Women's Emancipation* is not an exegetical analysis per se, this work illustrates the type of exegesis that Bint al-Shāṭi' may have been considering for the analysis of women in Islam. In this work, she indeed provides abundant scriptural proofs to corroborate her interpretation of an Islamic concept of emancipation applicable to today's Muslim women.

Bint al-Shāṭi' analyzes women's emancipation in terms of generations. There is the generation of the "society of the Turkish harem"[34] to which belongs the generation of her mother, who were for the most part illiterate, and her own generation, the generation of the "new women" who have witnessed the tremendous transformation of traditional Egyptian society.[35] In a similar fashion, women's emancipation will mean different things for these two generations.[36] For traditional "harem society," women's emancipation was understood solely as resulting in women's moral "perdition" and unleashing their natural female desire to "seduce." Consequently, women had to be protected—naturally by men—from *themselves* and from other men. Men became de facto guardians of women's honour and (moral) virtue,[37] an outdated conception Bint al-Shāṭi' criticizes:

> It was rather following the principle that man has imagined at the time of the harem and with which he has justified [women's] confinement. He became an expert at building walls and cages, without there being any shadow of the reality of woman herself in this [false] image, throughout the different centuries. Her honor has always been in her hands and not in those of ᶜAmrū and Zayd.[38]

The product of history, "new liberated Arab women" gave to women's emancipation another meaning. Terms like "free" (*ḥurra*) and "emancipation" (*taḥrīr*) have come to bear the symbolic weight of women's liberation movements and their fight for more rights (from the end of the 19th C onwards), whether through the efforts of reformists such as Qasim Amin or the struggle of feminists such as Doria Shafiq.[39] Bint al-Shāṭi''s discourse on women came long before the re-emergence of Islam and the (re-)assertion of male authority over women, characteristic of Islamism's defense mechanism against the radical restructuring of society.

Bint al-Shāṭi' shows a keen awareness of women's historical and social roles. During pre-Islamic times, women were deified and held positions of power in the Arabic peninsula, in Egypt, in Shām (Greater Syria), and in Iraq, such as the queens of Sheba and of Palmyra. During the Islamic period, women imposed their will, their existence, and became part of major events, in spite of being secluded behind closed doors and kept captive as was the Queen ᶜIṣmat al-Dīn Shajarat al-Durr who ruled over Egypt and Shām and who victoriously fought against the Crusaders.[40] Muslims are going back in time and are attempting to rediscover the obliterated traces of history. In a sense, the efforts of Bint al-Shāṭi' and those of a number of women of her generation are a prelude to Fatima Mernissi's rediscovery of the role of women in Islamic history.[41]

Bint al-Shāṭi' adds that the real difference between these two generations lies in the new "consciousness" (*wa^{c}ī*) women of her generation have come to develop. Women have re-evaluated their own existence—something immensely more profound.[42] She eloquently describes this new awareness in the following manner:

> This new Arabic woman realizes directly and fundamentally her existence, without begging or imploring [man] to graciously grant it—if he wishes, he grants, and if he wishes, he refuses—and without having to resort to subterfuge, slyness, and deceit in order to exercise her right to existence, something women of the harem had to do.
>
> By this, I mean that now I understand that, in life, my right is essential and fundamental, just as is the right of the man, equally and without having to conceive, as has the generation of my mother, that this right is merely offered, but rather, without having this right depend on the will of a man, or that it be determined by the fact that I bear a child or not, that I give birth to boys or that I have none.[43]

Women will rid themselves—and society—of similar false conceptions about their own freedom that have originated from centuries of "residues" of Islamic interpretation only once they will have realized and become conscious of the true foundation of this freedom.[44] Modern development forever changed traditional societies and has fostered the emergence of this new consciousness:

> Likewise, O friends, you see that the new woman focuses on Islamic principles in which there can be no place for suspicion or doubt, in what she exercises of progress and in the realization of what she desires for her free existence.
>
> You know and I know that this Islamic concept of woman's freedom (*ḥurriyya*) is not general and technical or obvious for everybody. Some of us continue to mistaken the meaning of freedom and what it entails. They do not

> distinguish between the state of being emancipated and the state of [moral] disintegration, between equality (*musāwāh*) and transformation [of genders], between liberty and licentiousness.
>
> Some of us continue in this matter, those for whom the manifestations of their freedom and their progress is reduced either to being a loaned, foreign merchandise which transforms the purity of her origin or its retrograde understanding, as residues of the society of the harem.[45]

Bint al-Shāṭi' conceives of women's freedom as an integral part of the Islamic religious paradigm. The new free Arab woman is alone responsible for her own virtue. She only demanded her freedom back in order to correct oppressive and erroneous views that were responsible for maintaining her captive, submitted and dependent. She reclaimed her freedom in order "to impose upon society the certitude that she is the one who carries a responsibility that she safeguards. The dignity of her femaleness arises out of [this personal responsibility] and not out of having it imposed upon her by the guardian of the cage or a chastity belt."[46] She adds:

> The insistence of the new free woman to take charge of the consequence of her freedom and the preservation of her virtue is at the heart of the Islamic concept of woman's freedom, in conformity with her religious legal capacities [to fulfill] her religious duties (*taklīf*) and to [assume] her responsibility.
>
> The guardianship (*wilāya*) of the father or the husband over the woman does not mean that they bear for her the consequences of her moral obligations and the responsibility to provide for her needs. It is rather up to the free Muslim woman, endowed with the capacity of discernment to bear directly the consequences; she is rewarded or punished according to her faith or her disbelief, of her virtue or her vice [as it is mentioned in the Qur'ān]: "Nor doth any laden bear another's load" [Q. 6:164].[47]

The first part of the verse omitted here by Bint al-Shāṭi' illustrates actually even better her intention: "Each soul earneth only on its own account." There are a number of other verses that enjoin the believers—women and men—to do good for which they will be rewarded and to avoid doing bad deeds for which they will be punished (e.g., Q. 33:35; Q. 40:40; Q. 48:5–6; Q. 4:124, etc.). Bint al-Shāṭi' grounds her notion of emancipation in her exegesis. The moral character of Muslim women's freedom comes to the fore with the following verse she cites and in which women are classified according to their degree of adherence to religious principles:

> Allah citeth an example for those who disbelieve: the wife of Noah and the wife of Lot, who were under two of Our righteous slaves yet betrayed them so that they [the husbands] availed them naught against Allah and it was said [unto them]: Enter the Fire along with those who enter. And Allah citeth an example for those who believe: the wife of Pharaoh [Lydia, the surrogate mother of Moses, and Mother of Righteousness] when she said: My Lord! Build for me a home with Thee in the Garden, and deliver me from Pharaoh and his work, and deliver me from evil-doing people; And Mary, daughter of ᶜImrān [cf. Q. 3:35] whose body was chaste, therefore We breathed therein something of Our spirit. And she put faith in the words of her Lord and His scriptures, and was the obedient' [Q. 66:10–12].[48]

Women's emancipation must, therefore, be understood in light of its moral foundation. For instance, Bint al-Shāṭi' wrote numerous biographies (not in a strict sense) that provided her with good opportunities to propose Islamic models of (feminine) virtues such as piety, modesty, devotion, loyalty, sacrifice, heroism or patience.[49] A closer examination of her position reveals that her argument rests on theological foundations. In as much as a woman's actions cannot be freely chosen, how then can her—moral and religious—responsibility be guaranteed? Women's individual freedom alone allows her to choose a virtuous life that conforms to her religious beliefs. The possibility to freely choose between good or bad actions alone gives meaning to the notions of reward and punishment guaranteed by divine retribution.[50] On the whole, her emphasis on free choice has affinities with Muᶜtazilī positions.

Bint al-Shāṭi' notes that equality has been conceived as either a "reversal of [natural] conditions," a "transformation of genders," and a "deterioration of the [natural] equilibrium of values," or as a "foreign imported" concept that transforms the real origin of the concept, that is, its Islamic roots. The former, a "retrograde" understanding of equality fostered a demand for the elimination of all distinctions between the genders and for complete equality[51] at the expense of women's true nature. The latter, a "foreign" understanding imported from the West transforms the true essence of equality between the genders that "is, in fact, an independent Islamic concept, established fourteenth centuries ago in the Book of Islam, the seal of the divine messages."[52] This "foreign imported" understanding constitutes yet another attack on Islam by Orientalism—which she severely criticizes[53]—one of Islam's major contemporary threats.

Bint al-Shāṭi' criticizes non-Islamic concepts of emancipation or equality that sever Muslim women from their religious rights and duties. By the same token, she presents a caricatured picture of freedom enjoyed by western women that amounts to mere sexual permissiveness. Nonetheless, she alludes to an objectification of women's bodies, where women become solely sexual objects. Cut from their Islamic heritage, women themselves fall prey to their appearances. Their new veils are those of their contrivances: "They have freed themselves from an old [type of] slavery, to fall prey to a more repulsive and oppressive contemporary slavery."[54] She notes:

> If the daughters of the pioneers have overcome the dangerous state of threading the rugged path from the walls of the harem and the desolated region of blind illiteracy to reach the horizons of light and consciousness (*waᶜī*), today's girls are going through a stage which is no less dangerous, because it is a stage in which concepts are all mixed up, distinctions are lost, and the measures of everything that pertains to the issue of woman and progress are disturbed. The nature of this stage is that the burden of it be without mercy for the new woman and that she pays a high price for all her wrong steps on the path or errors in understanding—her errors or the errors of society.
>
> The only way to avoid numerous sacrifices is to forever end this imagined and strange dispute between woman and man, or between woman and society. This cannot be real-

> ized from one side, for they [i.e., men] must be with her on the path, because she is your daughter, your sister, your partner and companion in life, your mother, and the creator of your future. Remember the verse of Allah about her and you: "And of His signs is this: He created for you spouses from yourselves that ye might find rest in them, and He ordained between you love and mercy. Lo! Indeed are signs for a people who reflect" [Q. 30:21].[55]

The idea of the "complementarity" of the genders is especially popular with commentators of the Qur'ān and it enables them to conform their interpretations to the legal differentiation between women and men. This idea is rather useful to explain away the differences between the genders by appealing to a natural order, at times, using paradoxical phrases like "equal though different." Although these differences are used to assert that women and men have complementary roles, a number of modern Muslim feminists who emphasize women's primary role as mothers and wives are eager to emphasize women's social as well as political roles. Moreover, Bint al-Shāṭi' does not conceive of this complementarity in terms of antagonistic wills.[56] She writes:

> The new woman has truly liberated her understanding of this equality. For her, the matter is unambiguous, and does not get mistaken for a transformation that eliminates the natural distinctions between male and female and the social distinctions between man and woman. For her, equality does not go beyond the [religious] rights and the corresponding duties (*wājibāt mutakāfa'a*). The man remains a man, and the woman remains a woman. None of the two genders is transformed and becomes an in-between!
>
> The new conscious Muslim woman does not conceive that there exists a competition or an antagonism between her and man. This is because competition only occurs between two contenders, and dispute only occurs between those who hold animosity towards [one another] or disagreements. We, liberated contemporary women, believe that man and woman are complementary (*mutakāmilān*). Each one of them needs the other to realize his/her perfect

> existence. Husband and wife are partners, founders of one social cell, companions in a life-long journey whose common life is realized with a single pulse. They become united in agreement, harmony, and complementarity. They do not split on account of a struggle over power or authority. [...] And they do not perceive that equality (*musāwāh*) clashes with the logic of nature (*fiṭra*) and natural laws (*qānūn ṭabīᶜa*) that recognize a complete equality neither between a man and another man, nor between a woman and another women, to say the least of the recognition of it between the two sexes.[57]

Islam is not the problem, but rather the solution. Muslim women must rediscover the true meaning of Islamic teachings that has been lost at the hands of centuries of erroneous interpretations. Although this idea of natural order and the necessary complementarity of the genders is grounded in the Qur'ān and the traditions, this does not prevent Bint al-Shāṭi' from trying to subtly subvert it. She does not dispute the natural, biological, or even social differences between the genders. Instead, she seeks to transcend these apparent differences by appealing to a more universal concept. The notion of "humanity," therefore, becomes central to her argument. This notion is grounded in the religious tradition. Bint al-Shāṭi' defines humanity as women's and men's equal religious duties and responsibilities. She writes:

> Today, if we exercise our essential and fundamental right in life, this is not something that befalls upon us or [something] foreign and imported, it is rather the Book of Islam in us that does not allude at all, by near or far, to the story of the creation of Eve from the rib of Adam. Rather, it establishes that we all come from a single soul (*nafs*)[58], and it refuses to deny the humanity (*insāniyya*) of woman, similar to the humanity of man, and in conformity with the unity of the origin: "O people! Be careful of your duty to your Lord Who createth you from a single soul and from it createth its mate and from them twain hath spread abroad a multitude of men and women. Be careful of your duty towards Allah in Whom ye claim [your rights] of one another, and towards

> the wombs [that bare you]. Lo! Allah hath been a watcher over you" [Q. 4:1]. Muslim women's freedom goes back to this established origin. According to the Islamic concept, it consists in the perfection of the humanity of woman, regarding everything that is related to this humanity among the rights, what they carry of religious duties (*takālīf*) and what follows from these.
>
> Our understanding of this Islamic concept of our freedom, of our rights and what follows from these is what distinguishes us from the generation of the harem.[59]

The ability to speak, to understand, and to reason are specific to the human species. The ability to acquire knowledge is, therefore, an integral part of this humanity. Consequently, access to knowledge cannot be denied to women. To do so is un-Islamic. She writes:

> Today, we consider knowledge a substantial element among the components of our humanity, in the sense that this humanity does not become complete in us and for us if its conditions of speech and reason, by which [we] are raised above the animal species, are not realized. And they share the same right as us in our common animality, which is constituted of nourishment, refuge, care and reproduction!
>
> From where comes this right we possess?
>
> It is not the modern West that has lent it to us. It is rather an established religious right that belongs to woman by virtue of her humanity. The first verse of the Revelation was revealed calling attention to knowledge as the exclusive possession of human beings: "Read: In the name of thy Lord Who createth. Createth human beings from a clot. Read: And thy Lord is the Most Bounteous. Who teacheth by the pen. Teacheth human beings which they knew not" [Q. 96:1–5].
>
> And *sūrat al-Raḥman* calls attention to utterance as the exclusive possession of human beings: "The Beneficent. Hath made known the Qur'ān. He hath created man. He hath taught him utterance (*bayān*)" [Q. 55:1–4].
>
> The Qur'ān guides us to what constitutes our humanity, that is, reason; if it petrifies or becomes defective, the

> human nature of human beings is transformed and they are no longer considered human beings, but descend to the lowest of levels of savage beasts: "Lo! The worṣt of beasts in Allah's sight are the deaf, the dumb, who have no sense" [Q. 8:22].
>
> The free Muslim woman does not accept that this change transforms her human nature, that the veils of ignorance and forgetfulness be pulled over her reason, her hearing, her sight, and that she becomes like livestock or is made to go astray. And Allah—the Most Exalted—says: "Having hearts wherewith they understand not, and having eyes wherewith they see not, and having ears wherewith they hear not. These are as the cattle—[nay,] but they are worse! These are the neglectful" [Q. 7:179].[60]

Education thus becomes a necessity for the realization of one's true humanity. Women can only fully partake in their God given humanity once they have developed their reason. This necessarily requires that they have an equal access to education. Although this is now an acquired right in most urban Muslim cities, the matter is, however, often different for women living in rural areas where traditional conceptions regarding education are still prevalent.[61] Historically, however, the conception of women's education in Islamic society differed greatly with modern conceptions of education:

> If the opportunity to learn was offered to one of our mothers, this privilege depended on her legal guardian (*walī amri-hā*). The new woman truly evolved if she believes that knowledge is her legal religious and human right, in conformity with her partaking in the human species. This right does not depend on the will of anybody, since no creature can transform her humanity and force her to live like a dumb and silent doll. The human being is distinct from dumb animal, with its capacity to speak that is realized only with [the use of] reason and utterance (*bayān*).
>
> This substantial difference is associated with the fact that our views of knowledge differ completely from the views of our mothers and our backward sisters. Women conceived, or society conceived for them, that knowledge was a kind

> of ornament and a luxury for rich families. During centuries of enslavement, slave girls were taught science, literature, and the arts in order that their price increase on the slave market, and in order that they may lend themselves to the pleasure of their masters—men—and animate their nightly entertainment and relieve them of the boredom and the displeasure that afflicted them. For the poor class, education of girls was a means of sustenance in order to obtain a morsel of bread.[62]

Today, education has another meaning. It is the right of every citizen. In modern societies, education becomes the first condition to women's greater social, political, cultural, religious, etc. roles. Bint al- Shāṭi' extends women's activities to the religious sphere of interpretation where women must play a greater role in the reassessment of these religious interpretations:

> But likewise, I also do not expect that, after us, our daughters will free themselves of the struggle which we have endured, we the ones who have threaded, before them, the perilous path of the transition phase, confronting a society that was not prepared to welcome the new woman. How more harsher that which we have endured! On the one hand, if we look, we see men among our people who want to transform our humanity in the name of Islam. They refuse that we learn and we work, that we comprehend (*nafqaha*) and we interpret (*nubayyin*). Our share is rather that we live like barbaric and numb dolls, enjoying the rattle of the shackles around our necks, our wrists, and our ankles like necklaces, bracelets and anklets. Is this what Allah wanted for us, Allah that created us and [men] from a single soul? This is not how our history has known Muslim women during the time of the Prophet of Islam—may peace be upon him—and the period of his rightly guided caliphs.[63]

Equal rights envisioned by Bint al-Shāṭi' extend far beyond the social sphere of education or work. Equal rights extend even to the religious sphere. She implicitly alludes to the right to exercise exegesis and jurisprudence (*fiqh*) by appealing to both the act of comprehension from which the name of the discipline of jurisprudence is derived and the study and analysis of the scriptures from which one of the names of the Qur'ān is derived—*al-Bayān*. Bint al-Shāṭi''s subtle position is equally radical and, in a sense, reflects her own intellectual and exegetical activities. She notes that:

> A number of them have reached the rank of religious leaders (*mashyakha*) in mysticism, jurisprudence, recitation of the traditions (*ḥadīth*), in Arabic sciences and its literary tradition. Moreover, one of them obtained the guardianship of the Islamic caliphate (*wilāyat al-khilāfat al-islāmiyya*) over Egypt and Sham, I mean "the Queen ᶜIṣmat al-Dīn Shajarat al-Durr" who led the final victorious campaign against the Crusaders.[64]

In 1956 Bint al-Shāṭi' had already written an article entitled "Will Women Become Religious Leaders (*shaykha*) at al-Azhar?" in which she predicted that admission to the oldest and most prestigious Sunnī institution of religious learning would be inevitable in the wake of the new social reality. She noted that history was the best witness: Was not ᶜĀ'isha, the preferred wife of the Prophet, the first and the most respected of *shaykhas*? And she was not alone. Bint al-Shāṭi' mentions the names of over twenty-eight women who became jurists (*faqīhāt*) and specialists of traditions (*muḥaddithāt*). Bint al-Shāṭi' seeks to show that women's real historical role within Islamic civilization greatly contradicts official interpretations of her social, religious, and political roles. She does this more than twenty years before Mernissi's similar feminist critique of 1993. Bint al-Shāṭi''s subtle position is, nonetheless, quite radical for the time. It reflects her intellectual endeavors. Women can and should participate in the religious discourse and the elaboration of religious interpretations, provided that they be well trained and prepared.

Bint al-Shāṭi' analyzes the Islamic concept of equality by going back to the scriptures. In a sense, she is implicitly proposing an exegesis by isolating a number of verses that mention that individuals are not similar. In doing so, she is not out to explain particular verses, but to propose an interpretation of equality by means of her "cross-referential" method, that is, by juxtaposing a number of passages where the term appears.[65] She writes:

> Our right to equality, according to its proper understanding, goes back to an Islamic foundation, established by clear texts from our firmly established book. The Qur'ān does not say at all: "Woman and man are not equal." Rather, what is found in it is:
>
> 1. "The evil and the good are not equal" [Q. 5:100];
> 2. "The dwellers of the Fire and the dwellers of the Garden are not equal" [Q. 59:20];
> 3. "Among you, those who spent [their goods] and fought before the victory are not equal. They are greater in rank than those who spent [their goods] and fought afterwards" [Q. 57:10];
> 4. "Believers who sit still—other than those who have a (disabling) injury—and those who strive in the path of Allah, with their wealth and their lives are not equal" [Q. 4:95];
> 5. "Say, are those who know and those who know not equal?" [Q. 39:9];
> 6. "The blind is not equal to the one who can see, and neither are darkness and light" [Q. 35:19].[66]

Four of the six verses Bint al-Shāṭi' quotes pertain specifically to religious aspects (i.e., nos. 1, 2, 3, 4), while two of them appeal to intelligence (no. 5) and to knowledge (no. 6). She uses these verses to circumscribe the moral and religious spheres the Islamic concept of equality encompasses and which she articulates in terms of religious rights and responsibilities that both women and men have towards God:

> The extent of equality or of its non-existence in the Book of Islam is in accordance with what is good or what is bad, with faith or unbelief, with being rightly guided or being led astray, with effort and exertion or abstention and prohibition, with knowledge or ignorance. It is not in accordance with maleness or femaleness.[67]

Bint al-Shāṭi''s critical approach to the Qur'ān inevitably encounters some difficulties. The spirit of the Qur'ān is derived from the written text. Therefore, her notion of equality must conform to the religious and the legal prescriptions of the Qur'ān. She writes:

> Our understanding of this equality is liberated by means of a return to the foundation of Islam. Woman recognizes that equality of nature (*fiṭra*) consists in the man's religious legal (*sharʿī*) and natural right regarding his "being in charge" (*qiwāma*) of her: "And [women] have rights similar to those [of men] according to what is equitable, and men are a degree (*daraja*) above them" [Q. 2:228].[68]

Bint al-Shāti' quotes the above passage of the Qur'ān (Q. 2:228). The idea of men "being in charge" of women is traditionally corroborated with such verses that place men a "degree" above women. Bint al-Shāṭi' is, however, quick to add that:

> The time has come for men to understand that the object of the "being in charge" that occurs in the Qur'ān is not merely a matter of maleness like in inheritance: "To the male the equivalent of the share of two females" [Q. 4:11]. Rather, this "being in charge," according to the Islamic concept, is a right belonging to manhood. And I do not like that we, the liberated Muslim women, be obliged to consent to our men satisfaction and pleasure, on account of this "being in charge."[69]

Bint al-Shāṭi' does not reject the notion of "being in charge." She refuses, however, to conceive of it, as it has traditionally been conceived, that is, as man's absolute authority over women. She adds:

> Likewise, the time has come for our men to understand that their religious legal right of "being in charge" of us is not absolute—of men, in general, over women, in general. It is rather restricted [as mentioned in the Qur'ān]: "Because Allah hath made the one of them to excel the other, and because they spend wealth [for the support of women]" [Q. 4:34]. Therefore, if a man is unable to fulfill this restriction, his right of "being in charge" disappears: "And men are a degree above them" [Q. 2:228], but, [only] after the origin of equality is established: "And [women] have rights similar to those [of men] according to what is equitable" [Q. 2:228].[70]

Bint al-Shaṭi' reduces this notion of "being in charge" to its social understanding. Man's responsibility is to ensure the material and financial well being of his family. The religious duty of the husband is to be the provider of the household. Modern interpretations offer similar social explanations for women's smaller share in inheritance: women preserve their personal wealth and are not required to contribute financially to the household. "Being in charge" cannot, therefore, be understood as the absolute authority or domination of men over women. No such right arises from men's nature. Bint al-Shāṭi' argues her interpretation by replacing the issue of "being in charge" in the original social context that can be discovered by means of a return to the scriptures themselves. She then argues that the Qur'ānic term of "degree" (e.g., Q. 2:228) used to demonstrate men's preeminence over women has to be understood in light of the context of the verse as well as in light of other passages. Other verses mention hierarchies that have nothing to do with the opposition of women and men, something other modern commentator are keen to note, e.g., Fazlur Rahman.[71] Consequently, equality between women and men cannot be understood in an absolute manner or arising from a particular nature (i.e., that of men), since even prophets were not all equal:

> The "degree" [e.g., Q. 2:228] alone refers to manhood and not to maleness with which the natural condition is preserved and criteria are well balanced, without abrogating our religious legal right to equality. Equality does not violate the religious duties of the mature and the responsibility of human beings. Messengers, indeed, were themselves [exalted above others] in degrees: "Of these messengers, some of whom We have caused to excel others and of whom there are some unto whom Allah spoke, while some of them He exalted [above others] in degrees" [Q. 2:253]. Believers and those most prominent in knowledge are [exalted above others] in degrees: "Allah will exalt those among you who believe, and those who have knowledge, to [high] degrees" [Q. 58:11]. The degree is, therefore, not such that it diminishes us, and it is not such that it lowers us below the level of men. Indeed, Allah has created them and us from a single soul.[72]

Bint al-Shāṭi' completes her exegetical analysis by turning to the traditions (*ḥadīth*). These traditions are reports dating back to the pristine period of the beginning of Islam, at the time of the Prophet and the Rāshidūn (from 11/633 to 41/661), the "rightly guided" caliphs. Traditions also provide information on the place of women during Muhammad's own lifetime. For this reason, a number of writers revert to these traditions to shed new light on women at the beginning of Islam.[73] Turning to traditions is a strategic move to appeal to the authority of those sources. Adopting an anti-andocentric interpretation or re-reading of Islamic history does this. Bint al-Shāṭi''s use of traditions is an early example of what may well be one of the first "feminist" oriented perspective, a strategy that has now become quite prevalent.[74] She gives examples of women that did play important roles within the nascent community (*umma*) of believers and that can serve as models for today's Muslim women:

> O, sisters and friends, I do not doubt that there is someone among you who may find something within themselves if they pause like I have and debate the conditions that Islamic society has, in the name of Islam, imposed on its women throughout long centuries. Perhaps, there is among you someone who says to themselves: 'What is it with this lady who talks about an Islamic concept of women's emancipation. When were women tackling courageously similar religious issues which are the specialty of the jurists among men?'
>
> Regarding this matter, I will not mention that the Prophet—may peace be upon him—recommended to his companions, and among them those who were most learned (*afqah*) in Islam: 'Take half your religion from this red hair;' for where do I stand *via-a-vis* the Mother of the believers, ᶜĀ'isha![75]

Bint al-Shāṭi''s first example consists of a tradition that is absent from the nine official and authoritative collections of traditions.[76] Aware of the contention over such traditions, she proposes a more authoritative tradition based on the report of a story recounted about ᶜUmar ibn al-Khaṭṭāb, the second caliph who ruled from 13/634 to 24/644:

> Instead, I will call your attention to the Commander of the Faithful, ᶜUmar ibn al-Khaṭṭāb, with whom a woman had an argument, when he was preaching in the mosque, over the ban on extravagant dowries for women. He had decided to confiscate whatever exceeded twenty *dirham*, and to deposit it in the public treasury. Historians of Islam reported that:
>
> A woman stepped out of the women's group and said to him, "You are not entitled to do such a thing, O, ᶜUmar." At the time, he was descending from the pulpit, while they were leaving. When he heard what she had said, he stopped and asked, "And why?" She answered, "Because God—the Most Exalted—says: 'And if ye wish to exchange one wife for another and ye have given unto one of them a sum of money [however great], take nothing from it. Would ye take it by the way of calumny and open wrong?' [Q. 4:20]." At that moment, the Commander of the Faithful returned to the pulpit and said his famous words that have continued to fill the ears of time: "A woman was right, and ᶜUmar was wrong."[77]

Bint al-Shāṭi' interprets this tradition[78] as a call on women to be critical of any given religious interpretation. Women are capable and should question the statements of any individual—even those of ᶜUmar, the second "rightly guided" caliph. This can be achieved only once they have had access to knowledge. Consequently, women must become learned in religious matter in order to be able to contest any particular situation or condition established by ancient religious interpretations, some of which are but successive erroneous judicial sedimentations that rob women of rights Islam guarantees them. Erroneous interpretations have come to consider women as deprived of any right to "object" to particular opinions and interpretations, or "discuss" them, and to question their legitimacy. Bint al-Shaṭi', like most reformists, goes back to the Sacred text which is more authoritative than any interpretation. Her call to women is quite explicit:

> Therefore, do not be afraid to discuss, like me, the Islamic concept of women's emancipation. Do not desist from opposing deeply rooted conditions established by pious

> predecessors among men of religion who considered that women are unable to supply refutations and objections. Did I not occupy such a position? Have I not been cited by respectable shaykhs. Allāh has honored me with those who have taught me religious jurisprudence, and guided me to specialization in the study of the Glorious Qur'ān. The Most Exalted has honored me with the [possibility] to deliver to you such a condensed call in which the mention of the illustrious testimonies of Muslim women in our honorable past, before the veil of ignorance and forgetfulness was imposed upon women's vision. So recite in humility and respect [the following verse]: "The Beneficent hath made know the Qur'ān, hath created human beings, and taught them utterance (*bayān*)" [Q. 55:4].[79]

Buds of an Islamic Feminism?

Bint al-Shāṭi' analyzes Muslim women's situation quite critically, in spite of what may be regarded as her conservatism in the social and political (her anti-leftist positions)[80] as well as exegetical realms—her "puritan"[81] or "anti-modern"[82] approach and her belief that Qur'ānic exegesis should be exercised only by specialists.[83] These different positions introduce a tension, even a contradiction[84] within her Islamic concept of women's emancipation. Her desire to preserve traditional Islamic values—maternity[85] or preventing women from becoming singers or dancers[86]—does not give her the latitude to reject such principles as the one of men "being in charge" over women. This does not, however, prevent her from questioning the interpretation of the absolute character of men's authority over women and from rejecting the idea that men are the ones in charge of the household if they are unable to acquit themselves of their religious duty or, for that matter, that they are responsible for women's moral behavior.[87]

The ambiguous stances adopted by Bint al-Shāṭi' may be the reason why, for some, she cannot be considered a feminist,[88] while she is, for others,[89] in spite of her negligible role in the history of Egyptian feminism.[90] But then again, Bint al-Shāṭi' states that she fought and struggled all her life to obtain more rights.[91] This did not prevent her from criticizing[92] the first generation of "Americanized" and "Europeanized" feminists for having deviated feminism from its true "national" and "Islamic roots",[93] while her own interpretation of Islam did not entail the imposition of the veil.[94]

Noteworthy is the fact that Bint al-Shāṭi' gave Muslim women a number of female models with her biographies: *The Mother of the Prophet* (1966), *The Wives of the Prophet* (1959; 1971b), *The Daughters of the Prophet* (1963a), *Sayyida Zaynab, the Heroine of Karbalā'* (1972), *Sakīna, the Daughter of Ḥusayn* (1965)[95] and *al-Khansā'* (1957), a poet converted to Islam by Muḥammad; she also published a work on contemporary Arab women poets (1963b). Moreover, she has criticized Arab society's negative attitude towards women and the inferior status it gives them. In her novels, *The Secrets of the Beach* (1952) and *The Master of the Domain: the History of a Sinful Woman* (1958), she describes numerous tragedies whose victims are women of rural regions.[96] Her collection of short stories, *Pictures of the Life of the Generation of the Pioneers; From the Harem to the University*, provides an homage to women who struggled during a period of radical social changes and also seeks to be a source of inspiration for younger women so that they may avoid the mistakes made by the women of the generation of Bint al-Shāṭi'.[97]

Her articulation of an Islamic concept of women's emancipation based on the scriptures, nonetheless, subtlety transforms the frame of reference of the concepts of equality, emancipation and rights in order to have them comply with an Islamic framework. Bint al-Shāṭi' engages in what Abu-Lughod has called "a complex dialogue with the colonial discourse."[98] Maintaining the notion of "being in charge" in her understanding of equality between women and men creates a hybrid concept that does not appear to overcome the paradox (even the contradiction) that it introduces. Bint al-Shāṭi' proposes a solution to this paradox. She appeals to human nature in its more universal sense: humanity and intellective capacities that women and men share. She constructs new references for these different concepts of equality, emancipation, and rights. New data are aligned with old ones that originate within the religious tradition and traditional social practices. The creation of a new hybrid culture takes a number of interesting forms as is attested with the multiple forms of contemporary "liberal"[99] or "modern" Islam.[100] In short, Bint al-Shāṭi' pleads for a critical approach through the renewal of exegesis.

Conscious of the potential of new Qur'ānic interpretations, Bint al-Shāṭi' proposes, admittedly quite subtly, an interpretation of women and Islam in tune with her time. She argues that Islam proposes notions of freedom and equality capable of providing the foundations for an Islamic concept of women's emancipation. She thus departs from traditional interpretations and returns to the Qur'ān. By the same token, she challenges erroneous traditional judicial interpretations that rob women of the rights that Islam guarantees them. The critical approach of Bint al-Shāṭi' has now become more common, as is testified by the later works of Fatima Mernissi. Scholars such as Mir-Hosseini are showing how centuries of interpretation of women's status and rights in Islam are now being openly questioned and challenged with unexpected and promising results.[101] Although full-fledged feminist theological visions have yet to be articulated, a number of voices have emerged that may prove to be crucial in the future.[102]

Appendix: Work of Bint al-Shāṭi' (not an exhaustive list)

1999 "Islam and the New Woman [trans. by Anthony Calderbank]," *Alif. Journal of Comparative Poetics*, 19: 194–202.

1991 (1953; numerous editions) *Ṣuwar min ḥayāti-hinna fī jīl al-ṭalīᶜa min al-ḥarīm ilā'l-jāmiᶜa* (Cairo).

1990 (vol. 1, 1962 and vol. 2, 1969; numerous editions) *al-Tafsīr al-bayānī lil-Qur'ān al-karīm*, 5th ed., 2 vols. (Cairo).

1986 (1967) *ᶜAlā al-jisr: Bayn al-ḥayāh wa'l-mawt: Sīra dhātiyya* (Cairo).

1984 *Tarājim sayyidāt bayt al-nubuwwa* (Beirut).

1978 (1972) *al-Qur'ān wa qaḍāyā al-insān* (Beirut).

1977 (1972; numerous editions) *al-Shakhṣiyya al-Islāmiyya: Dirāsa Qur'āniyya* (Beirut).

1975 (1973) *al-Isrā'īliyyāt fi'l-ghazw al-fikrī* (Cairo).

1972 (1952) *al-Sayyida Zaynab, baṭalat Karbalā'*, 6th ed. (Cairo).

1971a *al-Iᶜjāz al-bayānī lil-Qur'ān wa masā'il Ibn al-Azraq* (Cairo).

1971b *Wives of the Prophet*, trans. of the 3rd ed. with intro. by Matti Moosa and Nicholas Ranson (Lahore).

1971c *Muqaddima fī'l-manhaj* (Cairo).

1970 *al-Qur'ān wa'l-tafsīr al-ᶜaṣrī* (Cairo).

1969 *Maqāl fī'l-insān: Dirāsa Qur'āniyya* (Cairo).

1967 *al-Mafhūm al-Islāmī li-taḥrīr al-mar'a* (Khartoum, Cairo).

1966 (1953) *Umm al-nabī*, 2nd ed. (Cairo).

1965 *Sakīna Bint al-Ḥusayn* (Cairo).

1963a (1956) *Banāt al-nabī*, 3rd ed. (Cairo).

1963b *al-Shāᶜira al-ᶜArabiyya al-muᶜāṣira* (Cairo).

1959 (1954) *Nisā' al-nabī* (Cairo).

1958 (1942) *Sayyid al-ᶜIzba: Qiṣṣat Imrā'a Khāṭi'a* (Cairo).

1957 *al-Khansā'* (Cairo).

1956 "Hal tuṣbiḥ al-mar'a Shaykha lil-Azhar?" *al-Hilāl* (Feb.): 50–4.

1952 *Sirr al-Shāṭi'* (Cairo).

NOTES

1. Cf. Issa J. Boullata, "Modern Qur'ān Exegesis: A Study of Bint al-Shāṭi''s Method," *The Muslim World*, 64 (1974): 103–13; Kenneth Cragg, *The Mind of the Qur'ān. Chapter in Reflection* (London: George Allen and Unwin, 1973), 70–4; Andrew Rippin, *Muslims: Their Religious Beliefs and Practices.Volume 2: The Contemporary Period* (London: Routledge, 1993), 94.

2. Muḥammad Amīn, "A Study of Bint al-Shāṭi''s Exegesis," MA thesis, Institute of Islamic Studies, McGill University, 1992; Sahiron Syamsuddin, "An Examination of Bint al-Shāṭi''s Method of Interpreting the Qur'ān," MA thesis, Institute of Islamic Studies, McGill University, 1998; Yudian Wahyudi, "ᶜAlī Sharīᶜatī and Bint al-Shāṭi' on Free Will: A Comparison," *Journal of Islamic Studies*, 9.1 (1998): 35–45.

3. Miriam Cooke, "Arab Women Writers," in *Modern Arabic Literature*, ed. M. M. Badawī (Cambridge: Cambridge University Press, 1992), 449; Muḥammad Amīn, "Study of Bint al-Shāṭi''s Exegesis," 6–23; Valerie Hoffman-Ladd, "ᶜĀ'isha ᶜAbd al-Raḥmān," in *The Oxford Encyclopedia of the Modern Islamic World*, 4 vols., ed. John Esposito (New York: Oxford University Press, 1995), I, 4a-5b; Abāḥa al-Sabī'ī, "Bint al-Shāṭi'," in *Contemporary Arab Writers: Biographies and Autobiographies*, ed. Robert B. Campbell (Beirut-Stuttgart: Franz Steiner Verlag, 1996), I, 360–3 [in Arabic]; Joyce M. Davis, "Bint al-Shāṭi'," in her *Between Jihad and Salaam: Profiles in Islam*, (New York: St. Martin's Press, 1997), 167–79; Valerie Hoffman, "An Islamic Activist: Zaynab al-Ghazali," in *Women and the Family in the Middle East: New Voices of Change*, ed. Elizabeth W. Fernea (Austin: University of Texas Press, 1985), 233–54.

4. Syamsuddin, "An Examination of Bint al-Shāṭi''s Method," 52–73.

5. C. Kooij, "Bint al-Shāṭi': A Suitable Case for Biography?," in *The Challenge of the Middle East*, eds. Ibrahim A. El-Sheikh, Aart van de Koppel and Rudolph Peters (Amsterdam: Institute for Modern Near East Studies, University of Amsterdam, 1982), 70.

6. George Vajda, "Isrā'īliyyāt," *EI2*, IV, 221a-2a.

7. William M. Brinner, "An Egyptian Anti-Orientalist," in *Islam, Nationalism, and Radicalism in Egypt and the Sudan*, eds. G. Warburg and U. M. Kupferschmidt (New York: Praeger, 1983), 231, 233–44.

8. Bint al-Shāṭi', *al-Isrā'īliyyāt fi'l-ghazw al-fikrī* (Cairo 1975), 147–52; http://bahailibrary.org/books/biblio/antibahaipolemic.html, site consulted 30/03/2001.

9. Rippin, *Muslims*, 94.

10. Wahyudi, "ᶜAlī Sharīᶜatī and Bint al-Shāṭi' on Free Will," 35–45.

11. Cragg, *The Mind of the Qur'ān*, 70–4; Syamsuddin, "An Examination of Bint al-Shāṭi''s Method," 152–4; J. J. G. Jansen, *The Interpretation of the Koran in Modern Egypt* (Leiden: E. J. Brill, 1974), 65–76.

12. Issa J. Boullata, "The Rhetorical Interpretation of the Qur'ān: *Iᶜjāz* and Related Topics," in *Approaches to the History of the Interpretation of the Qur'ān*, ed. Andrew Rippin (Oxford: Oxford University Press, 1988), 152–4; cf. Bint al-Shāṭi', *al-Iᶜjāz al-bayānī lil-Qur'ān wa masā'il Ibn al-Azraq* (Cairo 1971).

13. Sahiron Syamsuddin, "Bint al-Shāṭi' on *Asbāb al-Nuzūl*," *The Islamic Quarterly*, 42 (1998): 5–23.

14. Jansen, *The Interpretation of the Koran in Modern Egypt*, 65–76.

15. Muḥammad ᶜAlā al-Sīd, "The Hermeneutical Problem of the Qur'ān in Islamic History," PhD dissertation, Temple University, 1975; Syamsuddin, "An Examination of Bint al-Shāṭi''s Method."

16. Boullata, "Modern Qur'ān Exegesis," 103–13; cf. Amīn, "A Study of Bint al-Shāṭi''s Exegesis," which depends on Boullata's study.

17. Bint al-Shāṭi', *ᶜAlā al-jisr: Bayn al-ḥayāh wa'l-mawt: Sīra dhātiyya* (Cairo 1986) and *al-Tafsīr al-bayānī li'l-Qur'ān al-karīm*, 5th ed., 2 vols. (Cairo 1990), 10; cf. Amīn al-Khūlī, *Manāhij tajdīd fī'l-naḥw wa'l-balāgha wa'l-tafsīr wa'l-adab* (Cairo 1961).

18. Hoffman-Ladd, "ᶜĀ'isha ᶜAbd al-Raḥmān," 4b-5a.

19. Boullata, "Modern Qur'ān Exegesis," 107; Jansen, *The Interpretation of the Koran in Modern Egypt*, 73.

20. Syamsuddin, "An Examination of Bint al-Shāṭi''s Method," 47–50, 73–82.

21. Rippin, *Muslims*, 94.

22. Bint al-Shāṭi', *al-Tafsīr al-bayānī*, I, 176–7 and II, 79–82; Idem, *Muqaddima fī'l-manhaj* (Cairo 1971), 133–4; Idem, *al-Shakhṣiyya al-Islāmiyya: Dirāsa Qur'āniyya* (Beirut 1977), 167–9; cf. Wahyudi, 37–40.

23. Jansen, *The Interpretation of the Koran in Modern Egypt*, chapter 4.

24. Boullata, "Modern Qur'ān Exegesis," 108.

25. Bint al-Shāṭi', *al-Qur'ān wa'l-tafsīr al-ᶜaṣrī* (Cairo 1970).

26. J. J. G. Jansen, "Polemics on Mustafa Mahmud's Koran Exegesis," in *Proceedings of the Ninth Congress of the Union Européenne des Arabisants et Islamisants*. Amsterdam 1st to 7th September 1978 (Leiden: E. J. Brill, 1981), 110–23.

27. Bint al-Shāṭi', *al-Qur'ān wa qaḍāyā al-insān* (Beirut 1978), 33; cf. Wahyudi, "ᶜAlī Sharīᶜatī and Bint al-Shāṭi' on Free Will," 37.

28. Sherifa Zuhur, *Revealing Reveiling: Islamist Gender Ideology in Contemporary Egypt* (Albany NY: SUNY Press, 1992), 43.

29. Valerie Hoffman-Ladd, "Polemics on the Modesty and Segregation of Women," *IJMES*, 19 (1987): 23–50.

30. Nov. 3, 1997: 10.

31. Bint al-Shāṭi', "Islam and the New Woman [trans. by Anthony Calderbank]," *Alif: Journal of Comparative Poetics*, 19 (1999):194–202.

32. *Al-Mafhūm al-Islāmī li-taḥrīr al-mar'a* (Khartoum, Cairo 1967); cf. Issa J. Boullata, *Trends and Issues in Contemporary Arab Thought* (Albany NY: SUNY Press, 1990), 121–3; Roxanne Marcotte, "Emancipation de la femme et exégèse qur'ānique chez Bint al-Shāṭi' (1913–1998)," *Studies in Religion / Sciences Religieuses*, 30 (2001): 277–92.

33. Margot Badran and Miriam Cooke (eds), *Opening the Gates. A Century of Arab Feminist Writing* (Bloomington and Indianapolis: Indiana University Press, 1990).

34. Cf. Fanny Davis, *The Ottoman Lady. A Social History from 1718 to 1918* (Westport CT: Greenwood Press, 1986)

35. *Al-Mafhūm al-Islāmī,* 4, 13.

36. Ibid., 7, 8–10.

37. Ibid., 8–9.

38. Ibid., 9.

39. Leila Ahmed, *Women and Gender in Islam. Historical Roots of a Modern Debate* (New Haven: Yale University Press, 1992), 202–6.

40. *Al-Mafhūm al-Islāmī,* 4, 5.

41. Fatima Mernissi, *The Forgotten Queens of Islam*, trans. Mary J. Lakeland (Cambridge: Polity, 1993).

42. *Al-Mafhūm al-Islāmī,* 5.

43. Ibid., 5.

44. Ibid., 5–6.

45. Ibid., 13.

46. Ibid., 9.

47. Ibid., 9.

48. Ibid., 9–10; cf. Idem., "Islam and the New Woman," 201.

49. Boullata, *Trends and Issues,* 121.

50. *Al-Mafhūm al-Islāmī*, 9.

51. Literally, "elimination of the 'n' (= *nūn*) of *niswah* (= women)" that results in *sawa* (= equal), Ibid., 10.

52. Ibid., 6, 10, 13.

53. Bint al-Shāṭi', *al-Isrāᶜīliyyāt*; Brinner, "An Egyptian Anti-Orientalist," 232.

54. *Al-Mafhūm al-Islāmī,* 14.

55. Ibid., 14–15.

56. Cf. Deniz Kandiyoti, "Emancipated but Unliberated? Reflections on the Turkish Case," *Feminist Studies*, 13 (1987): 317–38.

57. *Al-Mafhūm al-Islāmī,* 10–1.

58. Cf. Bint al-Shāṭi', *ᶜAlā al-jisr: Bayn al-ḥayāh wa'l-mawt: Sīra dhātiyya* (Cairo 1986), 139–41.

59. *Al-Mafhūm al-Islāmī,* 6–7.

60. Ibid., 7–8.

61. Nimat Hafez Barazangi, "Muslim Women's Islamic Higher Learning as a Human Right, Theory and Practice," in *Windows of Faith: Muslim Scholar-Activists in North America*, ed. Gisela Webb (Syracuse: Syracure University Press, 2000), 22–50.

62. *Al-Mafhūm al-Islāmī*, 7.

63. Ibid., 13–4.

64. Ibid., 4–5.

65. Syamsuddin, "An Examination of Bint al-Shāṭi''s Method," 47–50 and cf. 73–82.

66. *Al-Mafhūm al-Islāmī,* 11–2.

67. Ibid., 12.

68. Ibid.,12.

69. Ibid., 12.

70. Ibid., 12.

71. Barbara Stowasser, "Gender Issues and Contemporary Quran Interpretation," in *Islam, Gender, and Social Change*, ed. Yvonne Y. Haddad (New York: Oxford University Press, 1998), 38–9.

72. *Al-Mafhūm al-Islāmī,* 13.

73. Fatima Mernissi, *Le harem politique. Le Prophète et les femmes* (Paris: Albin Michel, 1987); Ahmed, *Women and Gender in Islam*; Aziza al-Hibri, "A Study of Islamic History: Or How Did We Ever Get Into this Mess?," in *Women and Islam*, ed. Aziza al-Hibri, et al. (Elmsford NY: Pergamon Press, 1982), 209–19; also cf. Shaḥrūr, on whom see Roxanne Marcotte, "Shaḥrūr, the Status of Women, and Polygamy in Islam," *Oriente Moderno*, 20 (2000): 313–28 and idem, "Le réformisme islamique revisité: l'interprétation de Shaḥrūr (1938—) et la condition féminine," *Studies in Religion / Sciences Religieuses*, 28 (1999) 437–64.

74. Mernissi, *Le harem politique*; Ahmed,*Women and Gender in Islam*.

75. *Al-Mafhūm al-Islāmī,* 15.

76. Ibid., 15; report also cited by al-Hibri, "A Study of Islamic History," 215.

77. *Al-Mafhūm al-Islāmī,* 16.

78. Report cited by al-Hibri, "A Study of Islamic History," 213.

79. *Al-Mafhūm al-Islāmī,* 16.

80. Kooij, "Bint al-Shāṭi': A Suitable Case for Biography?"67, 69, 70.

81. Boullata, "Modern Qur'ān Exegesis," 107; Jansen, *Interpretation*, 74.

82. Rippin, *Muslims*, 94.

83. Brinner, "An Egyptian Anti-Orientalist," 228–48.

84. Kooij, "Bint al-Shāṭi': A Suitable Case for Biography?"67.

85. Bint al-Shāṭi', "Islam and the New Woman," 187–201.

86. Davis, "Bint al-Shāṭi'," 176, 178.

87. Hoffman-Ladd, "ᶜĀ'isha ᶜAbd al-Raḥmān," 5a.

88. Joseph T. Zeidan, "Women Novelists in Modern Arabic Literature," Ph.D. dissertation, University of California, Berkeley 1982, 200.

89. Cooke, 449.

90. Badran and Cooke, *Opening the Gates*.

91. Davis, "Bint al-Shāṭi'," 176.

92. *al-Ahrām*, Nov. 13, 1997: 10.

93. Bint al-Shāṭi', "Islam and the New Woman," 197.

94. Davis, "Bint al-Shāṭi'," 168, 178; Bint al-Shāṭi', "Islam and the New Woman," 194.

95. 5 works in 1; cf. *Tarājim Sayyidāt Bayt al-Nubūwa* (Beirut 1984).

96. Analyzed by Zeidan, "Women Novelists in Modern Arabic Literature," 201–3; Paul Starkey, "ᶜAbd al-Raḥmān, ᶜĀ'isha [Bint al-Shāṭi']," in *Encyclopedia of Arabic Literature*, 2 vols., ed. Julie Scott Meisami and Paul Starkey (London: Routledge, 1998), 18a.

97. *Ṣuwar min ḥayāti-hinna fī jīl al-ṭalīᶜa min al-ḥarīm ilā 'l-jāmiᶜa* (Cairo 1991), 7–8.

98. Lila Abu-Lughod, "Feminist Longings and Postcolonial Conditions," in *Remaking Women. Feminism and Modernity in the Middle East*, ed. Lila Abu-Lughod (Cairo: The American University Press, 1998), 20.

99. Charles Kurzman, "Introduction. Liberal Islam and Its Islamic Context," in *Liberal Islam. A Sourcebook*, ed. Charles Kurzman (New York: Oxford University Press, 1998), 3–26.

100. Ziba Mir-Hosseini, *Islam and Gender. The Religious Debate in Contemporary Iran* (New York 1999).

101. Roxanne Marcotte, "How Far Have Reforms Gone in Islam?," *Women's Studies International Forum,* 26 (2003): 153–66.

102. Amina Wadud-Muhsin, "Alternative Qur'ānic Interpretation and the Status of Muslim Women," in *Windows of Faith: Muslim Scholar-Activists in North America*, ed. Gisela Webb (Syracuse NY: Syracuse University Press, 2000), 13–21; idem, "Qur'ān and Women," in *Liberal Islam. A Sourcebook*, ed. Charles Kurzman (New York: Oxford University Press, 1998), 127–38; idem, *Qur'ān and Women. Rereading the Sacred Text from a Women's Perspective* (Kuala Lumpur: Penerbit Fajar Bakti SDN.BHD, 1992); Riffat Hassan, "Human

Rights in the Qur'ānic Perspective," in *Windows of Faith: Muslim Scholar-Activists in North America*, ed. Gisela Webb (Syracuse NY: Syracuse University Press, 2000), 241–8; idem,"Feminist Theology: The Challenge for Muslim Women," *Critique: The Journal for Critical Studies of the Middle East*, 9 (1996): 53–65; idem, "Equal Before Allah? Women-Man Equality in the Islamic Tradition," *Harvard Divinity Bulletin*, 17.2 (1987): 2–4; idem, "On Human Rights and the Qur'ānic Perspective," *Journal of Ecumenical Studies*, 19 (1982): 51–65; Maysam J. al-Faruqi, "Women's Self-Identity in the Qur'ān and Islamic Law," in*Windows of Faith: Muslim Scholar-Activists in North America*, ed. Gisela Webb (Syracuse NY: Syracuse University Press, 2000), 72–101; Nighat Said Khan, *Voices Within: Dialogues with Women on Islam* (Lahore: ASR Pub., 2000).

Chapter 10

The Qur'ān in Egypt II: Sayyid Quṭb on Inimitability

Soraya Mahdi Hajjaji-Jarrah

> "*Siḥrun yu'thar*" which divorces man from his people, and from his children ... it was the statement of a man who was reluctant to become a Muslim, too insolent to give in to Muḥammad ... this statement testifies, more than all what the believers [may] say, to the Qur'ān's enthralling impact (*siḥr*) on the Arabs ... from the onset, ... consequently we must look for the wellspring (*manbaᶜ*) of the Qur'ān's spell ... before the meticulous legislation, before the lore about the universe and before the Qur'ān became a complete whole ... for the sparse early revelations did not include any of these later concerns ... they, however, possessed that original wellspring which the Arabs innately recognized and said "*in hadhā illa siḥrun yu'thar*."[2]

With this argument Sayyid Quṭb (d. 1966) undertakes the task of unraveling the source of the inimitability (*iᶜjāz*) of the Qur'ān in his *al-Taṣwīr al-Fannī fī'l-Qur'ān* and *Mashāhid al-Qiyāma fī'l-Qur'ān,* both completed in the 1940s.[3] By temporalizing his field of investigation to the early revelations, Quṭb has ostensibly broken away from the traditional exponents of the doctrine who cover the entire Book. The novelty of his approach goes even further. In his *al-Taṣwīr al-Fannī,* he *a priori* precludes the religious dimensions of the Qur'ān and unequivocally states that his study intends to deal purely and solely with the literary aspect (*al-wijha al-fanniyya al-baḥitha*) of the *iᶜjāz*. He argues that freeing the discussion from any thematic (*mawḍuᶜiyya*) "complications" is necessitated by the beautiful artistic rendition (*al-ᶜarḍ al-fannī al-jamīl*)[4] and by the temporal limitation of the investigation to when the Qur'ān was not as yet complicated by exegetical and syntactical studies.[5] However, what merits our attention is not to address Quṭb's literary appreciation of the Qur'ān, this Issa Boullata has amply covered; but to address what I call the "evolution" in Quṭb's concept of the *iʿjāz*.[6] I call it as such because as we shall see throughout this essay his positive findings and definitions of the *iʿjāz* are multifarious in the diverse periods of his life. For while he does indeed hold on to the fort of pure literary analysis of the Qur'ānic *iʿjāz* in his two studies, in the revised edition of his *Fī Ẓilāl al-Qur'ān* of 1959, Quṭb exhibits a phenomenal "change of heart." The transformation or evolution in his views, which include all approaches to any aspect of the Qur'ān, is so profound that he forcefully attacks the pure literary approach that he so intensely argued for and carried out in the 1940s. In his commentary he explicitly condemns "those who conduct stylistic or literary study *(dirāsa bayāniyya aw fanniyya)* of the Qur'ānic discourse." He confidently argues that those whom he calls inactive individuals, "will not be able to unravel the Qur'ānic reality in this slothful indolence (*hadhihi al-qaʿda al-bārida al-sākina*)." For the reality of the Qur'ān will never be revealed to "those who prefer leisure and security (*al-rāḥa wa'l-salāma*). Rather, experiencing (*dhawq*) the Qur'ānic discourse can only be attained by those who rush into Islam's deciding battle (*al-maʿraka al-taqrīriyya*).[7] That Quṭb, after joining *al-Ikhwān al-Muslimūn*, considers politico-religious activism as the locus of the life of the true Muslim, is a proposition whose validity has been established, and as such needs no demonstration. Once again what concerns us here is Quṭb's perception of *iʿjāz al-Qur'ān* insofar as it is multifarious, and it is to this extent that both his literary appreciation of the Qur'ān and his politico-religious activism will be relevant to us here.

An essential premise of this essay, therefore, is that one cannot speak of Quṭb's thought as a single uniform phenomenon, for one must account for the variegation in content and focus of his orientations, particularly after he adopted the tenets of political activism and religious radicalism. The evolution of his thought can be placed on a wide spectrum whose extreme ends represent liberal literariness and uncompromising politico-religious ideology. The differential between the stages of his thought is the fact that he revised the first thirteen volumes of his *tafsīr* which he wrote in 1952 before joining *al-Ikhwān al-Muslimūn*.[8] A mere perusal of the contents of the two editions reveals a considerable difference between them. A review of his 1940s studies of the Qur'ān and the revised edition of his *tafsīr* discloses an astonishing divergence.[9]

The ensuing essay, which is the first in a series of forthcoming articles, attempts to present a comparative study of Quṭb's approaches to the concept of *iᶜjāz* in the 1940s and 1959 which afford us perhaps the evidence of the significant changes and developments within his writings on the subject. However, it is instructive to note here that the radical leap in Quṭb's concept of the *iᶜjāz* from connoting a purely literary and largely secular definition, as we shall come to see, to becoming one of the vehicles of his politico-religious assumptions, did not occur precipitately. Rather the process of his thought went through an intermediate stage, as revealed in the unrevised edition of his *tafsīr*. We shall touch upon only three examples of this subsidiary stage in order to make our point. In the remainder of the study I shall limit my remarks to six Qur'ānic verses and Quṭb's divergent readings of the *iᶜjāz* in them during the different stages of his career.

In his first two major studies on the Qur'ān, Quṭb celebrates his original, and indeed ground-breaking discovery of the Qur'ān's uniform mode of expressions: *al-taṣwīr al-fannī* or artistic portrayal.[10] One of the defining and distinguishing features is its emotive, sensational and mental impact on the audience rendering *al-taṣwīr al-fannī* the efficacious style for both religion and literature. In terms of the Qur'ānic discourse, Quṭb explains that its cumulative effect on the human soul is the result of harmony between the artistic and thematic beauty (a*l-jamāl al-fannī wa'l-jamāl al-mawḍūᶜī*) of its discourse.[11] However, this sort of harmony remains at this stage a *terra incognita* for Quṭb and he focuses his attention, instead, on the purely artistic beauty of the Qur'ānic imageries, narratives, and scenes of resurrection. His focus testifies decidedly to an unwavering commitment to his pre-stated intentions which he manages to inject in his two studies to assert, as a reminder, that his interest in the Qur'ān now and in the future has but one purpose, *hadaf fannī khāliṣ maḥḍ*, purely and utterly artistic.[12] In fact, his faithful observance to and ostensibly exclusive interest in the Qur'ānic artistic rendition find expression, at times, even at the expense of ignoring the overriding theme of the Qur'ānic passage. Consider, for instance, Q. 2:127–8:

> And remember Abraham and Ismāᶜīl raised the foundations of the House "Our Lord accept (this service) from us, for You are the All-Hearing, the All-Knowing." "Our Lord make us Muslims to Your (Will), and of our progeny a people Muslim, bowing to Your (Will), and show us our places for the celebration of (due) rites; and turn unto us (in Mercy); for You are the Oft-Returning, Most Merciful.

Adhering to his approach, Quṭb takes a conscientious decision to overlook the contents of Abraham's and Ismāᶜīl's captivating *duᶜā* which forms the substratum of the two verses, and constitutes a quintessential link in the Qur'ānic view of the history of monotheism. Quṭb, instead, engages himself with the manner in which the Qur'ān animates the event, lending it immediacy and a palpable presence, to a degree that the listeners feel as though they were spectators of an actual scene before them. He points out that this lifelike presence is achieved through the dramatic development of the story where it transforms without a verbal link abruptly from narrative to prayer. He concludes that the mere but remarkable absence of a single connecting element is the secret of the scene's animation and hence the source of its *iᶜjāz*.[13]

Nevertheless, Quṭb is aware of the difficulty in drawing lines of separation between the literary and the religious dimensions of the Qur'ānic discourse. Consequently he realizes that his pure literary approach to the Qur'ān *iᶜjāz* may occasionally include religious references which could suggest that he is not conforming to his *a priori* intentions. Quṭb absolves himself from such deviation and attributes any religious references to "the innate nature of the Qur'ān [as a Book of religion.]"[14] Furthermore, even though Quṭb concedes the superiority of the Qur'ānic themes and the powerful attraction of faith (*al-ᶜaqīda*), at this stage he argues for the indebtedness of the Qur'ānic aims to its mode of *taṣwīr*.[15] In point of fact, Quṭb takes more of an emphatic stance to assert the legitimacy of his argument by implicitly rejecting the competence of the Qur'ānic themes to be the source of its *iᶜjāz*. The rationale for his contention is immediately given: had the Qur'ān used rationalism [to transmit its message] it would not have achieved any success.[16] Rather, it is through the indispensable Qur'ānic method of *taṣwīr* that its themes "have acquired their greatest value."[17]

Quṭb puts forward the principle element of the Qur'ān's sort of literary *taṣwīr*, namely, *al-takhyīl al-ḥissī wa'l-tajsīm* or the sensuous imaginative activity and palpability.[18] Through this element the audience gains immediate and concrete access to otherwise inaccessible abstract notions and supernatural phenomenon which constitute a major section of the Qur'ānic themes. To support his views Quṭb cites a number of verses, such as Q. 48:10, 39:67, and 8:17, which give anthropomorphic depictions of the most abstract Qur'ānic concept: God. Quṭb argues that these corporeal depictions where absolute abstraction and total transcendence are mandatory give emphatic evidence that palpable *takhyīl* constitutes the basis of the Qur'ānic mode of expression. From then on Quṭb advances his thesis by comparing and contrasting the Qur'ān's palpable depiction of abstract ideas, particularly its fundamental concepts of belief and unbelief with their presentation through rationalism. An examination of some of the examples involved may demonstrate how far Quṭb has proven the validity of his assumptions as well as how successfully he manages to separate mode of expression from themes.

Quṭb's treatments of Q. 24:39–40 and Q. 2:16–20 present an eloquent testimony to his thesis. He begins his discussion by pointing out how the mere theoretical exposition of the concept of the invalidity of the unbelievers' deeds reaches the mind and remains categorically stagnant. Expressing this notion through the Qur'ān's method of *taṣwīr* as in Q. 24:39–40, however, breathes life into it which stirs the imagination and sense perceptions:

> But the Unbelievers—their deeds are like a mirage in sand deserts, which the man parched with thirst mistakes for water; until when he comes up to it he finds it to be nothing: but he finds God (ever) with him, and God pays him his account: and God is swift in taking account. Or (the unbelievers state) is like the depths of darkness, in a vast deep ocean, overwhelmed with billow, topped by billow, topped by dark clouds. Depths of darkness, one above another. If a man stretches out his hand, he can hardly see it. For any to whom God gives not lights, there is no light.

Now, even though verse 39 portrays a remarkable and abrupt leap from the scene of a thirsty individual who is pursuing a mirage into

Judgment Day, it should come as no surprise that these religious implications do not seem to command Quṭb's attention. Instead, he concentrates exclusively on the aesthetic dimensions of the verses without even referring to the immediacy and decisiveness of the divine retribution. He marvels at the enchanting animated images of the verses which can neither be reproduced in a painting because of their narrative form, nor can the darkness of the sea underneath and the clouds above be captured on photographic image.[19]

For Q. 2:16–20 Quṭb dramatically amplifies how the Qur'ān expresses the abstract religious concept of error after guidance without, I must add, inflating the image:

> These are they who have bartered guidance for error, but their traffic is profitless, and they have lost true direction. Their similitude is that of a man who kindled a fire; when it lighted all around him, God took away their light, and left them in utter darkness, so they could not see. Deaf, dumb, and blind, they will not return to the path. Or (another similitude) a rain-laden cloud from the sky, in it are zones of darkness, and thunder and lightning. They press their fingers in their ears to keep out the stunning thunderclap, the while they are in terror of death. But God is ever round the rejecters of faith. The lightning all but snatches away their sight; every time the light (helps) them, they walk therein, and when the darkness grows on them, they stand still, and if God willed He could take away their faculty of hearing and seeing, for God has power over all things.

In these more involved verses the two components, namely, the religious and the literary, operate with equal competing force. Quṭb, however, manages with remarkable success to bring exclusively into prominence not only the imaginative and the original, but also the uncommon literary excellence of the Qur'ānic portrayal of the image. He wonders in the most glowing terms at the verses' arresting and vivid images of motion, loss and confusion by highlighting their most dramatic literary dimensions. "They [the erroneous] have lit a fire which provides them with some light. Suddenly through divine intervention, their light goes out leaving them in total darkness…or here is a rain storm…a sudden stroke of lightning brings in some illumination for a moment, they try to walk, but darkness descends and their loss continues...." Transmitting what seems to be his own acute perception of the imageries, Quṭb argues for the superiority of the Qur'ān's verbal tools to a painting or a motion picture. A more enjoyable ecstasy is achieved when "the imagination portrays the images and erases them, creates the movements and follows them and depicts the tones and watches them."[20] In his view this sort of *taṣwīr* not only influences the soul and senses, it also provokes the emotions. And in this emotive provocation lies the ultimate success of any literary work.[21]

It is now instructive to compare how Quṭb reads the above verses (Q. 2:16–20) in his 1952 unrevised edition of *Fī Ẓilāl al-Qur'ān*. Quṭb's approach to these verses heralds significant change in his discourse on the Qur'ān. He no longer seems to be rigidly adhering to his early exclusive proclaimed interest in the Qur'ān's mode of expression which he, in the 1940s, concedes to represent "an independent element of pure beauty ... free from all other purposes and concerns."[22] For even though his commentary on the verses remains largely literary, the verses now impart more than pure aesthetic ecstasy. They concurrently transmit a message innately related to the religious nature of the Qur'ān. His elucidation of the verses' powerful sense of confusion and motion is frequently intercepted by lengthy references to their religious implications. For Quṭb, this commotion now has a thematic as well as an aesthetic purpose, for "the movement in the whole scene does indeed depict the motion in the [human] conscience, it portrays the confusion between belief and the retreat to unbelief ... between the quest for guidance and the return to error."[23] Moreover, even though it is abundantly clear that Quṭb does not abandon his literary appreciation of the Qur'ānic extraordinary *taṣwīr*, his literary discussion imparts a lesser degree of emotional intensity than it did in the 1940s. For instance, in his analysis he does not attempt to magnify the image's sense of movement, nor does he emphasize the importance of the powerful emotions that can be stirred by them. Nor is this all. He makes virtually no attempt whatsoever to articulate the existence of emotional stimulation and its ultimate effect of utter enjoyment. Most remarkable indeed is Quṭb's own admission here of what seems to be a "coming to life" of his religious sentiments. Referring to his 1940s studies of the Qur'ān, he candidly states, "when I examined the Qur'ānic literary aesthetics in *al-Taṣwīr al-Fannī*, I perceived the *i^c^jāz* [purely] in the Qur'ān's mode of expression … I was not motivated by *al-^c^aqīda* then. This *^c^aqīda* has palpitated (*nabaḍat*) by these studies."[24]

A longer leap, and indeed a more substantial transformation in Quṭb's concept of *i^c^jāz*, finds expression in his 1959 revised edition of *Fī Ẓilāl al-Qur'ān* especially through his reading of the verses of the Qur'ānic *taḥaddī* or the Qur'ānic challenge. But we will deal with this later. The fervor of Quṭb's "conversion" to religion's extremism manifests itself as he introduces his commentary on the verses under discussion (Q. 2:16–20). The psychologically confused souls are no longer generic erroneous human beings. Quṭb now decisively identifies them. They are the hypocrites (*al-munāfiqūn*) of Medina and the hypocrites in the absolute sense. Moreover, this identification assumes a more defined purpose when Quṭb attributes the detailed Qur'ānic portrayal of the image to the magnitude of the gravely damaging role played by the hypocrites then and "at all times within the aggregation of the Muslims." These souls' successive loss of light is perceived by Quṭb as a Qur'ānic reference to divine retribution for their defection from belief.[25]

This kind of evolution in Quṭb's writings on the subject is by no means exceptional. In *al-Taṣwīr al-Fannī*, Quṭb contends that the Qur'ānic mode of *takhyīl* and *taṣwīr* can sometimes bypass the human attributes of mind and senses, by forging a direct link with the center of man's faith where the soul has direct contact with the unknown (*al-majhūl*). In this contact the combination of awe, enjoyment and pleasure which are derived by the soul, due to the mystery and remoteness of the unknown, are of primary importance. In order to support his argument, Quṭb cites several verses such as Q. 24:41 and 40:8. However, he appears to find more expressive power in Q. 6:59:

> With Him are the keys of the Unseen, the treasures that none knows but He. He knows whatever there is on the earth and in the sea. Not a leaf does fall but with His knowledge; there is not a grain in the darkness (or depths) of the earth, nor anything fresh or dry but is (inscribed) in the Record Clear (to those who can read).

Now quite clearly the central, if not *the* theme of the verse is divine omniscience. But for Quṭb it is not. In his reading of the verse his literary preoccupations are ever paramount, and the verse's religious component is fully controlled and creatively placed in the service of the literary consideration of his work. Equally important, for our purposes here, is his remarkably explicit indication of his secular interests in the 1940s. He begins his discussion by marveling at how the verse portrays the all-encompassing knowledge of whom he "boldly" calls the deity (*al-ilāh*). He continues to bring forward his secular interests by affirming that the tenor of this expressive verse is not merely intended to define omniscience; rather it imparts an extraordinary image that belongs to the realm of fantasy. Quṭb explains that through the verse's magnificent image the human imagination is able to follow all these falling leaves and hidden seeds which are only known to God. In this journey it travels to the furthest horizons and to all their unknown corners. It is the imaginative performance of such a breathtaking journey to the expansive unknown, he asserts, which fills the soul with awe and exaltation toward the omniscient God.[26]

On the same verse (Q. 6:59), Quṭb's attention in 1952 shifts from focusing on the journey of the human imagination to concentrating on the excellence of the verse's image in portraying the infinity of divine knowledge. It is an image, he explains, "of the All-Knowing God, nothing escapes Him in time or place, on land or in the sea, in the depths of earth or in the heights of space, whether dead, alive, moist or dry." Furthermore, these boundless spheres of time and space of divine knowledge are now outside of the limits and capacity of the human imagination which he so strongly supported earlier in the 1940s. The arresting features of the verse consequently change from its capacity to stir the human imagination, to its unmatchable conciseness in describing the minutest details of divine knowledge. Evidently pure literary considerations are here reconciled, by Quṭb, with religious exigencies. For Quṭb now, the marvelous union between the Qur'ān's literary excellence and its religious message is "indeed the *iʿjāz*."[27]

This short and indeed concise Qur'ānic verse captures Quṭb's attention in 1959 and he dedicates several pages and refers to it again in his commentary on Q. 10:38. In both places Quṭb integrates his altered concept of the Qur'ānic *iʿjāz*. The transformation in his orientation takes a clear turn when he focuses his attention on the former's thematic *iʿjāz*. Diametrically opposed to his reading of the verse in the 1940s, Quṭb holds now that the verse is intended to reveal a dimension of the substance of divinity (*ḥaqīqat al-ulūhiyya*): omniscience which is accessible to neither humans nor to their imagination. Moreover, while he marveled in the 1940s at the pleasures attained by the soul's traverse into the unknown, its imaginative journey is dropped altogether and the unknown takes an even stronger religious purpose than it did in 1952. It is now not only an exclusive divine territory, but synonymous with the only ascertained truth (*al-ḥaqīqa al-mustayqana*). Equally important is believing that this truth constitutes an integral component of the basis of the Islamic conceptualization of existence (*muqawwimāt al-taṣawwur al-Islāmī*).[28] It is this *taṣawwur* which informs Quṭb of his radically transformed view on the Qur'ānic *iʿjāz* whose primary constituent now is the Qur'ānic theme. His reading of two *taḥaddī* verses Q. 2:23–4 and Q. 10:38 can present us a view of this significant development in his concept of the *iʿjāz*:

> And if you are in doubt as to what we have revealed from time to time to Our servant, then produce a *sūra* like thereunto; and call your witnesses or helpers (if there are any) besides God, if your doubts are true. But if you cannot and you certainly cannot, then fear the fire whose fuel is men and stones, which is prepared for those who reject faith. (Q. 2:23–4)
>
> Or do they say "He forged it"? Say: "Bring then a *sūra* like unto it and call (to your aid) anyone you can besides God if it be you speak the truth!" (Q10:38)

In 1952 Quṭb perceives the Qur'ānic challenge of Q. 2:23–4 in terms of divine creative power. In his view "this incapacitating Book" is composed of letters referred to in the first verse of the *sūra* and are also available to humans. However, what humans can compose out of these letters and what God has created is beyond comparison.[29] Significantly in this edition of his *tafsīr* Quṭb reconciles the literary and thematic forces in constructing the *iʿjāz* of the Qur'ān.

And even though the themes are not clearly defined, they are, nevertheless, briefly designated in his commentary on Q. 10:38. They include the Qur'ān's sublime style, its unsurpassable social and legislative systems as well as its uncanny psychological effect.[30] Quṭb marvels here at this indissoluble union between themes and style as being the absolute *iʿjāz*. Aware of what he sees now as being his earlier "shortcomings" in perceiving the possibility of such a union, he attributes such "deficiency" in perception to "human fallibility and inadequacy" which prevented him from conceiving "the possibility of a remarkable perfection ... and of the harmony between all the parts in the larger whole."[31]

More significant is Quṭb's 1959 reading of the same verses (Q. 2:23–4 and Q. 10:38). It gives us a substantive comprehension and appreciation of what Quṭb now perceives as being the constitutive tenets of the Qur'ānic *iʿjāz*. In his commentary of Q. 2:23–4 they include the permanence and universality of the Qur'ān's challenge together with the Qur'ān's prophecies of future events. These remarks are by no means a rehashing of what had already been propounded about the Qur'ān's *iʿjāz*. Rather, Quṭb's conclusion here manifests a great deal of ingenuity. He explains that the *iʿjāz* of the *taḥaddī* is underscored by the historical fact that this challenge, as the Qur'ān has predicted, has never been and will never be taken up successfully throughout the ages. Hence this historical fact elevates the Qur'ān's authoritative prediction to a more wondrous status than the challenge itself.[32]

Politico-religious ideology, and indeed a passionate and genuine conviction inform Quṭb's elaborate discussion of the Qur'ānic *iʿjāz* through his commentary on Q10:38 in his revised *tafsīr*. His reading of the verse precisely exhibits, as intimated above, the crux of the divergence in his views on the *iʿjāz*. The Qur'ānic themes are strongly resuscitated, constructing the foundation of what is made to appear as an affinity between the Qur'ānic *iʿjāz* and Quṭb's politico-religious ideology.

In his detailed discussion of the Qur'ānic *taḥaddī* Quṭb incorporates large segments from both his *al-Taṣwīr al-Fannī*, significantly developed and enlarged, and his *Khaṣā'iṣ al-Taṣawwur al-Islāmī wa-Muqawwimātuh*. After a considerable and indeed

Quṭbian marveling at the Qur'ān's unmatchable mode of *taṣwīr*, the major portion of his reading of the Qur'ānic *i*ᶜ*jāz* is distinctly politico-religious and belongs to all things thematic. The Qur'ānic *i*ᶜ*jāz* now is firmly rooted in *al-manhaj al-Qur'ānī* or the Qur'ānic system which is ascendant and all-encompassing. In this *manhaj* the Qur'ān addresses the totality of man's creaturehood in the most concise, profound and clear manner. And herein lies the axis of its ascendancy. In its orbit its remarkable constituents evolve. On this level of his postulations, Quṭb brings in the oblique relationship between his ideological theory and the concrete human circumstances. On the one hand he holds that the most central characteristic of the Qur'ānic *manhaj* is that it is firmly grounded in *al-*ᶜ*aqīda* and proceeds from the All-Knowing, and hence it is based on absolute certain truth. All other systems and sources of knowledge, on the other hand, proceed from human conjectures and hence their conclusions are forever presumptive. At this point Quṭb is satisfied with arguing for the ascendancy of the Qur'ānic *manhaj* on strictly religious grounds. He holds that while human systems are always characterized by their fragmentary disposition, the Qur'ānic *manhaj* harmoniously incorporates all constituents of the whole. And in the same passionate spirit with which he marvels at the Qur'ānic style of expression, Quṭb expounds upon the religious concomitants of the Qur'ānic *manhaj*. In the comprehensiveness of this system "the seen is united with the Unseen, the reality of man and the universe with the substance of divinity, this world with the Hereafter, and the terrestrial existence with the Celestial Sphere." However, Quṭb explains that the Qur'ān maintains a divine gradient of importance between all the different components of its *manhaj*. In this gradation what is for Quṭb now a duet, namely, divine Lordship and man's servitude (*al-ūlūhiyya* and *al-*ᶜ*ubūdiyya*) occupy the paramount position, the reality of the unknown has a distinct place and the realities of man of the universe and of life take up their appropriate niche. In Quṭb's view this divine order constitutes the quintessential character of the Islamic conceptualization of existence. Interestingly, toward the end of this section Quṭb incorporates the 1940s link he forged between the Qur'ānic *i*ᶜ*jāz* and the very early recipients of revelation. However, the link now belongs to all things ideological. Consequently, he makes a conscious effort at relocating this link in which a connection between the Qur'ān's *iʿjāz* and his ideological activism is brought to the forefront. Quṭb tells us that elucidating the *iʿjāz* of the Qur'ānic *manhaj* in human terminology is inferior to experiencing it and to the Qur'ān's rendering of it. Empirical partaking in this *manhaj* was the privilege of the first Muslim community when the Muslims were receiving direct revelation while they were undergoing tremendous hardship to establish their community. It is this special atmosphere of direct receipt of revelation and the Medinese commitment that distinguishes the early Muslims' experience of the Qur'ānic *manhaj* from contemporary Muslims' knowledge of it. In his view these repercussions have become substantially greater as the Muslims today are no longer ardently pursuing the legacy of the pristine Islamic goals.[33]

The conclusion to his elaborate discussion of the *iʿjāz* of the Qur'ānic *manhaj* is a testimony to the perpetual presence of his literary creativity as he seeks further support from the Qur'ān for his ideology. In so doing he compares the miracle of the Qur'ān's building process to that of the universe. Citing several Qur'ānic references to the signs (*āyāt*) of divine creation, he marvels at how from the simplest material, such as the atom and cell, evolve the most complex forms of life and the largest creatures "and hereby utilizing the simplest and the most common features of creation, the Qur'ān establishes a vast all-encompassing conceptualization of this universe." For Quṭb, "it is the truth of this reality that will continue to be studied by the most learnt scholars till the end of time."[34]

The foregoing makes it abundantly clear that there are two, if not three, stages in the evolution of Quṭb's perception of the constituents of the Qur'ān's *iʿjāz*. In the 1940s, it was exclusively an *iʿjāz fannī*, where the Qur'ān's sublime literary beauty was isolated from its other properties which Quṭb believed had no relevance to enchanting the innately eloquent Arabs who attributed its enthralling effect to "*siḥrun yu'thar*."[35] Progressively beginning in the early 1950s, the definition of the *iʿjāz* encompassed the literary and thematic characteristics of the Book. In the final stage, absolute inclusivism (*al-iʿjāz al-muṭlaq*) constituted the distinguishing property of the Qur'ānic discourse. In Quṭb's view this included all that had been propounded about the subject and more.[36]

Well armed with an excellent command of *al-ᶜArabiyya*, an acumen for its beauties, and possessing a fine taste as well as a rich imagination, Quṭb invigorated the *iᶜjāz* literature and Qur'ānic commentary by concerning himself with the literary aspects of the Qur'ān. Earlier Muslims attempted to deal with these aspects, but as Issa Boullata has convincingly argued "they never conceived of them in the same forceful way as he did, nor did they see them integrated in a unitary theory in the manner he did."[37] To this extent Quṭb no doubt emerges as the most towering personality in the history of the *iᶜjāz al-Qur'ān* doctrine.

Ultimately Quṭb's approaches to the *iᶜjāz* doctrine must be evaluated from the perspective of his diverging disciplines and goals. In the 1940s, steeped in literary criticism, he was bound to be affected by the essential assumptions prevalent in this field of enquiry. His particular approach to the Qur'ān's literary aspects then reflects both the hermeneutical principles that guided his work and his own concept of evaluating a work of literature. In his book *al-Naqd al-Adabī,* Quṭb puts forward the principles with which to evaluate a literary work. In his view the value of such work cannot be determined by its goals and themes; rather its value is determined by the level of emotions it manages to evoke. Or better still, its value is measured by its capacity to traverse the readers from the coldness of the intellectual sphere and from the prosaic confinement of their everyday lives to the warmth of the realm of emotions where abstract facts can be perceived through sensations and sentiments.[38] Small wonder then that he zealously argues for these properties in the Qur'ān's *taṣwīr*.

By 1952, Quṭb's secular literary approach to the Qur'ānic *iᶜjāz* begins to be motivated by *al-ᶜaqīda*, as he himself acknowledges. It is noteworthy, however, that throughout his career he never wished to invalidate the literary components of the *iᶜjāz*. For even when he indisputably enters the "realm of themes", in 1959, as a major if not primary source of the *iᶜjāz,* his literary appreciation continues "unabated and is even developed."[39] It is Quṭb's *locus probans* for the *iᶜjāz* of the text, however, which is decisively altered.

In 1959 Quṭb's entire ethos is permeated by his activism as a radical ideologue. The evolution in his concept of the Qur'ān's *iᶜjāz* is part and parcel of a major shift in his orientation which motivated, among other things, the revision of the first thirteen volumes of his *tafsīr*. His ten-page discussion of the question represents a conscious and interested attempt to maintain a balance between the centripetal force of the text and the centrifugal energy of his ideological allegiance. This ideology is firmly grounded in a permanent Islamic conceptualization of existence whose principle concomitant is the Qur'ān's superior and all-comprehensive *manhaj* for man's life. His conviction in the ascendancy of this system assumes a crucial role in validating his call for an Islamic revolution in order to remove the *jāhilī* or corrupt ways of modern life.[40] Herein lies the heart of the matter for Quṭb's transformed views on the *i*ᶜ*jāz*. The politico-religious activist that he is, he is consistently, throughout his revised commentary, highlighting what he perceives as the Qur'ān's activist disposition (*ṭabī*ᶜ*at al-Qur'ān al-ḥarakiyya*). And this is no mere coincidence. Evidently Quṭb's audience in 1959 was derived primarily from the Islamist movements as compared to the literate circles of the 1940s. Nevertheless, I say this with reservations. For while the audience, as the final destination of a work, no doubt partakes in shaping the text, it must be asserted that the multifarious considerations that produced Quṭb's varied readings of the Qur'ān and its *i*ᶜ*jāz* never manage to displace "things Quṭbian". By that I mean in terms of style and presentation, his enormously intense and passionate approaches bear witness to his consistent love of *al-*ᶜ*Arabiyya* and its book par excellence. This Quṭbian hallmark remains strikingly evident even when he adopts the declamatory and polemic style in order to vindicate the program of the Islamic movements through the Qur'ānic discourse.

In the final analysis, undoubtedly Quṭb arrived at a remarkable unprecedented idea when he came upon the concept of *al-taṣwīr al-fannī* as a source for the *i*ᶜ*jāz* of the Qur'ān. Paradoxically, however, when he later on condemned *pure* literary approaches to the Qur'ān as a legitimate methodology for approaching the text and entrusted the issue to his ideology where the principle of politico-religious activism is largely considered controversial, he, in effect consigned an important avenue for the appreciation of the Qur'ān to the domain of controversial legitimacy.

NOTES

1. I wish to thank Professor Issa J. Boullata for his encouraging review and Professor Wael B. Hallaq for his constructive critique of the manuscript.

2. Q. 74:24: "This is naught but an inherited sorcery." Sayyid Quṭb, *al-Taṣwīr al-Fannī fī'l-Qur'ān* (Cairo 1966) 13 and 18. Referring here to al-Walīd ibn al-Mughīra and without claiming certainty of the stories, Quṭb introduces his study by citing his story and that of Umar ibn al-Khaṭṭāb as Muslim tradition has them. Both stories relay how the Qur'ānic uncanny effect enchanted the two powerful Meccan individuals, even though the latter reacted positively and the former negatively. Ibid., pp. 11–23. The English rendering of the Qur'ānic phrase (Q. 74:24) is the author's. All other English rendering of the Qur'ānic verses provided in addendum are the author's modifications of Abdullah Yusuf Ali, *The Holy Qur'ān: Text, Translation and Commentary* (Brentwood MD: Amana, 1989). All Qur'ānic citations follow numbering of the Egyptian standard edition unless otherwise noted.

3. For chronological information on the publications of these two studies as well as on Quṭb's articles that preceded them see Issa J. Boullata, "The Rhetorical Interpretation of the Qur'ān: *Iʿjāz* and Related Topics," in *Approaches to the History of the Interpretation of the Qur'ān*, ed. Andrew Rippin (Oxford: Oxford University Press, 1988), 150 no. 38 and idem, "Sayyid Quṭb's Literary Appreciation of the Qur'ān," in *Literary Structures of Religious Meaning in the Qur'ān* ed. Issa J. Boullata (Richmond: Curzon, 2000), 368 nos. 2, 3 and 10.

4. Sayyid Quṭb, *Mashāhid al-qiyāma fī'l-Qur'ān* (Cairo 1966), 10.

5. Quṭb, *al-Taṣwīr*, 25–26. I use the words 'artistic' and 'literary' in this essay interchangeably and in a liberal fashion to approximate them to the terms *fannī* used by Quṭb. Evidently Quṭb uses this term rather than *adabī* in order to transmit the notions of aesthetics, portrayal, literature, verbal creativeness, power of presentation and imaginativeness to name a few. Hence no one English term can exactly correspond to Quṭb's own notion of *fannī* in his discourse.

6. See Boullata "Sayyid Quṭb's Literary Appreciation of the Qur'ān," 354–71.

7. Sayyid Quṭb, *Fī Ẓilāl al-Qur'ān* (Cairo 1978), XII, 1863–4. For a discussion on how Quṭb justifies the need for *al-maʿraka* in Qur'ānic terms see Yvonne Haddad, "The Qur'ānic Justification for an Islamic Revolution: The Views of Sayyid Quṭb," *The Middle East Journal* 37 no. 1 (1983): 14–30.

8. I am referring here to Sayyid Quṭb, *Fī Ẓilāl al-Qur'ān* (n.p., 1953).

9. It is worth noting that in other than his 1940s studies under discussion, Quṭb appears to have argued elsewhere for the validity and legitimacy of pure literary approaches to the Qur'ān. His proposition is referred to in ʿAdnan Musallam's "The Formative Stages of Sayyid Quṭb's Intellectual Career and his Emergence as an Islamic Dāʿīya, 1906–1952," Ph.D. diss., University of Michigan, 1983. In support for pure literary approaches to the Qur'ān, Musallam maintains that Quṭb argued that "the nation had reached a stage of development which permitted intellectual and psychological luxury" and that the current situation was different from the stage of exegetical and legalistic approaches which were necessitated by the need to establish a legislative system. Ibid., 134. Quṭb's argument is remarkable. In that I mean that it gives an insight to Quṭb's idiosyncrasy in terms of how he perceived the status quo in the 1940s and of the magnitude of the later change in his perceptions. Besides Musallam's study of the historical realities that led to the evolution in Quṭb's thought, see also John Calvert's "Discourse, Community and Power: Sayyid Quṭb and the Islamic Movement in Egypt," Ph.D. diss., Institute of Islamic Studies, McGill University, 1993. Throughout this paper the years 1952 and 1959 are intended to refer to Quṭb's thought in his unrevised and revised editions of *Fī Ẓilāl al Qur'ān* respectively. 1940s refers to *al-Taṣwīr* and *Mashāhid* which were first published in this decade. Strictly as a by-product of our discussion, this essay may offer a refutation of the dogmatic view insisting on the static nature of Quṭb's thought. See, for instance, Naʿīm al-Ḥimṣī, *Fikrat iʿjāz al-Qur'ān*, intro. M. al-Bayṭār (Beirut 1980), 343–64. In his discussion of Quṭb's concept of *iʿjāz*, Ḥimṣī appears to labour under similar ideology as he attempts to verify whether or not Quṭb intended for his 1940s studies of the Qur'ān to represent his view on the *iʿjāz*.

10. For Quṭb's definition of *al-taṣwīr al-fannī* see Quṭb, *al-Taṣwīr*, 32–3. For excellent and concise English renderings of this definition see Boullata, "*Iʿjāz* and Related Topics," 151 and his "Sayyid Quṭb's Literary Appreciation of the Qur'an," 356. Quṭb is very critical of traditional discourse about the *iʿjāz* issue. In his view these traditional approaches, which rely on the principles of Arabic rhetoric, have continued to analyze and assess each Qur'ānic statement separately. They, consequently, have continued to be fragmentary and failed in finding the general principles and characteristics which distinguish the Qur'ānic verbal beauty from all human expression in Arabic literature. In Quṭb's view, al-Zamakhsharī (d. 538/1144) did succeed occasionally in perceiving some of the Qur'ān's literary beauty. Al-Jurjānī, however, is considered by Quṭb to have almost achieved a breakthrough for a scholar of his time, had he not been bogged down with the issue of "meaning and wording" (*al-lafẓ wa'l-maʿnā*). Quṭb, *al-Taṣwīr*, *passim*. Quṭb dedicates his book *al-Naqd al-adabī* to al-Jurjānī where he gives a brief discussion of al-Jurjānī's literary theory. See Sayyid Quṭb, *al-Naqd al-adabī: Uṣūluh wa manāhijuh* (Beirut n.d.), 147–52.

11. Quṭb, *al-Taṣwīr*, 26.

12. Quṭb, *Mashāhid*, 12. Quṭb stated that he intended to produce a series of his literary studies of the Qur'ān entitled *al-Maktaba al-Qur'ānī al-jadīda*. It was to include *al-Qiṣṣa bayna al-Tawrāt wa'l-Qur'ān; al-Manṭiq al-wijdānī fī'l-Qur'ān* and *Asālīb al-ʿarḍ al-fanniyya fī'l-Qur'ān* ibid., 8. Quṭb never produced this series, mostly, as Boullata remarks, "because Egyptian political life after the 1952 Revolution carried him away to other intellectual concerns." See Boullata, "Sayyid Quṭb Literary Appreciation," 354.

13. Quṭb, *al-Taṣwīr*, 51. Interestingly, the content of the *daʿā'ī* of these verses assumes a paramount importance in the two editions of *Fī Ẓilāl al-Qur'ān*.

14. Quṭb, *Mashāhid*, 12.

15. Quṭb, *al-Taṣwīr*, 193.

16. Quṭb, *al-Taṣwīr*, 192.

17. Ibid., 194.

18. Ibid., 73. I have settled here for the less-than-satisfactory English translation of what can correspond to Quṭb's notion of this particular element. Kamāl Abu Deeb has a better shot at it, albeit quite long. He states that in essence it is a method by which the presentation of an image as a reality is achieved through the concealment of any linguistic relationship between the similized and the similizing entity. Kamal Abu Deeb, *al-Jurjānī's Theory of Poetic Imagery* (Warminster: Aris and Phillips, 1979), 159.

19. Quṭb, *al-Taṣwīr*, 199.

20. Quṭb, *al-Taṣwīr*, 200.

21. Quṭb, *al-Taṣwīr,* 195–6., idem, *al-Naqd al-adabī*, 10–11 and 28.

22. Ibid., 23.

23. Quṭb, *Fī Ẓilāl al-Qur'ān* (1953), I, 19.

24. Ibid., XI, 82–3 no. 1.

25. Quṭb, *Fī Ẓilāl al-Qur'ān* (1959), I, 45–6.

26. Quṭb, *al-Taṣwīr*, 190–1.

27. Quṭb, *Fī Ẓilāl al-Qur'ān* (1952), VII, 69–70.

28. Quṭb, *Fī Ẓilāl al-Qur'ān* (1959), VII, 1108–13. It is worthy of note that "the Islamic vision" is often used to approximate Quṭb's phrase *al-taṣawwur al-Islāmī*. However, we are of the opinion that Boullata's "the Islamic conceptualization of existence" corresponds far more closely to Quṭb's notions and discourse; Boullata, "Sayyid Quṭb's Literary Appreciation," 365. For a condensed overview of Quṭb's discourse on the subject, see ibid., 365–7. This issue has been studied in more detail by Yvonne Y. Haddad "Sayyid Quṭb: Ideologue of

Islamic Revival," in *Voices of Resurgent Islam*, ed. John Esposito (Oxford: Oxford University Press, 1983), 67–98. In the revised edition of *Fī Ẓilāl al-Qur'ān*, Quṭb integrates the views he puts forward in his *Khaṣā'iṣ al-Taṣawwur al-Islāmī wa muqawwimātuh* (Cairo 1962). His last work *Maᶜālim fī'l-ṭarīq* (Damascus n.d.) is putatively taken by the Islamists and their foes to have been intended by Quṭb to be the manifesto for a universal Islamic revolution.

29. Quṭb, *Fī Ẓilāl al-Qur'ān* (1952), I, 21. Quṭb uses the term *ṣana'a* here in reference to the divine "creation" of the Qur'ān. This notion is also implied by Quṭb in his commentary on Q. 17:88 where he refers to the Qur'ān as a divine *ibdā'*. Quṭb, *Fī Ẓilāl al-Qur'ān* (1959), XV, 2249–50. Whether Quṭb holds the Muᶜtazilite doctrine on the createdness of the Qur'ān is a question that has yet to be investigated.

30. Quṭb, *Fī Ẓilāl al-Qur'ān* (1952), XI, 82.

31. Ibid., XI, 83 no. 1.

32. Quṭb, *Fī Ẓilāl al-Qur'ān* (1959), I, 48–49. In his *al-Taṣwīr al-Fannī* Quṭb rejects the Muᶜtazalite concept of *al-ṣarfa* introduced by al-Naẓẓām (d. 846). Al-Naẓẓām maintains "that the *iᶜjāz* of the Qur'ān consisted in God's preventing the Arabs from imitating it by turning them away from that potentiality and taking away their competence and knowledge" (cited in Boullata "*I'jāz* and Related Topics," 141–2.) Quṭb discredits al-Naẓẓām's concept and describes it as being "valueless." Quṭb, *al-Taṣwīr*, 15.

33. Quṭb, *Fī Ẓilāl al-Qur'ān* (1959), XI, 1788–90.

34. Quṭb, *Fī Ẓilāl al-Qur'ān* (1959), XI, 1793–4. Aside from the above categories of the *iᶜjāz* which Quṭb considers as being its perceptible *(mudraka)* components, he intimates that it also has a cryptic (*khafī*) dimension which cannot be rendered in human terminology. The existence of the latter is demonstrated, for instance, by the uncanny impact of the Qur'ānic recitation on listeners who are sometimes non-conversant with Arabic. Ibid., XI, 1786–7.

35. It is quite curious that Mustansir Mir does not make a reference in his "The Qur'ān as Literature," *Religion and Literature* 20 (1988): 49–64, to any of Quṭb's major literary studies of the Qur'ān.

36. As he progresses in writing his commentary, Quṭb concludes in his reading of Q. 52:37 that the principle of the Qur'ānic *iᶜjāz* is infinite (*ghayr maḥdūd*). Ibid., XXVII, 3450.

37. Boullata, "Sayyid Quṭb's Literary Appreciation," 358. For an overview of the Muslims' expositions on the Qur'ān's *iᶜjaz* from the ninth century to the twentieth century see idem, "*Iᶜjāz* and Related Topics," 139–154.

38. Quṭb, *al-Naqd al-Adabī*, 10–11 and 28.

39. Boullata "Sayyid Quṭb's Literary Appreciation of the Qur'ān," 354.

40. It is worth noting that while Boullata's article "Sayyid Quṭb's Literary Appreciation of the Qur'ān" represents not only a highly penetrating investigation of Quṭb's love and literary valuation of the Qur'ān, the study also reveals Boullata's own literary appreciation of the Qur'ānic *ᶜArabiyya* and an unmistakable sense of empathy towards one of its most outstanding exponents.

Chapter 11

The Qur'ān in Egypt III: Naṣr Abū Zayd's Literary Approach

Yusuf Rahman

The first modern Muslim scholar to employ a literary method in analyzing the Qur'ān was Amīn al-Khūlī (1895–1966). He is even regarded by Katrin Speicher as this method's spiritual father as well as the first to apply it.[1] Al-Khūlī was a literary critic who taught *ᶜilm al-bayān* and *tafsīr* at the Faculty of Arts in Fu'ad I (then Cairo) University, and edited a monthly journal on Arabic literature called *al-Adab*[2] from 1956 until his death in 1966. He broke new ground in proposing a new approach to Qur'ānic studies based on a literary point of view.

In his book *Manāhij tajdīd fī'l-naḥw wa'l-balāgha wa'l-tafsīr wa'l-adab,* and especially in the section on *al-Tafsīr,*[3] al-Khūlī argues that literary study of the Qur'ān consists of two steps: *dirāsat mā ḥawla'l-Qur'ān* and *dirāsat mā fī'l-Qur'ān*.[4] Here, it seems that al-Khūlī is in agreement with René Wellek and Austin Warren, the authors of *Theory of Literature,* who propose *extrinsic* and *intrinsic* approaches to literature.[5] Al-Khūlī's method has influenced many of his students, among them were Muḥammad Aḥmad Khalaf Allāh (1916–98), who wrote his PhD dissertation in 1947 on "al-Fann al-Qaṣaṣī fī'l-Qur'ān al-Karīm,"[6] and Shukrī Muḥammad ᶜAyyād (1921–99), whose M.A. thesis written in 1947 was entitled "Min waṣf al-Qur'ān: Yawm al-ḥisāb wa'l-dīn."[7]

However, because of the many objections raised against the literary approach to the Qur'ān in Egypt, especially against "*al-fann al-qaṣaṣī*,"[8] it was not applied very much after the time of Khalaf Allāh. Many students under al-Khūlī's direction—either for fear of the consequences or due to a shift in interests—wrote instead on Arabic literature.[9] Khalaf Allāh wrote his second dissertation on al-Rāghib al-Isfahānī's *al-Aghānī* while ᶜAyyād wrote on the Arabic translation of Aristotle's book on poetics. And if literary interpretations of the Qur'ān were attempted, they were more philological.[10]

However, in 1980s Naṣr Ḥāmid Abū Zayd revived al-Khūlī's tradition. Although he did not study directly under al-Khūlī, Abū Zayd has consistently asserted that he belongs to that tradition. In his works, he clearly states that he is applying a literary approach to the Qur'ān in response to al-Khūlī's call to study the Qur'ān as a literary text.[11] The purpose of this essay is to analyze and systematize his approach.

Abū Zayd's Presuppositions

In his article entitled "*Tafsīr* from Ṭabarī to Ibn Kathīr" Norman Calder writes that "[t]he qualities which distinguish one *mufassir* from another lie less in their conclusions as to what the Qur'ānic text means than in their development and display of techniques which mark their participation in and mastery of a literary discipline."[12] In other words, the methods employed by *mufassir*s may be considered more important than the result. It is also often said that different conclusions in interpretation are mainly due to the variety of methods used by interpreters.[13] But, aside from methods, the presuppositions adopted by interpreters are often far more influential in producing varying results than disagreements over method. Scholars frequently differ in their assessment of the same text. In the case of the Qur'ān, for example, the Ashᶜarites assumed its eternity, while the Muᶜtazilites were convinced of its createdness. Among Western scholars of the Qur'ān, John Wansbrough operated on the presupposition that the present Qur'ān was the product of editorial efforts some hundred years after the prophet, while the traditional views suppose it to be the text left by Muḥammad and published by the caliph ᶜUthmān b. ᶜAffān (d. 35/656).[14]

Presuppositions are involved in every aspect of the relationship of the interpreter to his text. Scholars commonly differentiate between presuppositions and prejudice; presupposition is the philosophical or theological starting point which an interpreter takes, while prejudice consists in personal factors which affect the judgment of the interpreter.[15] No one is more eloquent in his explanation of presupposition than the German theologian and hermeneut Rudolf Bultmann (1884–1967). In his influential work "Is Exegesis Without Presuppositions Possible?" Bultmann declares that "*there cannot be any such thing as presuppositionless exegesis,*"[16] because every one is conditioned by his/her individuality, biases and interests. In his other article "The Problem of Hermeneutics," he argues that to demand that an interpreter silence his subjectivity and individuality is a false ideal because it will destroy the very condition of interpretation, which is a "life relation" between interpreter and subject.[17] Bultmann, however, distinguishes presuppositions from prejudices. Exegesis, according to him, must be without prejudices, in that the latter must not decide in advance what the results of exegesis should be, or manipulate the text to confirm a particular opinion.[18] Commenting on the danger of prejudice in interpretation, Bultmann warns: "Every exegesis that is guided by dogmatic prejudices does not hear what the text says, but only lets the latter say what it wants to hear."[19] Pre-understanding, on the other hand, is an open assumption which will hear the text speak and be criticized or corrected by it during the encounter with the text.[20]

With this view in mind, I will identify Abū Zayd's presuppositions in his interpretation of the Qur'ān. Agreeing with hermeneuts and semioticians, Abū Zayd argues that the existence of a variety of methods and analytical-critical trends in the study of literary texts is due essentially to differing views in defining the nature of the text *(ikhtilāf fī taḥdīd māhiyyat al-naṣṣ)*.[21] His proposal is that "the Qur'ān is a text like any other text." In his book *Mafhūm al-naṣṣ,* for example, he states that the Qur'ān is a linguistic text (*naṣṣ lughawī),*[22] related to *(yantamī)* a specific culture or context.

He acknowledges that treating the Qur'ān as a text is not his own idea, but was proposed previously by Amīn al-Khūlī who called the Qur'ān "the greatest Arabic book" *(kitāb al-ᶜarabiyya al-akbar)*.[23] Al-Khūlī, however, according to Abū Zayd, was unable to pursue the ramifications of this idea. The contentious nature of his claim led to the removal of al-Khūlī from his post of professor of *tafsīr* at Cairo University, as well as to the university's refusal to examine the thesis of al-Khūlī's pupil, Khalaf Allāh, as it was first submitted, because he had applied his mentor's idea. No one knows better than Abū Zayd himself how much courage it requires to pursue such a course, one which can sometimes cost a person his life. But for the sake of scientific awareness *(intāj waᶜy ᶜilmī)* of the *turāth* (Islamic heritage), Abū Zayd has been willing to run that risk.

Because he holds the view that the Qur'ān has to be considered a text like any other, Abū Zayd does not see the need to have a special or "sacred" hermeneutics to uncover the Qur'ān's meanings. On the contrary, he insists that as a text it can be interpreted by any modern critical approach. This view was bitterly condemned by many scholars, especially the Islamists, since in their view the Qur'ān is superior to all other texts, being unique and therefore to be studied differently.[24] This was not the first time, to be sure, that such criticism has been directed at a scholar who would apply "secular" critical methods to their scriptures. Even in the fields of Old and New Testament scholarship, there are still some scholars who insist that inasmuch as it is the Word of God, scripture should not be the subject of human investigation or at least has to be approached by a special method. "It is bad hermeneutics," they argue, "if we do not interpret the Bible on its own terms, regardless of the question whether we are personally convinced of the Bible's divine status."[25]

Contrary to this "conservative" view which insists that scripture should not be treated like any other writing, "liberal" thinkers argue that the fact that the text is believed to have a divine origin and an authoritative status for a particular group of adherents should have no influence at all on interpretation. There is no "sacred hermeneutics" nor is there privilege given to these texts because of their authority. On the contrary, they must be treated like any other text.[26] Charles M. Wood, for example, makes the following interesting comment on the liberal position on this issue:

> [T]he fact that scripture is authoritative for a community does not mean that it must be regarded as authoritative by its interpreters, or that it must be interpreted as an authoritative text. Interpreters within or outside the community whose scripture it is may for various reasons disregard its authority—that is, disregard its character as scripture—on the grounds that for their particular purposes its authoritative character is either irrelevant or inadmissible.[27]

It seems clear that Abū Zayd goes along with this liberal view, and that he would also agree with Bultmann's assertion that "[t]he interpretation of biblical writings is not subject to conditions different from those applying to all other kinds of literature."[28] In his *Naqd al-khiṭāb al-dīnī*, Abū Zayd asserts his belief that religious texts are linguistic texts whose forms are the same as those of other texts in the culture (*anna al-nuṣūṣ al-dīniyya nuṣūṣ lughawiyya sha'nuhā sha'n ayyat nuṣūṣ ukhrā fī'l-thaqāfa)*.[29] Their divine origin, continues Abū Zayd, does not mean that they need a specific method suited to their specific divine nature, for if this were so it would imply that religious texts are beyond human understanding, except for those who have been granted a special power by God enabling them to understand them, and, as such, they are closed *(mustaghliqa)* for ordinary people.[30] Against those who object to the application of human understanding and method to divine texts, Abū Zayd argues that since the author of the Qur'ānic text [God] may not be subjected to scientific research, His speech/word which operates in human language is directed at human beings and is therefore linked closely to a specific context and culture, is certainly an appropriate field of study. And as such, it is subject to human understanding and method.[31]

Another consequence of assuming the Qur'ān to be a linguistic text, besides the effect of treating it as any other text, is that any qualified scholar, regardless of his/her religion, is equally capable of studying it. In an interview conducted by Navid Kermani, Abū Zayd states that the reason why he treats the Qur'ān as a text in the Arabic language is in order that Muslims, Christians and atheists alike can study the Qur'ān because Arabic culture is united with it.[32] Abū Zayd does not attempt to clarify this reason further, but if we may follow the argument of Graham N. Stanton, the author of "Presuppositions in New Testament Criticism," who addresses a similar issue in New Testament studies, the argument appears to be more logical, and one with which, I think, Abū Zayd would agree. Stanton argues that since interpretation involves dialogue with the text, the interpreter's belief is not at issue. The most important aspect of interpretation, however, is "willingness and readiness to run the risk that the pre-understanding with which he comes to the text may well be refined or completely renewed. He must be prepared to be interpreted by the text. That is the necessary presupposition with which he must attempt to operate."[33]

A corollary of this argument is that dialogue between the scholars is possible regardless of their faith. David W. Atkinson, for example, argues in his "Religious Dialogue and Critical Possibilities" that the "openness" initiated in modern critical theory may liberate a student of religion from exclusivism and allow him to learn other possibilities from other traditions.[34] Reporting on the Conference on "Qur'anic Studies on the Eve of the 21st Century" held in Leiden on June 10–12, 1998, where Western and Muslim scholars were invited to present their thoughts on the current state of the discipline, Abū Zayd—who had organized the conference—concluded that: "[T]he old clichés of orientalists versus Muslims seem very much to be a thing of the past,"[35] observing that these scholars came together in dialogue without difficulty. Dialogue, he states, can only be disrupted when one party claims to have the absolute truth and rejects the other.

Besides assuming that the Qur'ān is a linguistic text, Abū Zayd presupposes that it is also a cultural product (*muntaj thaqāfī*).[36] This understanding is based on the argument that since the Qur'ān took shape (*tashakkal*) during a period of more than twenty years in a specific context and culture, the latter obviously had a role in shaping (*tashkīl*) the former.[37] He finds additional support for his view in the process of revelation itself. He argues that when God revealed the Qur'ān to His messenger, He chose a human language as the code for revelation. And given that a language cannot exist in isolation from its culture since the latter is embodied (*tajassad*) in language, it is therefore impossible to separate the text from its cultural context.[38]

At the same time, Abū Zayd argues in *Naqd al-khiṭāb al-dīnī* for the humanity of the text (*bashariyyat al-naṣṣ*).[39] He does not, however, go so far as to say that the Qur'ān is a "human product" as John B. Gabeel and co-authors, for example, argue in the case of the Bible in their book *The Bible as Literature*.[40] Abū Zayd denies that the Qur'ān is man-made, stating only that it uses human language in its expression. Here he seems to echo Toshihiko Izutsu's words, which clearly must have influenced Abū Zayd's understanding of the Qur'ān as a linguistic text:

> And Revelation means in Islam that God "spoke", that He revealed Himself through language, and that not in some mysterious non-human language but in a clear, humanly understandable language. This is the initial and the most decisive fact. Without this initial act on the part of God, there would have been no true religion on earth according to the Islamic understanding of the word religion.
>
> It is no wonder then, that Islam should have been from the very beginning extremely language conscious. Islam arose when God spoke. *The whole Islamic culture made its start with the historic fact that man was addressed by God in a language which he himself spoke.* This was not a simple matter of God's having "sent down" a sacred book. It meant primarily that God "spoke." And this is precisely what "Revelation" means. Revelation is essentially a *linguistic concept.*[41]

To prove the humanity of the text, Abū Zayd makes a comparison between Jesus and the Qur'ān.[42] Both, according to Abū Zayd, are identified as *kalām Allāh* in the Qur'ān. Q. 4:171, for example, declares Jesus to be God's messenger and His Word *(rasūl Allāh wa kalimatuhu).* Similarly Q. 3:45 conveys the good news to Maryam about God's Word whose name is ᶜĪsā *(inna Allāh yubashshiruki bi-kalima minhu ismuhu'l-masīḥ ᶜĪsā ibn Maryam).* As for the Qur'ān, Q. 9:6 clearly states that it is the speech of God: *wa in aḥad min al-mushrikīn istajāraka fa-ajirhu ḥattā yasmaᶜa kalām Allāh,* "If any-one of the polytheists comes to you seeking your protection, protect him so that he may hear God's speech (*kalām Allāh).*"

Furthermore, as the speech of God, the Qur'ān was sent down to Muḥammad, just as Jesus was "conveyed to Maryam" *alqāhā ilā Maryam* (Q. 4:171). In both cases, Gabriel played the role of mediator coming in the form of a perfect man (*basharan sawiyyan)* to Maryam (Q. 19:17), and in the form of a bedouin (*aᶜrābī)* in the case of Muḥammad.[43] Basing himself on these verses, Abū Zayd concludes that both Words of God materialize (*tajassad)* into tangible form (*shakl malmūs):* into a created being in the case of Jesus, and into a linguistic text using human language in the case of the Qur'ān.[44] The humanity of the text in the case of the Qur'ān is due to its relation with the language and culture of a particular historical period.[45]

Jesus in Christianity	The Qur'ān in Islam
kalimatuhu (Q. 4:171)	*kalām Allāh* (Q. 9:6)
↓	↓
Maryam	Muḥammad
↓	↓
Jesus/ʿĪsā	Qur'ān

In his interview with Kermani, Abū Zayd further notes this comparison:

> Jesus in Christianity: Is he a God or a human being? This is a problem in Christian theology. The flesh and blood Jesus, who was born at a certain historical time and died at another, lived in Nazareth—this Jesus is a human being. This Jesus is the one we know. The Qur'ān, which we know, is Arabic. The Arabic language is a historical language. The Qur'ān was revealed at a certain historical time.[46]

On another occasion, to prove the close relationship between the Arabic language and the Qur'ān, Abū Zayd refers to the distinction made by the linguist Ferdinand de Saussure (1857–1913) between *langue* and *parole*. This reference points again to Abū Zayd's debt to Izutsu, who discussed this issue in an article which Abū Zayd had used.[47] The Qur'ān, according to Izutsu, represents the *parole* or speech-aspect of Saussurian terminology, while the Arabic language, used as a code-system for communication, is its *langue*-side.[48] While it is recognized that every community has its own *langue*, the Qur'ān clearly asserts that Arabic constitutes its own code: *innā jaʿalnāhu qur'ānan ʿarabiyyan laʿallakum taʿqilūna*, "We have made it an Arabic Qur'ān that you may understand" (Q. 43:3).[49]

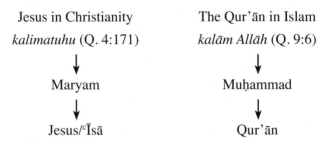

The dependence of the Qur'ān on the language of the Arabs confirms for Abū Zayd that the Qur'ān is closely related to Arab culture and society. This relation is further shown in the fact that its verses reflect the historical period of Muḥammad, as represented, for example, in the *asbāb al-nuzūl*, the *Makkī* and *Madanī* verses, etc.[50] These are some of the reasons used by Abū Zayd to argue for the context's role in shaping the text. However, he asserts that the relation between text and context is dialectical *(jadaliyya),* in that, not only does context shape the text but the latter also shapes the context and becomes the producer of culture *(muntij li'l-thaqāfa)*.[51] In this latter situation, the Qur'ān serves as subject *(fāᶜil)* and the culture as its object *(munfaᶜil)*.[52] The role of the text in shaping the culture may be represented in the existence of a plethora of Islamic *turāth* works which were produced by continuously re-reading the text and re-interpreting its meaning.

What is a Text?[53]

Having stated his assumption that the Qur'ān is a text, Abū Zayd goes on to define and explain the nature of Qur'ānic text in general. He suggests that before an attempt can be made at interpretation, "one must first define the nature of the text and examine the laws that govern the study of that text—not every interpretation is permissible."[54]

In his writings, Abū Zayd reports that many Islamists criticized him for describing the Qur'ān as a text. He tells of the case of an al-Azhar University professor who protested against the use of the word "text" in reference to the Qur'ān. The professor's argument was that:

> We have not seen in the history of the [Islamic] community anyone describe the Qur'ān other than by the names that God himself used such as *suwar* ([Qur'ān] chapters) and *āyāt* (verses); similarly we do not know of any [Muslim] scholar who dealt with the Qur'ān as a text (*naṣṣ*), because this is what is prohibited by God. They instead dealt with it as *tanzīl* (revelation) from God. [55]

Abū Zayd, however, argues that to refrain from treating the Qur'ān as a text or to disregard its textuality will lead to the fixation of its meaning. "When the meaning is frozen and fixed," Abū Zayd warns, "an authority emerges to claim itself as the only guardian power of Islam."[56] This authority then will manipulate the meaning of the Qur'ān to suit its own agenda and reject other possible interpretations.

The Semantic Meaning of *Naṣṣ*

As with the English term "text," derived from the Latin word *textus* meaning texture, structure, construction (whose root verb *texo* means to weave or compose),[57] its Arabic counterpart, *naṣṣ* or *naṣṣa* comes to mean to fix, lay down, compose, determine, arrange, set up or provide.[58] Abū Zayd, however, observes that in the classical period the term *naṣṣ* had a different meaning. In his research into the many usages of the term found in *Lisān al-ᶜArab* of Ibn Manẓūr (d. 711/1311),[59] he concludes that the main idea of *naṣṣ* is obviousness and clarity (*al-ẓuhūr wa'l-inkishāf)*.[60] Abū Zayd observes that in Islamic *turāth* the meaning of *naṣṣa* has developed from the perceptible connotation (*dalāla ḥissiyya)* into a semantic one (*dalāla maᶜnawiyya),* and finally into a technical term (*iṣṭilāḥ);* hence, from "to raise," or "to lift" as in *naṣṣat al-ẓabya jīdahā* (the female gazelle raised her neck) or *minaṣṣa* (the raised platform) to *naṣṣa al-rajula* meaning to ask someone about something, until finally coming to mean "to provide" or "to specify."[61] This development of meaning, however, still points to the idea of obviousness and clarity.

In the sciences of Qur'ān, as well as in *uṣūl al-fiqh,* according to Abū Zayd, the word *naṣṣ* refers to the clear verses of the Qur'ān (*āyāt muḥkamāt)* that need no explanation. As an illustration, he shows that al-Shāfiᶜī (d. 204/820) in *al-Risāla* defines *al-naṣṣ* as *al-mustaghnā fīhi bi'l-tanzīl ᶜan al-ta'wīl* (the revelation which does not need interpretation).[62] Similarly, al-Zamakhsharī (d. 538/1144), in his interpretation of Q. 2:7 uses the term *naṣṣa* to refer to *al-muḥkam al-wāḍiḥ al-bayyin alladhī lā yaḥtāj al-ta'wīl* as an opposite of *al-mutashābih.*[63] Abū Zayd further observes that, based on Q. 3:7 *Huwa 'lladhī anzala ᶜalayka 'l-kitāba minhu āyātun muḥkamātun hunna umm al-kitābi wa ukharu mutashābihātun,*[64] verses of the Qur'ān are divided by early Muslim scholars of the Qur'ānic sciences into four semantic levels. Those in the first category are called *al-naṣṣ,* meaning the clearest verses. The second category is that of *al-ẓāhir,* which are less clear since there are two possibilities for their meanings, of which the apparent meaning, however, is the more appropriate. The third category is that of *al-mu'awwal* (metaphorical) verses, i.e., verses whose hidden meaning is more appropriate than their apparent. The fourth and the last level is *al-mujmal* (the general).[65]

With these observations, Abū Zayd is trying to show that the term *naṣṣ* was widely used in the classical period to connote "clarity" and "obviousness." He is not certain, however, when and how this term came to take on its modern sense, i.e., the whole text.[66] He does note that, based on his study of Ibn Khaldūn's (d. 808/1406) *al-Muqaddima,* Aristotle's book on logic was once called *al-Naṣṣ* "the Text,"[67] and that Ibn Rushd (d. 595/1198) summarized that "Text" (*Talākhīṣ Ibn Rushd lil-Naṣṣ).*[68] The attribution of *Naṣṣ* to a book on logic, speculates Abū Zayd, may have been due either to its clarity in comparison with Aristotle's other books (which yielded different interpretations) or to its concentration on the general principles (*qawānīn kulliyya)* which regulate the process of reasoning and analogy.[69] With this observation, Abū Zayd would like to argue that the meaning of *naṣṣ* then has developed from its classical connotation to its modern sense of "the whole book."

The distinction between the modern sense and the classical one of the term *naṣṣ* is very important for Abū Zayd, because it is essential to his argument against the Islamists' understanding of the maxim *lā ijtihāda fīmā fīhi naṣṣ* "there is no *ijtihād* where there is a *naṣṣ*." In his *Maᶜālim fī'l-ṭarīq,* Sayyid Quṭb writes:[70] "If there is *naṣṣ,* the *naṣṣ* is the rule and there is no interpretation with *naṣṣ*. If there is no *naṣṣ,* then comes the role of interpretation." Quṭb and other Islamists after him understand the term *naṣṣ* here to imply the whole text of the Qur'ān, which consequently allows them to reject any interpretation of Scripture but a literal one. Abū Zayd, on the other hand, understands this term to refer only to the *muḥkamāt*; the other verses falling outside this category may still need interpretation.[71]

Many scholars, however, would raise an objection to Abū Zayd's identification of a text as the whole book (*kitāb kāmil),* because they would argue that even a one-line written statement, such as "There is no change," might be considered as a text. Paul Ricoeur simply defines a text as "any discourse fixed by writing."[72] In other words, it is the fixation of speech into writing that makes a text. Jorge J. E. Gracia in his *A Theory of Textuality: The Logic and Epistemology* has tried to provide a comprehensive definition of text. "A text is," according to Gracia, "a group of entities, used as signs, which are selected, arranged, and intended by an author in a certain context to convey some specific meaning to an audience."[73] These definitions indicate that the concept of text does not have to comprehend the complete book.

The Qur'ān as Text

Why is the Qur'ān called a text by Abū Zayd? Or to put it another way: What is the textuality of the Qur'ān in his opinion? While there are many names used to designate the Qur'ān, Abū Zayd asserts that the terms *waḥy*, "revelation," and *risāla*, "message," are its central designations, especially in his effort to define text. Acknowledging his debt to linguist Roman Jakobson's analysis of literary text, Abū Zayd sees a text as a form of communication or revelation act.[74] In every communication act, Jakobson writes:

> [t]he ADDRESSER sends a MESSAGE to the ADDRESSEE. To be operative the message requires a CONTEXT referred to ("referent" in another, somewhat ambiguous, nomenclature), seizable by the addressee, and either verbal or capable of being verbalized; a CODE fully or at least partially, common to the addresser and addressee (or in other words, to the encoder and decoder of the message); and, finally, a CONTACT, a physical channel and psychological connection between the addresser and the addressee, enabling both of them to enter and stay in communication.[75]

Context

Message

Addresser —————————— Addressee

Contact

Code

Following Jakobson, Abū Zayd sees the Qur'ān as a form or an act of communication, *waḥy,* comprised of six factors: a message *(risāla),* an addresser *(mukhāṭib/mursil),* an addressee *(mukhāṭab/mustaqbil),* a contact *(ʿalāqat ittiṣāl),* a code *(shifra/niẓām lughawī)* and a context (*wāqiᶜ wa thaqāfa)*.[76] From these elements, we may venture to describe his notion of text as "a message sent by an addresser to an addressee in a certain context through a contact using a special code," although Abū Zayd does not put it this way. And in the case of the Qur'ān, it is a message sent by God to His messenger through revelation in a certain context using the Arabic language.[77]

Wāqiᶜ

Risāla

Al-Mursil————————————*al-Mustaqbil*

ᶜAlāqat al-ittiṣāl

Shifra/Niẓām lughawī

It seems, however, that in his discussion of *waḥy,* Abū Zayd does not bother to differentiate between literary communication and day-to-day communication,[78] despite the fact that the implications of this difference are very important, especially in the activity of interpretation. For one thing, in literary communication the addresser and the addressee are not co-present but belong to different periods of time.[79] Where there is no dialogue or conversation in the form of question and answer between the writer and the reader, there is only one-way communication. In the words of Ricoeur, in a literary text "[t]he reader is absent from the act of writing; the writer is absent from the act of reading. The text thus produces a double eclipse of the reader and the writer. It thereby replaces the relation of dialogue, which directly connects the voice of one to the hearing of the other."[80] In the face-to-face communication, on the other hand, there is a possibility of checking and correcting the understanding from both parties in an act of communication (speaker and audience/I and you) through dialogue. Barbara A. Holdrege considers the relation between speaker and audience to be a personal one, since it involves face-to-face contact, while the relationship between the author and the reader is impersonal, in that the former has been replaced by the text he/she wrote.[81] In other words, in literary communication, the relationship is between the reader and the impersonal text.

Another distinction present between these two kinds of communication is the fact that in a literary text the context or the referent to which the addresser refers may be unknown to the reader.[82] In dialogic communication, on the other hand, both parties "are present not only to one another, but also to the situation, the surroundings and the circumstantial milieu of discourse."[83] It is therefore important to find the reference and the context, which the author sometimes inserted in the text during the process of interpretation.

Abū Zayd is aware of the oral aspect of the Qur'ān,[84] but since, I would argue, his concern is with the interpretation of the Qur'ān and the dialectical relation between text and context, he focuses mainly on the written text and discusses *waḥy,* the oral communication, in an attempt to prove the textuality of the Qur'ān.

It should be pointed out that the communication process in the Qur'ān is very complex. Many Western scholars of the Qur'ān have expressed doubts on God being the speaker of the revelation, since it is not clearly indicated in the Qur'ān. Besides, God is referred to in the Qur'ān not only as "I" but also as "He" and "We."[85] Similarly, Muḥammad is sometimes addressed as "you" or "he/him." As a believing Muslim, however, Abū Zayd holds an orthodox view on this issue.

Historicity of the Text

By stating that the Qur'ān is an act of communication, it (as Cesare Segre has pointed out in his *Introduction to the Analysis of the Literary Text* in the case of literary communication) "automatically brings to the fore its links with the culture, and the perspective thereby established is a historical one. The codes employed by the addresser, and his motivations as well, derive from the cultural context within which he is inserted, while the addressee will have recourse to the codes at his disposition in order to interpret the text."[86]

Similarly, Andreas Meier, who studies Abū Zayd's *Mafhūm al-naṣṣ,* deduces five theses that result from considering a text to be a linguistic text. He writes:

i. Religious texts are *linguistic* texts. They are constructed according to the structures and rules as every other linguistic text.

ii. Religious texts, as linguistic texts, are *human* texts. They are associated with the general condition of human thought and human speech and communication.

iii. Religious texts, as human texts, are *products* of human *culture*. They owe their genesis to a certain cultural context, through whose specific characteristics they are substantially and formally shaped.

iv. Religious texts, as products of human culture, are *historical* texts. They are, like every other product of human culture, subjected to the conditions of time and space.

v. Religious texts, as historical texts, are the subject of research through the historico-critical sciences using the standard methods, as these are applied also to all other historical texts.[87]

Abū Zayd defines historicity as "the occurrence in time" (*al-ḥudūth fī'l-zamān).*[88] Following the Muᶜtazilites, Abū Zayd argues that the Qur'ān is the speech of God and as such may be considered as one of God's attributes of action (*ṣifāt al-afᶜāl)*. Everything produced by these attributes is *muḥdath* (created), meaning it is created in separate moments *(laḥaẓāt)* of history. The Preserved Tablet (*lawḥ maḥfūẓ),* which is believed to contain the Qur'ān before it was sent down, is also considered by Abū Zayd to be created. If it is eternal, how could there be any eternal beings besides God, Abū Zayd asks hypothetically.[89] The extended time frame of the piecemeal revelation *(tanjīm),* the occasions of revelation, and the concept of *naskh* contain some further proofs of the historicity of the Qur'ān.

The belief in the historicity of the Qur'ān, for Abū Zayd, leads to the fundamental consequence that, since the prescriptions of the Qur'ān are very much linked to seventh-century Arabia, some of these prescriptions can no longer be applied in the present context. The changing of the context, therefore, invites new interpretation. This re-interpretation has to be performed not only with regard to the text of the Qur'ān, but also to other elements in the *turāth* of Islam, since these too are conditioned by the socio-historical context.

Abū Zayd's Method of Interpretation

For Meier, the concept of the text as an historical artifact requires that a scholar use "the historical-critical sciences [which] are the usual method in studying it."[90] This, of course, is valid on the whole but it must be qualified, since this method has been criticized by many scholars in recent years. Often applied in Qur'ānic studies as well as in Biblical interpretation, it is an approach that—to use the criteria outlined by John Barton[91]—examines the genesis, original meaning and historical reconstruction of the text, all of which questions are now considered *passé,* having been surpassed by the "new paradigm."[92] Robert Morgan, the author of *Biblical Interpretation,* for example, has criticized the historical-critical method on the grounds that "historical reconstruction of biblical persons, events, and traditions is an entirely legitimate activity, but possibly less fruitful for theology than the newly emerging literary approaches."[93] Stefan Wild also observes "a definite and irrevocable shift of attention" in Qur'ānic studies.[94] What all these scholars mean is that there has been a paradigm-shift in Biblical interpretation as well as in Qur'ānic studies from a diachronic approach, which examines the world behind the text, to a synchronic one, which takes a text as it is now available in its final form and evaluates its impact upon readers. In other words, the latter approach focuses on the world both within and in front of the text, not the one that lies behind it.

Nevertheless, as has been quite convincingly argued by Barton, the historical-critical approach focuses on more than just the diachronic aspect of the text—it also takes in its synchronic side. Historical approaches, continues Barton, "are predominantly literary in their interests … to untangle the complex interrelationships within and between complex texts."[95] To see how the text had influenced the early scholars as well as how they received and interpreted the text is a historical study which produces a history of interpretation. Finally, he proposes that the defining characteristic of Biblical interpretation is its "critical" tendency to ask questions unrestrictedly about the meaning of the text without fear of authority.[96]

Abū Zayd's approach might best be described as a critical study too. Not only is he critical of the Islamic *turāth,* but also of other authorities—whether that of the official discourse of Islam (*al-khiṭāb al-dīnī)* or that of the modernists. As he states:

> It is time now for a re-examination and transition to the period of liberation, not only from the authority of the texts, but also from every authority which hinders human journey in our world. We must undertake this (liberation) now and immediately before the flood sweeps us away.[97]

And this critical attitude is equipped by a variety of methods ranging from historical and textual interpretations to literary theory, such as hermeneutics, discourse analysis and semiotics.

The Meaning of the Text

There are at least three factors which are seen as determining the meaning of the text: the author, the text and the reader.[98] The author-centered interpretation (Romantic criticism) seeks to uncover the authorial intention, while the text-centered interpretation (New Criticism; Structuralism) asserts that the meaning can be found from the structure of the text. Finally, the reader-centered interpretation, usually known as reader-response theory, argues that it is the reader who creates and gives meaning to the text.[99]

In his discussion of the author of the Qur'ān, Abū Zayd has argued that God as well as the divine pre-existence of the Qur'ān are questions that lie beyond human reason. It is therefore impossible, argues Abū Zayd, to search for the meaning of the text in the authorial intention. He does not go so far as to say that the author is dead; he merely argues that reason cannot conceive of the metaphysics of God. And yet Abū Zayd may not be aware of the consequences of this judgment for the interpretation of other historical texts, especially in view of his opinion that the Qur'ān is a text like any other text. On the surface he seems to echo the argument of Ricoeur concerning authorial intention. With his theory of text Ricoeur asserts that when speech is fixed in writing, the text becomes *autonomous* from its author and the latter's intention.[100] This is because, by contrast with oral communication where the interlocutor can query the speaker directly, in the case of a text, we—as the reader—cannot speak directly to the writer to ask his intention. Even if we happen to meet the author, Ricoeur argues "we experience a profound disruption of the peculiar relation that we have with the author in and through his work."[101] That is why Ricoeur used to consider the author as already dead, and instead that we read only his posthumous works, regardless of whether he is still alive or not.

Having stated that the meaning of the text cannot signify the authorial intention, Abū Zayd similarly argues that neither can it be left to the text to speak of its meaning. In his many writings he often quotes the statement of ᶜAlī b. Abī Ṭālib (d. 41/661) *al-Qur'ān khaṭṭun masṭūrun bayna daffatayn lā yanṭuqu innamā yatakallamu bihi 'l-rijāl,* "The Qur'ān is a script written between two covers; it does not speak, but people speak through it."[102] In Biblical interpretation, Morgan equates texts with the dead men and women who "have no rights, no aims, no interests. They can be used in whatever way readers or interpreters choose. If interpreters choose to respect an author's intentions, that is because it is in their interest to do so."[103] In other words, it is the reader who gives meaning to the text.

Abū Zayd, however, does not agree with the view that the meaning of the text is constructed by the reader alone. He says that in the process of interpretation, the text is not a silent object that can be carried in any direction by any active reader. The relation between the reader and the text is not the relation of *ikhḍāᶜ* (forcing the text to submit to the reader) on the part of the reader and *khuḍūᶜ* (submission) on the part of the text. Rather, the relation between the two is dialectical *(jadaliyya)*.[104]

This dialectical relation between reader and text reminds us of the method proposed by recent scholars of literary theory and philosophical hermeneutics.[105] Wolfgang Iser, for example, in his *The Implied Reader: Patterns of Communication in Prose Fiction from Bunyan to Beckett,* argues that the meaning of the text "is not given by the text itself; [but] it arises from the meeting between the written text and the individual mind of the reader with its own particular history of experience, its own consciousness, and its own outlook."[106] Ricoeur also speaks of the dialectic between the world of the text and the world of the reader.[107] The world of the text is the text's claims, the horizon which it opens to the reader and the possibilities that it displays. This world of the text then encounters another world, that is, the world of the reader and his horizon of expectations.

As for how this dialectical relation operates, however, the debate still rages. The main question is: How do they meet? How does the reader construct the meaning from the text? James L. Machor has summarized this debate in his article "The Object of Interpretation and Interpretive Change,"[108] where he observes at least three groups: those who argue that the text possesses intrinsic formal features from which readers build meaning; others who propose that the reader constructs meaning through filling the gaps or blanks in the text; and finally, a third group that asserts the immanent meaning of the word. Abū Zayd, I believe, would advocate the ideas of the first group in constructing meaning/significance from the original meaning.

***Maᶜnā* (Meaning) and *Maghzā* (Significance)**

Unlike Ricoeur who sees the text as emancipated, or to use his important term "distanciated," from the author, the original context and the first addressee,[109] because of which the reader can "re-contextualize" the text, Abū Zayd still finds it an important prior step to know the historical meaning *(dalāla tārīkhiyya)* of the text. He is aware of the historical dimension of the text and thus its historical distance *(al-buᶜd al-tārīkhī)* from the contemporary reader, but the latter cannot jump to contextualize the text without understanding the original meaning of it. It is through a diachronic approach, by studying how the first generation understood the text, that the historical meaning of the text will be revealed. But, this meaning is not the final one for Abū Zayd. It needs to be followed with another step, which is to find its significance *(maghzā)* in the present context, or if we may use the distinction made by Biblical scholar Krister Stendahl between "what it *meant*" in the past and "what it *means*" in the present context.[110]

Surprisingly, Abū Zayd's distinction between *maᶜnā* and *maghzā* was adopted from E.D. Hirsch's distinction between "meaning" and "significance."[111] It is "surprising" because Hirsch was the main proponent of authorial intention while Abū Zayd is himself against it.[112] The latter has therefore had to make some adjustments to Hirsch's distinction. Let us see first how Hirsch distinguishes between the two. In his *Validity in Interpretation* Hirsch writes:

> *Meaning* is that which is represented by a text; it is what the author meant by his use of a particular sign sequence; it is what the signs represent. *Significance,* on the other hand, names a relationship between that meaning and a person, or a conception, or a situation or indeed anything imaginable.[113]

He further confirms that the author's meaning, which is represented in the text, is unchanging and reproducible;[114] its significance, on the other hand, changes.

While Abū Zayd accepts Hirsch's attribution of the stable nature of meaning and the changing character of significance, "meaning" in Abū Zayd's hermeneutics is not that imposed by the author, but the historical meaning as understood by the first addressees of the text. It is the canonical meaning—to use Raymond E. Brown's classification of meaning—that Abū Zayd refers to. In his *The Critical Meaning of the Bible,* Brown distinguishes between literal meaning which *meant* to its author, canonical meaning which *meant* to those who first accepted it as Scripture, and contemporary meaning which *means* today.[115] As has been pointed by Kevin J. Vanhoozer, Brown's third classification should not be considered as meaning but rather as significance.[116]

To support his distinction between historical meaning and significance, Abū Zayd examines the meaning of *ta'wīl* itself and analyzes the verses of the Qur'ān which contain that term.[117] He detects two different usages of the word.[118] The first he derives from the verb *āla 'l-shay'u—ya'ūlu—awlan wa ma'ālan,* which has the sense of *rajaᶜa* (to return).[119] On this basis *ta'wīl,* which is the verbal noun of the second form of *āla*, may be understood to mean, " to cause something or phenomenon to return to its original causes" (*irjāᶜ al-shay' aw al-ẓāhira ... ilā ᶜilalihā al-ūlā wa asbābihā al-aṣliyya*).[120] In *Mafhūm al-naṣṣ,* Abū Zayd says that *ta'wīl* means to uncover the hidden meaning *(al-dalāla al-khafiyya)* of an event, which means to reveal its real causes, to disclose its roots/origins.[121] It is in this sense that the prophet Yūsuf reveals the "origin" and the "source" of the food before it is served in the passage *qāla lā ya'tīkumā ṭaᶜāmun turzaqānihī illā nabba'tukumā bi-ta'wīlihī qabla an ya'tiyakumā* , "He said: the food which you are given shall not come unto you but I shall tell you its interpretation (source) before it comes unto you" (Q. 12:37).

The second meaning of *ta'wīl* derives, according to Abū Zayd, from *āla al-shay'—awlan wa iyālan* which means to put something in order and to manage it (*aṣlaḥahu wa sāsahu*).[122] Here, *ta'wīl* means to arrive at a goal through the exercise of care, management and improvement (*al-wuṣūl ilā 'l-ghāya bi'l-riᶜāya wa'l-siyāsa wa'l-iṣlāḥ*).[123] The term *ta'wīl* in the Qur'ān also used to mean *ᶜāqiba*, the outcome, the end, the result. For example, Q. 17:35, *wa āwfū 'l-kayla idhā kiltum wa zinū bi'l-qisṭās al-mustaqīm dhālika khayr aw wa aḥsanu ta'wīlan*, "Fill the measure when you measure, and weigh with right balance; that is good and better in the end" or Q. 4:59, *yā ayyuhā 'lladhīna āmanū aṭīᶜū Allāh wa aṭīᶜū 'l-rasūl wa ūlī 'l-amr minkum … dhālika khayran wa aḥsanu ta'wīlan*, "O you who believe! Obey God and obey the messenger and those of you who are in authority … that is better and more seemly in the end."

Based on his study of *ta'wīl,* Abū Zayd asserts that the process of contextual interpretation (*al-qirā'a al-siyāqiyya*) has to follow two steps: the first is to return (*rujūᶜ*) to the meaning in its historical and cultural context (*tārīkhiyyāt al-dalāla*); and the second, to arrive to the significance (*maghzā*) of the meaning in the present context.[124] The historical meaning is firm while its significance is changeable depending on the context. He further states that the *maghzā* has to be based on the historical meaning and is closely related to the latter.

Significance involves the relevance or the importance of the text's meaning. It is here, I think, where the reader plays a greater role. It is true that the reader also has a part to fulfill in discovering the historical meaning of the text, but since this meaning is determinate and stable, his role ends after discovering it. Finding the significance of that meaning, on the other hand, varies from one reader to the other, from one socio-historical context to the other. This will produce an endless process of interpretation and a diversity of interpretations, since the significance of the text differs from one person to another, from one time to another, depending on the development of the meaning of the language, on the one hand, and the changes in the socio-political context on the other.[125]

One of the strongest objections made to this theory is the charge of relativism, since absolute truth is held to be an illusion. Abū Zayd, however, provides some general principles to facilitate valid interpretation.

> The awareness of the difference between the original contextual "meaning" which is almost fixed because of its historicity and the "significance" which is changeable - in addition to the awareness of the necessity that the significance is to be firmly related and rationally connected to the meaning, will produce a more valid interpretation. It is only valid, however, as long as it does not violate the above mentioned methodological rules in order to jump to some "desired" ideological conclusions.[126]

This principle, for Abū Zayd, can lead to objectivity in interpretation. But it is not an absolute objective, since it will stand in the way of other possible interpretations—a far from desirable situation in that, as he himself admits, he cannot claim to be privy to absolute truth. The kind of objectivity that he is proposing is contextual objectivity or cultural objectivity,[127] a quality that is objective for specific contexts but not for all contexts.

Abū Zayd, Fazlur Rahman (1919–88) and Mohammed Arkoun (b. 1928)

In order to appreciate Abū Zayd's originality and his contribution to the modern approach in Qur'ānic interpretation, it is important to compare his method with those of other modern Muslim scholars. In the following, I will discuss Fazlur Rahman's and Mohammed Arkoun's approaches to the Qur'ān, which resemble Abū Zayd's insofar that they too have proposed the application of more modern interpretive methods to the Qur'ān. Another similarity between these scholars—and perhaps the most important one—just as Abū Zayd insists on defining revelation before interpreting the Qur'ān, Rahman and Arkoun too place an emphasis on understanding the meaning of revelation.[128]

The "traditional" position on this issue is reflected by Abdullah Saeed, who, in his "Rethinking 'Revelation' as a Precondition for Reinterpreting the Qur'an: A Qur'anic Perspective"[129] argues against a redefinition of the traditional concept of revelation *(waḥy),* stating that "a revision of the theory of Revelation in Islam is unwarranted; ... because ... a careful and literal reading of the linguistic evidence available, primarily in the Qur'an, does not support such a revision."[130] He further argues that if the purpose is to make the Qur'ān interpretable for the modern time, it is not the definition of revelation that has to be revised, but rather the method of interpretation.

I believe that Abū Zayd, Rahman and Arkoun would contest Saeed's thesis. Their determination to redefine *waḥy* and regard it in human and historical terms is meant to challenge the existing concept of the term that has dominated the Muslim world and to revive ones that have previously been banned and buried in Islamic history. In addition, contrary to Saeed's assumption, their attempt to revise the concept of revelation is based on their own understanding of the Qur'ān.

Fazlur Rahman's Theory of Double Movement

Basing himself on Q. 26:194, *nazala bihi 'l-ruḥ al-amīn ᶜalā qalbika li-takūna min al-mundhirīn,* "The Faithful Spirit has brought it (revelation/*tanzīl)* down upon your heart that you may be among the warners," Rahman argues in his major work *Islam* that the Qur'ān is both the Word of God and the word of Muḥammad.[131] It is this statement that has led to many objections on the part of his fellow-countrymen in Pakistan. Despite, however, the opposition he faced, Rahman retained this conviction till the end of his life. Commenting on this attitude in later years, Rahman states:

> I defended the idea of the verbal revelation of the Qur'ān, which is the universal belief. However, it seemed to me that the standard orthodox accounts of revelation give a mechanical and externalistic picture of the relationship between Muḥammad and the Qur'ān—Gabriel coming and delivering God's messages to him almost like a postman delivering letters. The Qur'ān itself says that the Angel "comes down to the heart" of Muḥammad. I stated that the

> Qur'ān is *entirely* the Word of God insofar as it is infallible and absolutely free from falsehood, but, insofar as it comes to the Prophet's heart and then his tongue, it was entirely his word.[132]

In *Islam & Modernity: Transformation of an Intellectual Tradition,* Rahman asserts further that this concept of revelation constitutes the basis of his project of Islamic intellectualism.[133] Unaware of the importance of this idea, Waheed Hussain criticizes Rahman's proposal.[134] Differentiating between the concepts of social practice and interpretive method in his analysis, Hussain questions how and why Rahman's idea of the Qur'ān as "the divine word literally revealed to the Prophet Muhammad" could become a practical interpretive method for interpreting the Qur'ān.[135] This question might not have arisen if Hussain had understood Rahman's motive in speaking in these terms, which was to challenge and refute the Ashᶜarite and the Ḥanbalite dogma, which claimed that the Qur'ān was not only the Word of God but also the "uncreated" and eternal Word of God—a concept that has long dominated Muslim thought. The latter view, according to Rahman, insists on the "otherness" of the Qur'ān and the "externality" of the Prophet in the process of revelation, neither of which solutions gives role to the Prophet Muḥammad. The Muᶜtazilites, on the other hand, to whom Rahman's idea refers, maintained the Prophet's involvement in revelation.

The Prophet's implication in the revelatory process, argues Rahman, is attested to in the Qur'ān which states that the revelation was sent down to the heart of Muḥammad (Q. 26:194) and that Muḥammad's speech was a revelation (Q. 53:3–4). Further proof of Muḥammad's involvement might be seen from the fact that many of the Qur'ānic verses deal with the historical context of Muḥammad. "The Qur'ān," for Rahman, "is the divine response, through the Prophet's mind, to the moral-social situation of the Prophet's Arabia."[136]

It is on this concept of revelation that Rahman bases his theory of interpretation. Rahman approaches the Qur'ān through an attempt to understand it in its socio-historical setting. According to him, each of the Qur'ān's pronouncements on social, moral, political and economic matters, had a background "rooted in the flesh and blood of history."[137]

The purpose of this historical approach is to determine the world-view or *Weltanschauung* of the Qur'ān which, according to Rahman, is ethical in nature. By applying this method, it is possible to distinguish between *prescription* and *description* in the Qur'ān.

Rahman is, however, best known for his "double movement" approach to interpreting the Qur'ān. The first movement is to move from the present situation to the time in which the Qur'ān was revealed. This enables the interpreter to evaluate the verse in the context of its socio-historical background, allowing him or her to grasp the purpose and original intention of the verse. The second movement is an attempt to interpret the ramifications of the verse in the face of the present socio-cultural situation.[138]

The first of these two movements, according to Rahman, consists of two steps. To understand the meaning of a given verse, the interpreter should study the historical situation surrounding its revelation. This step implies the absolute necessity of knowing the social and religious life of Arabia on the eve of Islam as well as its customs and institutions. In the light of this socio-historical background, it is then possible in the second step to derive general moral-social objectives from specific texts.

After determining these objectives, the scholar is ready to move from the general view achieved in the first movement to apply these Qur'ānic principles to society in the context of contemporary socio-historical situations. This requires a careful study of the present situation in order to implement correctly Qur'ānic values.

According to Ebrahim Moosa in his introduction to Rahman's posthumous book *Revival and Reform in Islam,* Rahman's theory of double movement is a condensation of E. Betti's (d. 1968) four canons that guide the exegete to reach and reproduce the original meaning of the text.[139] It is true that Rahman prefers Betti's "objectivity" theory to Gadamer's.[140] Like Betti, Rahman argues that an interpreter can reach objectively the original meaning of the Qur'ān. Unlike Betti, however, Rahman believes that this original meaning does not lie in the mind of the author but rather in the historical context to which the text/the Qur'ān responded.[141]

Abū Zayd's Contextual Approach

In comparison with Rahman, Abū Zayd proposes an even more logical and systematic theory of revelation. First, he asserts his understanding of the humanity and historicity of revelation by referring to the Qur'ānic text and comparing the human manifestation of the Qur'ān with that of Jesus as maintained by the Qur'ān. Next, his critical study of the traditional Qur'ānic sciences provides him with more proofs of the spatial and temporal aspects of revelation. Abū Zayd's application of Jakobson's theory of literary communication, as well as that of Saussure's differentiation between *langue* and *parole,* to the concepts of *waḥy* as well as to Arabic language and the Qur'ān, discloses further the involvement of humanity and culture in forming the revelation.

In his inaugural lecture as Cleveringa Professor in Leiden University, Abū Zayd explores this issue further. He distinguishes between three aspects of the Qur'ān: its content, language, and structure. Although the content of the Qur'ān is from God, Abū Zayd argues, it is expressed in human language, and therefore it is correlated with cultural and historical contexts.

As for the structure of the Qur'ān, Abū Zayd sees the human dimension of revelation in the fact that the Qur'ān was revealed piecemeal *(munajjam),* as well as in the process of the canonization of the Qur'ān. Inasmuch as it was revealed portion by portion, the Qur'ān responded to the needs and demands of the community. Another aspect of the human involvement with the Qur'ān consists in the human effort to collect, arrange and canonize the content of the Qur'ān.

In terms of theory of interpretation, on the other hand, Abū Zayd's contextual approach to the Qur'ān seems to be close to the double movement theory of Rahman. Though it is not quite clear whether Abū Zayd was influenced by Rahman's works, he does after all allude to double movement in speaking of the double meaning of the term *ta'wīl* and its use in the Qur'ān. He also discusses more comprehensively the different kinds of contexts—external and internal—that assist one in understanding the meaning and significance of the Qur'ān.

Arkoun's Strategies of Deconstruction

In the course of his discussion, Abū Zayd asserts that since the Qur'ān is a linguistic text (*naṣṣ lughawī*), the linguistic method is the only method (*al-manhaj al-waḥīd*) that may usefully be applied to the study of the Qur'ān, that it is "the only possible method in terms of its appropriateness with the topic of the study and its subject matter" (*innahu al-manhaj al-waḥīd al-mumkin min ḥaythu talā'umuh maᶜa mawḍūᶜ al-dars wa māddatih*).[142] However, it can be argued that this reduces the text to only one of its aspects, and closes the door to other perspectives which may yield valuable insights. When one claims that a particular method is the most authoritative one, one destroys the view of hermeneutics itself which admits different kinds of methods. Mohammed Arkoun for one rejects single-minded approaches to the study of the Qur'ān, and instead recommends a variety of approaches drawing from the humanities and social sciences.[143]

Like Rahman and Abū Zayd, Arkoun starts his project by discussing the notion of revelation. In his *Rethinking Islam: Common Questions, Uncommon Answers,* Arkoun writes:

> The question of revelation is more delicate, especially if one wishes to get beyond and renew "orthodox" teachings piously repeated within each of the monotheistic traditions. It is not a matter of ignoring or overturning these teachings; the science of religions today seeks rather to understand the theological and historical genesis of them, their ideological and psychological functions, their semantic and anthropological limits and inadequacies.[144]

What Arkoun wishes to accomplish by this deconstruction is to understand the reasons for the dominance of the orthodox view and its limitations, and to uncover other conceptions that have been forgotten. Defending himself against the charge of using Western ideas and methods in his studies, Arkoun maintains that the concept of a human and historical text with regard to the Qur'ān is to be found in the Islamic heritage itself. He refers to the Muᶜtazilite concept of the createdness of the Qur'ān, stating that this concept implies that the Qur'ān is in need of human mediation *(wisāṭa bashariyya)*.[145] By declaring that the Qur'ān is created, it asserts that the Qur'ān is manifested in human language, i.e., the Arabic language, and that human beings have the duty to understand and interpret it.

Arkoun differentiates between several levels of the Qur'ān.[146] The first is the Word of God that is related to the Heavenly Book, expressed in the Qur'ān as *al-lawḥ al-maḥfūẓ,* "the Preserved Tablet" (Q. 85:22) and *umm al-kitāb*, "Archetypal Book" (Q. 43:3). The second level is the Qur'ānic discourse which is the oral transmission of this Word to Muḥammad. This Qur'ān, which is also called by Arkoun "the prophetic discourse" *(al-khiṭāb al-nabawī),*[147] involves a discourse between three principal actors: God as the addresser, the Prophet as the first addressee, and men as the second addressee. The latter are those who accompanied the Prophet and heard the Qur'ān directly from him. This oral discourse was then transformed into a text *(muṣḥaf),* and finally elevated into the Official Closed Corpus. The transformation from oral discourse to written text, according to Arkoun, has three important implications: (1) radical changes to the linguistic and semiotic process in the Qur'ānic discourse; (2) the attribution of sacrality to the written text; and (3) the increasing role of written culture at the expense of oral culture.[148]

In the light of these three levels, Arkoun sees Ashᶜarite and Ḥanbalite theology as having assimilated the *muṣḥaf* with the transcendent Word of God, ignoring the successive processes of oral transmission and its transformation into a text. The Muᶜtazilites, on the other hand, maintained the createdness of the Qur'ān in its oral transmission to the Prophet in the Arabic language and in its specific historical context.

Besides the above implications, the role of oral discourse in the formation of the text makes the Qur'ān available to everyone, and makes it possible to be interpreted. It follows, therefore, Arkoun argues, that during the interpretation of the Qur'ān, one has to consider these three levels of the Qur'ān, especially the shift from the oral discourse to the written. In the former, particular attention has to be paid to the role of metaphor and the semiotic structure of the Qur'ānic discourse. In addition, the interpreted corpuses, which derive from the Official Closed Corpus, have to be taken into consideration in the process of interpretation.

Arkoun admits that his approach, which he calls "anthropology of the past" (*antrūbūlūjiyyā lil-māḍī),* following the French scholars Georges Duby, Alphonse Dupront and Jacques Le Goff, is still in a state of formation, and still at the level of theory.[149] However, this theoretical concept, which incorporates linguistic and anthropological analysis of the Qur'ān, according to Arkoun, has been successfully implemented by Jacqueline Chabbi in her *Le Seigneur des tribus: l'Islam de Mahomet.*[150]

This approach begins with the archeological excavation (*al-ḥafr al-arkiyūlūjī)* of the meaning of a word, its genesis and its genealogy through history from the past till the present. It further analyzes this word as it is used in the Qur'ān, by relating it to the socio-political context of seventh-century Arabia. Finally, the analysis of this word is extended to any works of *turāth,* such as annals or chronicles, collections of Prophetic traditions, biographies of the Prophet and his companions, compendia of *Isrā'īliyyāt,* and Qur'ānic exegeses, which discuss the word in question.[151] Here we can see the influence of the post-structuralist scholars, especially Michel Foucault (1926–84). The latter, in his *The Archeology of Knowledge* has suggested that an object of discourse "exists under the positive conditions of a complex group of relations."[152] It is therefore necessary, Foucault suggests, to analyze an object in its relation to other objects and to define its difference.

Arkoun argues that the purpose of this archeological analysis is not to determine the truthfulness or untruthfulness of a given account, but rather to deconstruct the social *imaginaire* which has been formed and structured by the phenomenon of the *muṣḥaf.* It seems that it is on this basis that Arkoun's deconstruction theory lies; that is, to consider the social *imaginaire* as the field of study. In his *Rethinking Islam Today,* where he outlines the strategies of his theory, Arkoun states:

> There is no possibility to interpret the whole literature derived from those Scriptures without taking into account the representations of Salvation perpetuated in the behaviors and the thinking activity of all believers, so that all history produced in the Societies of the Book is legitimized and assimilated by the *imaginaire* of Salvation, not by any "rational" construction. The theological and juridical systems elaborated by so-called "reason" are also related to the *imaginaire* of Salvation.[153]

As a historian of religious thought, Arkoun finds that this kind of approach, which studies the religious literature as the result of the believers' *imaginaire,* is richer than the philological approach that searches for lexical and thematic influences. On a practical level, however, Arkoun has not yet applied this theory comprehensively to interpret Qur'ānic verses related to contemporary issues, such as the role of women, for instance.

As we have seen, Abū Zayd's method of interpretation and the theory behind it resemble those of Rahman. Both began their projects by reviving the Muʿtazilite doctrine of "the created Qur'ān" through a redefinition of the concept of revelation. Their theories of interpretation, which are based on the historical dimension of the text, follow almost the same steps as well. Although Rahman took his hermeneutics from Betti and Abū Zayd from Hirsch, both came to the same conclusion: that there is a distinction between "historical values" and "moral values" or between "historical meaning" and "significance," and that it is possible to arrive objectively at the historical meaning. Despite this similarity, however, there is no evidence that the latter influenced Abū Zayd, who makes no reference whatsoever to Rahman in any of his works.

Abū Zayd has benefited in particular from modern and postmodern theories of interpretation, but his theory falls within the category of modernism rather than postmodernism. As Terence J. Kegan puts it, "[w]hat distinguishes postmodernism from modernism in both scientific and humanistic disciplines is the acceptance of the impossibility of arriving at objective certitude."[154] Abū Zayd insists that, with his theory, one can reach an objective understanding of the text as long as he or she follows the two steps faithfully. Mohammed Arkoun, on the other hand, has been influenced more by postmodernism in that he sees objective interpretation as being the result of the political, economic or religious power that justifies and legitimates a certain interpretation rather than another. His challenge to modern objectivism is further supported by his application of deconstruction. Besides challenging the notion of objective interpretation, this theory criticizes the hierarchical oppositions between inside and outside, speech and writing, and true and false. Arkoun proposes a theory of deconstruction to explain why certain dogmas prevail while others disappear from view.

NOTES

1. See Katrin Speicher, "Einige Bemerkungen zu al-Hulis Entwurf eines *tafsir adabi*," in *Encounters of Words and Texts: Intercultural Studies in Honor of Stefan Wild on the Occasion of His 60th Birthday, March 2, 1997, Presented by His Pupils in Bonn*, eds. Lutz Edzard and Christian Szyska (Hildesheim: Georg Olms Verlag, 1997), 4. Speicher's dating of al-Khūlī's death should be corrected from 1967 to 1966. See Kāmil Saᶜfān who writes that al-Khūlī died on Wednesday, the ninth of March 1966. Saᶜfān, *Amīn al-Khūlī* (Cairo 1982), 300. In his study of contemporary *tafsīr* methodology, H'mida Ennaifer (Aḥmida al-Nayfar) places al-Khūlī as one of the pioneers in modern era to reform *tafsir*. See Ennaifer, *Les commentaires coraniques contemporains: Analyse de leur méthodologie* (Rome: Pontificio Istituto di Studi Arabi e d'Islamistica, 1998), 74.

2. Published by al-Umanā' (Madrasat al-Fann wa'l-Ḥayat), Cairo.

3. Al-Khūlī, *Manāhij tajdīd* (Cairo 1995), 203–243. The first edition was published in 1961 by Dār al-Maᶜrifa, Cairo. The section on "al-tafsīr" was previously published in *Dā'irat al-maᶜārif al-Islāmiyya* (an Arabic translation of *EI1)*, V, 348–74, as a response to Carra de Vaux, the author of "tafsīr" in *EI1*, IV, 603–4.

4. Al-Khūlī, *Manāhij tajdīd,* 233ff.

5. R. Wellek and A. Warren, *Theory of Literature,* 3rd ed. (New York: Harcourt, Brace and World Inc., 1956), 71ff. Cf. al-Khūlī, *Manāhij tajdīd,* 258: *manhaj khārijī* and *manhaj dākhilī* in literary study.

6. This work has been printed four times. The first and the second were published in 1951 and 1957 by Maṭbaᶜat al-Nahḍa al-Miṣriyya, Cairo; the third printing was issued in 1965 by Maktabat al-Anglū al-Miṣriyya; and the last print was published by Sīnā li'l-Nashr and al-Intishār al-ᶜArabī (Cairo and Beirut) in 1999.

7. This work has been published under the title *Dirāsāt Qur'āniyya: Yawm al-dīn wa'l-ḥisāb* (Beirut 1980).

8. See, among others, the study of J. Jomier, "Quelques positions actuelles de l'exégèse coranique en Égypte révélées par une polémique récente (1947–1951)," *MIDEO* 1 (1954): 39–72; ᶜAbdelhamid Muhammad Ahmad, "Die Auseinandersetzung zwischen al-Azhar und der modernistischen bewegung in Ägypten von Muhammad ᶜAbduh bis zur Gegenwart," (Ph.D. dissertation, Universität Hamburg, 1963), 55–64; Rotraud Wielandt, *Offenbarung und Geschichte im Denken moderner Muslime* (Wiesbaden: Franz Steiner, 1971), 134–152; Marc Chartier, "Muhammad Ahmad Khalaf Allah et l'exégèse coranique," *IBLA* 137 (1976): 1–31; and Yvonne Yazbeck Haddad, *Contemporary Islam and the Challenge of History* (Albany NY: SUNY Press, 1982), 46–53.

9. Besides, al-Khūlī was prevented from teaching *tafsīr* and allowed only to teach Arabic literature.

10. Khalaf Allāh has also written some works on the Qur'ān, such as *al-Qur'ān wa mushkilāt ḥayātinā al-muʿāṣira* (Cairo 1967), *al-Qur'ān wa'l-dawla* (Beirut 1981), and *al-Usus al-Qur'āniyya li'l-taqaddum* (Cairo 1984). However, he does not use literary approach in these works. Marc Chartier has indicated in his "Muhammad Ahmad Khalaf Allāh et l'exégèse coranique," *IBLA* 137 (1976): 1–31, especially 16ff., that they tend to be apologetic.

11. See, for example, Abū Zayd, *Mafhūm al-naṣṣ: Dirāsa fī ʿulūm al-Qur'ān,* 4th ed. (Beirut 1998), 10, 19.

12. N. Calder, "*Tafsīr* from Ṭabarī to Ibn Kathīr: problems in the description of a genre, illustrated with reference to the story of Abraham," in *Approaches to the Qur'ān,* eds. G.R. Hawting and Abdul-Kader A. Shareef (London: Routledge, 1993), 106.

13. J. Wansbrough writes in his *Quranic Studies* "Results are, after all, as much conditioned by method as by material." See his *Quranic Studies: Sources and Methods of Scriptural Interpretation* (Oxford: Oxford University Press, 1977), 91. In a review of Josef van Ess's *Anfänge muslimischer Theologie,*" he also says "Method not merely conditions results, it may be selected to produce them." See *BSOAS* 43 (1980): 361. See also Issa J. Boullata's review of *Quranic Studies* in *Muslim World* 67 (1977): 307.

14. Except J. Burton who argues that the final text of the Qur'ān was produced by Muḥammad himself. See his *The Collection of the Qur'ān* (Cambridge: Cambridge University Press, 1977). For a summary of different theories of the collection of the Qur'ān, see A.T. Welch, "al-Ḳur'ān," *EI2* V, 404–6; Angelika Neuwirth, "Koran," in *Grundriss der arabischen Philologie,* ed. H. Gätje (Wiesbaden: Ludwig Reichert Verlag, 1987), 2: 101ff.; Claude Gilliot, "Coran: Les recherches contemporaines," in *Encyclopaedia Universalis,* ed. Jacques Bersani (Paris: Encyclopaedia Universalis, 1995), VI, 547ff. Wansbrough's thesis has led to many responses either to dismiss or to support his argument. I just would like to mention the recent ones: The special issue on "Islamic Origins Reconsidered: John Wansbrough and the Study of Islam," in *Method and Theory in the Study of Religion* 9, 1 (1997), ed. Herbert Berg; Berg, *The Development of Exegesis in Early Islam: The Authenticity of Muslim Literature from the Formative Period* (Richmond: Curzon, 2000), especially pp. 78–84; Jawid A. Mojaddedi, "Taking Islam Seriously: The Legacy of John Wansbrough," *Journal of Semitic Studies* 45 (2000): 103–14; and Rippin, "Introduction. The Qur'ān: Formative Interpretation," in *The Qur'an: Formative Interpretation,* ed. A. Rippin (Aldershot: Ashgate, 1999), xi-xxvii, especially xiv-xvii. See also the list of reviews of Wansbrough's works in Berg, *The Development of Exegesis in Early Islam,* 101–2, nn. 90–93.

15. Graham N. Stanton, "Presuppositions in New Testament Criticism," in *New Testament Interpretation: Essays on Principles and Methods,* ed. I. Howard Marshall (Exeter: Peternoster Press, 1977), 61.

16. Rudolf Bultmann, "Is Exegesis Without Presuppositions Possible?" in idem *Existence and Faith: Shorter Writings of Rudolf Bultmann,* selected, translated and introduced by Schubert M. Ogden (Cleveland: World Publishing, 1966, 5th printing), 290 (italics in the original).

17. R. Bultmann, "The Problem of Hermeneutics," in his *Essays Philosophical and Theological* (London: SCM Press, 1955), 255. See also p. 241, 242 and especially p. 252 where he defines presupposition to mean "*a previous living relationship to the subject,* which directly or indirectly finds expression in the text and which guides the direction of the enquiry." See also, "Exegesis Without Presuppositions?" 293, 294, 295.

18. Bultmann, "Exegesis Without Presuppositions?" 289; and idem, "The Problem of Hermeneutics," 255.

19. Bultmann, "Exegesis Without Presuppositions?" 290.

20. Ibid.

21. Abū Zayd, *Mafhūm al-naṣṣ,* 19.

22. Ibid., 9, 10, 18, 19, 25 *et passim.*

23. Ibid., 10, 19. See al-Khūlī, *Manāhij tajdīd*, 229, 230.

24. This assumption is mainly based on the idea of *iʿjāz* (the miraculous nature) of the Qur'ān. On *iʿjāz,* see, for example, Issa J. Boullata, "The Rhetorical Interpretation of the Qur'ān: *iʿjāz* and Related Topics," in *Approaches to the History of the Interpretation of the Qur'ān,* ed. Andrew Rippin (Oxford: Oxford University Press, 1988), 139–157. Rippin observes that many Muslims perceive the use of critical methods in the study of the Qur'ān as an "attack from the outside." See Rippin, "The Qur'an as Literature: Perils, Pitfalls and Prospects," *British Society for Middle Eastern Studies Bulletin* 10, 1 (1983): 41. On argument against non-Muslims' interpretation of the Qur'ān, see Muhammad Abdur-Rauf, "Outsiders' Interpretations of Islam: a Muslim's Point of View," in *Approaches to Islam in Religious Studies,* ed. Richard Martin (Tucson: University of Arizona Press, 1985), 179–88. For further objections to the study of the Qur'ān, see now David Marshal, *God, Muhammad and the Unbelievers. A Qur'anic Study* (Richmond: Curzon, 1999), 1ff.

25. T.E. van Spanje, "Contextualisation: Hermeneutical Remarks," *Bulletin of the John Rylands University Library of Manchester* 80, 1 (Spring 1998): 204. See also Sandra M. Schneiders, *The Revelatory Text. Interpreting the New Testament as Sacred Scripture* (New York: Harper Collins 1991), 22 who sees similar objections from some Protestants. She also finds some Catholics arguing that since the Bible is the Church's book, it is not subject to scholarly discussion and that only the hierarchical Magisterium are the authoritative interpreters of that Book.

26. Charles M. Wood, "Hermeneutics and the Authority of Scripture," in *Scriptural Authority and Narrative Interpretation: Essays on the Occasion of the Sixty Fifth Birthday of Hans W. Frei,* ed. Garrett Green (Philadelphia: Fortress Press, 1987), 4. The terms "conservative" and "liberal" are Wood's.

27. Ibid., 6.

28. Bultmann, "The Problem of Hermeneutics," 256.

29. Abū Zayd, *Naqd al-khiṭāb al-dīnī* (Cairo 1992), 197.

30. Ibid., 197.

31. Abū Zayd, *Mafhūm al-naṣṣ,* 27.

32. "Ich behandele den Koran als Text in arabischer Sprache, den der Muslim ebenso wie der Christ oder Atheist studieren sollte, weil sich in ihm die arabische Kultur vereinigt." Navid Kermani, "Die Affäre Abū Zayd: Eine Kritik am religiösen Diskurs und ihre Folgen," *Orient* 35, 1 (1994): 28–29. The complete interview has been published under the title "Die Befreiung des Korans: Ein Gespräch mit dem ägyptischen Literaturwissenschaftler Nasr Hamid Abu Zaid," in Abu Zaid, *Islam und Politik: Kritik des religiösen Diskurses,* trans. Chérifa Magdi (Frankfurt am Main: dipa-Verl., 1996), 191–213.

33. Stanton, "Presuppositions in New Testament Criticism," 69.

34. D. Atkinson, "Religious Dialogue and Critical Possibilities," *Religious Studies and Theology* 12, 2–3 (Sept. 1992): 26–27.

35. Abu Zayd, "Qur'anic Studies on the Eve of the 21st Century," in *ISIM Newsletter* 1/98, 46.

36. Abū Zayd, *Mafhūm al-naṣṣ,* 24,

37. Ibid., 26.

38. Ibid., 24.

39. Abū Zayd, *Naqd al-khiṭāb al-dīnī,* 197, 198, 206.

40. John B. Gabeel, Charles B. Wheeler, and Anthony D. York, *The Bible as Literature: an Introduction,* 4th ed. (New York: Oxford University Press, 2000), x.

41. T. Izutsu, *God and Man in the Koran: Semantics of the Koranic Weltanschauung* (Tokyo: Keio Institute of Cultural and Linguistic Studies, 1964), 152 (italics added).

42. Abū Zayd, *Naqd al-khiṭāb al-dīnī,* 195–196. See also Stefan Wild, "'We have sent down to thee the book with the truth …': Spatial and temporal implications of the Qur'anic concepts of nuzūl, tanzīl, and 'inzāl," in *The Qur'an as Text,* ed. Stefan Wild (Leiden: E. J. Brill, 1996), 137. This kind of comparison has also been made by W.C. Smith in "Some Similarities and Differences between Christianity and Islam," in *The World of Islam: Studies in Honour of Phillip K. Hitti,* ed. J. Kritzeck and R. B. Winder (London: Macmillan, 1959), 47–59, especially 56–8. Josef van Ess has documented other scholars who have done the same comparison in his *Theologie und Gesellschaft im 2.und 3. Jahrhundert Hidschra: eine Geschichte des religiösen Denkens im frühen Islam* (Berlin: de Gruyter, 1997), IV, 604, n. 1. Cf. Rein Fernhout, "The Bible as God's Word: A Christological View," in *Holy Scriptures in Judaism, Christianity and Islam,* eds. Hendrik M. Vroom and Jerald D. Gort (Amsterdam: Editions Rodopi B.V., 1997), 57–68, where he argues that Jesus is the Word of God that becomes flesh and the Bible the Word of God which becomes scripture.

43. Abū Zayd, *Naqd al-khiṭāb al-dīnī,* 196.

44. Ibid., 196. Sometimes he says the word of God is manifested *(tatajallā)* in the human language.

45. Ibid., 198, 206.

46. Kermani, "Die Affäre Abū Zayd," 31, my translation.

47. The article to which Abū Zayd refers is "Revelation as a Linguistic Concept in Islam," in *Studies in Medieval Thought, Journal of the Japanese Society of Medieval Philosophy* 5 (1962). The article is now reprinted in *God and Man in the Koran,* Chapter VII on "Communication between God and Man (II)—Linguistic Communication," 151–197.

48. See Izutsu, *God and Man in the Koran,* 152ff. for the discussion of the *parole*-aspect of the Qur'ān, and 185ff. for the *langue*-side.

49. See also Q. 12:2 *Innā anzalnāhu qur'ānan ᶜarabiyyan laᶜallakum taᶜqilūna.*

50. This issue will be discussed below. Abū Zayd seems to agree with the author of "al-Ḳur'ān" in *EI2* who also argues that the relation between the Qur'ān and Muḥammad is so close "that one cannot be fully understood without the other." See A. T. Welch, "al-Ḳur'ān," *EI2*, V, 402. See also Welch's "Muhammad's Understanding of Himself. The Koranic Data," in *Islam's Understanding of Itself,* eds. R.G. Hovannisian and Speros Vryonis (Malibu CA: Undena Publications, 1983), 15–52. Wansbrough, however, would argue against this historical account. See the latter's argument in A. Rippin, "Literary Analysis of *Qur'ān, Tafsīr,* and *Sīra:* The Methodologies of John Wansbrough," in *Approaches to Islam in Religious Studies,* 151–63. See also A. Rippin, "Muḥammad in the Qur'ān: Reading Scripture in the 21st Century," in *The Biography of Muḥammad: The Issue of the Sources,* ed. Harald Motzki (Leiden: E. J. Brill, 2000), 298–309.

51. Abū Zayd, *Mafhūm al-naṣṣ,* 24.

52. Ibid., 178.

53. It should be kept in mind that *naṣṣ,* which is usually translated as "text," means also in this discussion "literary text."

54. Abū Zayd, "The Modernisation of Islam or the Islamisation of Modernity," *Cosmopolitanism, Identity and Authenticity in the Middle East,* ed. Roel Meijer (Richmond: Curzon, 1999), 84.

55. Quoted by Abu Zayd in *al-Naṣṣ, al-Sulṭa, al-Ḥaqīqa: al-Fikr al-dīnī bayna irādat al-maᶜrifa wa irādat al-haymana* (Beirut 1995), 153; idem, "The Textuality of the Koran," in *Islam and Europe in Past and Present* (Leiden: NIAS, 1997), 43; idem, "Divine Attri-

butes in the Qur'an. Some Poetic Aspects," In *Islam and Modernity. Muslim Intellectuals Respond,* ed. John Cooper, Ronald L. Nettler and Mohamed Mahmoud (London: I. B. Taurus, 1998), 192.

56. Abū Zayd, "Textuality," 43; idem, "Divine Attributes," 192.

57. See Jorge J. E. Gracia, *A Theory of Textuality: The Logic and Epistemology* (Albany NY: SUNY Press, 1995), 7.

58. Hans Wehr, *A Dictionary of Modern Written Arabic* (Wiesbaden: Harrassowitz, 1979, fourth edition), 1135.

59. See Ibn Manẓūr, *Lisān al-ᶜArab* (Beirut 1956), 7 on "Ṣ": 97–9 (*naṣaṣa).*

60. Abū Zayd, *al-Naṣṣ, al-Sulṭa, al-Ḥaqīqa,* 150.

61. Abū Zayd, "Textuality," 44; idem, "Divine Attributes," 192; idem, *al-Naṣṣ, al-Sulṭa, al-Ḥaqīqa,* 150: (a) *al-dalāla al-ḥissiyya: rafaᶜa* (b) *al-intiqāl min al-ḥissī : naṣṣ al-umūr =shadīduhā* (c) *al-intiqāl ilā 'l-maᶜnawī : naṣṣa al-rajula = sa'alahu ᶜan shay' ḥattā yastaqṣiya mā ᶜindahu* (d) *al-dukhūl ilā al-iṣṭilāḥī : tawqīf wa taᶜyīn.*

62. Abū Zayd, *al-Naṣṣ, al-Sulṭa, al-Ḥaqīqa,* 151. Abū Zayd refers to *al-Risāla,* ed. Aḥmad Muḥammad Shākir (Cairo,1940), 14. I do not find on that page the term *naṣṣ* but rather *bayyin.* On page 21, however, in his discussion of *Kayfa al-Bayān,* al-Shāfiᶜī describes *naṣṣ* as *bayyin.* See also Majid Khadduri's translation of *Risāla* (Baltimore: The Johns Hopkins Press, 1961), 62 and 68, respectively.

63. Abū Zayd, *al-Naṣṣ, al-Sulṭa, al-Ḥaqīqa,* 154 (instead of Q. 2:17, it should read Q. 2:7. See al-Zamakhsharī, *al-Kashshāf* (Beirut n.d.), 50).

64. Many scholars have studied Q. 3:7. See, for example, Wansbrough, *Quranic Studies,* 149ff.; Leah Kinberg, "*Muḥkamāt* and *Mutashābihāt* (Koran 3/7): Implication of a Koranic Pair of Terms in Medieval Exegesis," *Arabica* 35 (1988):143–172; Michel Lagarde, "De l'ambiguïté (mutašābih) dans le Coran: tentatives d'explication des exégètes musulmans," *Quaderni di studi arabi* 3 (1985):45–62; and recently Jane D. McAuliffe, "Text and Textuality: Q. 3:7 as Point of Intersection," in *Literary Structures of Religious Meaning in the Qur'ān,* ed. Issa J. Boullata (Richmond: Curzon, 2000), 56–76.

65. Al-Suyūṭī, *al-Itqān fī ᶜulūm al-Qur'ān,* ed. Muḥammad Abū 'l-Faḍl Ibrāhīm (Cairo 1985), III, 8; see Abū Zayd, *Mafhūm al-naṣṣ,* 179; idem, "Textuality," 44.

66. Abū Zayd, *al-Naṣṣ, al-Sulṭa, al-Ḥaqīqa,* 157.

67. Ibid., 158. Cf. F. Rosenthal's translation of *al-Muqaddima* in Ibn Khaldūn, *The Muqaddimah: An Introduction to History* (New York: Pantheon Books, 1958), 3:139 where, instead of *al-Naṣṣ,* the word *al-Faṣṣ* is written, which is translated as "Text." See also M. Quatremere's reprinted edition of *Muqaddimatu Ibn Khaldūn* (Beirut, 1970), 3:110. However, *Tārīkh al-ᶜallāma Ibn Khaldūn* (Beirut, 1961), 1:910 writes *al-Naṣṣ.*

68. Abū Zayd, *al-Naṣṣ, al-Sulṭa, al-Ḥaqīqa,* 158. Cf. Quatremere's edition and *Tārīkh* where they read respectively *al-Faṣṣ* and *al-Qaṣṣ.* See *Muqaddimatu Ibn Khaldūn,* 3:217 and *Tārīkh,* 1:999.

69. Abū Zayd, *al-Naṣṣ, al-Sulṭa, al-Ḥaqīqa,* 158.

70. Quṭb, *Maᶜālim fī'l-ṭarīq* (Cairo 1988), 105.

71. Abū Zayd, "Divine Attributes in the Qur'an," 193.

72. P. Ricoeur, "What is a Text? Explanation and Understanding," in idem, *Hermeneutics & the Human Sciences,* ed. John B. Thompson (Cambridge: Cambridge University Press, 1995), 145.

73. Gracia, *A Theory of Textuality,* 4.

74. Abū Zayd clearly follows Jakobson's analysis. See *Mafhūm al-Naṣṣ,* 25. Cf. Jakobson, "Linguistics and Poetics," *Style in Language,* ed. T. Sebeok (Cambridge MA: MIT Press, 1960), 350–77.

75. Jakobson, "Linguistics and Poetics," 353.

76. See especially, Abū Zayd, *Mafhūm al-naṣṣ,* 24, 25.

77. Abū Zayd does mention that the Qur'ān is *risāla tumaththil ʿalāqat ittiṣāl bayna mursil wa mustaqbil min khilāl shifra aw niẓām lughawī*. See, *Mafhūm al-naṣṣ,* 24.

78. Ricoeur has discussed the transformation of Jakobson's six factors of oral communication to written text. See his *Interpretation Theory: Discourse and the Surplus of Meaning* (Fort Worth: The Texas Christian University Press, 1976), 26–37.

79. Cesare Segre, *Introduction to the Analysis of the Literary Text,* translated by John Meddemmen (Bloomington: Indiana University Press, 1988), 4.

80. Ricoeur, "What is a Text? Explanation and Understanding," 146–147.

81. Barbara A. Holdrege, *Veda and Torah: Transcending the Textuality of Scripture* (Albany NY: SUNY Press, 1996), 418–419.

82. Segre, *Introduction,* 4; Ricoeur, "What is a Text? Explanation and Understanding," 147–148.

83. Ricoeur, "What is a Text? Explanation and Understanding," 148.

84. See Abū Zayd, *Mafhūm al-naṣṣ,* 52–55; idem, "Divine Attributes," 190–191; and his review of Graham's *Beyond the Written Word* in *Die Welt des Islams* 35, 1 (1995): 150–2.

85. See the discussion on this in Welch, "al-Ḳur'ān," 402ff.; Neal Robinson, *Discovering the Qur'an: A Contemporary Approach to a Veiled Text* (London: SCM Press, 1996), 224ff. Cf. Rippin, "Muḥammad in the Qur'ān."

86. C. Segre, *Introduction to the Analysis of the Literary Text,* translated by John Meddemmen (Bloomington: Indiana University Press, 1988), 116.

87. Andreas Meier, "Gotteswort in Knechtsgestalt—ein islamischer Luther in Ägypten? N.H. Abu Zaids provokante Koranexegese als säkulare Reform des Islam," in *Begegnungen zwischen Christentum und Islam,* ed. Hans-Christoph Gossmann (Ammersbek bei Hamburg: Verl. An der Lottebek, 1994), 64 (my translation).

88. Abū Zayd, *al-Naṣṣ, al-Sulṭa, al-Ḥaqīqa,* 71.

89. Ibid., 72.

90. Meier, "Gotteswort in Knechtsgestalt," 64.

91. John Barton, "Historical-Critical Approach," in *The Cambridge Companion to Biblical Interpretation,* ed. John Barton (Cambridge: Cambridge University Press, 1998), 9ff.

92. Ibid., 12. Barton and Robert Morgan even call this "new paradigm" a "breakthrough" in Biblical interpretation that is "characterized as a shift in the focus of interest from past persons, events, traditions, literary forms, and conventions, to the now available texts and their impact upon present-day readers and hearers." See Morgan and Barton, *Biblical Interpretation* (Oxford: Oxford University Press, 1988), 221.

93. Morgan and Barton, *Biblical Interpretation*, 203.

94. Wild, "Preface," of *The Qur'an as Text,* viii. See also Issa J. Boullata, "Introduction," in *Literary Structures of Religious Meaning in the Qur'ān,* ed. Issa J. Boullata (Richmond: Curzon, 2000), x.

95. Barton, "Historical-Critical Approach," 14.

96. Ibid., 18–19.

97. See Abū Zayd, *al-Imām al-Shāfiʿī wa ta'sīs al-īdiyūlūjiyya al-wasaṭiyya* (Cairo 1992), 110.

98. See Walter Vogels, *Interpreting Scripture in the Third Millennium: Author-Reader-Text* (Ottawa: Novalis, 1993), 10ff. For a discussion in literary criticism, see M.H. Abrams, *The Mirror and the Lamp: Romantic Theory and the Critical Tradition* (Oxford: Oxford University Press, 1953), 3–29.

99. For a general survey of reader-centered interpretation, see S.R. Suleiman, "Varieties of Audience-Oriented Criticism," in *The Reader in the Text: Esseys on Audience and Interpretation,* eds. S.R. Suleiman and I. Crosman (Princeton: Princeton University Press, 1981), 3–45; and the many different approaches of this theory represented by the articles in that volume.

100. P. Ricoeur, "Phenomenology and Hermeneutics," in idem, *From Text to Action: Essays in Hermeneutics II,* trans. Kathleen Blamey and John B. Thompson (Evanston: Northwestern University Press, 1991), 32.

101. Ricoeur, "What is a Text?" 147.

102. Abū Zayd, *Naqd al-khiṭāb al-dīnī,* 56, 74, 87; *al-Naṣṣ, al-Sulṭa, al-Ḥaqīqa,* 113. See also an interview with Muḥammad Ḥusayn in "D. Naṣr Ḥāmid Abū Zayd yataḥaddath: Fahm al-naṣṣ bi'l-ḥayāh lā fahm al-ḥayāh bi'l-naṣṣ,"*Adab wa naqd* 10 (May 1993): 71. Abū Zayd refers to *Tārīkh al-Ṭabarī: Tārīkh al-rusul wa'l-mulūk,* ed. Muḥammad Abū 'l-Faḍl Ibrāhīm (Cairo 1979), 5:66 *wa hādhā 'l-qur'ānu innamā huwa khaṭṭun masṭūrun bayna daffatayni, lā yanṭuqu, innamā yatakallamu bihi 'l-rijālu.* See also G.R. Hawting's translation in *The History of al-Ṭabarī. The First Civil War* (Albany NY: SUNY Press, 1996), 17:103.

103. Morgan and Barton, *Biblical Interpretation,* 7.

104. Abū Zayd, *Falsafat al-ta'wīl: Dirāsa fī ta'wīl al-Qur'ān ʿinda Muḥyī al-Dīn Ibn ʿArabī,* 3rd edition (Beirut 1996) , 6.

105. For an overview of this method, see Marcel Dumais, "Sens de l'écriture. Reéxamen à la lumiere de l'herméneutique philosophique et des approaches littéraires récentes," *New Testament Studies* 45 (1999): 317ff.

106. Wolfgang Iser, *The Implied Reader: Patterns of Communication in Prose Fiction from Bunyan to Beckett* (Baltimore: Johns Hopkins University Press, 1974), 284.

107. See "World of Text, World of Reader," in *A Ricoeur Reader: Reflection & Imagination,* ed. Mario J. Valdes (Toronto: University of Toronto Press, 1991), 492ff.

108. See James L. Machor, "The Object of Interpretation and Interpretive Change," *Modern Language Notes (MLN)* 113 (1998): 1126–1150, esp. 1128ff.

109. See P. Ricoeur, "The Hermeneutical Function of Distanciation," in idem, *From Text to Action: Essays in Hermeneutics, II,* Trans. Kathleen Blamey and John B. Thompson (Evanston: Northwestern University Press, 1991), 83ff.

110. K. Stendahl, "Method in the Study of Biblical Theology," in *The Bible in Modern Scholarship,* ed. J. Philip Hyatt (New York: Abingdon Press, 1966), 196–209, esp. 199ff. See also Dumais, "Sens de l'écriture," 316, n. 16.

111. See, for example, Abū Zayd, *Mafhūm al-naṣṣ,* 229; *Naqd al-khiṭāb al-dīnī,* 116ff.; *Ishkāliyyāt al-qirā'a wa āliyyāt al-ta'wīl* (Beirut, 1994), 6, 48, 152; *Dawā'ir al-khawf: Qirā'a fī khiṭāb al-mar'a* (Beirut, 1999), 303; "The Textuality," 51; "Divine Attributes," 200. For Hirsch's distinction see his *Validity in Interpretation* (New Haven: Yale University Press, 1967), 8, 209–244; idem, *The Aims of Interpretation* (Chicago: University of Chicago Press, 1976), 1–13 and 17–49. Kermani argues that Hirsch's distinction was originated from G. Frege's between "Sinn" and "Bedeutung." See Kermani, *Offenbarung als Komunikation,* 12, n. 51. Hirsch himself admits that he adopted it from Frege, see Hirsch, *Validity in Interpretation,* 211.

112. Scholars have criticized Hirsch's distinction of "meaning" and "significance." See for the list of the critics in Paul R. Noble, *The Canonical Approach: A Critical Reconstruction of the Hermeneutics of Brevard S. Childs* (Leiden: E. J. Brill, 1995), 190, n. 9.

113. Hirsch, *Validity in Interpretation,* 8.

114. Ibid., 216

115. R. E. Brown, *The Critical Meaning of the Bible* (London: Geoffrey Chapman, 1981), 32ff. Noble calls the historical meaning "the text's intentional context," that is the meaning that relates to linguistic, social and cultural context when and where the author produces that text. See *Canonical Approach,* 197

116. K. Vanhoozer, *Is There Meaning in This Text?: The Bible, the Reader, and the Morality of Literary Knowledge* (Grand Rapids: Zondervan, 1998), 279, n. 293.

117. Abū Zayd finds that the word *ta'wīl* is mentioned seventeen times in the Qur'ān, while *tafsīr* only once. This explains that *ta'wīl* was used more often than *tafsīr* in the past. See Abū Zayd, *Mafhūm al-naṣṣ,* 226.

118. See Abū Zayd, *Mafhūm al-naṣṣ,* 229ff.; *Naqd al-khiṭāb al-dīnī,* 110ff.; *al-Naṣṣ, al-Sulṭa, al-Ḥaqīqa,* 167ff. Abū Zayd's discussion of the semantic meaning of *ta'wīl* is based on Ibn Manẓūr's *Lisān al-ᶜArab,* "a-w-l," XI, 32–40. Cf. I. Poonawala, "Ta'wīl," *EI2,* X, 390–2.

119. Ibn Manẓūr, *Lisān al-ᶜArab,* 11:32.

120. Abū Zayd, *Naqd al-khiṭāb al-dīnī,* 110. This definition is taken from *Lisān al-ᶜArab* of Ibn Manẓūr.

121. Abū Zayd, *Mafhūm al-naṣṣ,* 229.

122. Ibn Manẓūr, *Lisān al-ᶜArab,* 11:36.

123. Abū Zayd, *Naqd al-khiṭāb al-dīnī,* 111; *Mafhūm al-naṣṣ,* 230.

124. Abū Zayd, Mafhūm al-naṣṣ, 230; Naqd al-khiṭāb al-dīnī, 115ff.; Ishkāliyyāt al-qirā'a, 6.

125. Abū Zayd, "al-Manhaj al-Nafᶜī fī fahm al-nuṣūṣ al-dīniyya," *al-Hilāl* (March 1992), 56.

126. Abū Zayd, "Divine Text," 200–201.

127. Abū Zayd, *Mafhūm al-naṣṣ,* 240.

128. Cf. Farid Esack, *Qur'ān, Liberation & Pluralism: An Islamic Perspective of Interreligious Solidarity against Oppression* (Oxford: Oneworld, 1998), 63–73; and Richard C. Martin and Mark R. Woodward with Dwi S. Atmaja, *Defenders of Reason in Islam: Muᶜtazilism from Medieval School to Modern Symbol* (Oxford: Oneworld, 1997), 200–6.

129. In *Journal of Qur'anic Studies* 1, 1 (1999): 93–114.

130. Saeed, "Rethinking 'Revelation'," 95.

131. F. Rahman, *Islam,* 2nd edition (Chicago: University of Chicago Press, 1979), 31, 33.

132. Rahman, "Some Islamic Issues in the Ayyūb Khān Era," 299. See also Donald L. Berry, "Dr. Fazlur Rahman (1919–1988): A Life in Review," in *The Shaping of an American Islamic Discourse,* ed. E. H. Waugh, F. M. Denny (Atlanta: Scholars Press, 1998), 41.

133. F. Rahman, *Islam & Modernity: Transformation of an Intellectual Tradition* (Chicago: University of Chicago Press, 1984), 1–2.

134. See Hussain, "Interpreting the Tradition: The Modernist Argument and the Sources of Islam," *The American Journal of Islamic Social Sciences* 18, 1 (Winter 2001): 1–15.

135. Ibid., 10.

136. Rahman, *Islam & Modernity,* 5. For more discussion on this, see Ebrahim Moosa's "Introduction" to Rahman's *Revival and Reform in Islam: a Study of Islamic Fundamentalism,* ed. Moosa (Oxford: Oneworld, 2000), 13.

137. Fazlur Rahman, "Islam: Legacy and Contemporary Challenge," in *Islam in the Contemporary World,* ed. Cyriac K. Pullapilly (Notre Dame: Cross Road Books, 1980), 409.

138. Ibid., 415; Rahman, *Islam & Modernity,* 6ff.

139. Moosa, "Introduction," 19.

140. See Rahman, *Islam & Modernity,* 8ff. Cf. Earle H. Waugh, who mistakenly assumes that Rahman is closer to Gadamer whose position is that original meaning cannot be uncovered. See Waugh, "Beyond Scylla and Kharybdis: Fazlur Rahman and Islamic Identity," in *The Shaping of an American Islamic Discourse,* 21. Cf. Tamara Sonn, "Fazlur Rahman and Islamic Feminism," in *The Shaping of an American Islamic Discourse,* 126.

141. Rahman, *Islam & Modernity,* 8.

142. Abū Zayd, *Mafhūm al-naṣṣ,* 25, 27.

143. For his program, see *Lectures du Coran* (Paris: Maisonneuve et Larose, 1982), especially "Bilan et perspectives des études coraniques," v-xxxiii.

144. M. Arkoun, *Rethinking Islam: Common Questions, Uncommon Answers,* trans. and ed. Robert D. Lee (Boulder: Westview, 1994), 30,

145. M. Arkūn, "al-Mumkin al-Tafkīr fīh/wa al-Mustaḥīl al-Tafkīr fīh fī'l-Fikr al-Islāmī al-Muᶜāṣir," an interview by Hāshim Ṣāliḥ in *Qaḍāyā fī Naqd al-ᶜAql al-Dīnī: Kayfa Nafham al-Islām al-Yawm* (Beirut 1998), 278–279.

146. See M. Arkoun, "The Notion of Revelation: From *Ahl al-Kitāb* to the Societies of the Book," *Die Welt des Islams* 28 (1998): 62–89.

147. M. Arkūn, *al-Fikr al-uṣūlī wa istiḥālat al-ta'ṣīl: Naḥwa tārīkh ākhar li'l-fikr al-Islāmī,* trans. Hāshim Ṣāliḥ (London 1999), 30.

148. Arkoun, "The Notion of Revelation," 75.

149. Arkūn, *al-Fikr al-uṣūlī wa istiḥālat al-ta'ṣīl,* 43–44. See for example, Jacques Le Goff, *The Medieval Imagination,* trans. Arthur Goldhammer (Chicago: University of Chicago Press, 1985).

150. Paris: Noêsis, 1997.

151. See Arkūn, *al-Fikr al-uṣūlī wa istiḥālat al-ta'ṣīl,* 52–55.

152. See M. Foucault, *The Archeology of Knowledge* (New York: Pantheon Books, 1972), 45. In *Rethinking Islam,* Arkoun refers to this as the theory of intertextuality.

153. M. Arkoun, *Rethinking Islam Today* (Washington: Center for Contemporary Arab Studies, 1987), 21.

154. See T. J. Keegan, "Biblical Criticism and the Challenge of Postmodernism," *Biblical Interpretation* 3, 1 (March 1995): 1.

Chapter 12

The Qur'ān in Syria: Muḥammad Shaḥrūr's Inner-Qur'ānic Exegetical Method

Sahiron Syamsuddin

The dynamics of Qur'ān interpretation are never-ending; they began the moment the scripture was revealed to Muḥammad and they continue down until today.[2] Many different interpretations have been offered by both classical and modern exegetes; this is a result, according to Boullata, of "many elements in the text and its context, as well as in the relation of both to other texts and contexts." [3] As well, the receptors of a text are preconditioned by the "cultural and socio-political circumstances" that create a horizon of understanding. The dissatisfaction expressed by modern exegetes for earlier methods and interpretations may be viewed as proof of this dynamic.

At the end of the twentieth century there were many controversial thinkers who eagerly took up the study of the Qur'ān. One of them was the Syrian engineer, Dr. Muḥammad Shaḥrūr.[4] His new ideas concerning the Qur'ān and Islam in general have attracted the attention of many people in the Arab world. His first book, *al-Kitāb wa'l-Qur'ān*, was published in 1990. It offered a range of new findings in the field of Qur'ānic studies and quickly became controversial[5] and one of the best selling books in the Middle East.[6] Many scholars responded to it. Some people did not agree with his ideas at all and rejected them, while others attempted to take them into account. Those who rejected his ideas considered him as an enemy of Islam and a western and Zionist agent.[7] In Kuwait, for example, a book seller has said that Shaḥrūr's books are more dangerous that Salman Rushdie's *Satanic Verses*.[8] In some countries such as Saudi Arabia, Egypt, Qatar and United Arab Emirates, Shaḥrūr's books are formally banned.[9] In such a situation, Wielandt's theory is proven right; she wrote: "Muslime, die heutzutage innerhalb ihrer Religionsgemeinschaft ein wissenschaftliches Gespräch über neue hermeneutische Zugänge zum Korantext in Gang bringen wollen, haben es damit nicht leicht."[10] More followers of Shaḥrūr live in European and American countries than in Islamic countries[11] although there is some support for his work in Muslim countries. Sultan Qaboos in Oman, for example, has distributed Shaḥrūr's book *al-Kitāb wa'l-Qur'ān* to his ministries and recommended that it be read.[12] Some scholars, such as Wael Hallaq[13] and Dale Eickelman,[14] respect his new theories of Islamic law and his ideas on the reform of Islam, respectively. Arkoun considers him to be successful in bearing "witness to both the intolerable pressure of dogmatic control on Qur'ānic studies and the limits within which every discourse with hopes of innovation must be pursued."[15]

This essay will focus on the methodology which Shaḥrūr uses in interpreting the Qur'an: inner-Qur'ānic exegesis and the "paradigmo-syntagmatic" approach. With a few exceptions,[16] most other reflections on Shaḥrūr have been devoted to the study of his ideas and the Muslim reception of them and do not concentrate on his approach to interpreting the Qur'an. The approach that I use in this essay is a phenomenological one which means that I will describe what he says about the hermeneutical theory and how he then uses that theory; this will be illustrated by two examples, looking at the concepts of *rubūbiyya* ("world-mastery" of God) and *ulūhiyya* (the "worshipped-ness" of God) and the meaning of *islām* ("submission to God") and *īmān* ("belief").

Shaḥrūr on the Revelation of the Qur'ān and its Typology

Before introducing some of Shaḥrūr's theory about Qur'ānic revelation and typology, it must be pointed out that almost all of his findings are different from what previous exegetes have said. Experts in Qur'ānic studies over the ages have had various opinions on the nature of Qur'ānic revelation. In his *Mafhūm al-naṣṣ,* Abū Zayd[17] discusses the two main opinions which have emerged through history. The first opinion, followed mostly by Sunnī orthodox Muslims and some modern scholars like Aḥmad Khān,[18] is that the Qur'ān was revealed *verbatim* in word and meaning and that the angel Gabriel memorized it from the heavenly tablet (*al-lawḥ al-maḥfūẓ*) and then brought it down to the Prophet. In this case, the Prophet acted only as a receptor of the revelation. This opinion has, according to Abū Zayd, two consequences, namely (1) that an exaggeration of the holiness of the text has occurred and the Qur'ān has been changed from a "linguistic text" to an "imaginative text," and (2) a belief in the depth and the plurality of Qur'ānic meanings has emerged. The other opinion is that the angel Gabriel revealed the Qur'ān from God in the form of "inspiration" (*ilhām*), and the Prophet formulated it in the Arabic language. In other words, Muḥammad was involved in interpreting the divine revelation. Some modern Qur'ān scholars such as Shāh Walī Allāh, Muḥammad Aḥmad Khalaf Allāh and Asaf A.A. Fyzee[19] have held this opinion. However, Shaḥrūr has his own notion. Although it is to some extent similar to the first opinion, he offers new lines of argument and elaboration. Because of the fact that his theory of Qur'ānic revelation cannot be separated from his typology of Qur'ānic verses, the elaboration of his opinion on this subject must be undertaken first.

For Shaḥrūr, the *kitāb* (the Qur'ān as a whole) was revealed from God through Gabriel to the Prophet Muḥammad *verbatim* in the form of *inzāl* and *tanzīl*.[20] By the term *inzāl* he means "the change of something which existed in God's mind, and something which was preserved in the *lawḥ al-maḥfūẓ* or in the *imām al-mubīn*, all of which was not in a specific language like Arabic, Turkish or Chinese, from its humanly inaccessible form into the pronounced, listened and humanly perceivable form."[21] The term *tanzīl* is used to indicate "the objective transfer of the pronounced form from God to the Prophet through the Angel."[22] The *kitāb* is divided into three categories:[23] (1) *muḥkamāt / umm al-kitāb,* (2) *mutashābihāt / al-Qur'ān wa'l-sab*ᶜ *al-mathānī,* and (3) *tafṣīl al-kitāb*.[24] The *umm al-kitāb* ("the mother of the Book"), was revealed directly—in the form of *inzāl* and *tanzīl*[25]—from God to Muḥammad over a period of 23 years. It consists of verses that are concerned with human activities (*al-sulūk al-insānī*) in relation to legal and ethical matters, and are subject to *ijtihād* ("independent reasoning") according to the contemporary requirements of time and space.[26] Therefore, the results of the human interactions with the *muḥkamāt / umm al-kitāb* can differ over time. With this thesis, Shaḥrūr points out that the practical legal decisions of the Prophet (*sunna*) constitute the first human interaction with the *muḥkamāt*.[27] Just as in the case of religious rituals, the Prophet's explanations and applications must be followed all of the time. Multiple understandings and varied practical applications of the *muḥkam* verses are called *ḥanīfiyya* ("elasticity"), in which consistent legal aspects (*al-istiqāma*) that consist of *al-ḥadd al-adnā* (the "lower limit") and *al-ḥadd al-aᶜlā* (the "upper limit") are paid attention to and preserved.[28] Moreover, the *umm al-kitāb* is considered to be "subjective," in the sense that the application of legal and ethical norms, which are included in the *umm al-kitāb*, depends on the human choice (*al-ikhtiyār al-insānī*).[29] All such Qur'ānic aspects constitute the Prophet Muḥammad's *Risāla,* that is, the state of Muḥammad as receptor, informant and applicant of divine legal and ethical laws.

With regard to the *mutashābihāt*, to which the terms *al-Qur'ān* and *al-sabᶜ al-mathānī* belong and which were revealed from the *lawḥ al-maḥfūẓ* and *al-īmām al-mubīn* to the Prophet in the forms of *inzāl* and *tanzīl,*[30] there are two categories. The first is called *al-juz' al-thābit* ("the part that is consistent and never changes") which consists of the verses that concern the "general law" that regulates the universe from the beginning of its creation to the Day of Resurrection (*yawm al-qiyāma*). The other is *al-juz' al-mutaghayyir* ("the part that can change"). With this phrase Shaḥrūr means the verses dealing with aspects that can change according to causal factors, for example the change of wind, gender and historical events (*al-qaṣaṣ*).[31] Those verses are subject to *ta'wīl* ("deep interpretation") in accord with scientific premises (*al-araḍiyyat al-ᶜilmiyya*).[32] Unlike the *umm al-kitāb,* the *mutashābihāt* verses are "objective," meaning that their contents constitute the reality that exists beyond human awareness (*al-waᶜy al-insānī*), so that it does not depend on "human choice" (*al-ihktiyār al-insānī*).[33] Included in the *mutashābihāt* are the mysterious letters that are known as *al-sabᶜ al-mathānī*. These include *Alif Lām Mīm, Alif Lām Mīm Ṣād, Kāf Hā Yā ᶜAyn Ṣād, Yā Sīn, Ṭā Hā, Ṭā Sīn Mīm*, and *Ḥā Mīm*. These are all considered separate verses and appear in the beginning of certain *sūras*.[34] All the *mutashābihāt* are included into the concept of *al-nubuwwa,* that is, the state of Muḥammad as receptor and informant of revelations that are not related to legal and ethical laws, such as stories of previous prophets, the creation of creatures and eschatology.

The last type of Qur'ānic verses is called *tafṣīl al-kitāb* ("the explanation of the Book"). As far as Q. 3:7, on which the typology of Qur'ānic verses is based, has been studied, this type is introduced by Shaḥrūr for the first time. The term *tafṣīl al-kitāb* is used to indicate all verses that speak about the existence of all the types of Qur'ānic verses: *al-muḥkamāt*, *al-mutashābihāt,* and *tafṣīl al-kitāb*. It includes, for instance, Q. 3:7, 10:37, 11:1, 12:111, 39:23 and 41:3. Like *al-mutashābihāt,* this type is included in *al-nubuwwa,* because it only provides information about the *kitāb*.[35]

For Shaḥrūr, *al-kitāb* (the whole Qur'ān) is subject to interpretation or *ijtihād* (reasoning). In interpreting the *mutashābihāt* and applying the *ijtihād* to the *muḥkamāt,* Muslims do not have to depend on the exegetical products of previous exegetes, because they are nothing but historical achievements which are no longer suitable for current requirements. He even says: "We have to interact with the *kitāb* as if we could have received it from the Prophet yesterday."[36] To some extent, his hermeneutical theory coincides with that of Bultmann who insists on the signification and the contextualization of word of God within life as it is lived. As Weinsheimer explicates, Bultmann argued that "understanding the Word of God means understanding it as a call to salvation; and that modern man can interpret and appropriate the Word of God because he already pre-understood it, already knows what it would be mean to be saved, already recognizes the poverty of his existence and believes in the possibility of enriching it."[37] This idea contrasts to Bint al-Shāṭi''s opinion that the task of the interpreter is only to show the meaning of Qur'ānic verses as they were understood by the first Muslim generation—in other words, to grasp the original meaning.[38] In terms of exegetical praxis, it is evident that, in order to re-interpret the *kitāb*, Shaḥrūr uses the philological method that is supported by the method of inner-Qur'ānic exegesis and "paradigmo-syntagmatic" analyses.

Inner-Qur'ānic Exegetical Method and Paradigmo-Syntagmatic Analyses

The term "inner-Qur'ānic exegesis" is used here in the same sense as the term "inner-Biblical exegesis" is used by Michael Fishbane to indicate the way in which the cross-reference of some Biblical verses to other Biblical verses is done in order, in his terminology, to "re-use," "re-contextualize," "extend," "reformulate," "re-interpret" or "transform" them.[39] Like the method of inner-Biblical exegesis, the inner-Qur'ānic exegetical method suggests a the hermeneutical way of comparing all verses that deal with a same topic.[40] It is worthy of note that this method does not actually constitute a new method in the Qur'ānic interpretive tradition. The method derives from the concept *al-Qur'ān yufassir ba^{c}ḍuhu ba^{c}ḍan* ("one part of the Qur'ān interprets another part") that has been used from the beginning of Islamic exegesis. Its application can be seen, for instance, in the classical exegetical works of Muqātil ibn Sulaymān (d. 150/767), Ibn Jarīr al-Ṭabarī (d. 310/923), al-Zamakhsharī (d. 538/1144), Ibn Taymiyya (d. 728/1328) and Ibn Kathīr (d. 775/1373).[41] However, it is applied more systematically by interpreters in the 20th century, who call it as *al-tafsīr al-mawḍū^{c}ī* ("thematic interpretation").[42] In practice, interpreters apply this method in different ways, not only in the case of choosing verses but also in terms of analyzing them.

For Shaḥrūr, this methodological means has a justification found in Q. 73:4 in which the word *tartīl* appears. For him, that word does not mean "to read" as it is understood by the majority of interpreters. He says that the root of the word *tartīl* is *al-ratl,* that means "a rank or queue on a fixed order." On this basis, the so-called Qur'ānic methodology of *tartīl* means "to bring together all verses that deal with a same topic, and to arrange them beside one another for the purpose of interpretation."[43] This way should be followed because many Qur'ānic themes, such as the creation of universe, the creation of men, and the stories of previous prophets, are situated in different chapters of the Qur'ān. In order for interpreters to absorb a comprehensive sense of a certain topic, they should view the verses together and compare them.

For the purpose of absorbing a comprehensive understanding, Shaḥrūr utilizes a semantic analysis, using the paradigmo-syntagmatical approach. The paradigmatical analysis occurs when someone tries to grasp the meaning of a term by using another term which has a close or contradictory meaning.[44] In this case, however, Shaḥrūr agrees with Ibn Fāris who has said that in the Arabic language there is no synonym (*tarāduf*). Every word has its own specific meaning. However, any word can have more than one potential meaning (polyvalent word / *mushtarak al-maᶜānī*).[45] Unlike Nida who includes "overlapping, contiguous and hyponymous" words into synonymous types,[46] Shaḥrūr considers the three types as non-synonymous words. One of the factors that can give a clue for the most probable meaning of a word, out of its range of potential meanings, is the logical context in the text in which the word appears. According to Osborne, this is a syntagmatical analysis, that being one that reveals that the meaning of every word influenced by its linear connection to other words surrounding it.[47]

Whether synonyms exist in the Qur'ān or not is debated by scholars. Some people such as Sībawayh (d. 180/796), al-Aṣmaᶜī (d. 213/828) and Ibn Khālawayh (d. 370/980) said that one can find many synonymous words in it. Some others, like Ibn Fāris (d. 395/1004), Abū Hilāl al-ᶜAskarī (d. ca 400/1010) and al-Rāghib al-Iṣfahānī (d. 5th/11th C.) argued the opposite. This diversity of opinion originates from the different understandings of the nature of the language of the Qur'ān as to whether it is *tawfīqī* (a "divine guidance") or *iṣṭilāḥī* (a "social construction"). The belief that the language comes from God leads to the negation of synonym. Those who accept the existence of synonyms argue that language is a social construction and convention.[48] Shaḥrūr agrees with those who insist on the negation of the existence of synonyms. He states that there is a synonymous structure (*al-tarkīb*) in the Qur'ān,[49] arguing that because the Qur'ān is a divine revelation (*waḥy ilāhī*) and a divine construction (*ṣiyāgha ilāhiyya*), the choice of words in it is very accurate.[50] In addition, he also offers an analogical argument. He says:

> If we read a book in medicine or in engineering, written in whatever language, we see that the phenomenon of the synonym is not found. If one cell is different from another, even though the difference is very small, then the author will give it a new name in order to differentiate it (from the other). And, whenever an unknown measure (*ḥadd majhūl*) in mathematics differs from another, although the difference is very small, we see that the author will give them numbers that can differentiate them (S-1, S-2 or S-3). This

> is really for the scientific accuracy. How can we accept this phenomenon in these sciences that come from human beings, praise it, and call it a scientific accuracy, but on the other hand we insists that all signs in the Book of Allāh are the same.[51]

The paradigmatic and syntagmatic analyses constitute the most important ways in which Shaḥrūr discusses many Qur'ānic aspects. Two examples will be discussed in the following part in order to illustrate this method.

Application of the Method: The Concepts of *Rubūbiyya* and *Ulūhiyyah*

In the Qur'ān Allāh is referred as *al-ilāh* (the "worshipped" God), for example in Q. 47:19 and 22:33, and as *al-rabb* (the "Creator and Owner of the World"), for example in Q. 1:1 and 55:17. For Shaḥrūr, the two words have different connotations, even though they refer to the one God. It seems that he agrees with the assumption that every symbol (in this case: word) not only has a sense, but also a referent. However, it is possible that a word could have a sense that is different from that of another word, even though their referent is the same.[52]

The word *rabb* whose fundamental meanings are *milk* ("possessing") and *siyāda* ("mastery") has, according to Shaḥrūr, a sense of objective reality beyond human awareness. The *rubūbiyya* of Allāh constitutes a concept of mastery and possessing of Allāh over all of His creatures, regardless of whether they have an intellect or not, and whether they are believers or not.[53] Moreover, he insists that *rubūbiyya* is axiomatic and irresistible (*ṣārim, qāhir*), in the sense that, regardless of likes and dislikes, all creatures belong to God, are created by Him and are taken care of by Him. The creatures have no right to reject this fact. The only appropriate attitude is to accept that Allāh is the creator and the owner of all the creatures, because *rubūbiyya* is an objective reality that does not need recognition from the other side.[54] Q. 15:26 reveals that even *iblīs* (devil) can not reject the divine *rubūbiyya*. The acceptance of the divine *rubūbiyya* means also submission to the divine law (*sunnat Allāh*) that orders all creatures.[55] Therefore, for Shaḥrūr, the concept of *rubūbiyya* is related to the concept of *nubuwwa*.

Shaḥrūr explains the concept of *rubūbiyya* by exploring several examples of the use of the word *rabb* and other words whose meanings are subordinate to it, although they are not used in the context of the divine *rubūbiyya*. For example, the self-recognition of Pharaoh as *rabb,* as documented in Q. 43:51 and 79:24, is understood in the context of *milkiyya* ("possessing") and *siyāda* ("mastery"). In the two verses, Pharaoh called himself *al-rabb al-aᶜlā* ("the highest owner and master"), in the sense that Egypt, contents and all, was claimed to be his own possession that could be utilized however and whenever he liked, without any valid objection from anyone.[56] Another example is Q. 2:30. This verse affirms that Allah creates human beings as *khalīfa fī'l-arḍ* ("divine deputy in the world"). It means that He gives a part of His *sulṭa* ("power") to them, so that they can possess the world, master it and utilize it by paying attention to natural laws (*sunnat Allāh*).[57]

The concept of *rubūbiyya* is elaborated by Shaḥrūr, applying the inner-Qur'ānic exegetical method to the verses in which the word *rabb* with its varied contexts appears, such as Q. 2:30, 11:56, 12:41–2, 17:102, 18:27, 71:28, 78:37, and 79:24. Using the syntagmatic analysis he proves that the word *rabb* in these verses is connected to such words as *jāᶜil fī'l-arḍ khalīfa* ("to create a *khalīfa* in the world"), *khāliq kull shay'* ("to create all things") and *urzuq ahlahu* ("provide the [Meccan] people with means of subsistence"). This indicates that the concept of *rubūbiyya* is related to creation, possessing and taking care of the world.[58] This is why, in the verses that contain the begging to Allāh to forgive sins such as Q. 2:201, 5:83 and 71:28, the word *rabb* always appears.[59]

Unlike the concept of *rubūbiyya*, the concept of *ulūhiyya*, which conveys the sense that Allāh is the one God who is worshiped, is related to the free choice of human beings. In many verses human beings are ordered to worship only Allāh. However, they are given the freedom to follow or to reject this order. Since the order is directed to the creatures who have intellect, *ulūhiyya* comes in their hearts after *rubūbiyya*. The word *ilāh* in the verses, such as Q. 2:133, 2:163, 3:18, 6:19, 10:90, 11:50 and 23:32, is related to the concept of *tawḥīd* (monotheism), the prohibition of polytheism and the submission to the divine law (*sharīᶜa*). On this basis, Shaḥrūr includes the concept of *ulūhiyya* within that of *risāla*.[60]

Meanings of *Islām* and *Īmān*

The other example of the application of Shaḥrūr's method is concerned with the meaning of *islām* and *īmān*. In grappling with the two concepts, Shaḥrūr collects all the Qur'ānic verses in which the words and their derivatives appear. He begins his hermeneutical exercise by analyzing three verses in which the word *islām* is used: (1) Q. 33:35 which indicates the existence of communities of both *al-muslimūn wa'l-muslimāt* and *al-mu'minūn wa'l-mu'mināt*; (2) Q. 66:5 in which the word *muslimāt* is followed by *mu'mināt,* and (3) Q. 49:14 that reveals that the Prophet Muhammad has rejected the statement of bedouin, "We believe," indicating that they have not yet become *mu'minūn* ("believers"), although they are already *muslimūn*. Based on the three verses, Shaḥrūr understands that the community of *muslimūn-muslimāt* is different from the community of *mu'minūn-mu'mināt,* and that the attitude of *islām* comes before that of *īmān*.[61] Here, Shaḥrūr applies the paradigmo-syntagmatic theory to the two words (*muslimūn* and *mu'minūn*) such that when the particle *wāw* ("and") is inserted between them, this indicates that the two words are not synonymous—although whose meanings are overlapping—and they have different senses and referents. In addition, the appearance of the different words in the three verses gives a symbolic indication of the development of distinct existences.

Furthermore, Shaḥrūr cites ten verses in which the word *islām* and its derivatives are attributed to the previous people who had lived long before the Prophet Muhammad. In Q. 3:52, 3:67, 7:126, 10:42, 10:43, 10:90, 12:101, 51:35–6, and 72:14, the term *al-muslimūn* is attributed to Noah, Lot, Abraham, Jacob, Joseph, the *jinn*, the sorcerers who submitted to Moses, and the followers of Jesus. To him, this appearance shows that the attribute of *islām* does not belong only to the *umma* ("religious community") of the Prophet Muhammad.[62] The question then remains of what the meanings of *islām* and *muslimūn* are. Shaḥrūr responds to that by referring to Q. 2:62, 2:111, 2:126, 4:125, 5:44, 21:108 and 41:33. According to these verses, *islām* is believing in God (*al-īmān bi'llāh*) and the Day of Resurrection (*al-īmān bi'l-yawm al-akhīr*), and doing good actions (*al-ᶜamal bi'l-ṣāliḥāt*). Whoever attains these is called a *muslim,* regardless of whether he or she is a member of the religion of Muḥammad (*alladhīna āmanū*), Moses (*alladhīna hādū, al-yahūd*), Jesus (*al-naṣārā*), or any other. With this definition, *islām* constitutes *al-dīn* ("religion") which is accepted by God.[63]

Shaḥrūr theorizes that the *arkān al-islām* ("pillars of Islam") include three aspects: (1) belief in God, (2) belief in the Day of Resurrection, and (3) doing good actions, and that the right path may be found in every religion in the world and the reward of the hereafter may be received by anyone who follows that way. The first two *arkān* are regarded as theoretical aspects (*jānib naẓarī*), whereas the last is a logico-practical aspect (*jānib manṭiqī ᶜamalī*). This theory, he argues, is supported by Q. 2:111–12 which criticizes the Jews who had claimed for themselves the status of being the only religious group that would be given truth and safety on the Day of Resurrection, and who reject the Christians even though they had followed the same path of worship. Verse 112 affirms then that truth and safety belong to everyone who submits to God and does good actions (*man aslama wajhahu li'llāh wa-huwa muḥsin*).[64] Implicitly, Shaḥrūr wishes to suggest that such criticism can be made of any religious group that does the same thing as the Jews in the Qur'ān, even including followers of the Prophet Muḥammad.

Furthermore, Shaḥrūr explains that the antonym of the word *islām* in the Qur'an is the word *ijrām*. This word and its derivatives appear 68 times in the scripture. Etymologically speaking, the word *ijrām* means *qaṭᶜ* ("to cut"). In the legal dictionaries it is stated that those who steal, kill and rob are called *mujrimūn,* because, by doing bad actions, they "cut" their relation to society and social rules in order to satisfy their personal desires.[65] In the Qur'ān the meaning of the word, Shaḥrūr adds, is contrary to that of the word *islām*. Such Qur'ānic verses as Q. 28:78, 27:69, 30:12, 36:59, 55:41–3 and 77:18–19, relate syntagmatically the word *al-mujrimūn* to the attitude of unbelief in God and the Day of Resurrection. On this basis, the *mujrimūn* are understood as those who do not believe in God and the Day of Resurrection. They are called *mujrimūn* because they "cut" their relation to God.[66] More comprehensively, Q. 74:39–46 reveals that the *mujrimūn* are not only those who do not believe in God (*lam naku min al-muṣallīn*) and the Day of Resurrection (*nukadhdhibu bi yawm al-dīn*), but also those who do not do good actions (*lam naku nuṭ^cimu al-miskīn*), and do bad actions (*kunnā nakhūḍu ma^ca 'l-khā'iḍīn*).[67]

With regard to the concept of *īmān* in the Qur'ān, Shaḥrūr seems to be more cautious in interpreting the verses which contain that word and its derivatives. The inner-Qur'ānic exegetical method is applied not only for understanding the linguistic signs of the Qur'ān, but also for making sense of the logical structure which is inherent in its verses. For Shaḥrūr, the word *īmān* is polyvalent in its meaning. In several verses the word has the same meaning as the word *islām,* while in some other verses it means to "believe in the prophecy of Muhammad." This polyvalence is caused by the fact that, in some cases, the two words have the same potential meanings. To decide which potential meaning is relevant in a specific verse, Shaḥrūr's method requires that he analyze the context and the logic of the verse in question. In this case, Shaḥrūr quotes three verses he will analyze: Q. 4:136, 57:28, and 47:2; he says:

> In each of the three verses we can see that the verb *āmanū* and its conjugation are cited twice. The reason for that is that Allāh has ordered the believers to believe in Him and His Apostle and this cannot be understood unless they had not previously believed in His Apostle and his revealed book. As well, He orders the believers to fear Him and to believe in His Apostle which would not make sense if they had already feared and believed in His Apostle. The divine order for those who believe in Him and do good actions to believe in the revelation that is revealed to Muḥammad, cannot be understood unless they have not yet believed in the prophethood of Muḥammad. In order to understand the three verses we do not need a deep interpretation, since the verses are related to the meanings of *islām* and *muslimūn*. If we understand that *islām* means "to believe in God and in the Day of Resurrection and to do good actions," then we know that what is meant by *alladhīna āmanū* ("those who

> believe") in the three verses are the *muslimūn,* that is, those who believe in God and in the Day of Resurrection and do good actions.[68]

Shaḥrūr is thus arguing that the words *alladhīna āmanū* in the three verses refers to *alladhīna aslamū,* or *al-muslimūn* in a broad sense, that is, all human beings from the beginning to the end of the world who believe in God and the Day of Resurrection and do good actions. Unlike these three verses, the words *āmana, āmanū* and *al-mu'minūn* in other passages such as Q. 2:285 and 10:99, according to Shaḥrūr, are meant to be more specific, namely those who believe in the prophecy of Muḥammad, or the followers of the Prophet Muḥammad.

Given Shaḥrūr's understanding of the concepts of *islām* and *īmān* it is clear that his reading of the Qur'an affirms the importance of religious pluralism, supporting the idea that followers of different religions may live together and support each other for their human well-being. I certainly concur with Stefan Wild who considers Shaḥrūr as one of the interpreters who take the Qur'ān into consideration as a "legal work" (*Regelwerk*) that regulates the human life (*das menschliche Zusammenleben*).[69]

Concluding Remarks: Towards New Research

As this study has shown by its attention to two instances, Muḥammad Shaḥrūr uses the method of inner-Qur'ānic exegesis and the paradigmo-syntagmatical analysis. His theory and its application can be considered consistent throughout these examples. Nonetheless, this preliminary research needs further development both in extent and depth of critique. More extensive research might come to different conclusions. There are two additional reasons that suggest the need for further research. First, previous studies as cited in the introduction to this article do not provide any satisfying arguments against Shaḥrūr's ideas which might serve to highlight its distinctive attributes. The other reason is that many Islamicists, such as Wielandt and Boullata, still question the appropriateness of his hermeneutics. My personal discussion with these two scholars suggests that many people find his hermeneutics defective as an all-encompassing approach to the Qur'ān; Shaḥrūr lacks the historical and philological knowledge requisite for true Qur'ānic exegesis; and his desire for modernization makes him impose ideas and patterns on Qur'ān exegesis that are not necessarily justified by close textual analysis.

NOTES

1. A previous version of this essay entitled "Muḥammad Shaḥūr's Inner-Qur'ānic Exegetical Method and its Application in Interpreting the Qur'ān" was presented at the First World Conference for Middle Eastern Studies held on September 8–13, 2002 at the University of Mainz, Germany.

2. Amīn al-Khūlī, *Manāhij tajdīd fi'l-naḥw wa'l-balāgha wa'l-tafsīr* (Cairo 1961), 302.

3. Issa J. Boullata, "Introduction," in *Literary Structures of Religious Meaning in the Qur'ān,* ed. Issa J. Boullata (Richmond: Curzon, 2000), xi.

4. He was born in 1938. After Shaḥrūr finished his study in high school in Damascus at the age of 19, he left for Moscow to study engineering. In 1964 he went back to Syria, and departed in 1968 to Dublin to take a Master's program and a doctoral degree in the field of soil mechanics and foundation engineering. From 1977 on, he gave lectures at the University of Damascus. He is now retired. His books are *al-Kitāb wa'l-Qur'ān* (1990), *Dirāsa Islāmiyya muᶜāṣira fī'l-dawla wa'l-mujtamaᶜ* (1994), *al-Islām wa'l-īmān* (1996), *Mashrūᶜ mīthāq al-ᶜamal al-Islāmī* (1999), and *Naḥw uṣūl jadīda li'l-fiqh al-Islāmī* (2000). He has also written several articles published in magazines and journals including "The Divine Text and Pluralism in Muslim Societies," *Muslim Politics Report* 14 (August, 1997): 3–9, "Islam and the 1995 Beijing World Conference on Women," *Kuwaiti Newspaper*, reprinted in *Liberal Islam*, ed. Charles Kuzman (New York: Oxford University Press, 1998). In addition, he presented his ideas about the Qur'ān in relation to politics, human rights, and pluralism at several international conferences, for example at the MESA conference in Chicago in 1998.

5. See several of his findings in my review on his book *al-Kitāb wa'l-Qur'ān, al-Jāmiᶜah: Journal of Islamic Studies* 62 (1998): 193–6.

6. In Syria 13,000 exemplars were sold, in Egypt 3,000, and in Saudi Arabia 10,000. See Dale F. Eickelman, "Islamic Liberalism Strikes Back," *MESA Bulletin* 27, 2 (December 1993): 163.

7. Peter Clark, "The Shaḥrūr Phenomenon: a Liberal Islamic Voice from Syria," *Islam and Christian-Muslim Relations* 7 (1996): 337.

8. Eickelman, "Islamic Liberalism," 163.

9. Ibid, 163.

10. Rotraud Wielandt, "Wurzeln der Schwierigkeit innerislamischen Gesprächs über neue hermeneutische Zugänge zum Korantext," in *The Qur'an as Text*, ed. Stefan Wild (Leiden: E. J. Brill, 1996), 287. In this article, Wielandt discusses the many difficulties that Abū Zayd faced in Egypt when he introduced new hermeneutics to be applied to the Qur'ān.

11. Clark, "The Shaḥrūr Phenomenon," 341.

12. Eickelman, "Islamic Liberalism," 163.

13. See Wael B. Hallaq, *A History of Islamic Legal Theories* (Cambridge: Cambridge University Press, 1997), 245–54; and my review of *al-Kitāb wa'l-Qur'ān* in *al-Jāmiᶜah: Journal of Islamic* Studies, 193.

14. See Dale F. Eickelman, "Inside the Islamic Reformation," *Wilson Quarterly* 22, 1 (1998): 80–9.

15. M. Arkoun, "Contemporary Critical Practices and the Qur'ān," in *Encyclopedia of the Qur'ān*, ed. J. D. McAuliffe (Leiden: Brill, 2001), I, 428.

16. Previous studies on Muhammad Shaḥrūr's hermeneutical findings include Salīm al-Jābī, *Mujarrad tanjīm* (Damascus 1991, 1992, 1993) in which he rigorously criticizes Shaḥrūr's interpretative views; Muḥāmī Ṭāhir al-Shawwāf, *Tahāfut al-qirā'a al-muᶜāsira* (Beirut 1993) in which he shows the similarity of Shaḥrūr's views to Marxist ones and criticizes him on the basis of Islamic traditionalism; Jawwād ᶜAwāna, *al-Qur'ān wa awhām al-qirā'a al-muᶜāṣira* (Amman 1994) in which he tries to show the Marxist influence on his thoughts; ᶜĀdil al-Tall, *al-Nazᶜa al-mādiyya fī'l-ᶜālam al-Islāmī* (n.p. 1995) in which he compares the hermeneutics of Shaḥrūr to that of Muḥammad Iqbāl and Jawdat Saᶜīd, and tries to prove the influence of the materialistic method on their ideas; Jamāl al-Bannā, *Munṭaliqāt wa mafāhīm* (Cairo 1995) in which, on the one hand, he praises Shaḥrūr's innovative thoughts and, on the other hand, he criticizes his application of the philological method; Abū Zayd, *al-Naṣṣ al-sulṭa al-ḥaqīqa* (Cairo 1995) in which he considers Shaḥrūr's hermeneutics as *al-tafsīr al-talwīnī* ("ideologically colored interpretation"); Felix Körner, Muḥammad Šaḥrūrs Koranhermeneutik in *al-Kitāb wa l-Qur'ān*, MA Thesis, Otto-Friedrich University of Bamberg 2000, which is devoted to the analysis and criticism of Shaḥrūr's method of Qur'ān exegesis; Roxanne D. Marcotte, "Šaḥrūr, the Status of Women, and Polygamy in Islam," *Oriente Moderno* 20 (2000): 313–28, in which she analyzes Shaḥrūr's interpretive methods and his feminist ideas; Andreas Christmann, "'The Form is Permanent but the Content Moves': the Qur'ānic Text and its Interpretation(s) in Mohammad Shahrour's al-Kitāb wa'l-Qur'ān," *Die Welt des Islam* 43 (2003): 143–72, in which he explores Shaḥrūr's theories on the Qur'ān and its revelation. All these studies were done in response to Shaḥrūr's hermeneutical findings and his method that are found in his first book *al-Kitāb wa'l-Qur'ān*.

17. For the complete discussion, see Naṣr Ḥāmid Abū Zayd, *Mafhūm al-naṣṣ. Dirāsa fī ᶜulūm al-Qur'ān* (Beirut 1994), 42–52.

18. See Stefan Wild, *Mensch, Prophet und Gott im Koran. Muslimische Exegeten des 20. Jahrhunderts und das Menschenbild der Moderne* (Münster: Rhema Verlag, 2001), 35.

19. For more information, see Rotraud Wielandt, *Offenbarung und Geschichte im Denken Moderner Muslime* (Wiesbaden: Franz Steiner, 1971), 156–60.

20. For more information on the study of Shaḥrūr's theory of Qur'ānic revelation, see Christmann, "'The Form is Permanent but the Content Moves'," 143–72.

21. Shaḥrūr, *Naḥw uṣūl jadīda*, 125.

22. Ibid., 125.

23. Qur'ān scholars other than Shaḥrūr divide the Qur'ānic verses into two types: (1) *al-muḥkamāt* (the "clear" verses), and (2) *al-mutashābihāt* (the "unclear" verses). Nonetheless, their definitions of the two terms are varied. For more information, see for example, Jane Dammen McAuliffe, "Qur'anic Hermeneutics: The Views of al-Ṭabarī and Ibn Kathīr," in *Approaches to the History of the Interpretation of the Qur'an*, ed. Andrew Rippin (Oxford: Oxford University Press, 1988), 46–62; idem, "Text and Textuality: Q. 3:7 as a Point of Intersection," in *Literary Structures*, ed. Boullata, 56–76; L. Kinberg, "*Muḥkamāt* and *Mutashābihāt* (Koran 3/7): Implication of Koranic Pair of Terms in Medieval Exegesis," *Arabica* 37 (1988): 43–72; and my article, "*Muḥkam* and *Mutashābih:* an Analytical Study of al-Ṭabarī's and al-Zamakhsharī's Interpretations of Q. 3:7," *Journal of Qur'anic Studies* 1,1 (1999): 63–79.

24. For the detailed explanation, see Shaḥrūr, *al-Kitāb wa'l-Qur'ān: qirā'a muᶜāṣira* (Damascus 1990), 51–61.

25. Ibid., 157–66.

26. Ibid., 37.

27. Ibid., 21.

28. See ibid., 445–51. See also Hallaq, *History,* 245–54.

29. Shaḥrūr, *al-Kitāb wa'l-Qur'ān,* 104–5.

30. Ibid., 155–7.

31. Ibid., 74–81.

32. Ibid., 37.

33. Ibid., 103–4.

34. Ibid., 97.

35. Ibid., 113–22.

36. Ibid., 44; Eickelman, "Islamic Liberalism", 166.

37. Joel Weinsheimer, "Hermeneutics," in *Contemporary Literary Theory*, ed. G. Douglas Atkins and Laura Morrow (Amherst: University of Massachusetts Press, 1989), 124. See also Anthony C. Thiselton, *New Horizons in Hermeneutics* (Grand Rapids: Zondervan, 1992), 279–282.

38. ^{c}A@'isha ^{c}Abd al-Raḥmān Bint al-Shāṭi', *al-Tafsīr al-bayānī li'l-Qur'ān* (Cairo 1990), I, 17, and my book, *An Examination of Bint al-Shāṭi''s Method of Interpreting the Qur'ān* (Yogyakarta 1999), 45.

39. Michael Fishbane, *Biblical Interpretation in Ancient Israel* (Oxford: Oxford University Press, 1985); see also Thiselton, *New Horizons in Hermeneutics*, 39–40.

40. Shaḥrūr, *al-Kitāb wa'l-Qur'ān,* 197.

41. For some examples of their applications, see my book *An Examination,* 41–2.

42. Ibid., 41–4.

43. Shaḥrūr, *al-Kitāb wa'l-Qur'ān,* 197.

44. Grant R. Osborne, *The Hermeneutical Spiral,* 84–7.

45. Shaḥrūr, *al-Kitāb wa'l-Qur'ān,* 196.

46. Osborne, *The Hermeneutical Spiral,* 86.

47. Ibid., 90.

48. ^{c}A@dil al-Tall, *al-Naz^{c}a al-mādiyya fī'l-^{c}ālam al-Islāmī,* 354–60.

49. Shaḥrūr, *Naḥw uṣūl jadīda,* 189.

50. Ibid., 178.

51. Shaḥrūr, *Dirāsa Islāmiyya mu^{c}āṣira fī'l-dawla wa'l-mujtama^{c}* (Damascus 1994), 27.

52. Moises Silva, *Biblical Words and Their Meaning: An Introduction to Lexical Semantics* (Grand Rapids: Zondervan, 1983), 103.

53. Shaḥrūr, *al-Kitāb wa'l-Qur'ān,* 123.

54. Ibid., 125.

55. Shaḥrūr, *Mashrū^{c} mīthāq al-^{c}amal al-Islāmī* (Damascus 1999), 9.

56. Shaḥrūr, *al-Kitāb wa'l-Qur'ān,* 123.

57. Ibid., 123–4.

58. Ibid., 124–9.

59. Ibid., 128.

60. Ibid., 122–8.

61. Shaḥrūr, *al-Islām wa'l-īmān: Manẓūmat al-qiyam* (Damascus 1996), 31.

62. Ibid., 33.

63. Ibid., 37–8.

64. Ibid., 33–4.

65. Ibid., 39.

66. Ibid., 39–40.

67. Ibid., 41.

68. Ibid., 52.

69. Stefan Wild, *Mensch, Prophet und Gott im Koran,* 44–5.

Chapter 13

The Qur'ān in India I: Iqbāl and Gandhi on the Qur'ān

Sheila McDonough

In their formative years, Muḥammad Iqbāl (1877–1938), and Mohandas Karamchand Gandhi (1873–1947) were both exposed to, and affected by, the newly emerging academic discipline of the comparative history of religion. Each had received his secondary education in institutions shaped by the curriculum common to the British schools in India. Iqbāl was educated in the Presbyterian Mission school in Sialkot, and Gandhi in the Alfred High school in Rajkot.[1] In these schools, each learned something of the history of the world as a whole, and of his own culture as part of the wider context. Yet each also developed in his teens a critical perspective towards imperialism, and an incipient passion to find inspirational sources of resistance to British domination from within his own culture.

This essay will pose the question of how Iqbāl and Gandhi perceived the essential significance of the Qur'ān, and how did each of them fit his particular interpretation of the Muslim scripture into his developing structure of religious thought? As contemporaries in late nineteenth century India, they matured in the context of a British empire that seemed to young Indians was set to control the subcontinent for centuries. Nevertheless, each of these men felt unrest from his early years. Each of them was seeking some directive purpose that could help transform the future. Each thought that the key lay with religion.

Iqbāl's Beginnings

Most biographers of Iqbāl agree that Mawlawī Mīr Ḥasan, the teacher of Persian and Arabic in Iqbāl's secondary school, did much to convey to his young Muslim students the impulses to self assertion and change of the Muslim activist reformers, Sayyid Aḥmad Khān and Jamāl al-Dīn al-Afghānī. Mawlawī Mīr Ḥasan was one of a generation of Muslim scholars and teachers who tried to convey the revolutionary imperatives of these reformers to the younger generation of Muslims. The young Iqbāl seems to have been galvanized by this teacher to feel that his generation must take matters into their own hands. This Muslim teacher also transmitted to his students great love for, and comprehension of, the complex symbolism of Persian and Urdu poetry. In addition, Iqbāl's father, a Ṣūfī, taught his son to read the Qur'ān daily, and to try to experience the impact of the Qur'ān as the first Muslims had experienced it.[2]

Iqbāl himself began writing poetry in his teens. One of his early poems, *Himālah,* was published in 1900 when the young poet was 24. The poem tells us that the poet, who grew up in Sialkot in the foothills of the Himalayas, had turned to the mountains, looking for sources of inspiration. Even in his teens, Iqbāl wanted to overthrow the British domination of India; he hoped to find direction for that quest in his own cultural heritage. The mountains gave him a sense of vastness in time and space, and a feeling that that the oppressive power structures of the present could be transcended. He went to the mountains looking for *Sinai,* an experience of transforming power and directive purpose. He addressed the mountains as follows:

> The Kalīm of Ṭūr Sinai witnessed but one Effulgence
> For the discerning eye you are an embodiment of
> Effulgence....
> You are the *dīwān* whose opening verse is the sky
> You lead Man to the solitudes of his heart's retreat.[3]

Moses, the Kalīm of Ṭūr Sinai, the prophet whom God had addressed directly on Mount Sinai, had responded with effective action to his experience of a manifestation of divine power. The young Iqbāl speaks of looking again to the mountains for similar world-transforming insight and direction. Thus, the Qur'ānic image of Moses, as one who leads his people out of an enslaved condition, spoke directly to the Indian Muslim. The young poet combined this image of a liberating prophet with the mystery of the mountains. Apparently, Iqbāl experienced some form of overwhelming religious awareness in his early response to the mountains. All the main elements of the structure of his later religious thought are present in this early poem. He found guidance in contemplating the immensity of the created universe, and he also became aware of untapped reservoirs of creativeness within the depths of his own soul.

The symbols used in this poem continue to recur in Iqbāl's poetry throughout the rest of his life. *Sinai* is often used in later poems to indicate the possibility of an experience that could uplift and transform. The title of his first major collection of Urdu poems, *Bāng-i Darā* ["The Call of the Bell"], uses the caravan bell to symbolize the need for new vision to move the Muslim community forward in positive directions. Another collection is entitled *Ẓarb-i Kalīm* ["The Rod of Moses"].[4] The rod is symbolic of the capacity to overthrow the domination of the apparently powerful. According to the Qur'ān, Moses transformed a rod into a snake, and thus confounded the magicians of the Pharaoh. In the poetry, Pharaoh represents the might of the British Empire, as Iqbāl knew that power at end of the nineteenth century. Pharaoh was still immensely powerful when Iqbāl was young. Nevertheless, the young poet felt that the rod of transformative energy and vision was within reach.

In a speech to his community towards the end of his life, when the problems of conflict between the Muslim League and the Congress Party were severe, Iqbāl warned his people—"where there is no vision, the people perish."[5] This Biblical quotation, from Proverbs 29:18, was used by Iqbāl to warn the Indian Muslims to keep themselves rooted in the vision, conveyed by the Qur'ān, of the enduring source of guidance and hope latent in Prophetic experience.

Gandhi's Formative Years

When the young Hindu Gandhi had been in secondary school, he had been given the choice of studying Sanskrit or Persian. He tells us that he was briefly tempted to opt for Persian since it would be easier. He overcame this temptation and took Sanskrit. He did not have one particular mentor comparable to Mawlawī Mīr Ḥasan. However, he early developed antagonism to British rule, and to Christian missionaries. He tells us he was very angry when he learned that his father would have to wear English boots to attend a durbar for the British rulers. He was also offended by a Christian missionary whom he heard preaching on a street corner, and disparaging Hinduism as a crude religion. He was moved by a play in which he saw enacted the Hindu story of a hero supporting his aged parents. He also encountered, in the *Ramayana,* a dramatic presentation of the triumph of the persevering hero against evil powers. These traditional Hindu dramas gave him a sense of the ideals of filial devotion, the sanctity of vows, and the performance of duty in the face of antagonism from the world.[6] Later, he commented that, although he knew the heroes of the stories were mythological, and not historical, nevertheless he still found them inspirational. "These heros," he wrote, "are living realities for me, and I am sure I should be moved as before if I were to read those plays again today."[7]

Iqbāl and Gandhi had both grown up as Indians trained by the British educational system, and aware of the domination of the British over India. The British had developed this system of education as a means for educating Indians who would be able to work for the purposes of the British Empire within India. The Indian students in the British schools had been allowed some training in their own cultural traditions as a means of helping them develop a sense of their own background in the context of their service of the English system. These two Indians both went on to study law in London, the normal mode of education for Indians seeking to work for the British administration. Apparently, those who designed this educational system had not thought that knowledge of the indigenous cultural traditions might lead to revolutionary thinking. Each of these two future religious reformers developed within himself, as he matured, affirmations as to the liberating potential of his own tradition to help him transcend British dominance.

In Iqbāl's case, the Qur'ānic image of Moses as a bringer of liberating values served to inspire the young Muslim poet to hope to stimulate his people into moving out of their depressed colonial condition. In Gandhi's case, the drama of the *Ramayana* led him to think about the challenges of life in terms of a suffering hero struggling mightily against demonic forces. The young Hindu internalized the message that the ascetic courage of the hero could empower him against all the evil powers that were oppressing him. Gandhi's family came from the *Vaishnava* tradition of Hinduism. His mother's family was associated with the *Pranami* sect of the *Vaishnava* tradition. That tradition valued the poetry of Kabīr, and other medieval poets with links to Ṣūfism, as well as devotional Vaishnava poetry. This background shaped Gandhi's devotional life. He used the hymns and poems of medieval mystics like Kabīr often in the religious services [8] he conducted in his later life.

Gandhi and the Vegetarians

Gandhi did not go to university in India, as Iqbāl did, but rather opted to go directly to England to study law. Gandhi went to England in 1888, seventeen years before Iqbāl was to do so. As readers of Gandhi's famous *Autobiography* know well, the young Hindu was intimidated by his first experiences of British life, and briefly tempted to try to become as English as he could.[9] Perhaps Gandhi's early experiences of Hindu drama had encouraged him to think about life in terms of dramatic confrontations. He tells his own history as a dramatic story of struggle against the temptation to betray his roots. This danger was overcome by the power of his faithfulness to the vows, given to his mother, that he would not eat meat, nor indulgence in immoral practices. These vows led him, on the brink of great hunger, to discover London's vegetarian restaurants.

Here he encountered English vegetarians, many of whom were explicitly opposed to British imperialism, and to the aggressive claims of some Christians to be the heirs of the world's only civilized religious tradition. Many of Gandhi's new friends were socialists; they opposed British expansionist policies. Many also rejected Christian religious exclusivism, the notion that white English Christians were destined to world domination. These 19th century radicals were ready to move beyond the bounds of traditional Christian thinking, and to seek new insights from other world religions. The vegetarianism was sometimes symbolic of these radicals' urge to move beyond the arrogant blinkers of traditional European culture.

In chapter eleven of his detailed study of the Mahatma's early years, Gandhi's former secretary, Pyarelal, discusses at length the ideas and practices of the persons who made up the English Vegetarian Movement. In his words:

> It was a fascinating era, tense with new ideas and anticipation of fresh possibilities—the period of the Feminist and Suffragist upheaval, the Theosophist movement, Socialist and Anarchist propaganda, and of new currents in the Theatrical, Musical and Artistic worlds. The citadel of orthodox Christianity was crumbling under the assault of rationalist criticism; anthropology was shaking the structure of morality, science was undermining the bases of faith; and the onset of fresh discoveries was bringing about a dissolution of a number of hitherto regarded as "immutable laws" of nature.... It was in this world of widening horizons that Mohan [Gandhi] found himself during the formative period of his life.... The English Vegetarian Movement with which Mohan came in context in the eighteen eighties was part of a bigger movement of renaissance and idealism—the same that found expression in America in the Transcendentalism of Emerson, Thoreau and Walt Whitman.... In England, it was the economic and social conditions that were at sixes and sevens. The search for a new way of life here took the form of Nature and Humanitarian and Socialist movements."[10]

The young Gandhi met in the Vegetarian Movement many of the creative people who were active in the Fabian society, and in the other humanitarian organizations. He attended the funeral of the activist atheist Bradlaugh. He did not have direct contact with the academic study of comparative religion since he was not involved with any disciplined mode of study apart from his training in law at the Inns of Court in London. Gandhi's contact with the comparative study of religion was thus indirect. He came to know personally many English people who were trying to put new ideas about religion and society into practice. He developed enduring friendships with several of these vegetarians. Some of these English people later supported his work in South Africa, and welcomed him when he returned to London in 1931.

The leading academic scholar of world religions in the late nineteenth century, Max Mueller, had initiated the publication of the *Sacred Books of the East*. These translations played a significant role in familiarizing many English seekers with Eastern religious life and thought. Thomas Carlyle, in his renowned essay on the Prophet Muḥammad in *Heros and Hero Worship,* also brought the life of the Muslim prophet into the orbit of knowledge of the well educated English reformers. Gandhi tells us that reading Carlyle's essay in these early years in London made a significant impression on him. Gandhi also read Edward Arnold's translation of the Bhagavad Gita, an experience that seems to have crystallized in his mind confidence in the wisdom of that Hindu scripture. The fact that his English friends were exhibiting interest in these translations strengthened Gandhi's convictions about the value of the Hindu scriptures, and about the exemplary model of the Prophet Muḥammad.

There were a number of different perspectives present among the English vegetarians at this time, and two distinct currents of thought were becoming increasingly clear. One was the emphasis on healing the ills of the modern world by a return to nature, conceived as simple life, living by the fruits of one's own labor. Thoreau was one exponent of such a perspective, but it was developed in England particularly by Edward Carpenter and Henry Salt. The other current was that of the Fabians, Bernard Shaw, the Webbs and others, who were committed to working towards the development of an industrialized society to be organized in terms of social justice. These latter activists had little interest in returning to nature.

Later, in South Africa, Gandhi acknowledged that it was the perspective of Edward Carpenter, the return to nature, that was particularly attractive to him. Carpenter had said that a man is rich in proportion to the number of things he can do without. A number of land-based communities were formed to try to implement his ideas.[11] Gandhi's efforts to build such communities in South Africa, and later in India, were partly a result of the influence of Carpenter's ideas on the Hindu reformer. In sum, Gandhi encountered a creative ferment of ideas among the vegetarians he knew in England around 1889, and 1890, and he participated actively in the Vegetarian Movement there. He wrote a series of 10 articles for the Vegetarian journal, and attended a World Vegetarian conference. These experiences led him to feel that sympathetic persons who shared ideals, such as vegetarianism and a return to nature, might come from many different backgrounds.

The young Hindu understood that many of these English reformers were protesting the narrow exclusivism of the established beliefs and practices of their own societies. They were seeking to discover means of developing mutual respect and appreciation among adherents of different religious traditions. Such respect needed to have a theoretical framework that would somehow provide a basis for thinking about similarities in all traditions. Thus, although Gandhi was not involved in an academic study of the comparative history of religion, he did meet many of the English people who were trying to express some universal values in their lives. Many of them were trying to move away from the emphasis on one culture as the bearer of all truth, and towards a sense of religious life as a universal phenomenon. Many of these radical and reformist English thinkers also believed that a more universal sense of religious values could serve as a basis for the reformation of society.

Iqbāl and Arnold

Iqbāl was still a university student in Lahore while Gandhi was having his adventurous encounters with vegetarians in London. After completion of his studies in Sialkot, Iqbāl went on to study for BA and MA degrees at Government College, Lahore. His studies included English literature, philosophy and history. Next door to Government College was the Islāmiyya College, an institution for the study of classical Arabic and Persian thought. Iqbāl took courses there, too. Thus, his educational development continued the pattern of his secondary studies, namely, a thorough grounding in the western academic curriculum in the Humanities, as well as increasing familiarity with Persian and Arabic primary sources.

The English philosopher and historian, Thomas Arnold, moved to Lahore after the death of Sayyid Aḥmad Khān in 1898, and began work at both Government College and Islāmiyya College. Arnold had originally been recruited to teach at Aligarh. While working at that institution, he had become sympathetic to Sayyid Aḥmad Khān's efforts to refute the negative portrayal of Islamic history that was presented in the books of many western scholars. Sayyid Aḥmad Khān understood that Muslims needed western education in order to learn how to survive in the modern world, but he also knew that they would be threatened by reading western books that disparaged Islam as a crude and outdated religion. The Muslim philosopher, Shiblī Nuᶜmānī, also teaching at Aligarh, worked closely with Arnold. Shiblī and Arnold were young men in their twenties; each was stimulated by the encounter with the scholarship, and creative imagination of the other.

Arnold learned much about Islamic history and philosophy from Sayyid Aḥmad Khān and Shiblī. In his seminal book, *The Preaching of Islam,* first published in 1896, Arnold tried to refute the centuries old western theory that Islam had been propagated primarily by violence. The common project of Sayyid Aḥmad Khān, Shiblī, and Thomas Arnold was to produce writings, and educational curriculum for the young Muslims who were beginning to enter into the western university tradition. These Aligarh scholars wanted to help such students make the leap into modern modes of thinking without being threatened by the prevalent negative stereotyping of their religion and their values. When Arnold went on to Lahore, where he taught the young Iqbāl, he was following the approach that he had learned at Aligarh.

Arnold was also a product of the 19th century intellectual renaissance in Britain that was leading many people out of the narrowness of western focus on one cultural tradition only. Arnold had studied with Robertson Smith, a scholar whose seminal book, *The Religion of the Semites,* had been influential in bringing about a new awareness of the social context of ancient Semitic life. Arnold begins his own book, *The Preaching of Islam,* with a quotation from Max Mueller about the nature of prophetic experience, an experience that was now understood to go beyond the Biblical record.[12] Thus, Arnold knew and understood what Mueller was attempting to do by introducing the comparative study of religious life and thought into the western academic world. To speak of prophetic experience as a general category in the history of religion makes it more possible to acknowledge authenticity and sincerity in the religious experience of the prophet Muḥammad. Arnold was apparently ready to take this approach in teaching his Indian Muslim students.

When Iqbāl came under the influence of Arnold as a teacher, he was thus directly exposed to the early academic perspective of Max Mueller, and the other main founders of the academic study of the comparative history of religion. The young Muslim was learning to think about religious life in the context of the history of the world as a whole. Iqbāl's own later academic writings, his doctoral thesis, and his major work, *The Reconstruction of Religious Thought in Islam,* all assume this background of the history of the world's religions as the context for his own understanding of the origins and development of Muslim religious thought.

This angle was implicit in Iqbāl's intellectual development from his high school days; he seems always to have been concerned to articulate a Muslim perspective in the context of the wider human experience. Arnold's influence, and the transmitting of the perspectives of Sayyid Aḥmad Khān and Shiblī, through their own writings, through personal encounter, and also through Arnold's teaching, confirmed and strengthened in Iqbāl's mind the direction of his future interests. After completing his BA and MA degrees in Lahore, Iqbāl became a university teacher; he taught philosophy, English literature, and economics at Government College for 3 years. He continued also to study and teach at the Islāmiyya College.

Iqbāl had had a Hindu friend, Swami Ram Tirath, a mathematician and philosopher, whom he had known in Sialkot, and later in Lahore. The Muslim poet had been studying Sanskrit, and discussing Hindu philosophy, with this friend. Although this friend died in 1906, Iqbāl's interest in Hindu and Buddhist philosophy continued.[13] He wrote a poem when his friend died, saying that he had received much insight from their discussions.[14] His personal library contained books by Radhakrishnan and Tagore.[15] Later, in his doctoral thesis, Iqbāl discusses Hindu, Buddhist, Christian and Muslim philosophies of religion in the context of the history of human religious thought.

In sum, Iqbāl had achieved considerable intellectual maturity as a researcher and university lecturer before he left India. Under

Arnold's guidance, he had achieved a sophisticated grasp of the philosophical issues considered significant in the late nineteenth century. When he did go to England, in 1905, he went directly to Cambridge where he was enrolled as a research scholar. This had been arranged through Thomas Arnold, who had earlier returned to England himself. The young Muslim met philosophers from other traditions as peers with whom he could easily discuss the issues of the time. Iqbāl's encounter with English life and thought was thus different in many respects from that of Gandhi.

Gandhi in South Africa

While he was working as a lawyer in South Africa from 1890 to 1914, Gandhi's personal crisis crystallized. The political, social and economic domination by white racists in that country forced him to recognize that he would either have to accept the position of Indians as second class citizens, discriminated against by the law and the state, or resist. His earlier experiences in London with the vegetarian reformers, friends who had viewed him as an equal in their efforts to work for a better society, contrasted in his consciousness with the harsh refusal of the South African white society to respect his people and his culture. His decision to resist was joined in his mind with his conviction that good people from all religious traditions, Hindus, Parsis, Jews, Christians and Muslims would join him in the struggle. Gandhi was certain, because of his London experiences, that there were people in all traditions who were committed to equality and justice. He believed that many would join him in actively combating injustice.

Pyarelal devotes seventy-five pages of his analysis of Gandhi's developing beliefs and practices to the life and thought of the Russian religious radical, Leo Tolstoy. Tolstoy had been excommunicated by the Russian Orthodox Church, and had abandoned his privileged life as an aristocratic military man. While serving as Gandhi's secretary, Pyarelal had many opportunities to come to know well the workings of Gandhi's mind: he was convinced that the encounter with Tolstoy's thought in South Africa had helped focus the Hindu reformer's convictions. Pyarelal summarises Tolstoy's ideas as follows:

> Religion is a belief in certain supernatural occurrences, not in the necessity for certain prayers and ceremonies.... The essence of religion lies in the power inherent in man "to foreknow and to point out the way in which mankind must walk.... Still from time to time a man appears in whom the faculty has reached a higher development." Such were the Prophets or founders of the principal religions of the world.... If the transformation took place within the soul, the transformation in the world would follow."[16]

Gandhi was convinced that a transformation of this kind had occurred in the case of the Prophet Muḥammad, as in the instances of all the major founders, poets and exemplars of the various world religions.

In his years in South Africa, Gandhi was continuously in the company of Muslims who were ready to help him combat institutionalised racism. Many of these Muslims came from Gandhi's own Indian province of Gujarat, and shared a similar cultural background with him. Gandhi's father, grandfather, and other male ancestors, most of whom had been administrators in the service of local rulers, had centuries of experience in working with Muslims behind them. The coast where Gandhi was born had been visited for generations by Muslim ships and traders cruising between Africa and India.

A Muslim firm had employed him during his first trip to Africa. He spent twenty years there living with, and working with the Muslims who shared his hopes and concerns. The Hindu lawyer read the same books about the challenges of modern Muslim thought, especially the works of Amīr ᶜAlī and Shiblī, that his Muslim friends were reading. Gandhi seems to have blended this reforming view of the "spirit of Islam", with his own emerging perspective. This perspective was based on Tolstoy, the young Hindu's experiences in England, and his own researches, under the guidance of his Jain mentor, into the significance of the Hindu scriptures. He wrote to this mentor, Shrimad Rajchandra, for help in thinking about the variety of religions in the world; he received a reply in 1894 that seems to have settled the question for him. The answer was, "*Moksha* [release from ignorance] can be attained only by complete deliverance from the passions of hatred and attachment and the resulting ignorance."[17] This perspective shaped Gandhi's new modes of religious practice.

Gandhi returned to India in 1896, to raise money for the cause of fighting for justice in South Africa. He brought with him a "Green Paper" that described the oppressive laws in that African country, and complained against the discrimination against Indian Immigrants. Half the signatures to that document of protest were Muslims.[18] This indicates the widespread support and sense of common purpose that Gandhi enjoyed among his Muslim friends in South Africa. When he returned to Africa, he made many speeches to crowds of Indians. He increasingly quoted the Qur'ān and the *Ramayana* interchangeably. He claimed that honest response to the God of the Qur'ān, and to Rama, demanded that the oppressed Indians, whether Muslim or Hindu, rise to the challenge of combating the evils opposing them.

The Baptist Minister, Joseph Doke, who published his impressions of his personal encounters with Gandhi in 1909, said that Gandhi had explained to him that he did not like the term "passive resistance." He preferred to stress that doing good should mean an active response to evil.[19] The Muslim scholar, S. Abid Husain, has pointed out that many of the supporters of Gandhi's protest movement were Muslim traders. The Government of South Africa brought Indians into their country as indentured workers who were supposed to work on the farms for a period of years, and then return to India. This government was determined to prevent Indians staying in South Africa. They did not want Indian traders to develop an economic power base in the nation, because they would then threaten the prosperity of the white traders.

Gandhi understood the economic basis of this racist policy. Nevertheless, he was determined to fight against it. He was convinced that many of his Muslim friends would join him in his protest movement. In his own later history of his movement, *Satyagraha in South Africa,* Gandhi devoted a whole chapter to the efforts of one of the Muslim non-violent protesters, Ahmad Mohammed Kachhalia.[20] In the speech that had inaugurated the Satyagraha [non-violent resistance campaign], Gandhi said, "We all believe in one and the same God, the difference of nomenclature in Hinduism and Islam notwithstanding. To pledge ourselves with Him as witness is not something to be trifled with."[21]

Once his reform movement was underway, Gandhi took as self-evident that he and his Muslim friends believed in the same God. The notion of "pledge" was very important to him. As indicated in the above comment, he assumed that moral courage came from commitment to serve the good, and that this was done with God as witness. This language made sense to the Muslims who agreed to join him in protest against repressive government policies. The protesters had some degree of success, although they did not overthrow South African racism completely.

In 1909, returning on a ship from a trip to England, where he had failed to get the British government to agree to help his people resist oppression in South Africa, Gandhi wrote *Hind Swaraj,* an impassioned protest against the evils of western civilization, and an appeal to Indians to reject everything about that demonic system. He called his followers to return to nature, back to the ideals of ancient India.[22] Edward Carpenter is mentioned in this essay as exemplar of the ideal of returning to the natural way of life. In this manifesto, Gandhi has combined his personal concept of the ideal ancient Indian society of the Vedas with the ideals of the western protesters against the evils of the industrial age. *Swaraj* means self-government. Gandhi's manifesto was a challenge to young Indians to throw out imperialist domination, to revive the ancient Vedic ideals of a good society, and to bring peace and harmony to India.

Along with this affirmation, however, Gandhi continued to say that the Qur'ān was teaching him the necessity of working for the helpless. He wrote:

> God helps the helpless, not those who believe they can do something. Every page of the Qur'ān teaches me, a non-Muslim, this supreme lesson. Every *surut* of the Qur'ān begins "In the name of God the Compassionate and the Merciful." Let us, therefore, be strong in soul though weak in body.[23]

The Qur'ānic emphasis on compassion seems to have blended in Gandhi's mind with his vision of the ideal society of ancient India, the return to natural ways of life that would bring about a more sane human society. In 1909, Gandhi perceived the world as caught in a very tense situation in which the white racist society was determined to dominate all other peoples. In this context, Gandhi's manifesto, *Hind Swaraj,* conveys an imperative to cast all one's energy into the battle to resist racist oppression, and to create a new society based on harmony with nature. The tone of this manifesto is very intense; it is an impassioned call for a struggle to transform the world. The struggle is perceived as a conflict against an extremely strong dominating power.

Iqbāl's Manifesto

We observed that Gandhi's *Hind Swaraj* can be read as a vehement manifesto of opposition to what the Hindu reformer perceived as a corrupt and decadent social order, western racist and imperialist society. It was a call to Indians to embrace a total and non-violent rejection of that evil society. The call was to build a better world, a good social order in which the revolutionaries would undertake to restore justice and peace to the earth. Gandhi's passion on this occasion was stirred up after the British government refused to help the Indians do anything about the evils of South Africa. The passion that informs the manifesto surely indicates some of the pent up anger that Gandhi felt about the British refusal to help his cause in South Africa.

The Muslim author and retired judge, Amīr ᶜAli, had accompanied Gandhi in London on the Hindu reformer's formal visit to the British Secretary of State for Colonial Affairs. The two asked for support for the South African protest movement. They were firmly rebuffed.[24] Amīr ᶜAlī seems to have shared Gandhi's indignation about the so-called "civilized" people who refused to help fight racism. Amīr ᶜAlī published an article in 1908 entitled "Anomalies of Civilisation."[25] This Muslim author's anger against those who think that "wearing trousers makes a civilised person" resembles the outrage of Gandhi. The Muslim author is sarcastic about the alleged "civilized" values of the racist English, and he gives a number of examples of corrupt practices of imperialist regimes.

However, the Muslim author does not demand a total rejection of industrialized society in terms of a "return to nature." He seems to have shared Gandhi's indignation, but not to have reached similar conclusions as to what to do next. During this time, Amīr ᶜAlī founded the London branch of the Muslim League. The young student, Iqbāl, served as a secretary for the group. It is thus very likely that Iqbāl knew about the bad experience that Gandhi and Amīr ᶜAlī had with the representative of British colonial policy. Iqbāl's interest in the Muslim League continued for the rest of his life.

Iqbāl also wrote what might be considered his manifesto on the ship on which he was returning to India in 1908. As they passed Sicily, Iqbāl reacted to the sight of a remnant of a former Muslim civilization. His emotional reaction crystallized his feeling that Muslim history held examples of better civilizations than that which was currently dominating Europe. He writes of the danger of an immoral world order rooted in greed and domination. This manifesto was similar to Gandhi's in that both were calling on young Indians to reject the evils of racism and imperialist greed, and to look to their own cultures for better guides to direct their efforts. Iqbāl addressed Sicily:

> Now weep blood, oh eyes, for the tomb of the arts of Arabia stands there in sight
>
> Where the men of the desert whose ships made a playground of ocean once rushed to the fight—
>
> They who brought into emperor's throne rooms the earthquake, and swords in which lightnings had nested:
>
> Their advent proclaimed a new world—till the old was devoured their keen blades never rested;
>
> At their thundered *Arise!* A dead earth sprang to life, and man burst from the chains of unreason:...
>
> Tell your grief then to me; who am grief; who am dust of that caravan whose magnet you were:
>
> Stir my voice—let the picture glow bright with fresh colour, the ancient days' record declare!
>
> I go with your gift to the Indies, and I who weep here will make others weep there.[26]

Iqbāl thus lamented the loss of the highly developed cultures of medieval Muslim Spain and Sicily, cultures where people from different religious backgrounds had lived in a context of tolerance and peace, and where scholarship and prosperity had flourished. The poem indicates that, when the Qur'ān first brought forth new religious affirmations, emperors collapsed, unreason was abolished, and "a dead earth sprang to life." Iqbāl's message to the Indian Muslims was thus—turn again to the Qur'ān. Find in the Qur'ān courage and purpose to oppose tyranny, to build new forms of good political, social and economic life, and to banish unreason.

Behind this manifesto lay the Muslim poet-philosopher's experiences in his years in Europe. He had received much intellectual stimulation in his studies in Cambridge, and in Heidelberg, but he continued to think that the model of past Muslim societies, such as Umayyad Spain, and Sicily, represented a better ideal than that of 19th and early 20th century Europe. He perceived European society as shaped by racism, and virulent nationalism. He was well aware of the European nations' competition to divide up the riches of the world amongst themselves. Although he had not personally suffered discrimination in his university life, he was aware of widespread western contempt for Muslims.

Iqbāl's Academic Work

Iqbāl had received his doctoral degree from Munich for his thesis entitled *The Development of Metaphysics in Persia: A Contribution to the History of Muslim Philosophy*. The volume was dedicated to his teacher, Thomas Arnold. Iqbāl sought to stimulate new scholarship about Islamic intellectual history. He found some manuscripts in European libraries that would help demonstrate the vitality and originality of past forms of Muslim religious thinking. In the thesis, Iqbāl undertook to analyze medieval Muslim theological and mystical thinking from the perspective of the comparative history of religion. He tried to demonstrate the influence of environmental and cultural factors on the shaping of mental attitudes. By taking this approach to the relationship of ideas to their contexts, Iqbāl was indicating that he had a sophisticated grasp of the processes by which ideas change and develop over time. He assumed, as did most of the other scholars of his generation, that one could distinguish between an explicitly Semitic form of religious awareness, focused on the will, and an explicitly Aryan one, focused on knowledge.

The subjects he discusses include the pre-Islamic philosophical background in Persia, the impact on Muslim thought of the neo-Platonic Aristotelians, Islamic rationalism, the Ashᶜarite-Muᶜtazilite controversy, Ṣūfism, and later Persian thought. He deals with all these subjects from the angle of seeing the developing of Islamic philosophical thinking as a dialectical process in which the establishment of certain abstract ideas stimulates contrary ideas. What remains constant is the ongoing Muslim devotion to the Qur'ān, which shapes the way in which Muslims in different ages react to various metaphysical systems of thought.

From this thesis, one can see that Iqbāl was knowledgeable about Buddhist metaphysics, the Hindu philosopher, Sankara, and medieval Christian thought, as well as with 19th century German Christian religious thinkers such as Schleiermacher. The Muslim poet-philosopher had an overview of human religious thought as a whole that was as advanced as that of anyone of his generation. Iqbāl's approach to issues in Islamic philosophy, theology, and jurisprudence followed many of the directions that had been indicated by Shiblī. Iqbāl looked at intellectual history as a process during which people sometimes opt for "other-worldly" attitudes, and sometimes for a "this-worldly" approach. He looked at Muslim religious thinking as a dialectical process in which one fixed metaphysical position tended to stimulate an opposite position.[27]

The Ashᶜarite position was "other-worldly" in that events in this world were not seen as significant. Iqbāl considered this as an anti-rational position that had developed in response to extreme rationalism. Iqbāl quotes Shiblī's *ᶜIlm al-Kalām* as his source for this description of the medieval quarrel between the Muᶜtazilites and the Ashᶜarites.[28] Iqbāl wanted the Muslims of the present and future to move beyond the extremes of excessive rationalism, and excessive rejection of rationalism. He thought that a better understanding of the Qur'ān should enable to Muslims to value the world as a place in which believers could take concrete actions, so that values of justice, peace, and goodness could be manifested. The view he advocated was to be "in the world, but not of the world", working within time to make manifest in political, social and economic structures, the transcendent values of justice, goodness and peace.

Like Shiblī, Iqbāl considered the eleventh century mystic, al-Ghazālī (d. 505/1111), one of the greatest personalities of Islam. He believed that al-Ghazālī had helped bring about reformed modes of religious education that had influenced many subsequent generations of devout and creative Muslims. His own hope for the coming generations was that they also might be able to develop new institutions of learning that would stimulate renewed Muslim life and energy. He quoted the well-known passage in which al-Ghazālī indicated his rejection of all forms of theological and philosophical authority. "From my childhood I was inclined to think out things for myself"[29] Iqbāl clearly wanted his generations of Muslims to be equally independent in their thinking about religious values.

Iqbāl refers in his thesis to the writings of both Sayyid Aḥmad Khān and Shiblī in his discussion of these issues. He was aware of carrying on the thinking of his mentors with respect to comprehension of the Muslim past, and directions for the future. He summed up as follows his picture of the issues in the Muslim theology of the past.

> It is, therefore, clear that while the dialectic of Rationalism destroyed the personality of God, and reduced divinity to a bare indefinable universality, the anti-rationalist movement, though it preserved the dogma of personality, destroyed the external reality of nature.... The one saves nature, and tends to do away with the God of Theology; the other sacrifices nature to save God as conceived by the orthodox. The God-intoxicated Sufi who stands aloof from the theological controversies of the age, saves and spiritualises both the aspects of existence, and looks upon the whole Universe as the self-revelation of God—a higher notion which synthesises the opposite extremes of his predecessors....
>
> This extraordinary vitality of the Sufi restatement of Islam, however, is explained when we reflect on the all-embracing structure of Sufism. The Semitic formula of salvation can be briefly stated the words, "Transform your will"—which signifies that the Semite looks upon will as the essence of the human soul.... But the Sufi holds that the mere transformation of will or understanding will not

> bring peace; we should bring about the transformation of both by a complete transformation of feeling, of which will and understanding are only specialised forms. His message to the individual is—"Love all, and forget your own individuality in doing good to others."[30]

This discussion is entitled *The Origin and Qur'anic Justification of Sufism*. The title indicates that Iqbāl had no doubts about the Qur'ānic basis of the vitality which had developed among Muslims because of the Ṣūfīs.

On his return to Lahore, Iqbāl continued to reflect upon his experiences of Europe. He had studied in both England and Germany and had had good friends in both places. The war that broke out in 1914 represented to him the collapse of the immoral European civilisation. Iqbāl came to see the revival of Islam not only as a necessity for the recovery of the spiritual energy of his people, but also as an answer to the impasse that Europe had brought onto its people because of greed-dominated nationalism.

He published a major epic poem, *The Secrets of the Self,* in 1915. The poem indicates Iqbāl's idea that the proper understanding of the Qur'ān had been lost over the centuries because of "other-worldly" perspectives. The Ashᶜarite tradition, commonly taught to the religious leaders in the *madrasa*s, had failed to focus Muslim attention on the problems and possibilities of the experienced world. That "a-historical" attitude tended to turn Muslims away from thinking about what they could actually do to make concrete existence better.

The secret of the self was to use the creative potentiality manifest in all persons to learn to work more effectively in the world. The poet calls for the recovery of the original Qur'ānic perspective. This would mean recognition that the self must be growing towards God. Such growth was perceived as a means of liberating the kind of creative energy that could devise ways to solve the bewildering problems of war, and economic injustice. The self had to rediscover world-transforming creative energy. A few years later, Iqbāl published a second epic poem *The Mysteries of Selflessness*. Here he presented an image of the self as a candle that is burned up in giving light to other men. Often, in Iqbāl's poetry, the coming of Islam is equated with the destruction of priesthood and idolatry, with the creation of a society of free persons, each responsible directly to God, and with an emphasis on reason as a necessary tool for discerning how to implement values effectively.

Gandhi's Failure and Renewal

After the end of the European war in 1918, Gandhi joined the struggle in India to push the English into freeing India from imperialist control. His South African experiences had convinced him that the approach of non-violent action was the most effective way to lead oppressed peoples into victory over their oppressors. In the period of 1919–21, many Indian Muslims joined him in his efforts to lead a national movement of non-cooperation with British rule. The Hindu reformer also worked with the Khilafat movement, the movement to restore the Turkish Caliph to power, as a way of indicating his sympathy with his Muslim supporters.

The non-cooperation movement and the Khilafat movement both failed after 1922. Gandhi and other Indian leaders were imprisoned by their British rulers. Subsequently, Gandhi went into retreat by living in a village in 1926 and 1927, and withdrawing briefly from political action. This retreat represented to the Hindu reformer a time for reflection on failure, and a search for renewal. In this context, he wrote his mature reflection on what he had learned from life. The title was *Discourses on the Gita*. This series of lectures was delivered to those of his followers who were living in the Ashrams [religious communities] that he had established as a means of training non-violent activists for future movements of social change and reform. The series contains a summary of his fundamental ideas as to how life and religion should be understood.

He begins the series by acknowledging that the Hindu epic that contains the *Gita*, *The Mahabarata,* should not be understood as a record of historical events, but rather as a form of writing that conveys in an a-historical, timeless manner, the characteristics of the right way to live, *dharma*, with the wrong way, *adharma*. He insists that right and wrong are always the same in every generation. He writes:

> The *Gita* does not teach the path of action, nor of knowledge, nor of devotion. ... The *Gita* does not advocate any one of the three paths; I have from my experience come to the conclusion that it has been composed to teach this one truth which I have explained. We can follow truth only in the measure that we shed our attachment to the ego.... Krishna is the *atman* in us, who is our charioteer. We can win only if we hand over the reins of the chariot to him. God makes us dance, like the master in a puppet show. We are smaller than even puppets. We should, therefore, trust everything to God, as children to parents. Let us not eat uncooked stuff. Let Krishna the cook prepare and give us what food of grace He wills for our *atman*.
>
> The *Gita* does not decide for us. But if, whenever faced with a moral problem, you give up attachment to the ego and then decide what you should do, you will come to no harm. This is the substance of the argument which Shri Krishna has expanded into 18 chapters.[31]

Gandhi goes on to explain that the *atman* was never born and will never die.[32]He maintains that achieving a "one-pointed" mind is way to serve God.

> Along this path which I shall explain to you, one must hold one's intellect so firm that there is no wavering... We saw yesterday that those who hanker after enjoyment and power can never fix their intellect on one aim. Only a person like Hazrat ᶜAlī who is completely absorbed in God can succeed in doing so.[33]

This is an explicit example of Gandhi's assumption that Muslim devotion to service of God is essentially the same as that the Hindus. Since he used this example in speaking to the people living in his Ashram, he must have assumed that they agreed with this point. He goes on to explain that curbing the appetites is an essential discipline for growth in spiritual awareness. He again uses an Islamic example to illustrate his point.

> In the time of the Prophet, prayer, fasting and keeping awake at night were considered essential for subduing the

> *nafas* [this is a very good word denoting the sense-organs collectively; it also means desire]. The Prophet was often awake till two or three after midnight, and was never particular when and what he ate.... To the Prophet, fasting brought happiness, for it was an occasion when he could live constantly in the presence of God. ... Besides keeping awake thus, he would withdraw himself into solitude so that he might subdue the senses and be blessed with a vision of God. Jesus did likewise. He lived in solitude and fasted for forty days and subjected his body to the utmost mortification. At the end of forty days, he felt that he heard a mysterious voice that God was talking to him and that the veil which hid him from God had lifted.[34]

Thus, in spite of the experiences of the failure of the non-cooperation and Khilafat movements, Gandhi had not changed his basic perspective. He still assumes that people from different religious background can learn from their respective traditions the value of serving God by learning to subdue their appetites, and their greed. He continues to think that developing such control is a necessary prelude to working effectively to transform society. He goes on to explain that Europeans in the Middle Ages used to value spiritual practices like fasting, but that the Protestant reformation had led to spiritual confusion. He acknowledges that Luther had rightly criticized hypocrisy and superstition in the Church of his time, and tried to reform Christian life. Gandhi says that Protestants made the mistake of thinking that disciplines like fasting were all hypocritical. According to the Hindu thinker, this meant that the Protestants destroyed a potent means of realizing God.

He thinks that the India of his time may be making a similar error. He wants his listeners to understand that by rejecting the spiritual disciplines of fasting and self-control, Indians may be loosing their religious sensibility. He insists that rigorous fasting can be an excellent way to develop one's inner strength. He says:

> What is followed in the Roman Catholic church is also enjoined in Islam. The people who at present do evil things the name of Islam have little understanding of it. Those, on the other hand, who go on praying in their own homes, cer-

> tainly realize God. They give up all indulgences. One cannot indulge in pleasures and live a life of renunciation at the same time. If we understand the truth that we eat only to give the body its share, then we are fit to understand the *Gita*.[35]

Gandhi's interest in comparative religion appears again in his discussion of the significance of sacrifice.

> As we have the word *yajna* … [sacrifice] in our language, and the practice is enjoined in our dharma, so the Bible and the old books of the Jews too have corresponding words, and an idea similar to that of *yajna*. We find three things in the Koran: [1] animal sacrifices… [2] it refers to a practice which also obtained among the Jews, a father's sacrificing his son—Ibrahim does that; and [3] Ramadan, which is a form of sacrifice, that is, parting with or giving up something which is dear to us. In the same way, we see in the Bible the meaning of the terms sacrifice expanding after Jesus. … He told them that it was not a sacrifice to destroy other lives, that one should give one's own life as sacrifice. With that idea, he sacrificed his own life to for the eternal welfare of the world, for its spiritual welfare, for washing away its sins and not merely for feeding the people.[36]

In sum, Gandhi's commentary on the Gita can be seen to be his mature reflection, after his experiences of success and failure, as to what basic affirmations his followers should accept as guides to how to live. The influence of the English vegetarians is indicated by the reference in this commentary to the insights of Anna Kingsford, one of the vegetarians he had known in his students days in London.[37] He continues to affirm that the basic religious truths are the same in all religious traditions. These truths are that humans must learn to control their appetites, and to achieve a state of freedom from personal desire. Fasting, devotion, and spiritual exercises in all religious traditions have been developed to help people learn self-control. Gandhi thinks the modern western civilization is in distress because its people have lost their practices of spiritual discipline. He thinks India is in danger of similarly losing spiritual direction and focus. In his view, the transformation of social life into a good society of justice and harmony requires people from all traditions to practice the virtues of self-control and self-discipline. The evils of greed, and mutual hostility must be overcome by devout religious practice.

Iqbāl's Mature Reflections

We noted earlier that Iqbāl and Gandhi in 1908 and 1909 both wrote manifestos challenging their people to leave western civilization behind and to look for guidance in the wisdom of their ancestral traditions. *Hind Swaraj* and *Sicily* had appealed to young Indians to move away from the distracting illusions, and corrupt practices, of the west, and to seek guidance elsewhere. Many of those who responded to these appeals took active part in the revolutionary movements in India in 1919–22, and were disheartened when the revolutions failed. Twenty years later, in 1927 and 1929, after the collapse of the movements for the independence of India, we find both Gandhi and Iqbāl once again attempting to articulate their views as to the significance of their respective traditions for the problems of the present age. Each seems to have felt impelled to encourage his people to keep going in spite of discouraging failure, and the oppressive difficulties of life in the late 1920s.

Gandhi wrote his commentary on the Gita in 1927. Iqbāl, in 1929, delivered to an audience in Madras the lectures that became known as *The Reconstruction of Religious Thought in Islam*. Further, in 1932, Iqbāl's epic poem, the *Jāvīd Nāma, [The Pilgrimage to Eternity],* was published. It seems as though both authors felt similar urges to speak in the context of a world tormented by an economic depression, the continuing dominance of the British in India, and the unrest in Europe caused by the rise of fascism. Each independently felt compelled to express his mature thought as to how the members of his community should respond to the challenges of the present and the emerging future.

The background to Iqbāl's perspective in his *Reconstruction* lectures continues to be the comparative history of religion. His central thesis is that the religious experience of the Prophet Muḥammad was significantly different from the mystical experiences that occurred in other religions, and among Muslims. Iqbāl accepts as given that mystical experience occurs everywhere, and that such experiences are illuminating as perceptions of the depth of human consciousness in response to the vastness of the universe. However, he claims that the experience of the Prophet Muḥammad was different.

> The prophet's return is creative. He returns to insert himself into the sweep of time with a view to control the forces of history, and thereby to create a fresh world of ideals. For the mystic the repose of "unitary experience" is something final; for the prophet it is the awakening, within him, of world-shaking psychological forces, calculated to completely transform the human world.[38]

We noted earlier that Arnold had begun his book on *The Preaching of Islam* with a reference to Max Mueller's discussion of the nature of prophecy. Iqbāl's comments on the nature of prophecy as quoted above can be taken as the Muslim's elaboration of Mueller's idea. Iqbāl says that prophetic leadership not only judges human consciousness, but also evaluates the structures of human corporate existence. In so doing, the revelation to the Prophet calls upon believers to improve their social, economic, and political institutions. For this reason, the cultural worlds that Muslims have created, and can again create, as indicated by the symbol of Sicily in Iqbāl's early poem, remain proof of the validity of the Muslim revelation.

In the *Jāvīd Nāma,* addressed to the Muslims of the future, Iqbāl writes of a symbolic journey through the planets towards God. The journey can be taken both as a summary of the adventurous quest of the poet's own life, and as a model for generations yet to come. Iqbāl had been thinking about Persian poetry ever since his high school days; he continues to think about making his symbolic journey with Rūmī as his guide. Rūmī also had written about time and space. For example:

> "Answers from the Elements"
>
> A whole afternoon field inside me from one stem of reed.
>
> The messenger comes running toward me, irritated:
>
> *Why be so hard to find?*
>
> Last night I asked the moon about the Moon, my one
> question

for the visible world, Where is God?
The moon says, *I am dust stirred up*
when he passed by. The sun, *My face is pale yellow*
from just now seeing him. Water: *I slide on my head*
and face
like a snake, from a spell he said. Fire: *His lightning,*
I want to be that restless. Wine, *why so light?*
I would burn if I had a choice. Earth, quiet
and thoughtful? *Inside me I have a garden*
and an underground spring.

This world hurts my head with its answers,
wine filling my hand, not my glass.
If I could wake completely, I would say without speaking
why I'm ashamed of using words.[39]

One might say that Iqbāl also found that the world hurt his head. However, he did not stop writing. Iqbāl's *Jāvīd Nāma* can be looked at as his reflections on his twentieth century journey asking "Where is God?" With Rūmī beside him, Iqbāl portrays his questioning self traveling to the Moon, Mercury, Mars, Venus, Jupiter, Saturn, and Beyond the Spheres. He meets the Buddha, Hindu philosophy, Zarathustra, Tolstoy, and the pagans overthrown by the coming of Islam. From the Buddha, and Hindu philosophy, he learns to take love seriously; from Zarathustra to seek bravely for God; from Tolstoy to reject the exploitation of humanity; and from the pagans, to recognize that the revelation brought to Muḥammad has destroyed, and will destroy, idolatry, tribalism and racism.

Iqbāl thus indicates that much is to be learned from the many different religious traditions. If we take the journeys to the planets as symbolic of his own intellectual adventures, we can understand him to say that he learned different things at different times. Unlike Gandhi, he does not argue for the existence of one particular insight as the key to all significant religious thought. Gandhi thought non-violence was the key insight in all traditions. For Iqbāl, the significance of the Qur'ān was that the Muslims who accepted the revelation were freed from religious and political domination. They were stimulated to use their minds to devise new forms of common life. Non-violence, peace, would be one characteristic of a better society, but just economic and political institutions would also be necessary.

Iqbāl's Yes to history

Gandhi wrote his *Discourses on the Gita* in the context of the depressed mood among Indians in the late 1920s. We observed that Iqbāl's *Reconstruction of Religious Thought in Islam* was written in the same context, and perhaps for a similar reason, to clarify and re-affirm goals and values in a time of depression and confusion. Iqbāl's *Reconstruction Lectures* might well have a sub-title such as *Discourses on the Qur'ān in the light of the needs of the Indian Muslims in the late 1920s*. The lectures represent Iqbāl's effort to explain the relevance of Qur'ānic teaching to the pressing issues of the time.

Iqbāl knew that many Muslims of his time doubted that religion would any longer be relevant to life. He said religion would not continue to be relevant if religion were taken as a series of orders to be blindly obeyed, or as an attempt to construct a rational and credible metaphysical picture of the world of time and space. People in the modern world had to learn to think for themselves, and to use their minds, and not to follow old social and ethical codes blindly and uncritically. Following orders blindly would no longer serve to keep people religious. Also, no imaginative picture of the size and nature of the cosmos was any longer feasible in the light of the insights of modern physics.[40] Iqbāl had attended the philosopher Whitehead's lectures at Cambridge. The Muslim poet philosopher had a good grasp of the dilemmas posed by contemporary science to earlier forms of metaphysical thinking.

Iqbāl concluded that the Qur'ān could only be effectively understood as a catalyst to get the mind and imagination working.[41] It could not provide an inflexible moral code, or a credible picture of time and space. But it could encourage a person to develop a sensitive conscience, and confidence in his creative potentialities. Iqbāl thought of God as the source of vision. This is the implication of the need to hear a camel's bell; Muslims needed new insights in order to become effective in new contexts. Iqbāl quoted a Qur'ānic verse about the Prophet's vision of the Absolute: "His eye turned not aside, nor did it wander" (Q. 53:17).[42]

Iqbāl took this to mean that the human ideal, from the perspective of the Qur'ān, is not non-attachment, nor the extermination of the worldly self, but rather a strengthening of the creative, problem-solving, world transforming capacities of the individual person. He takes this verse to mean that the Prophet was focused on how to work to implement his vision, but was not annihilated by God. He quotes another passage: "Blessed by He whose hand is the Kingdom! And over all things is He potent. Who hath created death and life to test which of you is the best in point of deed: and He is the mighty and Forgiving" (Q. 67:2).[43]

The term "potent" is key to Iqbāl's understanding of the Qur'ānic imperative.. He was well aware that cynical atheism was developing among his people as a result of the collapse of the older civilizations, and the impact of new challenges. However, he defends the importance of religious life by arguing that the individual self only really discovers its full potentialities by focusing on the source of creative power that surges within from an external source that cannot be conceptualized. We cannot analyze what is happening when creative power surges within us. Iqbāl claims that religious experience is real, and universal. He thinks that the comparative history of the religions of the world attests to that universality. It is religious experience that can transform and redirect that creative capacities of individuals. This can happen in any tradition. However, Iqbāl also thinks that the Qur'ānic perspective has more to offer precisely because Prophetic experience focuses on actually changing the institutions that shape human life.

Iqbāl said that we can recognize that we are rooted in power from outside ourselves by noting that we cannot observe the source of the creativity that flows out of us. We know who we are by observing ourselves making decisions, forming plans, and acting upon these plans. None of this is predictable. It is freedom that makes us unpredictable.

> We appreciate the ego itself in the act of perceiving, judging, and willing. The life of the ego is a kind of tension caused by the ego invading the environment and the environment invading the ego. The ego does not stand outside this arena of mutual invasion. It is present in it as directive energy and is informed and disciplined by its own experience. The Qur'ān is clear on this directive function of the ego.
>
> And they ask thee of the soul, Say: "the soul proceedeth from my Lord's 'Amr' [Command] but of knowledge only a little to you is given." [Q. 17:85][44]

Thus the "soul", creative potentiality, is rooted in energy outside the self. But we can never directly analyze how this happens. There are thus significant differences in the ways in which Gandhi and Iqbāl understand the human soul. The former understood the soul as the battlefield, the battlefield portrayed in the *Gita,* in which the devotee should exercise his will to destroy all attachment to the world. Only then would he become an instrument of what God was doing for the world. In Vinoba Bhave's commentary on the Qur'ān, reflective of the thought of Gandhi, he referred to a number of Qur'ānic verses which he thought conveyed the same ideal of self conquest. For example, Q. 2:204 states, "And of mankind is he who would sell himself, seeking the pleasure of Allāh." Gandhi took Qur'ānic passages of this kind to refer to what they believed to be the universal religious teaching of the need for self-denial and asceticism. They assume that the soul is always, and in all contexts, a battlefield between personal appetites and desires, and the Absolute. They taught that only through the extinguishing of personal desires can the soul be free to serve God.

Iqbāl, however, did not use this metaphor of battle in his thinking about the soul. For him, the soul should be thought of as directive energy, energy that could be used to change the world. In his words: "And the recipient of Divine illumination is not merely a passive recipient. Every act of a free ego creates a new situation, and thus offers further opportunities of creative unfolding."[45] Thus, in Iqbāl's view, the self should not be "a passive recipient", a puppet. Problem-solving creativeness comes from the individual brave enough to take the world seriously and to engage with it in radical efforts to change institutions, ways of thought, and oppressive structures of domination.

This Muslim notion of the soul as creative potentiality is similar to the approach one finds in the widely read 20th century Christian author, Thomas Moore. In his best selling book, *The Care of the Soul,* Moore, basing himself on the insights of the Renaissance Platonist, Ficino, argues precisely that the soul is that part of human consciousness capable of transformation and creative potential.

Conclusion

Pyarelal tells us that the vegetarian reformers in England at the end of the 19th century were divided. Some said the world could be improved by a "return to nature". The others advocated a socialist revolution in order to use industrialism and modern science in the cause of building a future society in which social justice for all would be a dominating theme. The one tended to look backward, and the other, forward. Pyarelal says that Gandhi was more influenced by the "back to nature" reformers than by Shaw and the Fabians.

The opposite might be said of Iqbāl. Iqbāl tells us that history must be taken seriously in the manner of Ibn Khaldūn.[46] This meant that Muslims needed to learn much from the historical record; they must discern how to avoid the worst errors of the past. Iqbāl insisted that the traditional religious leaders of the Muslim community, the *ᶜulamā'*, had been misled by their education in the Ashᶜarite tradition to fail to take history seriously. They just thought of Islamic ideals as transhistorical, having no relevance to the on-going events in the world. Iqbāl's main message was that Muslims should give up this anti-rational approach and begin to use their minds to take seriously the evidence of history, and of modern science.

We began with the question as to how Gandhi and Iqbāl fitted the Qur'ān into their structures of religious thought. We have seen that Gandhi and Iqbāl both accepted the notion that religious experience happens in many places and times. Gandhi took from his experiences, in London and South Africa, the conviction that self-conquest was a necessary prelude to constructive action. This self-conquest was the method he had used to find the strength to resist racism in

South Africa. Gandhi thought that this imperative to self-conquest was the same in all religious traditions. He believed this "extinction of personal desire" to be the essential message of the Qur'ān, and of the Bible, as well as of the Gita.

Gandhi certainly worked in the world himself, and directed his followers to do so. Gandhi thought that the religious devotees could become instruments of God's purposes by surrendering themselves. He thought that God would make the world good, once humans eradicated personal greed, anger and lust from their consciousness. The phrase from the Gita—"act without regard for the fruits of action"—became the theme of the Hindu reformer's message. Iqbāl's phrases about allowing directive energy to surge into the self from outside might be viewed as a similar notion. That similarities exist in the two perspectives is unquestionable, since both these religious leaders conceived of humanity as needing to be rooted in the transcendent goodness, justice and mercy of the Absolute. Gandhi's religious thought was "this-worldly" in the sense that he was strongly oriented to fighting against social evils like racism and untouchability. However, he thought one needed to be an "otherworldly person" unmoved by personal desire or ambition, so that one could be used by God to make the world good.

Iqbāl said, however, that some mystics think of the self as a drop disappearing in the ocean of God, whereas others affirm that the self should retain some distinctive identity. From the Gandhian perspective, one might say, as Gandhi said about differences in Hindu and Buddhist metaphysics, that questions as to whether the end of life is complete absorption, or limited absorption, in the Absolute are unanswerable. Gandhi might have said that such differences in theories about the after life are irrelevant in day to day life.

There is no doubt, however, that Iqbāl thought that these questions were urgently important. Like other 19th century Muslim reformers, he thought that the Ṣūfism of absorption, the drop into the sea, had had the practical effect of making Muslims passive. He wanted to liberate his people from the depressed mentality of colonial subjects, and stir them into action. Hence his protest against theories of absorption. He wrote:

> The end of the ego's quest is not emancipation from the limitations of individuality; it is, on the other hand, a more precise definition of it. The final act is not an intellectual act, but a vital act which deepens the whole being of the ego, and sharpens his will with the creative assurance that the world is not something to be merely seen or known through concepts, but something to be made and re-made by continuous action.[47]

Iqbāl viewed consciousness as complex; faith, rootedness in transcendent goodness, was essential as a source of vision. The implementing of the vision required, however, the effective working of human minds to solve problems in specific contexts. We might affirm trust in justice, for example, but the implementation of justice requires direction and decision-making by human intelligence.

Iqbāl's main battle was against the servility and self-contempt that the conditions of colonialism had created among the Muslims of India. In his biography of the Prophet, Iqbāl's mentor, Shiblī, had followed the traditional portrayal of the Prophet's life. However, he added a new introduction, in which he stressed that the Prophet and the first Muslims had creatively changed the course of human history because of the new ways of living they had introduced.[48] It is this aspect of the Prophet's life that Iqbāl also takes as a guiding directive. He claims that the Qur'ān was liberating because it freed people from superstition, and from bondage to tyranny. Iqbāl wanted the Muslims of his time to become again problem-solving people. He wrote: "History … is the third source of human knowledge according to the Qur'ān. It is one of the most essential teachings of the Qur'ān that nations are collectively judged, and suffer for their misdeeds here and now."[49]

Gandhi and Iqbāl shared a common readiness to appreciate religious experience as a human possibility, not restricted to any one tradition. They differed, however, in their attitudes to the possibilities of genuinely new developments taking place within historical time. Gandhi showed little interest in the question as to whether anything new could happen. For Iqbāl, however, this notion was central. It meant, for him, that individuals and societies could learn from past mistakes, and go on to create better human institutions.

The essential characteristic of human consciousness, in Iqbāl's view, was that the present could be transcended, and the new could be created.

NOTES

1. Pyarelal, *Mahatma Gandhi—the Early Phase*, vol. 1 (Ahmedabad: Navijivan, 1956), 199–224.

2. Muhammad Iqbal, *The Reconstruction of Religious Thought in Islam* (Lahore: Ashraf, 1960 reprint), 181. In his annotated version, *The Reconstruction of Religious Thought in Islam,* annotated with commentary by Saeed Sheikh (Lahore: Ghulam Ali, 1986) Saeed Sheikh has commented that the Ṣūfī referred to was Iqbāl's father.

3. M.A.K. Khalil, trans. *Call of the Marching Bell, English Translation of Bang-i-Dara* (Lahore: Iqbal Academy, 1997), 65.

4. V. G. Kiernan, trans. *Poems from Iqbal* (Lahore: Iqbal Academy, 2000 reprint), 166–80, 204. See also, *Call of the Marching Bell,* 326, 351.

5. Syed Abdul Vahid (ed.),*Thoughts and Reflections of Iqbal* (Lahore: Ashraf, 1964), 195.

6. Rajmohan Gandhi, *Gandhi The Good Boatman* (New York: Viking 1995), 54, 55.

7. Pyarelal, *Mahatma Gandhi—the Early Phase,* 200.

8. Charlotte Vaudeveille, *Kabir* (Delhi: Oxford University Press 1974) I, 21. See also David M. Gracie (ed.), *Gandhi and Charlie: The Story of a Friendship* (Cambridge MA: Cowley Publications, 1989).

9. M.K. Gandhi, *Autobiography, The Story of my Experiments with Truth* (Boston: Beacon Press, 1962).

10. Pyarelal, *Mahatma Gandhi—the Early Phase,* 239.

11. Ibid., 249.

12. Thomas Arnold, *The Preaching of Islam* (Lahore: Ashraf, 1951 reprint), 1.

13. Annemarie Schimmel, *Gabriel's Wing A Study into the Religious Ideas of Sir Muhammad Iqbal* (Leiden: E. J. Brill, 1963).

14. M. A. M. Khalil, *Call of the Marching Bell*, 182.

15. Muhammad Siddiq, *Descriptive Catalogue of Allama Iqbal's Personal Library* (Lahore: Iqbal Academy, 1983).

16. Pyarelal, *Mahatma Gandhi—the Early Phase,* 662–701.

17. Ibid., 327–31.

18. *The Collected Works of Mahatma Gandhi* (New Delhi: Ministry of Information and Broadcasting, Government of India, n.d.), II, 52.

19. Joseph Doke, *M. K. Gandhi. An Indian Patriot in South Africa* (New Delhi: Ministry of Information and Broadcasting, Government of India, 1967 reprint), 101–5.

20. M. K. Gandhi, *Satyagraha in South Africa* (Ahmedabad: Navajivan, n.d.)

21. S. Abid Husain, *Gandhiji and Communal Unity* (Bombay: Orient Longmans, 1969), 56.

22. *The Collected Works of Mahatma Gandhi,* X, 24,25.

23. M. K. Gandhi, *The Hindu-Muslim Unity* (Bombay: Bharatiya Vidya Bhavan, 1965), 25.

24. *The Collected Works of Mahatma Gandhi,* VI, 113–26.

25. Amir Ali, "Anomalies of Civilisation" in *Memoires and Other Writings of Syed Amir Ali,* ed. Syed Razi Wasti (Lahore: People's Publishing House, 1968), 302–18.

26. V. G. Kiernan, trans. *Poems from Iqbal,* 31, 32,

27. Muhammad Iqbal, *The Development of Metaphysics in Persia* (Lahore: Bazm-i Iqbal, 1964).

28. Ibid., 61.

29. Ibid., 59.

30. Ibid., 82.

31. *The Collected Works of Mahatma Gandhi,* XXXII, 106–9.

32. Ibid., XXXII, 112.

33. Ibid., XXXII, 120–3.

34. Ibid., XXXII, 133, 134

35. Ibid., XXXII, 135.

36. Ibid., XXXII, 152, 153.

37. Ibid., XXXII, 219.

38. *The Reconstruction of Religious thought in Islam,* 124, 125.

39. Kabir Helminiski (ed.), *The Rumi Collection* (Boston: Shambala, 1998), 15.

40. *Reconstruction of Religious Thought in Islam,* 181.

41. Ibid., 14.

42. Ibid., 118–23.

43. Ibid., 119

44. Ibid., 102.

45. Ibid., 123.

46. Ibid., 157–9.

47. Ibid., 198.

48. Sheila McDonough, "Shibli Numani," in *Religion in Modern India,* ed. Robert Baird (New Delhi: Manohar, 1983).

49. *Reconstruction of Religious Thought in Islam,* 138–41.

Chapter 14

The Qur'ān in India II: Tablīghī Jamāᶜat and the Qur'ān

Alan M. Guenther

The Tablīghī Jamāᶜat, a movement established in India in the 1920s, has received increasing attention in academic circles. Until recently, it had largely been ignored by scholars, unlike a number of other Islamic groups emerging in the twentieth century, because as a movement it avoids all political involvement and has produced no new or radical religious philosophies. But its massive following and resulting impact on Muslim religious life in South Asia and other parts of the world has stimulated research. Organizing rallies that attract more than one million people in Pakistan and Bangladesh[1] and being a major player in the spread of Islam in the West makes it important that it be examined and compared to contemporary movements. The early history of the movement, its growth and guiding ideology, and its spread around the world have been explored.[2] Other studies have analyzed the movement in the context of other "fundamentalist" movements,[3] in the context of Ṣūfism in the Indian subcontinent,[4] in its approach to *daᶜwa*,[5] and through an examination of its chief text.[6] Because of its increasing visibility and influence as a movement for reform, a study of its use of the Qur'ān is beneficial, since generally, reformers and reform movements tend to appeal directly to the authority of the Qur'ān and the *sunna* rather than the accumulated weight of tradition. This paper seeks to develop such an understanding by examining two of the movement's most influential leaders, Muḥammad Ilyās and Muḥammad Zakariyyā, and the writings of the latter specifically on the subject of the Qur'ān.[7] This examination reveals the uniqueness of the movement in that it has not claimed to offer any new interpretation of Islam to meet the challenges of modernity, and would actually oppose such independent reasoning (*ijtihād*) while supporting the following of traditional interpretations (*taqlīd*).[8] As a movement it approaches the reform of religion and religious practice more in terms of "faith renewal" rather than modernization or revivalism.[9] This paper seeks to situate the movement's particular understanding of the Qur'ān in the broader pattern of its leaders' acceptance of a continuation of the medieval scholarship that preserved and expanded the Qur'ānic commentaries (*tafsīr*) for many centuries. Thus a particular focus will be the educational heritage of each, and their participation in the various educational movements of their time.

Muḥammad Ilyās: His life and thought

Though the founder of the Tablīghī Jamāᶜat, Mawlānā Muḥammad Ilyās (1885–1944), did not write any commentary on the Qur'ān or propose a fresh approach to its interpretation as some of his contemporaries such as Mawlānā Abū'l-ᶜĀlā Maudūdī and Amīn Aḥsan Iṣlāḥi, he has been the most influential figure in the history of the movement and in the shaping of its approach to the Qur'ān. His parental heritage linked him closely to the scholarly tradition of Shāh Walī Allāh (d. 1762) of Delhi and his sons.[10] His father earned his fame as a teacher of the Qur'ān.[11] With respect to his scholarly credentials, he was firmly grounded in the Deoband school. He had given *bayᶜa* to Rashīd Aḥmad Gangohī (1829–1905), who had been instrumental in founding the academy at Deoband and was well known as a teacher of *ḥadīth*.[12] He had been brought to study under him by an older brother, Mawlānā Muḥammad Yaḥyā in 1896. Three years after the death of Rashīd Aḥmad, he went to the academy at Deoband where he studied Ḥadīth with Mawlānā Maḥmūd al-Ḥasan.[13] He associated with key *ᶜulamā'* in the Deoband group such as Mawlānā Ashraf ᶜAlī Thanawī, Maulānā ᶜAbdur Raḥīm Rā'ipurī, and Mawlānā Khalīl Aḥmad while he was at the school at Saharanpur, the Maẓhīrul ᶜUlūm, a sister school to the one at Deoband, as well as outside of the academic setting including on several journeys to Mecca.[14] Those of the Deoband group were committed followers of *taqlīd-i shakhsi*, encouraging each Muslim to follow a single *ᶜālim*, "trusting him completely as his definitive guide to the law," an attitude reflected in the work of Ilyās as well.[15] This association indicates the foundation of orthodox interpretation on which he built his movement calling Muslims to active participation in *tablīgh*.

The Tablīghī Jamā^c^at also became linked with the Nadwatul ^c^Ulamā' academy in Lucknow, which has had a strong tradition of Arabic scholarship[16] One of the most famous *^c^ulamā'* from the academy who closely identified himself with the movement for a while was Mawlānā Abū'l-Ḥasan ^c^Alī Nadwī (1914–1999) who wrote a highly sympathetic biography of the founder, Muḥammad Ilyās.[17] Yet despite this grounding in the Indian Muslim scholarly community, Muḥammad Ilyās came to doubt the effectiveness of religious schools (*madrasa*s) alone to bring about the revival of religion for which he looked.[18]

Muḥammad Ilyās was also committed to Ṣūfism, and his movement reflects that influence. He was initiated into the Ṣābiriyya branch of the Chistiyya order, as well as into several others, the characteristics of which were reflected in his beliefs and practices.[19] Like the Chistiyya, he consistently refrained from involvement in the state and political affairs and did not extend his missionary activities to non-Muslims to seek to convert them, while his practice of *dhikr* and his adherence to the *sharī^c^ah* were more like those of the Naqshbandiyya. The Maẓhīrul ^c^Ulūm where he began his teaching career was one of the largest schools in the sub-continent, second only to the one at Deoband, but it "came to be considered less intellectual and more Ṣūfī in orientation than Deoband."[20] The seven core teachings of his movement, namely 1) the creed (*kalima*), 2) prayer (*namāz*), 3) religious knowledge (*^c^ilm*) and the remembrance of God (*dhikr*), 4) respect (*ikrām*) for all Muslims, 5) sincerity (*ikhlāṣ*) of motives, 6) donation of time (*tafrīgh*), and 7) abstention from useless and worldly talk, also reflected Ṣūfī ideals.[21] "Ilyās adopted Ṣūfi terms and practices such as *dhikr, murāqaba* and *chilla* with certain changes, to popularize Ṣūfism and create a better understanding of it among the masses; at the same time he sought to eliminate the abuse which had crept into Ṣūfī orders contributing to their unpopularity among certain sections of the community."[22] His letters to Nadwī reveal a strongly mystical perspective, containing discussions of the being (*wujūd*) of God and man, inner (*bāṭin*) and outer (*ẓāhir*) realities, and the essence (*dhāt*) of God.[23] Thus, like other scholars of his era, he combined the classical Islamic sciences and mystical practices with a commitment to reform, a combination also influencing his approach to the Qur'ān.

After teaching at the Maẓhīrul ᶜUlūm, he returned to his home at Nizamuddin near Delhi to take over responsibility for the mosque and school begun and operated by his father and oldest brother in 1917.[24] Here he taught all levels of students, but did not restrict his teaching to the standard syllabi or texts common in the *madrasas* at the time. It was also while teaching at this school that he became more involved with the Mewati community which became so central in his early efforts at *tablīgh*.[25] Beginning with the belief that education was the key to reforming the religious life of this nominally Muslim group, he moved out of Delhi and established elementary religious schools (*maktabs*) in Mewat, a vast region in Central India, south of Delhi.[26] But he soon became convinced that the proliferation of schools would never be sufficient to bring about the change in religious and cultural practices he desired, since without a genuine attachment to faith, parents did not consider religious knowledge worth the economic sacrifice of sending their children to school. Furthermore, if it were only children who were educated, the impact on the community would be slight since they were exempted from religious duties by their age. Adults would generally not be free to attend the *maktabs*. These convictions led him to consider alternatives, specifically calling Muslims to join *jamāᶜats* or groups for the purpose of propagating the fundamental tenets of Islam, namely the proper recitation and meaning of the *kalima*, the profession of faith, and the practice of prayer (*namāz*).[27]

Maulānā Ilyās had gained the respect of the Muslims of Mewat as a consequence of his assistance to the community in social and religious reform. In 1932, he decided to increase his activity in the region, through holding gatherings of those interested, and sending out small groups to other villages and regions. This activity culminated in a large gathering of notables of the area where the chief objectives of the Tablīghī Jamāᶜat were stated and its program officially launched.[28]

The system of *tablīghī jamāᶜats* accomplished a dual purpose of a broad preaching of the tenets of Islam and the training of individual Muslims. Those joining the bands of preachers would spend time perfecting their own knowledge of Islam and listening and learning from the behavior of spiritual mentors for a specific period of time during which they left their home areas and traveled about villages and cities inviting Muslims to join their instruction classes in local *masjids*.[29] The foundation of this approach was based in the Qur'ān, on the following two verses:

> You are the best community sent forth unto mankind; you command that which is reputable and you prevent that which is disreputable and you believe in Allah. (Q. 3:110)
>
> And let there be of you a community calling others to do good and commanding that which is reputable and prohibiting that which is disreputable. (Q. 3:104)[30]

The result of their activity was a remarkable change in the religious character of the Mewati population, with numerous *masjids* built, Hindu practices given up, and more *ᶜālims* produced.[31] Interestingly, the study of the Qur'ān did not become a major feature in the movement which tended to focus on religious devotion expressed in the correct performance of the rituals of worship. The movement was not founded on a new approach or interpretation of the Qur'ān, but on the practical necessity of teaching the masses the basics of Islam.

His attitude to religious knowledge

The attitude of Muḥammad Ilyās towards scholars and the acquisition of religious knowledge gives further insight into the reasons for the absence of any distinctive *tafsīr* emanating from the new movement. Though evolving from a context rooted in traditional scholarship, the efforts of the Tablīghī Jamāᶜat to communicate effectively to the masses resulted in a break with that tradition, at least in methodology. Muḥammad Ilyās emphasized that religious knowledge did not mean withdrawal from society and from pursuing legitimate means of livelihood, nor could it only be acquired through books and Arabic *madrasas*, since the presumption of such restrictions caused many to disqualify themselves from religious knowledge.[32] He also considered it necessary to begin at an earlier stage of teaching before moving on to such more advanced religious instruction as *tafsīr* would entail. "To talk of the more advanced branches when the plant of Faith had yet to take root in the hearts was unreasonable and premature."[33] He thought that theological education had become a formality instead of a means of correction in a society where religion had become mere ritual.[34] Though deploring empty ritual, he was still a strong proponent of the external aspects of faith, as was seen in his disappointment with a celebrated young scholar who had completed his study of the Qur'ān in one of the schools of Mewat, but was clean-shaven and "from his face and dress there was no sign that he was a Muslim."[35] This reflects a fundamental principle of the Tablīghī Jamā^c^at that access to truth is routed not through theoretical knowledge but through its practice.[36]

The inability of the *^c^ulamā'* to appreciate and participate in Muḥammad Ilyās' system of *tablīgh* was a source of concern for him. Ilyās believed that *tablīgh* was a method for bringing the *^c^ulamā'* and the common people together. He wanted them to be active participants in the mission, not just lending their vocal support in speeches and sermons. He remarked in a letter to Maulānā Muḥammad Zakariyyā, "I have long been of the view that unless educated persons called at the doors of the common people and went from town to town and village to village like ordinary men, the Movement would not be successful because learned and forceful discourses of the Ulema could not have the same effect on the masses as their physical participation."[37] But they remained hesitant because the quiet constructive work was obscured in the political agitation and upheavals in the first half of the twentieth century. Furthermore, little was known about the work since Ilyās avoided publicity and had difficulties communicating with other *^c^ulamā'*.[38] Nadwī sums up the attitude of the religious scholars of his time thus:

> It was, thus, difficult for those who had been brought up in that atmosphere to realise that there was anything else for them to do than to establish Maktabs and Madrassas, teach the Quran and the Sunnat, issue religious decrees, refute the innovations in Faith and attain self-purification through the path of *Tasawwuf*.[39]

Nevertheless, Ilyās did not give up on religious schools, but saw their decline as a misfortune. He continued to direct his followers to respect the *^c^ulamā'* and believed with the revival of religious ardor of the masses, the schools would once again prosper.[40] But the Tablīghī Jamā^c^at also "challenged the monopoly on religious guidance of the *^c^ulamā'* and the shaykhs, while proclaiming respect for them and engaging many of them in its work" through its unique belief that all Muslims, not just those educated in the traditional religious disciplines, were teachers.[41] Interestingly, though, Ilyās appealed not to a "return to the Qur'ān" as a solution, but to the disciplines of the creed and prayer as central to the identity of Muslims in order to stimulate that ardor. His preference for beginning with these two disciplines reflected the social realities of the Mewati context in which he began his work. The Meos of Mewat were by all contemporary accounts only nominally Muslim, and would not have been attracted by complex theological reasoning.[42] Ilyās and his early disciples did not focus on denunciations of non-Islamic practices which abounded, but rather on the cultivation of faith, with the confidence that it would result in the people changing their lives according to the Law of God.[43]

Ilyās did, however, disapprove of the approach to religious knowledge as practiced in the universities which he credited with bringing about a change in one's mental outlook that resulted in religious knowledge being seen in relation with the world rather than with God.[44] He lamented the fact that some Muslims were dependent on non-Muslim Orientalists for the acquisition of religious knowledge or of Arabic. With such an ambivalent attitude towards classical scholarship and decidedly negative perspective of modernist educational institutions, Ilyās naturally devoted himself more to the raising up of groups of missionaries rather than to the production of *tafsīr* or any other books for that matter.

This disdain for *kitābi ᶜilm*, or book knowledge, continues to be shared by most Tablīghī leaders and workers today. Workers are "discouraged from reading any books other than those written by Mawlānā Muḥammad Zakariyyā and Mawlānā Manẓūr Nuᶜmānī, the two scholars whose works are prescribed as texts for all Tablīghī workers."[45] They remain suspicious of scholarship, especially that of Muslims attempting to rationalize faith in light of modern society. Their emphasis on people becoming good Muslims through personal contact and participation in *daᶜwa* and not through books is stated succinctly by Nuᶜmānī, who broke with Mawdūdī after assisting in the founding of the Jamāᶜat Islāmi when he said, "Tablighi work is not a book, it is action."[46] Metcalf has described the

Tablīghī Jamā^cat as "not an intellectual movement that encourages speculation and breadth."[47] This characterization seems at odds with the large book store near the center of Jamā^cat activities in New Delhi, but the diversity of books sold and shipped around the world is limited to a few, primarily the collection of writings by Zakariyyā known as *Tablīghī Niṣāb* or *Faḍā'il-i A^cmāl*, published in Urdu, English and a number of other languages.[48] The section of this text devoted to the Qur'ān is analyzed below. Manẓūr Nu^cmānī wrote a book entitled *The Quran and You*, but it is more a systematic theology of Islam defining the primary beliefs of Islam and grounding those beliefs in quotations from the Qur'ān, and has practically no teaching on the Qur'ān itself.[49]

Muḥammad Zakariyyā

Mawlānā Muḥammad Zakariyyā (1898–1982), son of Ilyās' brother Yaḥyā, was well known as Shaykh al-Ḥadīth at the Maẓhīrul ^cUlūm at Sahāranpūr where his uncle had also taught. Though the author of over eighty published and unpublished works in both Arabic and Urdu, including commentary notes (unpublished) on the Qur'ān in both languages, he is revered within the movement primarily for the collections of Ḥadīth declaring the virtues of the repetition of the name of God (*dhikr*), prayer, *tablīgh*, the Qur'ān, and fasting which are published along with stories of the Companions in the aforementioned *Faḍā'il*.[50] As to his academic upbringing, he was a graduate of the academy at Deoband, which was known for disseminating *ḥadīth*, and had been a disciple of Maulāna Rashīd Aḥmad Gangōhī, whom he succeeded as spiritual guide.[51] He had served as the head teacher of *ḥadīth* at Sahāranpūr, where he was working when requested by his uncle Ilyās and another scholar to compile a selection of forty Ḥadīth on the virtues of the Qur'ān, the first of the series, in 1929.[52]

In his handling of *ḥadīth*, Zakariyyā demonstrated an approach to history characteristic of the Tablīgh movement. For him the only history that mattered was the mythological history always potentially present, the "type" that was to be recreated.[53] Unlike Sir Sayyid Aḥmad Khān (1817–1898) and Shiblī Nu^cmānī (1857–1914) who utilized the body of traditions to write fresh histories of the life of the Prophet, Zakariyyā's purpose was to make immediate parallels with the current context and prescribe proper behaviour. He also ignored Muslim glory in the recent historical past along with its decline under conquest and struggle for reassertion in his direct appeal to the age of the Prophet and his Companions.[54] "The issue for Tablighis is not to trace linear change and causality but to identify moments when individuals have followed the pristine example of the Prophet; the goal then is to relive his time."[55] This approach would have a direct effect on his interpretation of the Qur'ān, he would not seek to understand the text as containing universal principles to be extracted from historically-specific accounts through the use of consistent hermeneutical principles. Rather he assumed the specifics to be directly applicable to his context without extensive interpretation.

Faḍā'il-i Qur'ān

The book, *Faḍā'il-i Qur'ān*, was the first in a series of books written by Maulānā Muḥammad Zakariyyā, beginning in 1929. The series was not initially written for the Tablīghī Jamāᶜat, but a number of the books in the series were later compiled into the larger *Faḍā'il-i Aᶜmāl* which has become the primary textbook for those participating in a *tablīghī jamāᶜat*.[56] Initially published together in the 1950s under the title, *Tablīghī Niṣāb* (Curriculum for Tablīgh), the title was changed in 1985 to its current form, *Faḍā'il-i Aᶜmāl* (Merits or Virtues of Practice). This collection was initially suggested by Ilyās when pressed to fix a syllabus for knowledge (*ᶜilm*).[57] He suggested it be used for solitary as well as communal readings, for memorization and for recitation.[58] The booklet whose subject matter is the Qur'ān consists of forty *aḥādīth* gathered by Zakariyyā that spell out the virtues of the Qur'ān. The forty are followed by another set of seven and a summary review of all which specifies the benefit accrued by a Muslim from reading, studying, memorizing, reciting, and teaching the Qur'ān.[59]

A major focus of the work is the benefit of reciting the Qur'ān and the proper methodology. Zakariyyā begins with outlining the rules of reverence for recitation, both outward—specifying washings, posture, speed of reading, weeping, and inflections of voice, and inward—realizing the glory of the Qur'ān, bearing in mind the transcendence of God, being free from distractions and doubts, and meditating on the meaning when it is understood (8–10). Some of the rules of pronunciation especially with respect to words and letters of which the Urdu enunciation is less precise than the Arabic, he takes from a commentary by Shāh ᶜAbdul ᶜAzīz Dihlavī (1746–1824) (28, 52).

In the context of detailed instructions on the use of the Qur'ān, Zakariyyā emphasizes the relatively greater importance of understanding its meaning. While understanding is not required for recitation (30), mere recitation of the words is considered the lowest degree of excellence while learning the Qur'ān with its meanings and intent is the highest (12). At one point he also discusses the idea that reading the Qur'ān is superior to reciting it from memory (41–2). In other places, he suggests that reading and memorizing are ranked higher than prayer (14), and acquiring religious knowledge is more virtuous than worship (74–5). He quotes a *ḥadīth* from the Prophet predicting the rise of a people who would develop recitation into an exact science, laboring over the correct pronunciation of each letter, but all for a "worldly motive" with little thought for the hereafter (88). From this Zakariyyā concludes that reciting in a pleasing voice is of no avail if there is no sincerity and the motive merely temporal benefit. Another necessary corollary is that sincerity required acting on the precepts learned (20–1).

Zakariyyā repeatedly mentions those in his society who considered the memorization and recitation of the Qur'ān to be useless and "a sheer waste of time and mental energy to repeat its words without understanding them" (11, 35, 87, 99). This is one of the few times he departs from his custom, which also characterizes the Tablighī Jamāᶜat as a whole, of accenting the positive commands and not focusing on prohibitions and criticisms.[60] He identifies those who look on learning the Qur'ān as useless as "our national leaders" who obstruct rather than assist in propagating the Qur'ān (99). The context suggests that he is not indicating the British regime or other non-Muslim political leaders, but those Indian nationalists of the Muslim community promoting Islamic dress and other aspects of national culture in newspaper articles and speeches (98). He regards with concern the passing of laws for compulsory secular education for children and the neglect of the Qur'ān. These leaders had criticized the religious teachers for teaching only to make a living and not out of love for the Qur'ān. Zakariyyā rebukes such an attack on the intention of the teachers, but suggests elsewhere that he recognizes there is some truth in this criticism, and counsels them to be motivated only by love for teaching (89–90). This attitude is consistent with the views of Ilyās on education as discussed earlier, in that non-religious instruction is viewed with suspicion.

Since reading and writing with understanding is desirable, Zakariyyā presents the requirements for correctly interpreting the Qur'ān. The requirements reflect Zakariyyā's concern that only those fully qualified participate in this activity. While listening, reading, memorization, and recitation are activities required by all, interpretation is limited to a few. His concern demonstrates his commitment to *taqlīd* and rejection of independent *ijtihād*, the validity of which was often asserted by other reformers. This argument for restricted access to interpretation is based on the Qur'ān's outward (*ẓahr*) and inward (*baṭn*) aspects—the outward being its words which can be recited properly by all, and the inward being its meanings and underlying ideas, the understanding of which varies with the readers (p. 23). In part, this emphasis also reflects that those who formed the majority of the Tablīghī Jamāᶜat, those to whom these instructions were addressed, were not *ᶜulamā'* but people less educated in the religious sciences. The activation of non-*ᶜulamā'* for such a purely religious activity was a new phenomenon. And since Zakariyyā still held the *ᶜulamā'* in high regard it is not all that surprising that he chose not to address the details of Qur'ānic exegesis in these instructions because exegesis, in his mind, should only be done by those fully qualified.

The fifteen subjects of learning presented by Zakariyyā as requirements for attempting a commentary on the Qur'ān are consistent with those taught by the classical exegetes (24–6). He begins with four areas of grammar: 1) philology (*lugha*), 2) syntax (*naḥw*), 3) etymology and conjugation (*ṣarf*), 4) derivation (*ishtiqāq*). The next three he terms knowledge of oratory (*ᶜilm al-balāgha*), consisting of 5) knowledge of semantics (*ᶜilm al-maᶜānī*), 6) knowledge of figures of speech (*ᶜilm al-abyān*), 7) knowledge of rhetoric (*ilm al-badīᶜ*). Similar in focus is 8) knowledge of the art of pronunciation (*ᶜilm al-qirā'a*). He then lists several branches of Islamic learning in which excellence is also required: 9) knowledge of the fundamentals of faith (*ᶜilm al-ᶜaqā'id*), 10) principles of jurisprudence (*uṣūl al-fiqh*), 11) occasions of revelation (*asbāb al-nuzūl*), 12) abrogation (*nāsikh wa mansūkh*), 13) knowledge of jurisprudence (*ᶜilm al-fiqh*), and 14) knowledge of relevant *aḥadīth*. The final requirement, one which Zakariyyā considers the most important, is the gift of understanding bestowed by God (*ᶜilm-i wahabī*). This last skill does not seem to be restricted to mystical knowledge in Zakariyyā's perception. He declares that it is not beyond the capacity of anyone to acquire it, since all that is needed is for one to act on the knowledge already achieved and to turn away from the world (27). His listing of these branches of knowledge developed during the medieval period of Islamic scholarly activity seems at variance with his tendency to skip over this period and appeal directly to the authority of the Prophet and his Companions. As if aware of this discrepancy, he inserts the justification that the *Saḥāba* acquired the necessary knowledge of the Arabic language naturally as their mother tongue, and reached a depth of knowledge in the other sciences by means of the "illuminating contact" they had with the Prophet (27). As such they had no need to acquire these fifteen subjects of learning, nor spell them out for posterity. Subsequent generations without this *natural* facility developed the necessary disciplines to aid understanding.

A person attempting to write a commentary without using these tools would be basing it on his personal opinion, which, Zakariyyā declares, is prohibited (27). He laments, "An unbecoming present-day fashion is that even those who possess little or no Arabic vocabulary proceed to introduce their personal opinion on the basis of vernacular translations of the Qur'ān (23–4). His distrust of the self-proclaimed scholars who were familiar with only translations of the Qur'ān is also demonstrated in another quote of his: "The true meanings of the Holy Qur'an can be understood by those who have dived deep into its Verses and are well-informed on this subject."[61] In yet another criticism of those of his contemporaries interpreting Islam in light of modernist ideals, he states that complete knowledge of the Qur'ān is withheld from three categories of people—those who lack necessary knowledge, those who persist in sin, and those who tend to rationalize all aspects of faith (27–8).

Interestingly, in this book on the Qur'ān he very seldom quotes from it; and when he does, it is without comment. In one instance in his booklet *The Virtues of Tabligh*, he does offer the opinions of six commentators briefly, concluding with his own opinion.[62] The pattern that is more typical of his writing and of the Tablīghī Jamā^{c}at in general is to quote verses as proof texts to support an argument, without discussing other possible meanings of the text.

A recurring theme throughout Zakariyyā's discussion on the Qur'ān is its wondrous nature and inimitability (*i^{c}jāz*). Mastering the sciences of interpretation is necessary to understand its miraculous constructions (25). Its excellence is revealed in its "beautiful composition, wonderful coherence, the right choice of words, the proper development of arguments, narration of past events and prophesies about the future" (44). He argues, "Of all the infinite number of excellent attributes that one can imagine, the Glorious Qur'an is found to be superior and matchless in respect of all of them" (93). The Qur'ān is also described as the basis of the religion of Islam, and its preservation and propagation would determine Islam's very existence (12). Since its discourse is superior to that of other books, reading and teaching it would also be superior to reading or teaching other materials (13). The interconnection between the divine origin of the Qur'ān and its propagation is demonstrated in the Ḥadīth predicting the one who recites to be in the company of angels (17). Zakariyyā describes the Qur'ān as having been transferred from the Preserved Tablet in the heavens by angels; those who recite the Qur'ān have the same occupation, that of conveying it to others.

Chief among the excellencies of the Qur'ān is, of course, that it is God's own revelation. It has its origin from Him and, as His speech, is one of God's attributes (92–3). As the speech of the Master of masters, the Emperor of all kings, and the all-powerful Monarch, the necessary response of mortals is humility and reverence resulting in progress in the path of nearness to God (8). Not only was the Qur'ān the revelation of God, it was the final revelation. All previous books were summed up in it (66). The chain of revelation (*waḥy*) ended with Muḥammad, further revelations could not come.

The Qur'ān was the speech of Almighty God and contained the knowledge of prophethood (*nubuwwa*) (73). Again, the practical facet of *iᶜjāz* was emphasized in that knowing the divine origin of that which one was memorizing would impact one's lifestyle in a positive manner, leading to obedience.

Seeing the Qur'ān as the Speech of God, the Word of One whom Muslims love and seek, demonstrates the mystical roots of Zakariyyā's thinking. Not only would the glory of the Qur'ān and its divine origin inspire all-consuming awe, this communication from the Beloved would sway one's heart with "emotion of Heavenly love" (7–8). Throughout his discourse, Zakariyyā returns repeatedly to the image of the lover and his Beloved. The one who recites is called upon to attempt to "visualize the real beauty and limitless bounty of our Beloved Allāh" (8). The Qur'ān is personified as one who will intercede for those who read it, respect it, and follow its commands, on the Day of Judgment, resulting in God expressing His pleasure in those for whom it interceded (22–3, 71). "We find in this life that the pleasure of the beloved is considered to be the most coveted gift. Similarly in the life Hereafter, no bounty shall compare with the pleasure of our Beloved Almighty Allāh" (23).

At the conclusion of his presentation of the forty-seven *aḥadīth*, Zakariyyā states the purpose of describing the beauties and virtues of the Qur'ān is to cultivate a love for it, since love for the Qur'ān is needed to develop a love for God and vice versa (91).[63] The outcome of love is obedience, "When a person falls in love with someone, submission and obedience to the beloved becomes his habit and second nature" (91). A person is drawn to love another by seeing a beautiful face or hearing a sweet voice. A partial glimpse inspires one to hunger to see more, while neglecting to pay attention to the beloved causes love to grow cold (91–2). God as the source of all beauty and elegance, Whose loveliness knows no bounds, has expressed that excellence in the Glorious Qur'ān which is superior in beauty to all other things (92–3). Gazing on this beauty, ever longing to see more, should then be the preoccupation of every Muslim. The *aḥadīth* offered by Zakariyyā should not be enough to content the true scholar, he concludes, but should spur one to greater contemplation of its beauties (102–3).

Somewhat related to the mystical perspective of the Qur'ān is its use in magical formulas for cures. In detailing the virtues of the first *sūra*, *al-Fātiḥa*, Zakariyyā lists numerous cures attributed to its recitation. In addition to its recitation, he seems to view with favor practices using it in amulets, licking its writing, blowing or applying saliva in connection with its reading (78–9). Though this would seem a departure from orthodox uses of the Qur'ān, he claims as his authority the book, *Maẓāhir-i Ḥaqq*, an Urdu translation by Muḥammad Quṭb al-Dīn of the *Mishkāt al-Maṣābih* (80).

Conclusion

The use of the Qur'ān by the Tablīghi Jamāᶜat has been heavily influenced by its founder, Muḥammad Ilyās and its chief writer, Muḥammad Zakariyyā. Fully trained in classical Islamic scholarship, they held to a traditional interpretation of the Qur'ān and advocated *taqlīd* or strict adherence to this interpretation. They were also fully committed to the mystical Ṣūfī traditions and incorporated that perspective in their emphasis on *dhikr*, reciting the Qur'ān, and on imagining God as the Beloved with the Qur'ān as communication with His lover. However, the absence of any volume of *tafsīr* or even of the principles of commentary, apart from Zakariyyā's collection of *aḥadīth*, reflects more the social element of those initially involved in Ilyas' movement of *tablīgh*. His work among the religiously uneducated Meos produced in him a vision for teaching the masses the basics of faith. The teaching was to be done by non-specialists recruited from those same masses. The emphasis was not to be on abstract theologizing, but on personal contact, direct involvement in *tablīgh*, and a simple basic message of six injunctions and one prohibition. These were certainly based on the Qur'ān, but not on a new approach to its interpretation, or a new hermeneutic derived from the changing intellectual or political context.

The expansion of the movement has continued among the common people, while intellectuals and *ᶜulamā'* have tended to treat it with disdain or simply ignored it. The basics of the movement have remained the same—"The organization of the Tablīgh is both the means of action and its aim."[64] Those of the *ᶜulamā'* who have participated in the movement have continued with the simplicity of its founders. The continuing use of Zakariyyā's collection of *aḥadīth* has been a key factor in maintaining continuity. His approach to the Qur'ān in his book on its virtues remained within the orthodox-Ṣūfī nexus. While praising the superiority of the Qur'ān, he is much more apt to use the *ḥadīth* in support of his arguments. In his view, the primary use of the Qur'ān is in recitation. Understanding its meaning is not required, though definitely preferred, but private interpretation is not permitted. In general, the movement has a somewhat ahistorical view of the text, where the Qur'ān as well as the *sunna* are seen as patterns for current behavior, not a text within a historical context from which principles must derived through the use of appropriate hermeneutical tools.

NOTES

1. Barbara D. Metcalf, "New Medinas: The Tablighi Jamaᶜat in America and Europe," in *Making Muslim Space in North America and Europe*, ed. Barbara D. Metcalf (Berkeley: University of California Press, 1996), 111.

2. Muhammad Khalid Masud, ed., *Travellers in Faith: Studies of Tablīghī Jamāᶜat as a Transnational Islamic Movement for Faith Renewal* (Leiden: E.J. Brill, 2000).

3. Mumtaz Ahmad, "Islamic Fundamentalism in South Asia: The Jamaat-i-Islami and the Tablighi Jamaat of South Asia," in *Fundamentalisms Observed*, ed. Martin E. Marty and R. Scott Appleby, The Fundamentalist Project (Chicago: University of Chicago Press, 1991), I, 457–530; Barbara D. Metcalf, " 'Remaking Ourselves': Islamic Self-fashioning in a Global Movement of Spiritual Renewal," in *Accounting for Fundamentalisms: The Dynamic Character of Movements*, ed. Marty and Appleby, The Fundamentalist Project (Chicago: University of Chicago Press, 1994), IV, 706–25; Yoginder S. Sikand, "Charisma and Religious Revivalism: The Case of the Islamic Tablighi Jamaᶜat Movement among the Meos of Mewat," Diss. Jawaharlal Nehru University, New Delhi 1994.

4. M. Anwarul Haq, *The Faith Movement of Mawlānā Muḥammad Ilyās* (London: George Allen and Unwin, 1972), 15–76, 167–80.

5. Christian W. Troll, "Two Conceptions of Daᶜwā in India: Jamāᶜat-i Islamī and Tablīghī Jamāᶜat," *Archives de Sciences Sociales des Religions* 87 (1994): 115–33.

6. Barbara D. Metcalf, "Living Hadīth in the Tablīghi Jamaᶜāt," *The Journal of Asian Studies* 52 (1993): 584–608.

7. I would like to thank Professor Issa J. Boullata for his comments on an earlier draft of this paper prepared for his seminar on the modern exegesis of the Qur'ān.

8. Ziya-ul Hasan Faruqi, "The Tablīghī Jamāᶜat," *India and Contemporary Islam: Proceedings of a Seminar*, ed. S. T. Lokhandwalla (Simla: Indian Institute of Advanced Study, 1971), 67.

9. "Introduction," in *Travellers in Faith*, xxix.

10. Muhammad Khalid Masud, "The Growth and Development of the Tablīghī Jamāᶜat in India," in *Travellers in Faith*, 4.

11. Ibid., 5.

12. Sayyed Abul Hasan Ali Nadwi, *Life and Mission of Maulana Mohammad Ilyas*, trans. Mohammad Asif Kidawi, 2nd English ed. (Lucknow: Academy of Islamic Research and

Publications, 1983), 9. This is a biography of the founder by a respected Indian ^{c}*ālim* known to have strong sympathies for the movement.

13. Nadwi, *Life*, 11.

14. Nadwi, *Life*, 14–15. This association with Deoband and its political successors in Pakistan, the Jamā^{c}at ^{c}Ulamā'-i-Islam, has continued till today; Ahmad, "Islamic Fundamentalism," 523.

15. Barbara D. Metcalf, *Islamic Revival in British India: Deoband, 1860–1900* (Princeton: Princeton University Press, 1982), 143.

16. Metcalf, "New Medinas," 112.

17. Christian W. Troll, "Five Letters of Maulana Ilyas (1885–1944): The Founder of the Tablighi Jama^{c}at Translated, Annotated and Introduced," *Islam in India: Studies and Commentaries*, vol. 2 *Religion and Religious Education*, ed. Christian W. Troll (Delhi: Vikas Publishing House, 1985), 150. On Nadwī, see Ahmad Mukarram, "Some Aspects of Contemporary Islamic Thought: Guidance and Governance in the Work of Mawlana Abul Hasan Ali Nadwi and Mawlana Abul Aala Mawdudi," D. Phil Thesis, University of Oxford, 1992.

18. Masud, "The Growth and Development," 6–7.

19. Ibid., 6.

20. Metcalf, *Islamic Revival*, 133.

21. Haq, *The Faith Movement*, 66; for expanded versions, see: Faruqi, "The Tablīghī Jamā^{c}at" 64–6; Ahmad, "Islamic Fundamentalism," 513–4.

22. Haq, *The Faith Movement*, 73.

23. Troll, "Five Letters," 152–4, 156, 159.

24. Nadwi, *Life*, 18–21.

25. Yoginder Sikand, "The Emergence of the Tablīghī Jamā^{c}at among the Meos of Mewat," *The Bulletin of the Henry Martyn Institute of Islamic Studies* 13 no. 3–4 (1994): 7–18; see also, Haq, *The Faith Movement*, 100–125; "Introduction," *Travellers in Faith*, xxx-xlii.

26. Nadwi, *Life*, 28–32.

27. Nadwi, *Life*, 33.

28. Masud, "Growth and Development," 10.

29. Nadwi, *Life*, 35.

30. As found in Haq, *The Faith Movement*, 73.

31. Nadwi, *Life*, 40.

32. Nadwi, *Life*, 49, 145.

33. Nadwi, *Life*, 132, 138–9. He defined the root as *tablīgh*, 141.

34. Nadwi, *Life*, 154.

35. Haq, *The Faith Movement*, 108.

36. Mohammad Talib, "Construction and Reconstruction of the World in the Tablīghī Ideology," in *Travellers in Faith*, 60–1.

37. Nadwi, *Life*, 52.

38. Nadwi, *Life*, 55.

39. Nadwi, *Life*, 131.

40. Nadwi, *Life*, 133; see also pp. 139–40 for an account of his disillusionment with teaching in *madrasa*s and his belief that leading people to God would result in the restoration of the schools and Ṣūfī centers. See also, Troll, "Five Letters," 160.

41. Metcalf, "Living Hadīth," 589–90.

42. Sikand, "Emergence" 8–14. For a discussion on the Islamic nominalism of the people of Mēwāt, see "Introduction," *Travellers in Faith,* xxx-xlii.

43. Sikand, "Emergence," 14.

44. Nadwi, *Life,* 115.

45. Ahmad, "Islamic Fundamentalism," 516.

46. Ahmad, "Islamic Fundamentalism," 516.

47. Barbara D. Metcalf, "Meandering Madrasas: Knowledge and Short-term Itinerancy in the Tablighi Jamaᶜat," in *The Transmission of Knowledge in South Asia: Essays on Education, Religion, History, and Politics*, ed. Nigel Crook, SOAS Studies on South Asia: Understandings and Perspectives (Delhi: Oxford University Press, 1996), 54.

48. Metcalf, "Living Hadith," 585; Muhammad Khalid Masud, "Ideology and Legitimacy," *Travellers in Faith*, 81–5.

49. Mohammad Manzoor Nomani, *The Quran and You*, trans. Mohammad Asif Kidawi (Lucknow: Furqan Book Depot, 1971).

50. For a bibliography of his works see, Muḥammad Zakariyyā, *Muslims' Afflictions: A Study of Causes and their Remedy*, trans. Iftikhar Ahmed ᶜAlavi, ed. Sadruddin ᶜAmir Ansari (New Delhi: Kitab Bhavan, 1977), 1–14.

51. Metcalf, "Living Ḥadīth," 585.

52. Muḥammad Zakariyya, *Virtues of Quran, being English Translation of Urdu Book* Fazail-e-Quran, part 5 of *Teachings of Islam*, rev. ed. (1976; Delhi: Dini Book Depot, 1980), 5.

53. Metcalf, "Living Hadīth," 593.

54. Metcalf, "Living Hadīth," 594.

55. Metcalf, "New Medinas," 119.

56. Masud, "Ideology and Legitimacy," 81–2.

57. Troll, "Five Letters," 166, 174.

58. Metcalf, "Living Hadith," 599.

59. The subsequent page references included in the text are from the 1976 edition (published in Delhi by Dini Book Depot in 1980) of Zakariyyā, *Virtues of the Quran*.

60. Nadwi, 143; Metcalf, "Living Hadīth," 587–9.

61. Muḥammad Zakariyyā, *Virtues of Tabligh, being English Translation of Urdu Book* Fazail-e-Tabligh, part 4 of *Teachings of Islam*, rev. ed. (1976; Delhi: Dini Book Depot, 1980), 19.

62. Zakariyya, *Virtues of Tabligh*, 19.

63. This section is peppered with brief selections of Persian and Urdu poetry, absent in some of the English translations.

64. Felice Dassetto, "The Tabligh Organization in Belgium," in *The New Islamic Presence in Western Europe*, ed. Thomas Gerholm and Yngve Georg Lithman (London: Mansell Publishing, 1988), 163.

INDEX

(See also Qur'ānic Verses Index on page 357)

Arnold, Edward, 291
Arnold, Thomas, 292–95, 293, 301, 310
al-Ash^carī, Abū 'l-Ḥasan, 127–28, 134–35
Ash^carite doctrine
acts occur at will and decree of God, 146–47
and anthropomorphization of God, 134–35
founding of, 127–28
Iqbāl on, 302, 304, 315
as orthodox theology, 130
on Qur'ān as eternal Word of God, 250
al-Rāzī and, 129–31
See also Rāzī, Fakhr al-Dīn al-
aṣlaḥnā (curing barrenness), 15–16
Atkinson, David W., 232
author-centered interpretation, 243–44, 245–46
authority
of Islam, 27
of men over women, 59–60, 184, 189–90, 196–97, 200
of messengers, 197
of Prophetic *ḥadīth,* 154*n*14, 154*n*16, 163, 198
of Qur'ān, 60–61, 71, 219
of al-Rāzī, 128–29
of scripture/texts, 230–31, 235, 242–43, 303
of al-Suhrawardī, 161
of Zakariyyā, 167
al-Awārd (Zakariyyā), 169–70, 173
^cAwārif al-Ma^cārif (al-Suhrawardī), 160–62, 163–64, 169–70, 175*n*4
āyāt, types of, 20–21
āyat al-ghār, 107, 108–15, 116–17
āyāt muḥkamāt, 125
^cAyyād, Shukrī Muḥammad, 227
al-Azhar, 194

B

al-Baghawī, 41
al-Baghdādī, 134
Baha'i faith, Bint al-Shāṭi' on, 181
balance *(mawzūn),* 17
balance of right and wrong *(mīzān),* 11–14, 17, 20–21
banū Isrā'īl. See Israelites
al-Bāqillānī, 134
al-Bāqir, 42
barrenness *(^cuqm),* 16, 20
Barton, John, 242, 262*n*92
bāṭin al-Qur'ān (inner Qur'ān), 161
battle of Harra (682 CE), 80
al-Bayhaqī, 134
Bayt al-Maqdis. *See* Jerusalem
bayyināt (Clear Signs), 35–36
behaviorism, 31*n*15
believers
in Abū Bakr as Companion, 111
clarity regarding source of the Qur'ān, 240
hearts of, 170
and prayer, 165–66
al-Rāzī's beliefs about, 152–53, 158*n*68
Bell, Richard, 77
benefits
al-Suhrawardī on, 160–62
of *muḥkam* verses, 144
of *mutashābih* verses, 156*n*52
from reading, reciting, and teaching the Qur'ān, 329–30
Bernidaki-Aldous, Eleftheria A., 49–50
Betti, E., 251–52
Bhagavad Gita, Gandhi's series on, 305–9
Bhagavad Gita (Arnold, trans.), 291
Bhave, Vinoba, 314
Bible
the blind and blindness, 50, 58
description of Israel, 74*n*12
exhortations to remember, 36–37
Gandhi on, 308
inner-Biblical exegesis, 271–72
interpretation of, 230, 242, 244, 259*n*25, 262*n*92
Iqbāl's quote from, 287
Jacob's renaming and the twelve tribes, 68–69
literal, canonical, and contemporary meaning, 246
passages of reproof, 67
on Sodom prior to its destruction, 74*n*12
as Word of God, 260*n*42
The Bible as Literature (Gabeel, et. al), 232
Biblical Interpretation (Morgan), 242
Bint al-Shāṭi' (^cĀ'isha ^cAbd al-Raḥmān)
beliefs and boldness of, 180–81
biographical information, 179, 180
feminism of, 200–202
The Islamic Concept of Women's Emancipation, 179–80, 183–84, 185–94
Jewish Sources in the Intellectual Razzia, 181
list of major exegetical works, 182–83
"Will Women Become Religious Leaders at al-Azhar?", 194
works of (partial list), 202–3
See also exegesis of Bint al-Shāṭi'
bio-psychical basis, 10–16, 20–21, 31*n*18

grammar, exegesis and, 331
great derivation technique, 4
The Great Exegesis (al-Rāzī), 112–13, 126, 131–32. *See also* exegesis of Q. 3:7 by al-Rāzī
groups *(jamāᶜats),* 324
guardianship *(wilāya)* of fathers or husbands, 186
guardians of orphans and widows, 23–24
guidance
  blindness as lack of, 55, 56, 57–58
  Quṭb on error after, 214–15
  submission to guidance from God, 13–14
  tawfīqī, 273–74
Guillaume, Alfred, 66

H

ḥadīth (traditions)
  ᶜAbd al-Malik's study of, 90
  on Bayt al-Maqdis, 74*n*15
  Bint al-Shāṭi''s interpretation of, 198–200
  Islamic tradition and Israelites, 71–73, 99
  Jews role in, 38
  on Muḥammad's heavenly journey, 73*n*8
  prophetic *ḥadīth,* 154*n*14, 154*n*16, 163, 330
  al-Rāzī's use of, 132, 156*n*47
  on *al-ṣuḥba* concept, 110
  al-Suhrawardī's use of, 160, 161, 162–66
  transmissions of, 34
  Zakariyyā's collections of, 328, 329, 334, 335
Hadrian, Emperor, 79, 102*n*13
al-Ḥajjāj, 89, 97, 106*n*97
Hallaq, Wael, 268
Ḥanafī, Ḥasan, 181
Ḥanbalī jurist tradition, 160
Ḥanbalite dogma, 250
ḥanīfiyya (elasticity), 270
harmony *(ṣalāh),* 9–12, 17
al-Ḥasan al-Baṣrī, 40
Ḥasan, Mawlawī Mīr, 285–87
hawā (lower desires), 13–14, 15, 25
heavenly paradise of Israelites, 67–68
Hebrew Bible. *See* Bible
hermeneutical findings, studies on Shaḥrūr's, 281*n*16
hermeneutical process
  Abū Zayd's rejection of, 230
  meaning vs. significance, 246–48
  of al-Rāzī on *ghār* event, 113
  for Suhrawardī scholars, 159
  and al-Suhrawardī's treatise, 161
  ta'wīl as a tool for, 132–33, 135
Heroes and Hero Worship (Carlyle), 291
hijra. *See* Muḥammad's emigration to Medina
ḥikma (divine wisdom), 19
al-Ḥillī, al-ᶜAllāma, 115–16
Himālah (Iqbāl), 286–87
al-Ḥimṣī, Naᶜīm, 224*n*9
Hind Swaraj (Gandhi), 298–99, 309
Hirsch, E.D., 245–46, 263*n*111, 274*n*112
historic-critical interpretation, 242, 245, 246–47, 249
historicity of Qur'ānic text, 240–41
history, learning from, 315, 317
history, mythological, 328–29
Holdrege, Barbara A., 239
Holy Land, 65, 78
Hūd b. Muḥakkam, 38–39
hudā (God's guidance), submission to, 13–14
al-Ḥudaybiyya incident, 122*n*37
Ḥudhayfa, 88
human behavior, 6–9, 20–21
human beings
  body of, 11–15, 27–28, 172–73
  physiology of, 10–13, 15–16, 20–21, 58–59
  rational dimension of, 12–15
  relationship to universe, 17–21
  specific terms used in Qur'ān, 182
  world transforming capacities of, 313, 314–15, 316–17
humanity, realization of, 190–93, 201
humanity of the Qur'ān, 232–33, 252–53
human psyche *(nafs),* 13–15, 17–18, 28, 172
human soul
  developing mind and imagination, 312–13
  as directive energy, 314–15, 316–17
  divine/natural infusion, 31*n*15
  growing towards God, 304–5
  individual (woman's) responsibility for, 186–87
  Plato on, 31*n*12
  Qur'ān on, 314
humility, al-Suhrawardī on, 164
ḥurriyya (freedom of women), 185–89, 192–94
Husain, S. Abid, 297
Hussain, Waheed, 250
hypocrisy, 7–9, 14

I

Ibn ᶜAbbās, ᶜAbd Allāh, 11, 14, 40, 41, 116, 164
Ibn Abī Dā'ūd, 89
Ibn Abī Hadhara, 110

N

O

P

T

U

QUR'ĀNIC VERSES INDEX

Mizan Publications
Distributed by Islamic Publications International

On the Sociology of Islam Lectures by Ali Shari'ati tr. by Hamid Algar
Pperbk ISBN 978-0-933782-00-6 $9.95

Marxism and Other Western Fallacies: An Islamic Critique by Ali Shari'ati tr. Robert Campbell
Pperbk ISBN 978-0-933782-06-8 $14.95 Hdbk ISBN 978-0-933782-05-1 $24.95

Constitution of the Islamic Republic of Iran tr. Hamid Algar
Pperbk ISBN 978-0-933782-07-5 $7.95 Hdbk ISBN 978-0-933782-02-0 $14.95

Islam and Revolution: Writings and Declaration of Imam Khomeini
tr. Hamid Algar
Pperbk ISBN 978-0-933782-03-7 $24.95 Hdbk ISBN 978-0-933782-04-4 $34.95

The Islamic Struggle in Syria by Umar F. Abd-Allah
Hdbk ISBN 978-0-933782-10-5 $29.95

Occidentosis: A Plaque from the West by Jalal Al-i Ahmad tr. Robert Campbell
Pperbk ISBN 978-0-933782-13-6 $14.95 Hdbk ISBN 978-0-933782-12-9 $29.95

The Contemporary Muslim Movement in the Philippines by Cesar Adib Majul
Pperbk ISBN 978-0-933782-17-4 $9.95 Hdbk ISBN 978-0-933782-16-7 $19.95

Fundamental of Islamic Thought: God, Man and the Universe
by Ayatullah Murtaza Mutahhari tr. Robert Campbell
Pperbk ISBN 978-0-933782-15-0 $9.95 Hdbk ISBN 978-0-933782-14-3 $19.95

Social and Historical Change: An Islamic Perspective
by Ayatullah Murtaza Mutahhari tr. by Robert Campbell
Pperbk ISBN 978-0-933782-19-8 $9.95 Hdbk ISBN 978-0-933782-18-1 $19.95

Principles of Sufism by Al-Qushayri tr. B. R. Von Schlegell
Pperbk ISBN 978-0-933782-20-4 $19.95 Hdbk ISBN 978-0-933782-21-1 $29.95

Society & Economics in Islam: Writings & Declarations of Ayatullah Sayyid Mahmud Talighani tr. by Robert Campbell
Pperbk ISBN 978-0-933782-09-9 $24.95

Published by Islamic Publications International

Challenging the New Orientalism: Dissenting Essays on the "War Against Islam" by M. Shahid Alam
Pperbk ISBN 978-1-889999-45-6 $19.95 Hdbk ISBN 978-1-889999-46-3 $29.95

Surat Al-Fatiha: Foundation of the Qur'an by Hamid Algar
Pperbk ISBN 978-1-889999-00-5 $7.95

Sufism: Principles and Practice by Hamid Algar
by Hamid Algar Pperbk ISBN 978-1-889999-02-9 $7.95

Jesus In The Qur'an: His Reality Expounded in the Qur'an by Hamid Algar
Pperbk ISBN 978-1-889999-09-8 $7.95

Understanding The Four Madhhabs: The Facts about Ijtihad and Taqlid by Abdal Hakim Murad (T.J. Winters)
Pperbk ISBN 978-1-889999-07-4 $3.00

The Sunnah: Its Obligatory and Exemplary Aspects by Hamid Algar
Pperbk ISBN 978-1-889999-01-2 $7.95

Imam Abu Hamid Ghazali: An Exponent of Islam in Its Totality by Hamid Algar Pperbk ISBN 978-1-889999-15-9 $7.95

Wahhabism: A Critical Essay by Hamid Algar
Pperbk ISBN 978-1-889999-13-5 $16.95 Hdbk ISBN 978-1-889999-31-9 $26.95

Path of God's Bondsmen From Origin to Return by Najm A. Razi
Tr. by Hamid Algar
Pperbk ISBN 978-1-889999-33-3 $39.95

Social Justice in Islam by Sayyid Qutb
Translation Revised & Introduction by Hamid Algar
Pperbk ISBN 978-1-889999-11-1 $24.95 Hdbk ISBN 978-1-889999-12-8 $34.95

Roots of the Islamic Revolution in Iran/Four Lectures by Hamid Algar
Pperbk ISBN 978-1-889999-26-5 $14.95 Hdbk ISBN 978-1-889999-27-2 $24.95

Principles of Islamic Jurisprudence: According to Shi'i Law by Muhammad Baqir al-Sadr Tr. by Arif Abdul Hussain Translation Revised by Hamid Algar
Pperbk ISBN 978-1-889999-36-4 $19.95 Hdbk ISBN 978-1-889999-37-1 $29.95

Jihad & Shahadat (Struggle and Martyrdom in Islam) Essays and Addresses by Ayatullah Mahmud Taleqani, Ayatullah Murtada Mutahhari & Dr. Ali Shariati Edited by Mehdi Abedi & Gary Legenhausen.
Pperbk ISBN 978-1-889999-43-2 $24.95 Hdbk ISBN 978-1-889999-44-9 $34.95

What Is To Be Done (The Enlightened Thinkers and an Islamic Renaissance) by Dr. Ali Shariati Edited & Annotated by Farhand Rajaee
Pperbk ISBN 978-1-889999-41-8 $24.95 Hdbk ISBN 978-1-889999-42-5 $34.95

Theoretical Studies in Islamic Banking and Finance Edited by Mohsin S. Khan & Abbas Mirakhor
Pperbk ISBN 978-1-889999-40-1 $29.95

Man & Islam by Dr. Ali Shariati. Translated by Dr. Fatollah Marjani.
Pperbk ISBN 978-1-889999-39-5 $14.95

Hajj by Dr. Ali Shariati. Translated by Ali A. Behzadnia & Najla Denny.
Pperbk ISBN 978-1-889999-38-8 $14.95